COMPLETE BOOK OF OUTDOOR COOKERY

COMPLETE BOOK OF OUTDOOR COOKERY

MEL MARSHALL

DRAWINGS BY CHARLES BERGER

OUTDOOR LIFE BOOKS
NEW YORK

VAN NOSTRAND REINHOLD COMPANY
NEW YORK CINCINNATI TORONTO LONDON MELBOURNE

Published by
Outdoor Life Books
Times Mirror Magazines, Inc.
380 Madison Avenue
New York, NY 10017

Distributed to the trade by
Van Nostrand Reinhold Company
135 West 50 Street
New York, NY 10020

ISBN: 0-442-26437-2

**Library of Congress Cataloging in
Publication Data**

Marshall, Mel.
  Complete book of outdoor cookery.

  Includes index.
  1. Outdoor cookery.   I. Title.
TX823.M278   1983   641.5'78   83-2223

Manufactured in the United States of America

CONTENTS

PART II: TRAIL COOKING

PART III: COOKING FISH AND GAME

ACKNOWLEDGMENTS

My thanks for help in furnishing data, photos or photo subjects, product samples for testing, and for sharing their time, knowledge, and experience go to L. L. Bean Co.; Tracy and Dale Boeing, Paula Cross of Dacor; Bill Danchuck of Koolatron Industries; Betsey Drake, Vince Gonzalez, Patricia Lee of Better Living Labs; Edith McCaig, Katie McMullen, and Betty Crosby of the Coleman Co.; Pecci O'Conner of Hammacher Schlemmer; Jack Sable of Skylab Foods; Anne Secours of Orvis; Jay Van Brunt of Ducane Co.; Jerry Waggoner, Bill Wallum of Leyse Aluminum; Don White of Jenn-Air; John Willard, Don Wilson of Richmoor Foods.

A special note of thanks also: to Henry Gross for editing the manuscript through all its convolutions with patience and insight and gentle firmness.

There are a number of others I'd like to thank, good hunting and fishing companions of years gone by, and I only wish they were still here so that I could acknowledge the woodslore and camping lessons they passed on to me, some of which are passed on to you in the following pages.

M. M.

INTRODUCTION

Cookbooks don't really belong outdoors. When you're away from civilization, communing with nature in the fresh air under a smog-free sky, there are better ways to spend your time than thumbing through the pages of a cookbook.

That's why parts of this book emphasize principles that can be applied to all outdoor cooking. Once you're familiar with them, you can carry them in your head, and armed with basic knowledge of outdoor cookery, you won't need to carry the book into camp with you.

This is in accord with the old woodsman's saying (which I just made up), "If you're sure about the trail you want to follow, all your going will be smooth." You may find that you must take a few steps off to one side of the trail or the other, but if your destination is fixed firmly in your mind, you'll reach it.

Of course, some new trails are hard to follow even if you're reasonably certain that you know their most distinctive landmarks. For the difficult trails, you need a map or you're apt to wind up at the base of an unscalable cliff. Look on parts of this book which go into details as to quantities, ingredients, cooking times and so on, as the map or chart you consult when starting out on an unfamiliar trail.

None of these parts will be so complicated that you can't carry them with you in your mind. The philosopher who said, "Hunger is the best sauce," must certainly have been thinking of outdoor cookery, for fancy sauces and complex combinations of ingredients aren't really necessary when appetites have been whetted by a pleasant day spent outdoors. Simplest is generally best when you're cooking in camp.

This is as true today as it was a couple of hundred years ago. Then, the rugged mountain men would start out for a season of trapping with a generous supply of powder and lead, but only a sack of salt in their necessary bags to handle their needs for food. If they'd acquired a taste for luxury, they might add a little bag of sugar flood. Damage was done, and more importantly the fear of greater damage was created.

Inevitably, there was a reaction. Hunters and fishermen complained loudly that the wildlife habitats which their license fees were paying to maintain were being spoiled by irresponsible freeloaders. Many landowners closed their acres; state and federal agencies responsible for maintaining public lands imposed or tried to impose access restrictions.

Whether or not the fear of damage and the complaints were fully justified is beside the point. Some of these were almost certainly an overreaction, but this did nothing to nullify their effects. Bit by bit, the open countryside was shrunken by signs that warned everyone, guilty or innocent, to keep off. The careful were barred as well as the careless.

This does not imply that there are no more open spaces left for the outdoorsman to enjoy. There are, but as a rule those using the countryside, whether private or public, must be much more aware of the need to use open areas carefully and to respect their integrity more.

In numerous areas, there are now restrictions on campers that did not exist or were not enforced before. Although campfire permits have long been required in national parks and forests, the rule was only loosely enforced until the mid-1960s.

Campers will now find their gear being checked in some national recreation areas, and in those where there is fire danger, they will be required to carry a camp shovel that can be converted to a grubbing tool. Many state as well as national parks prohibit the use of deadfall wood, trees or limbs, in cooking fires. In places where this ban applies, campers must use pressed logs in stoves placed at specified spots or must have artificial fuel camp stoves, again at specified campsites.

As this is being written, plans are being made to close the floor of Yosemite Valley to all auto traffic and consequently to overnight camping and cooking. This type of restriction may spread to other parks with similar problems of overcrowding.

There is a point to this lengthy exposition, though we've been a long time arriving at it. We've at last realized that, given modern mechanization and mobility, easy access to wild and semiwild areas is a blade with two edges. If such areas are to be preserved, their use must be monitored and controlled to prevent irreversible damage.

Today, it's not enough that you are a careful camper, one who respects the environment, one who does not litter, who buries garbage and removes trash. On public land — the only semiwild land readily and easily available in many areas for those who want to enjoy outdoor cooking as part of a day-long or overnight stay — you may find that you'll have to go prepared to use artificial fuel for your cooking fire, and if overnight camping is not allowed, have an early supper instead of singing into the night around the dying embers of a campfire.

Presented with the alternative of closing wild and semiwild environments, controls on their use is certainly preferable. And there are some plusses which we haven't yet noted that will make the price of controls seem smaller.

HUNTING AND FISHING

In the present and even more in the future you are likely to find new varieties of game and fish on your favorite hunting grounds, lakes, and streams. Better understanding of habitat requirements has led to greater use of wild and semiwild lands, chiefly through establishing in them carefully selected European, Asiatic, and African game species. Cross-breeding or hybridization of both animal and fish species is becoming more commonplace, and these "new" forms of wildlife are being distributed, often experimentally, to supplement declining types of native fish and game.

This is all to the good, of course. When I began as a boy to hunt and fish, the varieties of both game and fish were much less extensive than today. Admittedly, both were less sophisticated, but so were guns and tackle. Access to open land was easier, but transportation was more primitive; so was camp gear. For the record, let's try to strike a balance sheet.

Upland bird shooting was pretty much confined to quail in the South, doves in the Southwest, and in the Northeast grouse were getting scarce. Pheasant were relatively rare and limited in distribution, chukars were unheard-of, the prairie chicken had been written off as an almost-extinct species.

Today, the scattergunner finds pheasant almost everywhere, chukar in many areas, the prairie chicken is making a comeback in the Southwest, and quail distribution is vastly improved. Ducks Unlimited has done a magnificent job of improving waterfowl availability, and today the shotgunner has a better chance of taking home the makings of a duck dinner than he'd had since the great flights began to diminish in the early 1900s.

Small game was the same mix of rabbits and squirrels that we now have, and the small game situation has changed very little.

Big-game hunting has undergone some changes. Nationwide, deer predominated as they do today, with antelope and elk in the western plateaus. Aoudad and Barbary sheep had not been introduced in the West, nor had the new antelope species now relatively common on the high ranges. Today's southeastern boar hunts did not exist. Moose were scarce even then, elk a bit more plentiful, but the decline of the elk was beginning. This decline has now been arrested and should ultimately be cured. Bears were more plentiful in the western mountains, and controls were put on bear hunting early enough to protect the bruin from the dip that the elk suffered.

Despite the ravages of "acid rain" in sections of the North and Northeastern United States, which has had an adverse effect on once-splendid trout waters, fishing has generally improved. True, in many areas the fishing is for hatchery trout in artificial impoundments, but without these there would be very little trout fishing left today.

Yesterday's bass were either smallmouth or largemouth and both were shrinking in size and numbers. Hybridization has produced new strains, such as the Florida giants; watershed rehabilitation and additions of new open-water areas have widened the bass fisherman's horizons.

Striped bass were saltwater fish yesterday; today the striper is as much at

and one of coffee or tea, but like the Indians from whom they'd learned, the old mountain men knew how to live off the land.

They knew that wherever they went in what was then an almost untouched country, they'd find enough game to keep them well fed, and they knew which plants were edible and which should be avoided. Even well in the 1900s, old Ben Lilly, the legendary mountain-lion hunter of the Southwest, would start out for a six-month hunt with a pound of salt and five pounds of cornmeal in a gunnysack as his only provisions.

We can't make do with such frugality today, for things have changed since the mountain men ranged. They stopped to shoot a squirrel or rabbit for a meal, cleaned and cooked it then and there, ate and moved on. Today, with universal refrigeration and fast transportation, a lot of us prefer to defer the pleasure of cooking our game until we're back in our home kitchen. We know that waiting will give the meat a chance to age and improve its flavor.

Perhaps we're also willing to wait because cooking at home gives us a chance to put the big pot in the little pot, which is an old Southern expression for fancy cooking. With that thought in mind, there are included some recipes for home cooking of your trophies of the streams and fields and forests.

So, we eat grocery store food in camp, and even victuals from the supermarket taste better when they're cooked and eaten under the open sky, surrounded by towering trees or on the rim of a plateau looking out over a expanse of rolling countryside.

Most of us have found, though, that today we can't always depend on having

fuel handy in some of the places we like to camp, so we'll look at equipment such as camp stoves and their uses. In fact, we'll be surveying the entire broad spectrum of outdoor cooking and eating, as well as the equipment that is associated with them.

We'll cover camp baking, cooking without utensils, how to prepare a real barbecue and clambake, and trail cooking for those times when you want to get along with the basic foods that you can carry in a light backpack. We'll even get back to the days of the mountain men by giving a bit of attention to survival foods and the wild plants that can still be harvested and eaten safely in some parts of the country.

THE CHANGING OUTDOORS

What this book really tries to do is to update outdoor cookery and present it in all its contemporary aspects. The outdoors is no different from a town or city in one way: it is constantly changing. If yesterday's mountain men could return, they would not always recognize the land we know today as the land they left, any more than an individual long absent from almost any town or city would recognize old landmarks.

Part of the change has been due to nature's innate cussedness, sending such things as floods and earthquakes, forest fires and volcanic explosions to ravage huge areas. Part of the change has been due to man's innate cussedness in trying to tailor the land to suit his needs.

In this book, we're not going to argue the pros and cons of changes in the outdoors, or take an advocate's position regarding praise or blame. We'll simply note some of the changes and let you be the judge. The countryside has been changing from time immemorial, and will continue to change. In urban areas, however, man has been solely responsible for the changes. In the outdoor environment, the responsibility has been divided between man and nature.

Whether we like it or not, in the immediate past the changes, for better or worse, have been accelerated. In this latest period, one of the greatest parts man has played in the outdoors is trying to preserve its flavor, its unique features, so that future generations can enjoy them.

Let's look for a moment at some of the changes that have taken place, not only in the outdoors, but in outdoor cooking, so that we can perhaps understand them better.

During the years just before World War I and up to the time of World War II, cooking over an open fire was generally confined to only two groups. On the one side there was a relatively small number of respectable citizens, primarily hunters and fishermen, whose enjoyment of foods cooked outdoors was considered a mild but forgivable form of madness, an eccentricity of those who enjoyed getting smoke in their eyes and ashes on their steaks. At the opposite end of the scale, the only other outdoor cooking was that carried on by hoboes in their jungles on the wrong side of the railroad tracks.

Even during this recent era, the countryside were generally open. In almost all parts of the United States there were substantial tracts of semiwild or wild lands and open streams free from pollution. The public lands, national parks and forests, drew relatively few visitors and only the mildest of restrictions were imposed on the activities of those who camped, hiked, hunted, or fished within their borders. By and large, those who did use the open land respected it, were careful of their fires, buried their garbage and litter, and left unspoiled the spots they'd used.

World War II and the urbanization which followed it changed this attitude. Veterans escaping from the standardizations of C-rations and of the military mess hall; factory and office workers fleeing the mass-produced foods of the cafeteria or travelling canteen, took to the countryside and the backyard grill. Overnight, both the outdoors and outdoor cooking suffered from instant popularity.

"Suffered" is used advisedly. Technology overwhelmed the open spaces and lack of experience on the part of the users of those backyard grills resulted in some pretty sorry meals.

Perhaps the outdoors had the most difficult time. Off-road vehicles, surplus jeeps in the beginning and more specialized types of transport later on, zoomed and varoomed into places that had once been semiwild, accessible only by packhorse or on foot. Some of these off-road vehicles were manned by the heedless or careless, a few, sadly, by slobs and wreckers.

Litter appeared where there had never been litter before. Debris-strewn campsites marred the once-clean wild and semiwild spots. Spray-painted graffiti appeared on cliffs, boulders, and the boles of trees. Streambeds tossed back the shine of aluminum cans and the glint of bottle glass. During the period of the counterculture, with its accompanying protest against urbanization, the tide reached its

home in Arizona, Nevada, Oklahoma, Texas and Tennessee as it originally was on the coasts. The kokanee was an exotic a few years ago, found in only one or two western lakes; now it is following the striped bass into widely distributed artificial impoundments.

Until the late 1950s, steelhead and coho were unknown to the upper Midwest, and the Great Lakes were being rendered fishless by the sea lamprey. Today many of the streams tributary to the Great Lakes offer superb steelhead fishing; offshore in the lakes themselves coho abound, and the sea lamprey has been eliminated.

When I began to hunt and fish, it was still possible to reach good fishing water within a half-day of driving from most metropolitan areas. Keep in mind that much of the driving then was at a top speed of 35 miles per hour over unpaved roads and sometimes wagon ruts. It was an equally short trip to find good hunting. Today, better roads and vehicles have managed to keep the situation much the same, though that half-day drive will take you twice as far and the wilderness you reach won't be quite as wild.

You be the judge. I've tried to make up my mind on the plus and minus sides, and fall somewhere in the middle. But perhaps I'm just prejudiced.

OUTDOOR COOKING TODAY

There is one thing I miss. Until the 1960s, I'd never used a portable camp stove, and the first day of a hunting or fishing trip always ended with a cookout. There'd be a bed of coals from deadfall limbs picked up close by, with birds or rabbit or squirrels spitted over it, or liver from the first deer lightly sauted in a heavy cast-iron skillet, or grilled fish taken during the evening rise from the lake or stream beside the camp.

Today, a bed of coals isn't always possible, for the camp may be in a controlled area where only bottled gas or gasoline-fueled camp stoves can be used. There isn't always game or fish the first night. Sometimes the areas closest to the campsites have been worked too hard by previous campers to be quickly productive; at other times the trip has been longer than those old half-day drives and the campsite is reached too late for anybody to hunt or fish.

However, on the positive side of the ledger, I've learned to do pretty well with a camp stove or a small charcoal grill in places where open cooking fires aren't allowed, and how to use grills and camp stoves are among the things we'll be sharing later on. And the differences between today and yesterday are quickly overlooked in the sheer pleasure of being outdoors again.

We've finally reached the end of this introduction and are ready to move on. In the chapters that follow, you'll find both basic principles and details of ways to cook different kinds of outdoor foods, including fish and game, in different ways and different places. All of them, I hope, will make your meals tastier, easier to prepare, and generally more enjoyable.

MEL MARSHALL
Phillips, Texas

I

CAMPGROUND COOKERY

1 EQUIPMENT FOR CAMPGROUND COOKERY

Before thinking about equipment, let's agree on just what we mean by "campground." There are several kinds of campgrounds, each one calling for a slightly different approach by the cook as well as for different types of equipment.

First, there are the roadside campgrounds which are now found along most major highways. These are the spots which more and more travelers are using today to escape the banality of the fast-food joints that clutter up our roadsides, where you'll be served food that tastes pretty much like the plastic containers in which it's served. Facilities at these roadside rests are limited to some kind of grill and a table.

Second, there are commercial campgrounds. These are almost always located near popular recreational areas, and offer tent sites, rec vehicle parking, or cabins with minimal accommodations; usually in addition to a bed and a communal bath a cabin will have a tiny kitchen as well as an outdoor cooking area. When you stop at this kind of campground you'll almost always be expected to provide your own utensils and, most of the time, your own stove and fuel.

Third, there are wilderness and semiwilderness campgrounds or designated areas where camping is permitted. In controlled campgrounds, such as those in state and national parks and forests, you may be required to use a camp stove. In wild and semiwild areas, you can use wood picked up from your camp area, limbs of deadfall trees, or logs chopped from the trunk of such a tree. In this kind of camp, you're strictly on your own, and you'll be getting as close to the primitive as is possible today.

This opening chapter is chiefly concerned with hardware, the kind of equipment you'll need to function as a camp cook in each of the three types of camps already described. This includes equipment such as grills and/or stoves, utensils, cooking accessories, and tableware. Food selections and recipes will come in later chapters; so will the art of preparing a bed of coals and using the coals for cooking. Other chapters will cover specialized campground and cabin cooking.

Really expert camp cooks will rise above inadequate equipment. They can get food to cook thoroughly in pans that heat unevenly whether they're preparing a dish over open coals or on a camp stove. They can even cook a full meal without pans, using an improvised grill or spit. Let's face reality, though. Having the right kind of gear will save the beginner's bacon and make the expert's job easier.

Many roadside camps or rest stops provide stone or cement firepits with metal grill tops, or metal fireboxes; these are usually adjacent to some sort of table and overhead shelter. All of us have seen these facilities in public campgrounds and recreational areas and at highway rest stops. They follow a pretty predictable pattern. They will give you a place in which to build a fire safely, using wood or pressed logs or charcoal. (The use of these fuels will be covered later on.)

What we're concerned with at this point is the kind of outdoor cooking equipment that you'd be carrying. The range of choices is broad, and your selection depends on the places at which you'll be doing your campground cooking.

In some cases, the simplest kind of quick-cooking equipment will serve your needs for short roadside stops, or even for more extended stops if you can get along with the limited menus that this basic gear makes possible.

You might want a portable stove fueled by bottled gas or a grill that uses charcoal or some other kind of man-produced fuel. There are dozens of styles and types of these on the market, and we might look at a few typical examples from the standpoints of cost, safety, convenience, portability, and use.

Your needs for an extended camping trip where you'll be cooking over a firepit will be very basic, even simpler than the small grills which were first mentioned.

GRILLS

For many years the only camp grill I used was a simple metal lattice or grid with legs made from ⅜-inch metal rod slit to accommodate the corners of the grid. It was—and is, for I still use it on occasion—compact and easy to carry, and had no moving parts to go awry, yet it accommodates all the cooking needed to feed four people.

In a later section of this chapter, do-it-yourselfers will find details showing how to make several inexpensive outdoor grills, but unless you're sure that you can light an outdoor cooking fire and find fuel for one at the spot where you intend to camp, carry an artificial fuel camp stove as a precaution.

Let's look now at some of the options you have in manufactured grills, which you'll find at outdoor equipment stores or which you can get through the mail-order sources listed in one of the book's appendices.

By far the simplest portable grill and the easiest to set up and use for quick casual cooking is one called the Qwik-Cook Grill. It's so simple that it looks primitive, as well it might, for it's an adaptation of a bucket-grill used by African natives to cook a piece of meat quickly with no fuel other than a few rolled-up wads of dry grass or a couple of handfuls of bark.

In its civilized version, this grill looks like a trio of sheet-metal rings when telescoped for traveling, and extends to a 14-inch-high cylinder without a top. Ex-

This is the Quik-Cook grill. Its three sections nest together with the food basket in a carrying box that is only 16 inches square.

Assembling the grill is a two-minute job, fitting together the three sections.

Wad four full sheets of newspaper—or the equivalent in dry grass or brush—into grapefruit-sized balls, drop them into the grill, and light them.

Grill cooks thin chops, fish fillets, and then meat patties. Sections cool to the point where they can be handled without gloves in less than five minutes.

tended for use, a wire grid is laid across the top and a half-dozen sheets of wadded-up newspaper put in the bottom and lighted. Fat from the cooking meat drips onto the papers in the bottom and keeps them burning. It is not for use with long-burning fuel such as charcoal or pressed logs, just wadded-up newspaper or dry grasses.

This grill will cook a steak or chop, a patty of ground meat, or a filleted fish in less than 10 minutes. With a mid-point refueling it will handle a split chicken or one that's been cut up. You can't use it to boil water for tea or make a pot of coffee or to cook anything except the foods already mentioned, though it will also toast slices of bread and heat biscuits or buns. However, if you are willing to accept its limitations, it's a simple piece of equipment that requires no liquid or gas fuel, is compact, needs no adjustments, and is easy to carry in a car trunk. Though it's light in weight, it's a bit too bulky to be practical for backpacking.

Next in terms of portability is our old friend the hibachi. This oriental import has been around a long time, and is somewhat more versatile than the grill just described, since it's made of cast iron, uses charcoal for fuel, and will provide cooking coals over a period of time extended enough to allow some vegetables to be cooked on it. You can do a good job with roasting-ears, eggplant, and tomatoes (preferably the small variety known as cherry tomatoes), and can also bake an apple or a halved potato.

A hibachi occupies very little room in a car trunk, though you'll need to carry charcoal as well as the grill. Its chief disadvantage is its weight and the fact that once you get it hot enough to cook, it takes a long time to cool down. The

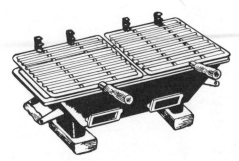

Every year, hibachis are sold by the thousands. However, since they are made of cast pig iron they have limited lifespans. You can make yours last longer by cleaning it after each use and keeping it out of the rain.

weight of a hibachi makes it unsuitable for backpacking.

There's a huge array of more conventional pressed sheet-metal charcoal grills bulkier than the hibachi. Most people call these grills barbecue grills or simply barbecues. These are usually round, and most of them have detachable legs which fold when the grill is being transported. A grill of this kind, 14 to 20 inches in diameter, is quite light in ratio to its bulk. This type of grill can be cooled very quickly and kept relatively grease-free simply by lining the bottom with metal foil and removing the foil and charcoal together as soon as the meal has been cooked. Usually the grill will be cool by the time you've eaten.

Of course, you won't be extending your menu choices very much by using a grill of this kind instead of the hibachi; the chief advantage such a grill offers is the extra size, which allows you to cook a greater quantity of food and brew a pot of coffee at the same time. And, you'll still be required to carry charcoal, perhaps a can of starter fluid, when you use this type of grill.

Lightweight pressed-metal grills fold into compact units for easy packing. When grills are opened, there is ample room to prepare food for four people. Fuel tray is usually adjustable to regulate heat.

Wire grills come in an infinite number of sizes and designs, have folding legs to make storage easy.

Larger model of the traditional wire grill has a 3-foot-long cooking surface. When using a grill of this type, be sure to anchor it securely by pressing the legs into the ground.

Sheet-metal rings for containing fires are found in some campgrounds. Reinforcing rods welded in place allow minimum cooking room, so many outdoorsmen bring along a discarded oven rack and lay it on top of the existing rim.

This unique grill design is popular in the Midwest where gusting winds can make open fires hazardous. Fire is built deep in the ground so there's less chance of sparks flying into the woods.

Popular in both campgrounds and picnic areas are stand-up grills with adjustable shelves for regulating the heat. Don't be squeamish about laying your steaks right on the grill; the metal will be sterilized after several minutes of exposure to the hot coals.

Larger version of the stand-up grill is ideal for family reunions or gang cookouts. The 5-foot grilling surface will hold 25 steaks, and you can lift one end or the other to produce some medium rare and others well done.

CAMP STOVES

There are two basic kinds of camp stoves: liquid-fueled and gas-fueled. The former came first, and it's still very much a part of the camp-cooking scene, in spite of the one-dollar-per-gallon-plus price of the unleaded gasoline it must have. The gas-fueled type uses canned or cylinder-packed butane/propane, and can be adapted to use large pressure containers of these gases. Most of the stoves of this type have two burners; some have three.

Light camp stoves make any attractive spot a meal-stop. The most economical, both in purchase price and operation, use unleaded gasoline for fuel or the stove manufacturer's special fuel which is available in sporting-goods stores.

Stoves of similar design use propane for fuel. These are more expensive to buy and operate, but they are much safer and easier to use.

There are small single-burner gas-fueled stoves, but these are more suited for backpackers than for general camp use, and we will look at these in a later chapter.

Basically, your choice of a camp stove will be decided by personal preference: Do you prefer to carry your fuel in liquid or gas form? The gasoline used by liquid-fueled stoves is usually carried in gallon cans. Butane or propane for stoves using this type of fuel is available in cylinders or canisters of several sizes, some of them large enough to give two or three days of use without the need to change cylinders. The tanks of liquid-fueled stoves are pressurized by a plunger-type pump integral with the stove, and you'll find you must use the pump at least two and possibly more times per meal cooked.

All these stoves depend on a fuel-air mix for efficient operation, and both types have adjustments which allow you to regulate fuel pressure to get optimum efficiency at any altitude at which they may be used. In performance, both kinds are about evenly matched.

There is a great similarity between different makes of these stoves in appearance as well as performance. In all of them the burners are contained in a metal body which, when closed, becomes a carrying

Everyone likes toast for breakfast, but no one knows how to make it in camp. One idea is to punch holes in the bottom of a coffee can, place the open end on top of several glowing coals or over a stove-burner flame, then toast the bread on top. Or, buy an inexpensive toaster (right) that fits on top of a stove burner, folds flat for easy storage.

case. All have side-shields which fold into the lids and can be extended to shield the burners from dangerous or annoying drafts. All of them weigh about the same.

Some of the gas-fueled types require a separate gas container for each burner; in others a single fuel container serves all burners. I've used both types, and find that each one has its advantages and disadvantages. Single-container stoves are a bit ticklish to adjust, and if both burners are used often will exhaust a fuel container fairly rapidly. Multiple-container types require that an additional supply of cylinders or cans of gas be carried if you want to get the fullest use of the stove. Again, this comes down to a matter of personal preference.

If your camp vehicle is a van or pickup, where a bit more bulk and weight isn't tremendously important, and you're going to be cooking for a large group, you might opt for a gas-fueled stove converted to use large containers of butane. One of these large cylinders will hold enough fuel to cook three meals a day for a couple of weeks. The initial cost of a setup of this type will be substantially higher than will be a stove using the small cylinders, and before making up your mind whether to go this route you will probably want to do some serious figuring.

UTENSILS

Nothing contributes more to a camp cook's peace of mind than having the proper utensils to do the job well. Trying to cook in a pot or pan unsuited for the type of fire you're using drives outdoor cooks up the wall and leads to their uttering sulfurous expletives that may well shed a bit of their sulfur into a dish that's being prepared.

It's impossible to overemphasize the importance of choosing utensils compatible with the kind of cooking fire you're using. Almost any kind of reasonably sturdy utensils will serve if you are going to be cooking over a camp stove; basically, these don't differ much from a kitchen range. There are a number of nested aluminum cooking kits available that are very satisfactory for use on camp stoves.

Remember, though, that a bed of glowing coals is far, far hotter than the flame from a camp stove, even if the utensils are placed above the coals on a grill. If cooking is done directly on the coals, the pots and pans selected must be thick enough and rugged enough to take the heat. Their handles must be metal, not wood or plastic. You can get by with utensils which have wooden handles, sometimes even with those having plastic-insert or plastic-sheathed handles, when cooking on a camp stove. You cannot use these kinds of utensils on or over a bed of coals.

Utensils used on coals must also be thick enough or sturdy enough so that they will not warp under the intense heat put out by coals. They need to be made from a material that will hold heat when a pot or pan is lifted off coals for a few minutes to prevent food from burning. Any material that meets the two foregoing tests will be one that distributes heat evenly without developing hot spots.

For direct on-coals cooking, pressed aluminum is the least satisfactory of all metals. Pressed-aluminum utensils invariably warp, develop hot spots, and overcook. Some utensils made from lightweight cast aluminum will crack or shatter when exposed to the direct heat of cooking coals. Thin pressed-steel utensils share with aluminum the flaw of warping. We'll go into the use of graniteware utensils in detail a few paragraphs further along.

Over the years I've relied almost totally on cast-iron cooking pots and skillets for cooking over direct coals. I've found cast iron to be ideal except for one thing: It's as heavy as an unexpiated sin. Recently, my attention was caught by a new line of cooking utensils made by the Revere Company. These new pots and pans are made by bonding a layer of heat-conducting copper between two layers of stainless steel; the handles and lid-grips are made from brass riveted to the body of the utensil. Before putting these new utensils to the test of coals, I weighed my cast-iron pots and pans and the comparable pieces from the new Revere line for comparison.

My shallow 10-inch cast-iron skillet, which I favor for bacon and ham because it has slanted sides which allow fat to be drained off easily and quickly, weighed in at a healthy 5 pounds. My 8-inch "four egg" skillet tipped the beam at 3 pounds, and the top and bottom halves of my all-time favorite 11-inch double skillet which also functions as a shallow Dutch oven, weighed 5 and 6 pounds respectively, for a total 11-pound heft. The deep, heavy bean and stew pot with its lid weighed 14 pounds, and a cast-iron Dutch oven came very near that weight. The total weight of the cast-iron cooking utensils was 33 pounds.

In the new steel-clad/copper-core Revere set, the heaviest piece was a 3-quart pot with lid, which weighed 2¾ pounds. The 2-quart pot weighed 2¼ pounds, and the three skillets, 8-inch, 10-inch, and 12-inch sizes, each weighed within a few ounces over or under 2 pounds. Total: 11 pounds.

Admittedly, I haven't used these new pieces for 30 years or so, as I have the cast-iron utensils, but judging from the quality of their workmanship, if I'm still cooking outdoors 30 years hence, I'll still be using them. The few times I've tested these pieces over coals, they've performed as well as the cast-iron pieces, and are much easier to clean and pack because their bottoms don't accumulate the greasy black crust that makes it necessary to wrap each cast-iron piece in several layers of newspapers. The new utensils can also be packed in about one-third of the space the cast-iron group requires.

Regretfully, feeling somewhat like a traitor to old friends that have shared a lot of campfires, I've retired all the cast-iron pieces except the double skillet. This one I'm keeping because I've never found any real substitute for it. However, the total weight of the new battery is 20

This is the old battery of cast-iron utensils which has been my standby for many years. Small and medium-sized skillets flank big double skillet which can be used either as two large skillets or a Dutch oven. In a pinch, the double skillet could cook for 6 campers, as the depth of its large bottom half makes it a good stew pot.

pounds instead of 33, so getting the necessary box from car to camp is a lot easier.

This 20-pound heft includes a new cast-aluminum Dutch oven, which has now replaced my cast-iron standby. Developed by the Leyse Company, a firm which specializes in heavy-duty professional cooking utensils, this is the only Dutch oven of modern design and fabrica-tion I've found which can hold its own in competition with the cast-iron Dutch ovens that have been used for several centuries.

If I were going on an extended camping trip during which most of the cooking would be done over direct coals, I'd want to add my medium-sized Dutch oven to the utensils list. To me, the Dutch

When the weight of cast iron is prohibitive for the type of trip you're taking, consider copper-clad stainless steel. It weighs one-third less.

My newest discovery is shown here beside the heavy cast-iron Dutch oven which it will replace. The lightweight Dutch oven is made of thick cast aluminum and has the recessed lid which is needed to hold a layer of coals. Its weight is a fourth that of the cast-iron model. So far, the aluminum oven has cooked well and hasn't warped.

oven is the most versatile of all camp utensils. It makes baking possible, eases the job of preparing a big batch of stew or beans, and can also be used to cook soups and chowders.

If you want to cook for a couple, there are Dutch ovens as small as 3 quarts. A few antique Dutch ovens may be numbered arbitrarily, beginning with #2, which hold about 2¾ quarts; modern ovens are sized in quarts from 3 to 20, which is big enough to cook enough food for a harvest crew or a roundup gang.

One of the great virtues of a Dutch oven, of course, is that it's the one utensil which makes possible unattended cooking on coals. A Dutch oven on a camping trip that is going to last a week or longer relieves the cook of a lot of pot-watching and enables him or her to join in other activities.

Admittedly, cast-iron utensils require a bit of attention to perform properly. They must be seasoned when new, and then if food is burned in them—making the use of a heavy-duty scouring pad necessary—they may require reseasoning.

Both are simple jobs, but a bit messy, and are best done outdoors. Here's the procedure:

Fill the utensil almost level-full with lard, and heat until the lard smokes. Remove the pan from heat and let it cool naturally. Don't try to hurry the cooling. When cool enough to be handled with bare hands, pour out the lard and wipe the inside of the pan dry with paper towels. Return it to the coals quickly, let it heat until the residue of fat clinging to its interior surface starts smoking, then wipe it while hot with a dry rag or with paper towels.

After a cast-iron utensil has been seasoned, never scour it with a soap-impregnated metal pad or with any abrasive cleaning agent. If a stew or some other dish cooked in it leaves a heavy film or residue, fill the utensil with water, add a tiny bit of mild soap, and bring it to boiling heat. Pour out the soapy water and scald the inside with boiling water, then wipe dry. Once a cast-iron utensil has been properly seasoned, very few foods will stick to it. However, some modern detergents will break down the seasoned interior surface, so don't use these any more than you would a metal pad or steel wool.

There are two other types of cookware that can be considered satisfactory for use over direct coals. One is heavy-duty graniteware. This material is relatively light in weight, is not given to warping, and is easy to clean. It can be used with equally good results on coals or on a camp stove.

pot. There are a number of makers of graniteware, and their products are about equally satisfactory.

If the unrelieved black of cast-iron utensils turns you off, porcelain-coated cast-iron utensils in an array of rainbow colors are also suitable for use over coals. Their coatings are fused on, but because they have heavy cast-iron cores, they are not at all susceptible to chipping. I've used utensils by Le Cruset and Dansk on

Graniteware utensils can be used on coals and are lightweight, but because of their tendency to chip have limited life. In my necessary box, graniteware is confined to a teakettle, dishpan, and the gallon-size coffee pot shown here.

Graniteware has one major drawback. It must be packed and handled carefully, for it will chip if banged against a rock or the corner of a grill. Graniteware is made by fusing a molten glass-based coating onto a steel base. If it gets chipped, tiny slivers of this coating may sneak into food, and ingesting them is a definite no-no for human innards.

A graniteware coffeepot can be considered safe, as any slivers will sink to the bottom and be thrown out with the grounds. You can get both skillets and pots of graniteware, but I'll still confine my graniteware for camp use to a coffee-

coals in camps and have never had one damaged. These two makers, incidentally, are the only ones I know of whose utensils have integral porcelain-coated handles. Other makers of porcelain-coated cast-iron utensils equip their skillets with wood or plastic handles, which makes them useless for over-coals cooking jobs. However, cookware of this type is even heavier than plain black cast-iron utensils.

Of the utensils just described, only the copper-cored stainless and those of graniteware are suitable for use with camp stoves. Cast-iron utensils don't heat

Nested cooking kits are extremely popular with many campers. Aluminum is not the best metal for cookware, and plastic plates are not the most desirable for eating. But if weight is a consideration, such cooking kits are a good compromise.

quickly enough over these stoves to be really efficient; you spend as much time waiting for a skillet to reach cooking temperature as you do in cooking, and waste a great deal of fuel just heating the utensil.

If you're going to be using a camp stove, regardless of its type, your choice of utensils extends beyond the new copper-cored stainless Revere utensils or those of graniteware. In fact, any good pressed-steel, or pressed or cast aluminum pots and pans will do well on camp stoves or when used on a grill above a bed of coals.

Some utensils are made by fusing a thick coating of vitreous porcelain to a cast-iron core. These are suitable for use directly on coals.

Both steel and aluminum utensils will reach cooking heat quicker than cast iron, and the moderate heat from a camp stove's burner—much less intense than that from coals—will not cause them to warp unless they're left empty on a burner for a long period of time. To save weight, choose utensils with metal handles. You'll be quite safe in using either wood- or plastic-handled utensils on a camp stove, but a pot holder or two will weigh little and take up almost no room at all.

Wise camp cooks avoid preparing stews or soups or using a Dutch oven for baking on a camp stove. For dishes that require extended cooking time, camp stoves aren't practical because they are extremely extravagant of fuel. It's much more practical, if your taste in camp foods runs to stews, to carry one or two cast-iron or stainless-clad copper pots and cook dishes that require long simmering over a small bed of coals—if you can use

A deep aluminum pot, such as this 5-gallon model, has many uses in camp. Make soup or stew for a crew of 20, wash dishes, haul water to camp, or soak your feet after a long hike.

open coals for cooking where you're camping.

You can, of course, take the grid off the top of a grill and cook a stew or a pot of soup on the bed of charcoal in your grill. Or, you can use a loaf pan on a hibachi for stewing. There's no law that says a stew or soup must be cooked in a round pot. Oversized loaf pans that fit snugly on top of hibachi grids can give you a bit of extra use from this kind of grill.

To complete your list of cooking-associated needs, you should by all means have a graniteware coffeepot, teakettle, and dishpan. Coffee that's kept hot in an aluminum pot quickly takes on an unpleasant taste, and one of the great pleasures of camping is topping off a meal with old-fashioned boiled coffee.

Also, in most camps, I heat dish-washing water in the dishpan as the coals of the cooking fire are dying out, then add enough cold water from the water bucket to bring the temperature down to a bear-

able level. The teakettle should always be kept filled and close to the boiling point; you'll want hot water for diluting stews and soups as they cook and for the cook's helper to use in scalding dishes after they've been washed.

That's right, the cook's helper. No self-respecting camp cook will wash dishes. That job goes in rotation to members of the party who haven't done any cooking chores.

TOOLS FOR COOKING

Put three good knives at the top of your list of cooking tools, if you're going to be doing anything beyond grilling meat patties or precut chops and steaks. The three are an 8-inch chef's knife, an 8-inch butcher knife, and a 3-inch or 4-inch paring knife or a 6-inch utility knife. Add an 8-inch steel and a lightweight cutting board, and you're in business.

You can use your regular kitchen knives in camp, of course, if they're good ones. In choosing knives, "good" doesn't necessarily mean "expensive," though you'll pay more for a good-grade kitchen knife than you will for one of the kind you pick off a carded display rack in a supermarket.

Avoid stainless steel; I know of no stainless steel yet made that will hold an edge long enough to make it a practical tool for a working cook. "Stainless" is a misleading term, anyhow. Stainless steel stains just like other steels, while a high-carbon steel blade will with use acquire a patina that makes it virtually stain-free and rust-free.

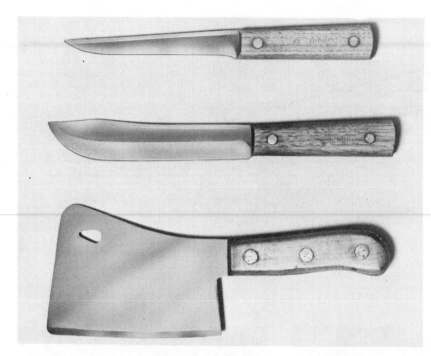

There are only two essential camp knives, a utility knife and a butcher knife (top). If it's a hunting camp, a cleaver is a worthwhile addition for preparing game.

Put an edge on the knives with a coarse emery stone and finish the edge on an Arkansas stone. Use plenty of oil when sharpening. If you've chosen well, you'll only have to give your knives a stone-edge once or twice a year, provided you use the steel religiously at least two or three times a week.

What else you'll need in outdoor cooking tools will depend on the kind of cooking you'll be doing, specifically the type of heat you will use. Regular kitchen-type cooking tools: large spoon, fork, spatula, or pancake turner are all you'll need if your heat source is a small grill or camp stove.

If you're going to be cooking over coals, then you'll want to make the job easier by getting a long-handled spoon, pancake turner, and a pair of long tongs, all with insulated grip areas. The long handles will keep your hands and wrists from being cooked along with the food and the insulated grips will protect your fingers.

Forget about kitchen forks when you're grilling meat. Use tongs to turn the meat instead of a fork. You can turn meat in a pan with a fork, because the juices released by the tines will be collected in the pan. However, if you stab a fork into a steak or chop that's being cooked on a grill or over coals, the juices dribble into the cooking fire and are lost forever. This makes the meat dry and savorless, and also causes flame flare-ups.

Unless you're cooking large numbers of meat patties or chops or steaks, use a latching grill that you can turn by hand and save time as well as labor. Latching grills are now available shaped for cooking fish as well as in straight-sided versions to accommodate flat cuts of meat. The one flaw in this kind of grill is that all the

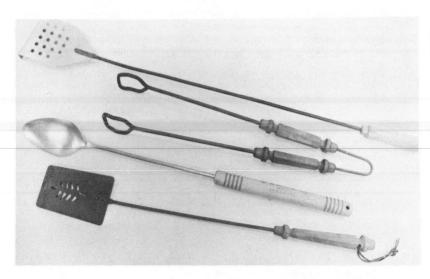

For cooking on a camp stove or small grill, ordinary wooden-handled kitchen tools do quite well. Undoubtedly your spatula will see the greatest use.

Never use a fork to spear meat and turn it on a grill; the precious juices will escape. Use wooden handled tongs instead. On short notice, this ingenious backyard cook contrived a unique grill by igniting a bed of charcoal in a wheelbarrow and laying an oven grate on top.

One utensil that is extremely handy for outdoor cooking is this pot-grabber. Use it to lift any type of pot or pan that doesn't have a handle, or to cook foods right in their cans.

pieces it contains are cooked to the same degree, so if you want to deliver steaks that are rare, medium, and well-done, you'll have to remember when each steak must be removed. Actually, you're better off cooking each one separately.

For basting meat as it cooks, you can carry some clean cloth along and tie a pad of it to a long branch to make a basting swab and save carrying this essential in your necessary box. Most of the basting swabs you'll find in stores have handles that are too short to make them practical for outdoor cooking, anyhow.

Be lavish with pot holders. These don't fit precisely into the category of tools, but let's say they do where outdoor cooking is concerned. Big pieces of old terry-cloth towels make good pot holders for camp cooking. There are also insulated gloves made for outdoor cooks, if your hands are unusually sensitive.

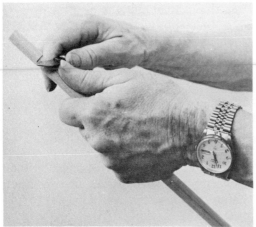

For basting on a grill or spit, cut and peel a long, straight branch (or use a length of dowel) and cut a shoulder in the business end.

The only mistake you may make when buying pot holders is not buying enough. Heavy, insulated gloves are best when cooking over an open fire.

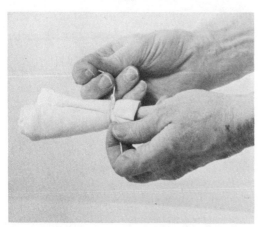

For a swab, fold a small piece of cloth to put all ravelled edges inside the folds, and tie it to the stick. The shoulder keeps the cloth from slipping off; when the cloth wears out, a new swab is easily attached.

This isn't an impressively long tool list, but to repeat an earlier note, where outdoor cookery is concerned, simplest is almost always best.

TABLEWARE

Go by one rule of thumb when choosing tableware for camp use: the heavier and sturdier, the better. After earlier remarks about weight-saving, this may seem contradictory, but it makes sense when you consider the matter for a moment. Lightweight aluminum or tin plates allow food to chill fast in the cool outdoor air. There's nothing less appetizing than eating from a plate smeared with congealed fat or hardened pan juices.

Graniteware plates and serving bowls cool a bit more slowly, but they're fragile, as has already been noted. Heavy crockery such as that used in second- and third-rate restaurants can be placed beside the grill or firepit and allowed to heat while a meal is being cooked. It will keep food warm and tasty long after a similar serving on a thin tin plate has gotten chilled and lost its savor.

Plastic tableware saves weight, just as tin or aluminum does, but it not only has all the quick-cooling vices of these metals but a few of its own, such as heat-sensitivity, which precludes warming of plates and platters unless they're immersed in hot—but not boiling—water. Boiling water will cause some plastic plates to warp; they're designed to withstand the temperature from a hot-water kitchen faucet, which is much lower than that of water poured from a bubbling kettle. And many plastics have a tendency to scratch, which reduces their useful life.

Paper plates? Please don't. The only outdoor tableware you can choose that's worse than paper is Styrofoam.

As for cutlery, you can probably assemble enough from your kitchen discards to equip your necessary box. If you're starting from scratch, get stainless steel or heavily tinned cutlery for the longest useful—and consequently most economical—life.

SUPPLIES

Keeping a small box of regularly used cleanup items inside the necessary box will save a lot of time and trouble. These items aren't numerous, but they do make camp cooking a lot easier and save the cook's helper when he or she starts getting things ready for the next meal.

Incidentally, the time to do this is as soon as the dishwater's hot after everyone's finished eating. Putting off a chore of this kind makes it rougher to handle. Grease and food congeal on plates left standing, and to get cold pots and pans clean takes half again as much boiling water as you'll need if the utensils are still warm when the cleanup's started.

You'll find only three cleanup items essential, and perhaps one or two others handy, so you won't need a big box to hold them. The essential items are a good

Clean-up is quick and easy if you have the right supplies. Don't use soap-impregnated steel-wool pads as they will rust. Much better are copper scouring pads. Add a plastic bottle of detergent, several sponges, and a dish towel; all fit compactly in a large cigar box.

dishwashing soap—not a detergent, but a soap—either in bar, flake, or powdered form; a few nonscratching abrasive pads; and a sponge.

Ask any camp cook and he'll tell you the one thing he reaches for most often is paper towels. These are put within easy reach by a rope holder to keep them high and dry.

Handy if there are a lot of dishes to be washed are a rubber scraper, and a couple of balls of the cleanser-impregnated coppery metallic curls that were made popular under the trademark of Chore Boy. Use these for cleaning soot off the bottoms of cooking utensils to prevent it from building up and making the pot or pan less efficient. Be sure to carry twice as many paper towels as you think you'll need. Burn them when they're used.

PACKING AND STORAGE

Old-time outdoorsmen always carried what they called their "necessary bag." It was usually a small soft-leather bag with a drawstring closing that contained the basics necessary for survival if a pack animal fell down a cliff and took with it what the pioneer scouts considered luxuries, such things as store-bought foods, cooking pots, and so on.

A mountain man's necessary bag might hold a twist of parchment containing salt, a flint-and-steel, a needle and thread, a plug of tobacco, a supply of spare caps for the scout's guns, some lint for packing a wound. We've come a long way from the old necessary bag, but today's campers will profit by keeping all their camp cooking gear together in today's equivalent, which I long ago named a "necessary box."

Wooden boxes make the best necessary boxes, and it's hard to find good ones any more, but they're about the only kind that are satisfactory to use when you're hauling camp kitchen gear around. Wooden boxes last. They not only protect your equipment while traveling, but serve as storage containers during the times they're not in use. If you store cooking gear in cardboard boxes, the boxes can't be stacked, because their sides will buckle.

When using the same boxes you can establish a packing routine that gives you a snugly nested rattle-free load trip after trip, year after year. If you use cardboard boxes, you seldom find two that are the same size, and those big enough to handle

For packing food, utensils, and other cooking gear, most experienced campers use lightweight wooden boxes such as the one shown here. Build them yourself from ¼-inch plywood, or buy them for $3 apiece from a fish market.

A small box will keep tableware together and easier to pack. Don't rob tableware from your kitchen; keep a supply for camping so it always is ready.

cooking equipment are too flimsy to last very long, so you're constantly having to reestablish your packing pattern.

To get a good sturdy wooden box or two, you might have to make your own. I did, about 30 years ago when I was spending more time in wilderness or semiwilderness camps than at home, and am still using those boxes to haul my cooking essentials. If your gear's packed in wood, the pots don't get dented, dishes don't get broken, and hammering up a couple that will fit your exact needs will save a lot of time and trouble if you go out oftener than once a year.

Plan to pack in nests as much as you can, small items inside bigger ones. Make a few extra boxes from thin hardboard to hold such things as table cutlery and your

Combination boxes you can make yourself serve triple duty. Transport your gear in them, then in camp lay them on their sides and attach legs to create an open-ended cupboard and a small table or work surface on top. Ideally, the box should measure about 1½ by 2 feet. From 2 x 2 lumber, cut legs about 24 inches in length, then drill a hole in the center of one end of each to accommodate a table-leg hanger bolt (available in hardware stores). Screw a bolt securely in each leg. Tee nuts can then be attached to the box, in predrilled holes.

cooking knives. Carry your groceries and other expendable supplies in corrugated cardboard boxes which you can use for kindling, because you won't be going home with those groceries if your trip's been a good one.

MAKING YOUR OWN COOKING GEAR

In this section you'll meet a couple of make-it-yourself camp grills and the camp stove which I consider the ultimate one for any outdoor cooking, the sheepherder stove. Unhappily, a sheepherder stove's not really portable enough to be practical in any but a base camp that's going to be used for a long time, and it must be a camp that can be reached by a pickup truck or pack animals.

Grills are another matter, so we'll look at a couple that can be made easily and inexpensively as well as a spit that will roast any cut of meat up to the size of a quartered carcass of a deer or wild boar. In a later chapter you'll find a section in which grills and spits you can improvise will be described, but here we're looking at easily transported metal grills.

To start with the simplest, let's look first at a portable grill that can be used over a firepit.

GRILLS

For grill Number 1 you need a piece of stamped metal mesh, such as is used widely in plants and factories for stairway treads and overhead walkways. A lot of used mesh of this kind winds up in scrap metal depots, and you'll probably be able to find a piece at such an establishment; 50 cents to a dollar will buy a section about 14 by 24 inches, which makes a very satisfactory-sized grill. The dimensions of this grill aren't really important, though the practical size limit is about 24 by 36 inches; in bigger pieces the mesh used tends to sag in the middle.

In addition to the mesh you'll need 8 feet of ⅜-inch or ½-inch concrete reinforcing bar—called "rebar" by builders—which will set you back about 75 cents or a dollar at a building supply store or a ready-mix concrete plant. Have the bar cut into lengths 24 inches long. The sellers are used to cutting this material for buyers and usually make no charge for cutting.

That's your grill. To use it, pound the rod into the ground at the corners of your firepit and attach the mesh at the height you wish with a twist or two of stovepipe wire, as shown in the photos. The heat from your cooking coals sterilizes the mesh, so don't worry about the food you cook on it picking up germs.

For grill Number 2, your basic requirement is a rack for the oven of any standard kitchen range. Most appliance stores take old ranges in trade on new ones and frequently simply junk the old range. Ask any appliance dealer, and they'll probably have one on hand which you can buy for a few cents—perhaps the dealer will give you one just to get rid of it.

One thing always stored in my combo box is a home-made grill that consists only of four lengths of reinforcing rod and a square of metal mesh. Stovepipe wire holds the grill in place once the rods have been pushed into the ground.

Just be sure you get an oven rack, though, not a shelf from a refrigerator. Refrigerator shelves are usually made of light metal and aren't designed to withstand heat. Also, they are cadmium coated and shouldn't come into contact with food.

You'll also need an 8-foot length of aluminum angle; this can be found at building supply and hardware stores in widths from ½ inch to 1 inch, and any width is adequate for the job.

First, clean the oven rack with steel wool or emery cloth to make it easier to work with. Use a hacksaw or saber saw fitted with a metal-cutting blade and cut the angle stock into four 18- to 24-inch lengths.

Still using the saw, cut along each piece of the angle stock from one end as shown for a distance of 1 inch to 1¼ inches. Make a second cut at right angles at the end of this cut to remove one side of the angle stock. These four pieces are the legs of the grill.

Use long-nose pliers as illustrated to start a curving bend in the flat section formed at the end of the angle, then crimp this curve around one side or one end of a corner of the rack. Repeat this operation at each corner of the oven rack.

Use adjustable-jaw pliers or locking-jaw grip pliers for this part of the job; they'll make it easier. Don't crimp the curved section of the leg too tightly; leave it loose enough for the legs to be folded down along the ends of the rack.

That's all there is to the job. To use your grill, simply push each leg into the ground over the firepit. The legs are purposely made longer than you might usually require, for there are places such as the beach, where you'll have to push

You can make another type of grill from an oven rack and four lengths of aluminum angle. Use a hacksaw to cut a portion of the angle away at each end, then bend it with pliers. The legs support the grill yet easily fold for convenient storage.

them in deeply to keep your grill firmly planted, and other places where rocks are scarce and you may have to rim your firepit with a bank of earth to keep it safe. If you make a shallow firepit and encircle it with stones, the legs can be laid out straight and the corners of the grill rested on the stones.

About 6 to 8 inches above the level of the coals is the proper height for the grill itself. On it you can cook steak or fish or vegetables, or it can be used to support cooking utensils. For carrying, fold the legs against the rack and secure them with a twist of wire.

Be sure to keep the grill clean; let the heat of the coals burn off grease and wipe the rack well before packing. It can be kept rust-free when stored for winter by rubbing it well with a piece of suet—but don't use bacon fat or the fat from any cured meat or any prepared solid shortening, as cured fats contain salt and some of the solid shortenings have antioxidant chemicals in them which will cause the metal to rust.

SPIT

For roasting small game or large pieces of meat over a bed of coals, a spit is the easiest utensil to use. If you want a suitable spit, you'll have to make your own or have it made, for I know of no factory-made spits suitable for use over coals. You might consider making two spits, one for small game and another for large roasts. They can be made very inexpensively from standard sizes of iron rod available at any well-stocked machine shop or metalworking shop.

We'll start with the large-sized spit, which will be a bit easier to make than a small one. The tools needed are a butane torch or welding torch, a vise, a ball-peen hammer, locking pliers, a file or grinding wheel (a wheel chucked into a portable drill will be adequate), and a drill.

From a machine shop or metal-working shop, buy a 4-foot length of ½-inch-square iron rod, an 18-inch length of ½-inch-wide strap iron, and a ¾-inch No. 8 hex bolt with nut. These items are for the spit itself; if you don't want to depend on finding a forked branch to support the spit, also get a 4-foot length of ⅜-inch round stock.

Scribe marks 6 inches and 14 inches from one end of the ½-inch rod, and with a butane torch at pinpoint flame adjustment heat the rod at the 6-inch mark until it can be bent in the vise at a 90-degree angle, as shown in the illustration.

Again following the illustration, heat and bend the rod to a 90-degree angle at the 14-inch mark. Make the second bend in line with the first 90-degree angle to form a crank-handle. This is the shaft and handle of your spit.

If you don't have a suitable torch, you can have a welding shop do this bending for you, of course.

Put the spit-shaft aside and form the holding-tine. Cut a 10-inch piece off the length of strap iron. Make in-line 90-degree bends in this 10-inch length at marks scribed 3 inches, 1 inch, and 6 inches from one end. (Look at the drawing of the tine and you'll see the shape it must take.)

Grind or file the 6-inch end to a tapering point and thin the edges and tip as shown. This will be the end of the tine which will be inserted in the meat being roasted.

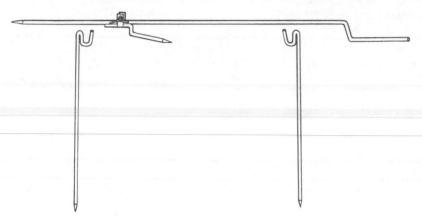

Homemade spit of square iron rod is equipped with a holding tine to prevent roast from slipping. You can make the support rods, too, or use forked sticks.

To attach the tine to the spit, bend the remaining piece of strap iron into a U-shape that will slip over the tine and spit, and drill concentric holes in the upper section to take the hex bolt. When tightened, the bolt will turn the U-shaped section into a clamp, and the tine and spit-rod will be held together firmly.

An option is to cut the strap iron into two lengths and braze it to the end of the tine, if you have welding equipment, or if you want to have this job shop-done. As you'll see in the photos, this is the way my spit-tine was made, and as a minor refinement, a short length of rod was also brazed to the nut to do away with the need for a wrench or pliers to tighten the nut.

To hold the spit over the coals, bend a 1-inch-deep U in one end of each piece of the ⅜-inch round rod and sharpen the other end to make it easy to drive the supports into the ground.

A smaller-diameter spit can be made the same way, to the same longitudinal dimensions, but the smaller cross-section shaft won't support a really heavy roast. However, a smaller-diameter spit is very handy for use when cooking small game and birds.

You'll find as I have that a spit with a square shaft is a lot easier to use than a round one. The square shaft holds the spit in place when turned, even if the meat on it isn't centered to balance its weight exactly. We'll get to directions for using the spit in a later chapter.

SHEEPHERDER STOVES

This is my favorite of all stoves to be used in a camp where I'll be cooking over an extended period of time. The stove got its name from the Western sheepherders, whose working habits are a bit different from those in more settled areas.

Sheepherders in the wide, wide West will keep a flock for a couple of weeks, perhaps even for a month, in one locality, by which time the sheep will have consumed every bit of edible foliage. Then

Factory-made sheepherder stoves come in a wide range of sizes and designs. Not only do they heat your tent in bitter-cold weather but also can be used for cooking.

the herder must move his camp to a fresh grazing range, perhaps 30 to 50 miles distant, where he'll stay for a week or two. Most Western sheepherders live in small horse- or mule-drawn caravans, like those of the old-time gypsies, or a scaled-down, very basic version of a modern motor home without any conveniences such as plumbing or kitchen facilities.

Virtually all sheepherders cook outdoors on a stove which is amazingly versatile. A sheepherder stove can be used as a conventional range, cooking on its surface with pots and pans, or on the flat metal top of the stove itself. But the stove can also be used as a grill if you don't mind a bit of stray smoke, as a griddle, or for sautéing and—special bonus—for baking.

It's the cook's best asset in a camp which will be used for several weeks, and in an all-summer camp I'd hate to be without one. But, the sheepherder stove has two drawbacks. First, because it's a woodburner, a lot of natural fuel needs to be readily available. Second, it's not an easy stove to pack into a remote camp.

Basically, a sheepherder stove is a rectangular metal trough with its open side placed over a firepit. It has a collar or flange at one end to which a length or two of stovepipe is fitted, and a hinged door is set in the opposite end. Lengths of metal rod go across the open or bottom end from side to side, spaced closely enough to serve as a grill with the door open, and also providing a rest for utensils when baking.

You can forget about skillets when you're using a sheepherder stove; swab off the flat top, oil it well, and use the entire surface as a griddle for pancakes, bacon, eggs, steaks, chops, fish, potatoes, or whatever. Put stewing or soup pots on the flat top when it's not in use as a griddle. Leave the door open and use the reinforcing bars across the bottom as a grill, or use the compartment as an oven and whip up biscuits, a cake, or a pie.

There aren't any dimensions or specifications connected with a sheepherder stove. The smallest practical size, though, is roughly 36 inches by 24 inches wide by 14 inches deep. Expand it if you like, in ratio to those dimensions. The sketches give you all the information needed to make one. The body is bent of heavy-gauge sheet metal. The gauge isn't critical, but you want metal that's thick enough to resist warping from heat yet thin enough to heat easily with a minimum of fuel. Sheet metal $\frac{3}{32}$ inch thick is a pretty good compromise.

You can make a sheepherder stove any size you wish; let's compromise this time on one that will have a top cooking area 2 by 3 feet and sides one foot high. For the body of the stove get a piece of sheet metal 4 by 5 feet, and in its center scribe the lines outlining its top. You'll have a 12-inch square of surplus metal to remove at each corner. When these have been cut out, bend the sides up to form an open-topped box and weld the corner joints. The open side of the box formed is actually the bottom of the stove, of course.

Get a metal stovepipe collar (or flange) and weld it in the center of one of the short sides—these are the ends of the stove—and cut out the interior metal. Cut a rectangle from the end opposite the stovepipe collar for the door, which can be any size you like. In this imaginary stove, let's say the door will be 9 inches high by 16 inches wide. The width of the door is

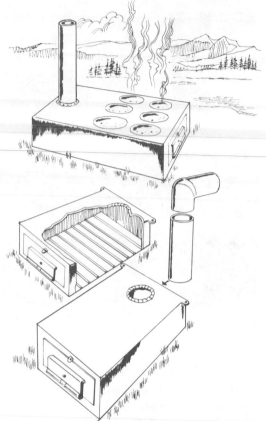

Following the general guidelines given here, you can also make your own sheepherder's stove, or have a metalworking shop tackle the job. It shouldn't be larger than 3 feet wide by 4 feet in length. A collar should be brazed on the top at one end for the stovepipe (be sure to use an asbestos collar where the pipe goes through the tent roof) and there must be some type of flap door at one end for adding wood. Some stoves have an added refinement of bars welded across the open bottom, allowing the stove to be used as an oven as well as a surface cooker. Meats and pancakes can be cooked right on the griddle-like surface.

parallel to the top of the stove, of course, and the 3-inch space at the top of the door will accommodate hinges that allow the door to be swung up.

Attach the hinges and fashion a handle for the door which will be welded to the bottom edge. A reinforcing piece of narrow strap iron should be welded along the bottom of the end in which the door is cut, to reinforce it and serve as a doorstop. If you want to use the interior of the stove as an oven or a grill, weld ⅜-inch rods across the bottom (open) side on the narrow dimension, spaced on 4-inch centers, starting 12 to 14 inches from the door. These will hold baking pans or a roasting pan when the stove is placed over a shallow firepit.

For all practical purposes, the sheepherder stove is now finished. Sit it over a firepit with the open side down, fit a length of straight stovepipe into the collar, a second length into the first, and top off the second with a 45-degree elbow that can be turned as needed to keep the wind from blowing smoke back in the cook's eyes. The elbow finishes the job. All you have to do then is build a fire and start cooking.

If you don't have the facilities to make a sheepherder stove yourself, get a metalworking shop busy on the job. Use it as a patio stove during the noncamping months. Just remember, you'll need a pickup truck or van to haul it to camp and back, and plenty of wood for fuel. But once you've used a sheepherder stove, you'll never be without one until you give up outdoor cookery altogether.

Now, we've just about covered the field of equipment. We'll deal with the problem of preserving foods in camp in the next chapter, in which we'll also be looking at foods and fires and basic cooking procedures.

2 PLANNING MEALS

Camp meals needn't suffer from lack of variety or be any less well cooked than those at home, even if you don't have a food store close by where you can do last-minute shopping.

Plan your menus in advance for your entire stay in camp. As a rule of thumb, allow approximately 2 to 2¼ pounds of food per day per adult or teenage camper, 1½ pounds per day for children. These are raw weights of unprepared foods, not the weight of cooked foods. The figure given takes into consideration the discards such as meat bones, potato peelings, and so forth, but before weighing remove and discard all inedible parts of fresh foods such as carrot tops or the comparable discardable portions of other fresh vegetables, and don't include the weight of any food cartons in your calculations.

Buy all the nonperishable staples you're going to need in advance and pack them separately. This includes packaged foods like flour, cornmeal, macaroni or spaghetti, breakfast cereals, cookies,

crackers, dry beans, rice, and so on. Take boxed, packaged noncrushable foods such as cereals out of their cardboard containers and carry them in plastic bags to save weight and bulk. Also in the staples category are such fresh vegetables as potatoes, onions, carrots, green peppers, cabbage, and similar fresh foods that don't require chilled or refrigerated storage.

Buy perishables at the last possible moment and put those that must be kept chilled in whatever kind of cool-container you are using. In Chapter 3 you'll find a pretty complete discussion of the choices you have, and there are a few storage containers covered in that chapter which you can make yourself.

There are some foods which must be avoided, of course. Today's methods of food handling and processing are so totally dependent on freezing and refrigeration that some traditional camp foods are no longer safe or suitable for campers to include in their menus unless they're prepared to refrigerate them.

To save space when packing, remove the contents from cardboard boxes and place in sturdy plastic bags closed with twist-ties. Be sure to include the panel of directions.

Freeze-dried foods like this sumptuous shrimp dinner allow outback dining never experienced by our grandparents. Many such foods are expensive, but they're also extremely lightweight, require no preservation, and can be prepared in minutes.

CURED MEATS

To get a bit of perspective on the problem facing today's camper, it's necessary to go back a few years in the history of food preservation.

Until fairly recently, three traditional methods besides canning were used in preserving meats. These were salting, air-drying, and smoking. Salting gave such foods as salt pork and salt cod or herring long storage life without refrigeration. Air-drying was used in the preparation of foods such as jerky and some·types of sausage; the drying was originally done in the open air during hot summer days, and when the air became too polluted air-drying moved indoors where warm, filtered air was blown over meats hanging in a screened, enclosed area.

Smoking was used to produce hams and bacon and some types of sausage. In some cases the meats to be smoked were first soaked in a brine solution; in others they were merely rubbed well with salt or buried in salt or sugar or a mixture of salt or sugar and crushed peppercorns for several weeks to draw out the juices, and then suspended from racks or rafters to be smoked.

Fuels used to create the smoke varied, but seldom were they burned in the same room in which the meat was hanging. The fires producing the smoke burned in a separate room or building, and the smoke was ducted into the curing chamber. Hickory was the most widely used wood, but some smokehouses used a combination of hickory and other woods. Corncobs were a traditional fuel in some areas. After the meat was dried by smoking, it was then dried still further by being hung in an aging room for periods ranging from a few days to a year or more.

Regardless of the variations used, the smoke-curing process was and still is time-consuming and costly. Its greatest virtues lie in the distinctive flavors that could be imparted to meats cured this way, and the fact that such meats could be stored without being refrigerated for an almost indefinite period during which their flavor mellowed and their quality generally improved. Rarely did a well-smoked ham or side of bacon mildew or rot or deteriorate in quality. Nor did meat cured in this fashion have in it the carcinogens which so alarm today's nutritionists who caution against the use of what is currently and, to the shame of our government agencies such as the USDA and the FDA, legally labeled "smoked."

Traditional smoked meats—ham, bacon, sausage—began suffering only after the arrival of artificial refrigeration which begat freezing, for freezing was followed by the chemists with their test tubes, singing a siren song of fast preservation to the meat packers.

Although bacon and ham and some sausages are still labeled as being smoked, the traditional process has been replaced by one of pickling with chemical solutions injected under pressure. The cured meat is then coated with other chemical solutions by brushing or dipping to give it a flavor which imitates that of the traditional smoking.

During the early 1960s, when one of the nation's largest meat packers opened a new packing plant, its press releases stated proudly that in the new plant the time required to cure a side of bacon was only 9 minutes and a ham could be cured in less than 20 minutes. The press release then described in some detail the automatically controlled devices used to inject the curing solutions into the meats being treated.

Today, it is virtually impossible to find in the average retail food store any uncanned meat product which will remain edible for more than a few days without the aid of refrigeration. Even some canned meat products today require refrigeration before the can has been opened.

This is a sweeping statement, and its only virtue lies in its truth. No meat-packing firm whose products are distributed nationally produces bacon, ham, or sausages cured by the traditional methods which once allowed them to be stored for many months without refrigeration.

What are sold as cured meats today are actually meats which have been pickled chemically. Not only do these products purporting to be ham and bacon bear little resemblance in taste to the traditional ham and bacon, but the modern curing process actually seems to encourage the development of maggots. These little white grubs which seem to appear spontaneously in decayed meats will usually be noticed in 6 to 8 days in bacon; in some types of sausages in 8 to 12 days; and in ham within 6 to 8 days after these various kinds of "smoked" or "cured" meats have been left unrefrigerated.

This is not hearsay being repeated. During two successive summers a few years ago, while working on a book about the Sierra Nevada Mountains, I camped from the beginning of snowmelt to snow-fall—late April to mid-September—in the cool clean mountain air at altitudes of 6,500 to 8,000 feet.

This mountain terrain was very familiar. Though I'd had no chance to visit it for a dozen years or so, I'd spent summers in it for some 20 years; in my cooking, I was simply following long-established routines. In the camp cooler described in Chapter 3, I'd been accustomed to keeping ham and bacon for as long as a month. Because my camp was some 40 miles from the nearest store and required a mile of hiking, eight miles of driving over no road at all, and ten more miles of unpaved and unattended road to reach pavement, I went into town for supplies only once in every two weeks.

My regular purchases included a small piece of slab bacon, and as long as the cooler was buried in snow, the bacon stayed good between trips. Once the refrigeration of the snow was lost, maggots began to appear in the bacon. After three tries with bacon from two different stores, I gave up and switched to ham, only to have the ham develop maggots, too, before it was all cooked. After that, I swore off cured meats until I could find out a reason for the maggots. What my research uncovered, I've related in the preceding paragraphs.

There are still a few small meat processors who do produce smoked hams and bacon and sausages by the traditional methods of curing and smoking. These producers generally sell by mail order and their prices are high, but if you want cured meats they are your only source of supply. I'm sure the labels on products of the large packing companies that describe their products as being "smoked" are quite literally true; if the meats are exposed to smoke for only a few minutes at some stage of their processing, this labeling can be legally justified. But the cold fact is that you cannot buy genuinely cured meats in your friendly neighborhood supermarket.

This leaves the camper with one of

two alternatives. You can invest in a portable refrigerator, or plan your camp menus without bacon, ham, or sausages. Fresh meats will keep safely without refrigeration for a longer period than you can keep today's mass-produced cured meats in edible condition.

Depend on bacon or ham, then, for only the first few days of your camp stay. You might consider serving salt pork rather than bacon; salt pork is frankly pickled, but it does not seem to suffer the deterioration that today's much more expensive bacon does. It must be kept cool, but need not be refrigerated. Trim off the rinds and discard them, slice the meat about ¼ inch thick, rinse the slices and wipe dry with a paper towel, roll in flour, and fry over brisk heat.

All commercially produced eggs today are unfertilized, and only fertilized eggs go bad quickly, so eggs in the shell will stay fresh for several days without refrigeration. You should be able to enjoy them in any camp lasting less than a week. If you're going to be traveling over rough country to your campsite, pack fresh eggs in a cardboard carton in the cornmeal you'll be using to make cornbread, or in a carton of oatmeal or other cereal.

FRESH MEAT

Beef will stay fresh longer than other meats, though you should take special precautions when transporting and keeping ground beef. Have the meat ground to your order, and ask the butcher to scour his grinder blades before putting the meat through it. Do not let the meat be pressed into a solid mass, or heat-sealed in a plastic wrap. Wrap it loosely in waxed paper or butcher's paper, refrigerate it thoroughly, and keep it as cool as possible until it's cooked.

If these precautions are taken, ground beef will last up to a week in normal temperatures, though during periods of extreme heat three to four days is a safer storage period. You should avoid completely the thin steaks run through the fiber-mangling blades of the butcher's "tenderizer." This treatment carries bacteria into the slits made by the tenderizer and meats which have passed through it go bad quickly.

Beef is the mainstay of most camping menus, of course, and steaks come first to mind, sizzling on a grill over a bed of coals, so we'll look at them first.

Don't just sigh and shake your head mournfully while thinking that because of high meat prices steaks are out of reach. To paraphrase a certain Mr. W. Shakespeare, There are more steaks in Heaven and on Earth than are dreamt of by the average menu-planner. Of course, unless they're seasoned with imagination and cooked with skill, some of the lesser-known steaks are less than heavenly when they get to the table.

For the moment, let's put aside the expensive steak cuts which just about anybody can grill successfully. These choice cuts really need no more than to be swabbed with butter now and then as they sizzle on the grill. Their success depends more on the cook's timing than on his or her advance preparation. But don't take for granted that the steaks bearing these expensive names you see on them in the

Steaks are one of the easiest meats to prepare over coals. Just be sure they are not cooked so long they are shoe-leather tough.

butcher's case are actually entitled to the designations with which they're honored.

To get your money's worth in a butcher shop today, you've got to do your homework and study up on meats until you're able to make an educated guess as to the area on a steer's carcass from which a steak actually was cut.

Prime-cut steaks, T-bone, porterhouse, and top sirloin steaks all come from the central third of the steer's spine; the fourth prime cut, filet mignon, is taken from the tenderloin, a long soft muscle running along the spine. At a glance, filet mignon looks very much like a rib-eye steak, which is cut from the much more solid muscle beween ribs and backbone. However, close inspection will show that while a filet mignon has virtually no grain and no connective tissue, a rib-eye steak has a slightly coarser meat, visible graining, and some connective tissue.

A short while before starting this book, I happened to be standing at the meat section of a supermarket when I saw a man studying very closely a section of the case holding a display of steaks labeled filet mignon. While I was still trying to decide what to buy, this customer pressed the butcher's call button, and when the butcher arrived, pointed to the filets.

He said with a puzzled frown, "I think one of your helpers must've made a mistake in labeling those as filet mignon."

Taking a quick look, the butcher shook his head. "No," he replied, "I'm sure the labels are correct."

"I still think you're wrong," the customer insisted, picking up one of the packages. He went on, "Look here. The meat in this steak's got a diagonal grain, and it's got a lot more connective tissue in it than you'll ever see in tenderloin."

Now the butcher was looking concerned. He took the package and examined it closely, then asked the customer, "You're not a butcher, are you?"

"Not a professional. But I've cut up a few beef carcasses and I know where this meat came from and it wasn't the tenderloin."

"You know, I think you're right," the butcher agreed, realizing he was in a sticky situation. He took a grease pencil from his pocket. "I'll just mark this down to the rib-eye price for you." He scratched through the price on the label.

"You might as well mark the whole bunch down," the customer told him. "I'll buy all of them at that price."

"Now, hold on!" the butcher protested. "This one might be mislabeled, but the rest of them are filet mignon!"

"Would you like to go through all of them with me and see how many are mislabeled?" the man suggested.

After a moment's hesitation, the

A wise shopper learns to recognize various cuts of meat. These are called "breakfast steaks." They're tasty, but since they're not true steaks (they come from the flank) you shouldn't pay steak prices.

cuts, but you'll encounter steaks taken from them on butchers' counters at prime-cut prices. The cuts are labeled "tournedos," "medallions," "breakfast," "cottage," "skirt," or other names that disguise their unsteaklike origins, names which give no hint as to the section of the beef carcass from which they were cut.

It seems to me that we're partly to blame if we've overpaid some butchers for meat, because until recently we've been quite unconcerned about labels. For a long time, we've accepted secondary and utility meat as steaks. Example: "strip" and "shell" steaks come from the poorest steak section on a steer, the thin, tissue-laden flank.

Secondary and utility cuts can be grilled successfully, if you marinate them, or they can be pounded with a mallet to tenderize them and rolled with ingredients that will further tenderize and add flavor to them when cooked. But they're candidates for Dutch oven cooking, not for grilling.

As for other meats, lamb lends itself well to both grill and spit cooking, and will stay fresh for several days under camp storage conditions if you wipe the pieces with a damp cloth every day or so to keep them from drying out. Pork should be cooked within the first two days. Poultry keeps badly without artificial refrigeration. Unless you can get freshly killed chickens from a market that does on-premises slaughtering, use supermarket poultry early during your camping stay. This is equally true of turkey. If you enjoy the dessicated meat of frozen chickens, let them thaw naturally and cook them at once.

Large chunks of meat such as roasts will keep better than steaks or chops. Before leaving for camp, chill the meat well

butcher shook his head. He said, "No. I'm pretty busy right now. But if you want all twelve of these steaks, you can have them for the rib-eye price."

Now, I've no idea whether the knowledgeable customer got one filet mignon or ten or eleven, but I do feel pretty sure he wasn't overcharged for his rib-eye steaks. After inspecting the meat counter, I began to wish my perceptions had been as sharp as his were. But the point of this story is that unless you do your homework, you can be overcharged, either by accident or design, at just about any butcher shop or supermarket meat department.

Meat cuts *can* be identified by bone structure and grain pattern if you want to take the time to study a bit. In today's butcher shops, cuts that were never sold as fancy steaks before are labeled with new names.

Take round steak, chuck steak, flank steak, and arm steak. They are classed as secondary or utility cuts, not prime steak

without allowing it to freeze and keep it as cool as possible until it's cooked. Raw meat thawed after being frozen goes bad very quickly and should be cooked at once.

If at all possible, when you buy a chunk of meat to take to a camp where the meat may be kept for several days before being cooked, get an untrimmed piece, with a thick layer of fat. The fat serves as insulation, and by cutting from the edge away from the fat the freshness of the chunk will be preserved. Every time a large piece of meat is cut, the cut surfaces begin to deteriorate. After chilling it, just before you take off for camp where it will not be cooked at once, wrap the meat in 6 to 10 thicknesses of paper, then in a blanket. In camp, keep it as cool as possible, using the methods you'll find in Chapter 3. All red meats will keep for several days when they are handled this way.

Usually, you can buy a large cut for steaks, and another of a lower grade for stewing meat. Slice or cube only what you need for the meal you're preparing. Remember that all the foregoing applies primarily to beef or lamb. Pork will not keep as long as either of these, and of course liver or tongue and all the other variety meats should be avoided. In a later section we'll get into the preservation of game and fish.

One of the secrets of keeping meat fresh by using the methods given here is never to let it warm up. Keep it in your refrigerator bag or camp refrigerator until the ice is gone, then transfer it at once to the cooler. If you're caught by an unexpected spell of warm weather in a camp area that's usually cool, you can generally salvage all the meat you've brought along by cooking it. Then, cool it as well as possible and store it as you did when it was fresh. Cooked meat stays good much longer than raw, and it's better to eat warmed-over meat than to lose the mainstay of your meals.

SAUSAGES

If you've been planning a traditional wienie roast for any youngsters you may have along, or just to bring back your own first experiences with outdoor cooking, my suggestion is that you read very carefully the labels on any wieners you might be thinking of buying. After reading the labels, your enthusiasm for a wienie roast might be sadly dampened. When the wiener first came to be a low-cost staple in the U.S. diet, it was a good food product, made of trimmings from beef and pork, modestly spiced, and encased in a skin made from the intestines of small animals.

In the beginning days of wiener popularity, the skin came to be dyed with a food coloring called Red #2. This dye was indeed a carcinogen, though generations of youngsters ate wieners and seemed to suffer no ill effects. But the point made here is that originally the wiener was an all-meat product, lightly flavored, a food in which the flavor was enhanced by cooking. It was also a food which could absorb and exchange flavors when cooked with a vegetable in a sort of stew.

If you read the labels on today's wieners, you'll find that they're made from what our British cousins bluntly call offal. Into the modern wiener go such marginally edible substances as tripes, beef lips, beef cheeks, pig's ears, and similar gristly portions of animals. The Red #2 dye is now banned, but in its place are such goodies as nitrates and nitrites.

What is more to the point is that the modern wiener is compressed into molds and cooked completely; its flavorings are so thoroughly locked into its marginally meaty body that it can neither absorb nor transmit any other flavors. Sadly, because I did enjoy real wieners, I gave them up a number of years ago, and you'll find no recipes calling for them in the following pages.

There are some sausages that will keep almost indefinitely without refrigeration. These include good Italian salami—the small hard salamis, about 1¼ inches in diameter, not the big soft salamis—Spanish *chorizos,* and French *saucissons secs.* In many towns, specialty food stores, delicatessens, and ethnic

shops can supply you with these. They are all hard-cured and are designed to be sliced very thinly and eaten uncooked.

FLAVOR ENHANCERS

One of the best flavor enhancers that you can carry on a camping trip is a supply of beef stock. Make your own. It will be better than canned broths, and the broths made from bouillon cubes are principally salt, which costs less when bought in its pure state. Here's a recipe for beef stock:

When refrigeration may be a problem, stick with dried or smoked meats (real smoked meats, not those merely injected with an artificial smoke flavoring). Salami, sausage, knackwurst, and others are favorites, but you may have to shop in ethnic groceries to find them.

BEEF STOCK

> 1 large soup bone or 2 pounds beef trimmings
> 1 to 2 quarts water, to cover the meat plus 2 inches
> ½ cup vinegar
> 2 Tbsp salt

Boil the soup bone or meat trimmings briskly for 30 minutes; reduce to simmer, and periodically ladle off any scum that forms on the surface. Cook 4 to 6 hours.

Strain the stock and refrigerate. Skim off all fat. Store in a jar or other sealed container. Keep as cool as possible until used. Dilute as required for use.

Another quick and easy flavor booster which takes 30 to 45 seconds to prepare in a skillet is the following:

BLACK BUTTER SAUCE

2 Tbsp butter
1 Tbsp white vinegar

Heat butter in a small saucepan until it begins to turn brown. Dash the vinegar into the bubbling butter and swirl the pan to mix. Pour over fried eggs (fried soft in butter) or vegetables while still bubbling hot.

VEGETABLES

When it comes to choosing vegetables, try to buy from stands where fresh vegetables are kept without being refrigerated. Most supermarkets keep their vegetable bins as cold as their refrigerators, and once vegetables have been so thoroughly chilled by artificial refrigeration, their unrefrigerated storage life is drastically reduced. Don't overlook the opportunity of buying farm-fresh produce along the road after you get off the freeways.

In some places you may even today pass roadside stands where farm crops are sold to passing motorists, and if you pass a field of something that looks ripely succulent, the farmer who grew the crop will probably be so complimented by your asking that he'll gather enough to supply your needs.

When stocking up for a camping trip, the ubiquitous but versatile white potato will still be the most important, but don't overlook sweet potatoes or yams, which can be cooked in their skins either over a charcoal grill or buried in the ashes of a firepit. Butternut squash, which travel and keep well, are a good alternative to potatoes. So are summer squash, which can also be cooked without a pan.

Take along a lemon or two and when you cook a bland vegetable such as squash, squeeze a bit of lemon juice over it after sprinkling on salt and pepper. There are very simple sauces which you can carry with you or which can be prepared quickly in a skillet, and these can be used on both vegetables and meat.

Onions must be on the list, of course, both white and the bigger, sweeter red variety or the sharper yellow kind. Carrots and turnips go well in stews and add to their variety. Fresh tomatoes are relatively frail, but if you choose those that are a bit too firm for immediate use they'll ripen if placed in the sun. Cabbage, eggplant, mushrooms, cauliflower will all keep for a week or so without refrigeration. Most of the leaf vegetables, the lettuces and their kin, wilt too quickly and lose their charm.

In the dried food department, there are beans such as pinto, lima, kidney, and white; black-eyed peas and split peas, the latter for a big pot of succulently thick soup. There's also rice to vary the potato routine, and pastas to give a change from both.

When combining camping with fishing, hunting, or hiking, always plan several easy one-pot meals. Freeze-dried meals, or those which are merely dehydrated, make meal preparation a joy at the end of a long day. Simply add hot water . . .

. . . stir . . .

. . . and serve!

Unless you want to lay in something against a rainy day, leave canned foods behind. About the only really useful canned foods in a camp are tomatoes and evaporated milk. Freeze-dried, pouch, and retort foods keep indefinitely without refrigeration, but unless you're backpacking there's not much point in using them when you can enjoy cooking and eating fresh food.

For desserts, concentrate on fresh fruits that will keep fresh: apples, oranges, plums, grapes, tangerines. Avoid today's bananas; the big banana importers refrigerate bananas for shipment now, and the green-tipped bananas that once ripened slowly now rot at the same time they ripen. Peaches and pears are very chancy; often when they're taken off refrigeration they deteriorate with lightning rapidity. Your limited refrigerator space is too valuable to be used for fruit; save it for meats.

PLANNING MENUS

Going back once more to the beginning, when you plan menus for outdoor meals, keep things simple. Too much equipment, too many pots to watch, too many dishes lead to confusion. The best outdoor cooking is almost always that which is done in one pot. Preparing dishes that require elaborate sauces, a string of pans, a lot of mixing and blending should be done in a home kitchen, or reserved for cooking in a patio close enough to a kitchen to ease the precooking steps. Gussying up a meal in a kitchenless camp puts a lot of extra strain on the cook, and cooks should be able to enjoy the meals they prepare just as much as do the others who eat them.

Over the years, my experience has been that camp cooking can pretty well be based on serving a generous breakfast and supper and letting noon meal be a sort of catch-as-catch-can affair. In camp, there are always things that keep intruding on the noon hour, so if the day's started and ended right, midday will pretty much take care of itself.

One way to start breakfast off with a bang is to make a fresh pot of coffee just before turning in for the night. Put the steaming coffee into a vacuum bottle so that a prebreakfast cup can be poured at once, without waiting. Start a fresh pot, of course, to go with breakfast and for leisurely after-breakfast sipping while deciding where to fish, hike, or whatever.

Breakfast, in the absence of ham or bacon, can be made a filling meal in several ways. Biscuits left from last night's supper can be split and browned in butter in a skillet while eggs are cooking. Toast can be made this way, too. Whether eggs are being fried or scrambled, they should be cooked slowly, at the edge of a bed of coals or in a pan raised above the coals on a grill. If you're using a camp stove, turn the flame low.

Incidentally, don't overlook a breakfast omelet, made with some hearty filling such as cheddar cheese or cottage cheese. There's a breakfast dish which I've never heard called anything except a "gluptkin," which is made by breaking a couple of soft-cooked eggs into a bowl over torn-up chunks of buttered toast or biscuits and bits of crisply fried bacon broken up into small pieces. Eat it with a spoon, of course. And put hotcakes high on your list of breakfast foods (see recipes in Chapter 6).

One thing that main outdoor meals have in common with all similar meals: they should be planned around a substantial meat course. If you're having a spit-cooked roast, bake potatoes in the coals and serve something simple such as herbed sliced tomatoes as a salad, a piece of fruit for dessert. If you tire of potatoes with your steak, try baking a hard-shelled butternut squash on the coals; the squash will take longer to cook than the steaks, so start it about a quarter-hour earlier.

Make a stew or two, but space them a day or more apart. Put any vegetables you have into the stew pot after browning the meat, and let it simmer through a long afternoon.

Whatever you do in your menu planning, don't make the common mistake of repeating dishes too often. Outdoor appetites are hearty, but repetition dulls even the heartiest. A little bit of planning not only makes buying supplies easier, but keeps a camp livelier and happier.

3 PACKING AND STORING FOOD

We've still a way to go before we can really start cooking. Now that you've assembled your kitchen battery and planned the meals you're going to cook, let's devote a bit of attention to transporting them. We'll expand the definition of the word to include packing supplies as well as getting them to your campsite safely, and then keeping them in good condition until you're ready to use them. Any military commander will tell you that logistics is half the battle, and though the problems you'll face fall far short of those involved in a military maneuver, preplanning is the only way to solve them.

Item one in packing your camp grub is to put all the nonperishable staples in cartons that won't be disturbed until the campsite is reached. While you were planning your meal schedule, you'll have scheduled for early cooking foods that must be kept cool or refrigerated. You'll also have bought the nonperishable items and packed them before leaving home. Then, at the last stop before taking off for

a camp in wild or semiwild country, all the perishables will have been bought and packed.

Equally important, you'll have reached a decision on what you're going to do about eating en route, for you don't want to break into the boxes of staples before you get to camp.

What you decide to do will have been based on the size and composition of your group, the distance you'll be traveling, and the condition of your budget. Your options are to stop and cook at roadside stops or, if the trip involves overnight stays, at public or commercial campgrounds. You might equally well have decided that you prefer to carry no foods at all for the trip, but to buy what you need on a meal-to-meal basis.

Or, if you feel that you don't want to do any cooking along the way, you can stop and eat at restaurants, and give yourself a break after spending a lot of time and effort getting ready and in view of the camp cooking you'll be doing later on. A compromise decision would be to breakfast at a restaurant, snack at noon on foods bought locally, and treat yourself to dinner when you stop for the night.

One thing's certain. If you have a meal or two at some of the general run-of-the-mill roadside beaneries, you'll enjoy and appreciate good camp cooking a great deal more.

If you do decide to cook or carry something to snack on during the trip, you'll need to segregate the foods destined to be cooked in camp from those consumed on the road. Finger foods are the answer, of course, unless it's an exceptionally long trip with overnight stops. But whatever you do, don't break into the foods you've planned to cook in camp, and throw those carefully thought-out menus all askew.

How you pack depends a great deal on what you're packing. Staples don't present many problems. There are a few tricks I've picked up in packing, dating back to the days when cars were built without trunks and were considerably shorter and narrower than today's machines. Oh, you could get a trunk if you wanted to buy one as an extra-cost accessory, and mount it on brackets outside the tonneau at the back. Most of these add-on trunks were about 16 inches wide, 18 to 20 inches deep, and spanned the back end of the car, which in those days made them around 24 to 26 inches long.

They weren't very roomy, but they did have more space than a running-board luggage rack, which enclosed a space about eight inches wide and eight inches deep and extended along the running

Insulated bags are ideal for brief outings. Here, the large compartment holds two thermos bottles. The smaller compartment holds two plastic boxes plus other small essentials.

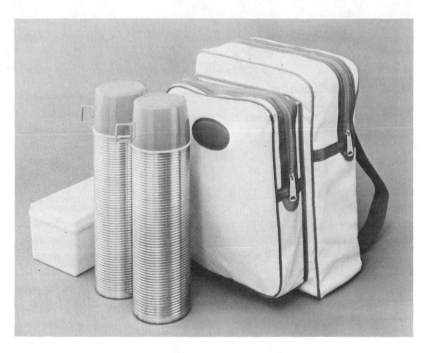

board three to four feet. Anything carried in a running board rack had to be covered with a canvas tarpaulin if you wanted to keep it relatively free from dust when the weather was dry and keep it dry when the rains fell.

Some of the tricks used in packing for a trip to camp that were used then are still valid today. For instance, using a number of small cardboard cartons instead of one or two large ones is as good packing judgment when traveling in the roomier cars of today as it was when using yesterday's cramped vehicles.

To transport eggs, use a crushproof egg carton available in camping supply stores. Or, bury eggs in corn meal or in a flour sack.

Cartons about 10 by 12 by 16 inches are just about ideal. They're light to lift when full, and easy to fit into odd corners of a car's trunk. You can segregate your food by types, mark each carton with the kind of foods it holds, and pack with the heavier boxes and boxes containing foods which a little crushing or squeezing won't harm forming the bottom layer.

Label each box, of course, to guide you in placing them when you unload at your campsite. There, you'll want to arrange the boxes so that foods which will be used first, or foods used most often, will be almost instantly accessible. When two cartons are half-empty, move the contents of one into the other and use the surplus box for kindling. Strips torn from corrugated cardboard boxes rank very high as kindling, especially in wet weather.

Cartons of this kind are best suited for dry staples such as cereal foods, rice, pastas, flour, sugar, and canned foods. If you have a wooden necessary box for your cooking utensils, and haven't fitted it with legs to use as a fireside cooking table/cabinet, rig a cover for it that will enable you to use it as storage for foods such as fresh fruits and vegetables.

These don't keep well in cardboard cartons because they're semimoist and will cause cardboard boxes to disintegrate fairly quickly, yet most of them don't need cool storage such as will be described later. Fitted with a top, a necessary box—or even two such boxes, if you're a constant camper—can serve as a seat as well as provide storage.

Remember, cardboard cartons aren't animalproof. Field mice and chipmunks can get into them, so cover the stacked boxes with a tarp, well roped, when camp's going to be deserted for any length of time. In areas where small, hungry, and agile animals are numerous and where you're going to be camped very long, double-seal the seams and corners with duct tape, which will foil most small critters that might come prying. When a carton's not going to be opened for quite a while, sealing its opening as well will keep out insects.

REFRIGERATION

Keeping perishable foods fresh in a camp with primitive or often no refrigeration requires some kind of schedule on which these perishables are to be used. This, of course, is why you've already planned your menus and have a list that shows exactly the items you need to buy before leaving that last shopping place.

And you've almost certainly provided some kind of cooling for those perishables during an extended stay in camp. There are a number of ways of doing this, so let's look at them here. Our look will extend from the simplest to the fanciest.

Perhaps "refrigeration" isn't the precise word to use in describing the facilities that are usually available to campers. More often than not, "cooling" might be more accurate, but there is refrigerated storage in several degrees of chill available to campers today, as we'll see as we look at the options. Remember that sources of supply for the items described in the following paragraphs are given in the appendix.

Jumbo-size refrigerator bags do not offer the same cooling efficiency as conventional camp coolers. But they are cheaper and lighter, so for brief outings often the preferred choice.

REFRIGERATOR BAGS

While traveling, and for brief periods while in camp, the simplest and least expensive way to provide cool storage is with a refrigerator bag. These bags are made from canvas or vinyl, are insulated with some sort of thermally efficient material such as fiberglass or Styrofoam,

While cracked, cubed, or block ice is traditionally used in camping coolers, don't try to use it in insulated refrigerator bags. Instead use a plastic bottle with liquid refrigerant permanently sealed inside. Place the bottle in your home freezer overnight, then transfer to your refrigerator bag where it will stay frozen for about 12 to 15 hours.

have waterproof, leakproof linings and tight-closing tops. The largest refrigerator bags with which I'm familiar are about 18 by 10 by 12 inches. Their efficiency is roughly comparable to that of an old-time icebox cooled with cakes of ice.

In them you can store a quantity of prechilled perishables such as eggs and meat and milk, together with ice or dry ice or one of the several kinds of refrigerant gels in sealed packages. These gels are prefrozen in your home freezer or the freezing compartment of a refrigerator; they will stay frozen for 16 to 18 hours, depending on the efficiency of your container and the outside temperature. If you are carrying frozen foods, their presence in the bag will add to its cooling efficiency. Refrigerator bags should never be carried in a car trunk or exposed for a long period to direct sunshine.

There are several types of camping coolers available at reasonable prices. This one has a metal housing with thick foam insulation between steel layers. Draincock at one end releases melted ice water.

Some campers prefer coolers made entirely from pressed foam, plastic, or molded fiberglass. Their cooling efficiency is about the same as coolers made of metal, but they are strong and rustproof.

PORTABLE ICE CHESTS

Next on the list come the metal camp ice chests that are also cooled with ice, dry ice, or a refrigerant gel. These are more efficient than refrigerator bags, because they can be sealed more tightly and are better insulated. They will also carry a larger quantity of food. Coleman and other manufacturers offer them in several sizes. A good ice chest will keep food chilled for 48 to 64 hours with dry ice, 24 to 36 hours with ice or a refrigerant gel. Precooling of both food and icebox will prolong the storage periods; so will keeping them closed as much of the time as possible.

Actually, these metal/plastic ice chests are incredibly efficient. On one occasion during midsummer I carried a small ice chest well packed with prefrozen steelhead and salmon from the far northern border of California across the blistering heat of the deserts of Nevada, Arizona, New Mexico, and on to half-past

Miniature coolers are popular with the go-light crowd. This type, made of molded, insulated plastic, has a gullwing lid that opens when you press a button. Use these coolers for quickie outings, or in conjunction with a larger cooler on extended trips.

Texas. Of course, the fish were frozen to begin with, and I put a 2-pound chunk of dry ice in at the beginning of the trip and replenished it at the midway point. But— the fish were still frozen solid after three days and two nights on the road.

REAL REFRIGERATORS

At the deluxe end of the scale, there is now on the market a truly portable refrigerator that uses electronic semiconductors to replace the power-hungry compressor mechanism found in large refrigerators and freezers. There are three sizes of these miniature refrigerators, holding approximately 10, 20, and 40 pounds of food respectively.

These refrigerators operate on the principle of the heat pump, and can be reversed to keep food cold or warm. The degree of cold or warmth can be adjusted.

They operate by being plugged into a car's cigarette lighter, or with a converter, on household current. If your car is to be parked close to your campsite, you can run the engine a few minutes each day to avoid excessive drain on the battery and have genuine refrigeration during your entire stay in camp.

KEEPING FOODS COOL IN CAMP

Even if your campsite is too isolated to consider refrigeration, there are several ways to provide for limited cooling that will help keep foods in good condition until you're ready to cook them. Items that are not highly perishable can often be kept fresh for several days in one of two ways. The first is by simply turning your sleeping bag inside-out and wrapping already cool perishables in it. The other, which is most satisfactory if your campsite is in mountainous terrain where the air is dry and cool, is to provide a well-ventilated container that allows the food to be bathed in a flow of cool air at night, and keeping the container in a breeze-washed, shaded spot during the day.

Such a night-cooler doesn't have to be fancy—just a wooden or metal framework covered with a screen to protect the stored food from insects and allow a constant circulation of air around its contents. An old birdcage lined or covered with fine-mesh screening will work quite well.

For many years I've used a camp cooler which began its life during World War II as a sterilizer for army field hospi-

This is the WWII hospital-instrument sterilizer which I converted into a camp cooler by inserting fine mesh screen to keep insects out. The following picture sequence shows how you can convert a minnow bucket liner the same way.

tals. Camp refrigerators weren't around in the mid-1940s when I bought the sterilizer for something like 75 cents at a war-surplus store. It's a round tanklike container made of stainless steel, about 14 inches high and a foot in diameter, pierced generously with half-inch holes, with a snap-closed steel latching top and handle. I lined it with fine-mesh screen to keep insects out.

In early-season camps at high altitudes, foods to be kept cool are placed in pressure-sealed plastic bags before putting them in the cooler, and the cooler is buried in a snowbank; at my favorite altitude and camping spots, snowbanks are usually around until late in June. After snowmelt, or when my camp is in a warm climate, the cooler's put in a stream or anchored in the shallows at the edge of a lake and then through the day it's moved as necessary to keep it in the shade.

Even after buying a camp refrigerator, I still use the cooler when camping in isolated areas for long periods; it works long after the ice in my refrigerator has melted.

Though the stainless-steel cooler's fancier, its basic construction is virtually the same as the inner compartment of a fisherman's minnow bucket. If you've an old minnow bucket that you've retired, pull out its inner compartment, put in a screen lining, and you've got it made.

Or, you could duplicate this simple type of cooler in a somewhat larger size by cutting a top of plywood to fit a milk bucket, and drilling holes in the bucket's sidewalls. You could also cut rounds of galvanized sheet metal for the ends and solder wire mesh to the edges. If you make this kind of container, be sure to line it with fine-mesh screen, for the openings in the wire mesh are large enough to admit insects.

If the air isn't cool around your campsite, the chances are there'll be a cool-water stream or lake close by any site you might choose for an extended camp. Put perishables in press-to-seal plastic bags, place the small bags in a larger plastic bag, and anchor the bag in the shallows. Weight the big bag with a rock or two if necessary and press all the air from it before sealing it to keep it submerged. Foods stored this way, surrounded by cold water, will generally stay fresh for as long as a week.

There are some precautions you should take when using this kind of preservation/storage. Fresh raw meat should not be crammed into the small storage bags. Use a separate bag for each piece of meat and avoid folding such thin cuts as steaks. Don't crowd fresh vegetables; fill the bags about half-full so they'll stay thin and flat. Be sure to press the sides of the bags closely around their contents and exhaust all air from the bags before closing them.

Use only the inner, perforated section of the minnow bucket. If the outer shell is not damaged, take it with you to camp as a handy water bucket.

Cut a piece of screen to overlap by an inch or two when placed inside the bucket. Fit the screen smoothly inside around the inner wall of the bucket, and your camp cooler's ready to go to work. The holes allow air or water to pass over the food placed inside, while the screen keeps out airborne or aquatic insects.

Using cool water is only one way of utilizing a gift from nature to lengthen food storage time. Another natural cooler can be devised by using the earth itself. Even in warm climates, digging down a couple of feet will usually bring you to a layer of soil appreciably cooler than the air's ambient temperature. Use this natural phenomenon to create cool storage that will keep most vegetables fresher and will also be more satisfactory for meats than surface storage, though not as satisfactory as underwater storage in a stream or at the edge of a lake.

Dig a hole the size needed to hold the provisions to be kept cool; how deep it is will vary from place to place. Along seashores or beaches and close to large streams you might need to go down only a foot or so beneath the warm surface layer of sand or soil. Line the hole with black agricultural plastic. When you buy the plastic, ask for 5-mil material. For easy access, cobble up a cover from branches held together with wire. Place the cover over the hole and spread a layer of plastic material over it, then shovel on a layer of dirt—only a few inches will be required in most cases.

One final thought: if you're new to camping, you might think such painstaking care is unnecessary when you're storing food for a short time. Don't underestimate. Until you've been caught foodless and hungry in an isolated camp, whether through some unforeseen catastrophe of nature or by your own heedlessness, you won't realize just how important food is. No amount of care you take, no amount of time spent in assuring yourself that grub will be available when you want or need it, is ever wasted.

4 BASIC CAMPGROUND COOKING

Cooking, yes, but don't look for recipes just yet. Basics must be our first concern, items of information a camp cook needs to master a very specialized style of cooking.

You won't encounter a long list of hard and fast rules which those who cook outdoors must follow. Camp cooking isn't like the schools of cooking in which master chefs of a bygone era laid down rigid specifications covering ingredients and proportions and procedures which their disciples still observe.

Remember that traditional schools of cooking developed in kitchens, where almost all ingredients and procedures can be standardized, while camp cooks seldom encounter exactly the same conditions twice. If an ingredient called for by a recipe isn't on hand, the camp cook can't run down to the corner and buy what he needs; chances are the nearest store is miles away. He or she must make do with what's available.

Campground cooking, then, is an individual art in which each cook makes his own rules based on general principles, the conditions prevailing at the place and time where he's cooking, and the ingredients he has to work with. Of course, camp cooks follow some basic procedures common to all outdoor cooking, but most of these are based on natural laws and common sense. There are also a few traditional dishes, most of which evolved over a long period of time through the cumulative knowledge of several generations of cooks. Most of these dishes were originally based on regional foods or conditions.

So, the purpose of this chapter isn't to bind you into a straitjacket, but rather to point you in the right direction, after which you can find the path that's most comfortable for your own feet.

You may very well know much of what you'll read in the next 20 or so pages, but there's no way for me to be sure of this. On the assumption that you're just beginning as an outdoor chef, what we're setting out to do now is to establish guideposts and landmarks that will start you on the right trail and keep you from getting off it.

When you're cooking in a kitchen, on a range that has dials you can set to maintain even oven temperatures, knobs you can use to regulate surface burners, timers to warn you when a dish you're cooking is done, then precisely timed recipes are invaluable. In campground cooking, unless you're using a butane or gasoline stove, you're pretty much on your own in determining heat ranges and cooking times.

There are other variables as well that you must consider in outdoor cooking, and one purpose of this chapter is to help the novice camp chef understand what to look for in judging these variables. With experience, what you garner and store in your memory banks from this chapter will help you to identify them. Then, as you continue cooking outdoors, the process of adjusting cooking times to changes in fuel, altitude, and other conditions that affect a dish will become almost instinctive.

You'll make the required adjustments without really thinking about them, just as you'd measure a half-teaspoon of salt just by pouring the right quantity in your cupped palm instead of reaching for a spoon.

COOKING ON CAMP STOVES

Every outdoor cook who's ever used a camp stove sooner or later comes to accept the limitations they impose. I always take a camp stove on trips to places where I'm not sure about the availability of wood, or when I'm going to an area where use of campfires is prohibited. Usually, even if the camp is in a familiar spot where there's plenty of firewood available I'll carry the stove unless I've an exceptionally heavy load of other gear, for a camp stove has a definite place in the camper's scheme of things.

In early-season camping, there's almost always a threat of a soaking rain which makes outdoor cooking an unhappy job, both because of wet wood and because nobody really enjoys cooking in the rain, whether it's a downpour or a drizzle. In late-season camps where snow's a possibility, a sudden snowstorm can be as inhibiting as a heavy rainfall. At such times, being able to cook a meal or two under shelter is very appealing indeed.

Because cooking on a camp stove is very much like cooking on a regular kitchen range, you really need very little in the way of suggestions to be able to use one efficiently. The chief thing to remember is that the burners of camp stoves, whether gasoline- or butane-fueled, are somewhat smaller than those on most kitchen ranges, so foods will cook a bit more slowly, and you'll be tempted to turn the flame up higher.

This is a temptation to avoid. Accept the slower cooking time in order to conserve fuel. Remember, there's no pipe connecting your camp stove to a gas main, no wires drawing current from an electric cable, either of which will give you an endless quantity of fuel or energy. The usefulness of a camp stove is limited by the quantity of fuel you can pack into camp. Once the bottles of butane or can of

When there's doubt about the availability or dryness of wood, a camp stove is a valuable asset. This camper contrived a makeshift table for his stove by lashing dead branches between two trees, allowing him to cook standing upright.

gasoline you've brought along are used up, the stove does nothing except take up space.

All camp stoves have a point at which the small amount of extra heat derived by boosting up the flame uses more fuel than a slightly shorter cooking time will save. This point of maximum energy efficiency will vary slightly in each stove, so it'll be up to you to do a bit of experimenting—preferably at home, where you quite literally have fuel to burn—to determine that special point.

Generally, the point of greatest fuel efficiency in either a gasoline- or butane-fueled camp stove is reached when the first tinge of yellow begins to show at the tips of the flamelets from the burner orifices. This is something you can see with your naked eye in a shaded area, but difficult to see in the bright sunlight, so make

your adjustments in the shade of a tent or fly. As a rule, when the point of greatest efficiency is reached, the top of the flames from the burner orifices will just be touching the bottom of the pan over the burner.

Make your tests by putting a measured amount of water in a saucepan and checking the length of time required for bubbles to form on the bottom of the pot at various flame heights. Remember to start each timing test with fresh, cool water. As you increase the height of the flame, you'll reach a point where the time required to form bubbles on the pan's bottom stays within a second or two of being the same. The lowest setting at the point where increasing the height of the flame doesn't appreciably speed up the formation of bubbles is the most efficient.

Scratch a mark on the backplate of

the burner knob to mark that point. If the stove you're using has no backplate around the adjusting knobs, but is of the type where you simply turn a small buttonlike knob to adjust flame height, use strips of masking tape on the knob and at the edge of the opening its shaft passes through. You won't need the marks after you've used the stove a short time, but they'll be useful to anybody else who might be sharing cooking chores with you in camp—someone who isn't familiar with the stove.

One more thing you should keep in mind about those small burners. Instead of the flame they emit covering the entire bottom of a pan, the small-diameter burners tend to concentrate the heat in the center. It's a good idea to stir food being cooked a little more often to keep burned spots from forming on the pan's bottom. And, if you're using a frying pan, move the eggs or whatever the food might happen to be so they'll cook evenly.

There is one other adjustment you'll have to make if the altitude of your camp is radically different from the one to which you're accustomed, and this will apply whether your cooking is being done on a camp stove or a bed of coals. As you go from a lower to a higher altitude or vice versa, the atmospheric pressure changes, and you must add or subtract from your normal cooking times to compensate for the changes.

If you go from a 2,000-foot altitude to the 6,000-foot level, the rule of thumb I've worked out over the years is to increase the cooking time by about 10 percent per thousand feet for foods being roasted or sautéed and 20 percent per thousand feet for foods being boiled or stewed. When going from 2,000 feet to sea level, you'll decrease cooking times in the same ratio. This may not seem like a great deal of change, but it is, especially if you're cooking a pot of beans or a stew.

This brings us back to the point made at the beginning of this section, about the limitations of camp stoves. They're fine for brewing a fresh pot of coffee at breakfast, when you don't feel like waiting for a freshly lighted campfire to burn down to cooking coals. They're good as gold when you want to frizzle a panful of eggs and make skillet toast, or cook a meat patty or a thin cut such as a chop. But camp stoves really aren't suitable for long, slow, low-heat simmering of dishes such as stews or beans. These belong on a bed of glowing coals.

BROILING OVER COALS

Now, let's get to the firepit, because that's where your camp cooking efforts will be tested to the greatest degree. The first thing to remember is that you don't cook over a blazing fire, but over a bed of glowing *coals*. And the word "glowing" is the place where our discussion of campfire cooking starts.

All coals glow; when they stop glowing they become embers and when the embers get cool enough for you to pick them up and handle them bare-handed they're cinders. With this in mind, let's examine the degree to which live coals glow and try to establish a kind of standard color scheme, for it's this which gives you

FIREMAKING BASICS

Tools for cutting firewood: a bowsaw, hatchet, and small splitting axe.

Have all materials ready in advance before you begin building a fire. After tinder has ignited very small pieces of wood, add progressively larger sizes. For cooking purposes, no wood should be larger in diameter than your wrist, for it takes too long to burn down to coals.

Efficient fire designs have one thing in common: they allow oxygen to circulate freely so the initial flames are full and robust. This particular fire-starting design is called the log-cabin lay.

The teepee lay is good for making a quick fire. As soon as the burned sticks fall over, place thick logs on either side on which to lay your grill.

The keyhole lay is popular because you can keep a robust fire going continually and rake additional coals as needed into the actual cooking area.

a visual indication of how much heat a bed of coals is emitting, and the degree of heat determines your cooking time.

We've all heard the phrase "white heat," and this is the color that appears in a bed of coals when it's fresh and being fanned by a brisk breeze. A bed of coals can stay white-hot for only a short time. As soon as the solid combustible elements in wood have burned away, the flames die. Immediately after this, and for a relatively short time—the time depends primarily on the velocity of prevailing winds and the manner in which the wind sweeps across the firepit—the coals fade from that incandescent white to yellowish and then quickly darken to bright red.

This is the earliest stage at which you should try to begin cooking. Actually, it's the first stage at which you can get close enough to the firepit to cook and still be comfortable enough to think about cooking.

From bright red, coals darken to cherry-red, then to a dark red which sometimes looks purplish. Soon after they reach that stage—again, how soon depends on the wind blowing across them— the coals become embers. Embers from a hardwood fire stay hot enough to cook for a relatively lengthy period of time compared to their earlier color transitions. You can cook an egg in a skillet or make toast or keep a pot of coffee warm on embers.

As soon as the coals reach the cinder stage, they're useless for cooking, but still dangerous to their surroundings. Buried in some of the seemingly dead cinders there is quite likely a bit of unconsumed combustible material which even a mild breeze can fan into flames. For this reason, firepits should always be doused with water or covered with earth before being left unattended. Water's preferable if the firepit is to be used again the next day or for another meal, for the unconsumed combustibles in the cinders will be brought to life by a fresh fire.

TYPES OF WOOD

The period during which your cooking should be done is when the coals are in the span of colors or shades ranging from bright red to the point at which no discernable color remains in them. How long this span lasts when measured in minutes will depend on the kind of wood you're using, as explained earlier.

Different kinds of woods produce different kinds of coals, and you need at least a passing familiarity with these differences. Hardwoods, such as oak, ash, hickory, and beech produce solid, long-lasting coals that throw off very intense heat. You need a bed of coals only 3 or 4 inches thick, and a single bed of coals will see you through the preparation of any dishes that aren't required to simmer a long time; but if you're cooking stew or soup you'll probably have to be ready to move your cooking pot to a fresh spot at least once.

Coals produced by softwoods such as pine, fir, sycamore, and elm give a less intense heat and do not last as long; you'll need a bed of coals at least 6 inches deep before you begin to cook and your pots will have to be moved fairly often.

So-called trash woods such as aspen, tamarack, cottonwood, larch, basswood, and spruce leave light, feathery coals that will be caught by any breeze which may be blowing and alight on food, so cooking coals from these woods must be watched closely and fanned carefully. You'll also need a much deeper bed of coals to begin with, and will have to move your cooking pot more often.

Some woods, notably Douglas fir, cypress, redwood, and cedar, are spark-tossers. Be careful that you don't begin to cook over coals left by these woods until all the sparks have stopped popping, or you'll have cinders in your pans. Incidentally, pay no attention to the myth that if you use coals from a resinous wood such as pine or fir or cedar you'll have a meal which tastes like the resin.

You will, if you try to cook over the flames while the sparks are still popping. However, the sappy resins contained in these woods will all have burned away by the time your fire has been reduced to a bed of coals suitable for cooking. You may get some popping sparks when the heat reaches a small deep pocket of resin, but the bulk of the objectionable resinous sap will have vanished. There won't be enough to flavor your food in the small trickle of smoke that comes from your cooking coals.

Coals under a grill or spit on which food is cooking need to be replenished occasionally. Use a branch to rake away the ashes that have formed on top of the coals, working very gently to keep from causing the ashes to blow up onto the food. Then, just as gently, push fresh coals from around the perimeter to the center of the cooking area, a bit at a time.

To be sure you'll have a continuing supply of fresh coals for a long session of cooking, keep two or three pieces of wood burning at the edge of the firepit furthest from the cooking area. Put the ends of the fresh wood on the coals and as the ends

burn, push the pieces further in. That way you'll always have new coals ready to replace those that have burned to ashes.

Coals produced by charcoal are comparable to those left by the preferred cooking woods. You'll have a long-lasting bed of coals and need only about a 2-inch-deep layer when your fuel is charcoal.

JUDGING COALS

There's a technique of judging the heat emitted by a bed of coals by feel as well as by color. If you've done any amount of cooking on coals, you probably know it, and quite likely learned it more by instinct than design. Beginning outdoor cooks will become aware of this technique as they gain experience, but reading a description of the method and an analysis of how and why it works can shorten the learning period.

To newcomers, though, a word of advice: Please approach learning this technique with caution and don't expect to acquire it overnight. Because no two human bodies have sensory organs which react precisely the same, the technique is difficult to describe. It involves placing the palm of your hand above the grill at the edge of the coals for just a few seconds, to sense the degree of heat the coals are emitting.

Hold your hand palm-down 6 to 8 inches above the surface of the grill. If you can keep it there only two or three seconds, you have high heat from bright coals. Five to seven seconds indicates medium-bright coals and medium heat. Seven to ten seconds exposure tells you the coals are getting dark.

FAST CHARCOAL STARTER

The fastest way to start charcoal is to take an old coffee can with both ends cut out and make holes along the bottom rim with a beer opener. Then cram the can with wadded-up newspaper.

Add charcoal and light paper through one of the bottom holes. The can acts as a chimney; the charcoal is ready to cook over in only a few minutes.

If you don't have a prepared fire site, add a small grill and cook on the top of the can.

When you first begin learning this method, *be very careful not to hold your hand too near the coals or expose the hand to their heat for more than a few seconds.* Coals can be very, very deceptive in appearance, for there are several factors which contribute to the degree of heat they are radiating. These factors include the kind of wood used, the depth of the live coals, the speed and direction of the wind, and the X factor, which is the sensitivity of your own nervous system.

This latter is called the pain threshold, and varies greatly in different individuals. A degree of heat that a person with a low pain threshold can stand for five seconds may be unendurable for one with a high threshold. If you have a low pain threshold you run the risk of getting the palm of your hand blistered if you bring it

When using an open fire pit, it's necessary to judge the coals to determine when they're ready for the type of cooking about to be done. First check their color, then use the palm-down testing method described in the text.

too near the coals and hold it there too long. You may not even be aware that you're absorbing enough heat to raise blisters until the damage has been done.

Move cautiously, then, in learning to judge the heat emitted by a bed of coals by holding your hand near it. Observe the coals carefully, and mark their color in your mind. After you've experimented for a while, you'll acquire the ability to judge within a few seconds just how long will be required to grill a steak or chop over that particular bed of coals.

Your own nervous system is more sensitive than the very finest thermometer in this respect, for you'll be judging the *quality* of the heat as well as its degree of intensity. Once you've acquired the knack of doing this, you can tell almost to a second when a piece of meat being grilled or spit-cooked has been cooked to the desired degree.

While you're learning to judge the intensity of a bed of coals by radiation, you'll also be learning to gauge its intensity by color. The next thing you'll acquire is the ability to match cooking times to the kind of meat you're cooking. Beef, pork, and lamb require different degrees of heat, different cooking times, and different treatment in preparation, such as whether the meat has been marinated, whether it will be basted while it is cooking. The degree of fat in the meat, the shape and thickness of the cut being cooked also play a part in judging the time.

Another factor which influences the timing, as we've already seen, is the distance from the coals to the food being cooked. Only a few of the patio grills I've seen over the years offer any way to adjust the span between the cooking coals and the grill, and most of them provide too little space between the two. If you cook on a grill or spit with only an inch or so between the food and your heat source, the food will be burned on the outside before it's cooked on the inside, unless you're grilling thin strips of bacon.

As was mentioned in Chapter 1, in the pages devoted to make-it-yourself grills, the grills illustrated are provided with legs that can be driven into the ground to bring the grilling area itself the desired distance from the coals, about 6 to 8 inches. If you skipped over that portion because you're not interested in making a grill, it was also noted that not all camp firepits can be made to uniform specifications because of differences in the terrain.

As you gain expertise in using an outdoor grill, you'll soon make the food-to-coals distance adjustment just as automatically as you do the adjustments for timing and the allowances made for coals of different heat intensities. One of the endless fascinations about outdoor cooking is that when you get into camp you also get away from the set situations provided by backyard and patio grills. Each new camp offers a different challenge.

TIMING BROILED FOODS

When you're cooking food in a pot or pan, testing to determine whether it's done is an easy matter. You can find out very quickly whether the beans in a pot are still hard, or whether the meat in a stew is done, or the potatoes are getting mushy. When you're sautéing in a pan, all you need do is take it off the fire for a moment and insert the tip of a knife or a fork into a piece of meat. A quick look at the juices released will tell you how much more cooking is needed, if any.

It's not quite as simple when you're cooking on a grill, whether the grill's over an outdoor firepit or the coals in a patio grill. In the first place, you shouldn't be using a fork to handle meats being cooked on a grill; tongs are much better.

If you open the seared surface of a piece of meat being cooked in a pan, the juices are captured in the pan and partly reabsorbed by the meat. Stab a piece of meat being cooked on a grill, and the juices keep flowing and are lost forever. What's of even more personal concern to you is that while you're testing, your hand and arm are stretched above the firepit. This puts a sensitive part of your body into the same situation that the food is, cooking over the heat of the coals. Timing by sight, then, becomes very important.

Please don't expect to find precise timing given here; all that can be offered is an approximation. If you've read the pages immediately preceding this, you'll understand why giving any kind of accurate timing is next to impossible. But we'll try for a few averages, and leave you to adjust the timing according to the conditions prevailing when you're cooking.

Beef steaks and lamb chops 1½ inches thick or less, cooked on a grill over nice cherry-red coals, should suit average tastes when cooked 5 to 7 minutes per side. Cut off a minute for medium-rare, a minute and a half for rare. Pork should always be cooked until the center of the slice is white; this means 6 to 8 minutes per side. For cuts of 1 inch to 1½ inches thick, increase the times given by one-third.

Cut-up pieces of chicken ought to be cooked over coals just a bit brighter than

Tailor your firepit to the size of your party. A large pit such as this one can easily provide food for six to ten people. A pot of *frijoles borrachos* is resting on the coals, skillet biscuits are ready in the pan, and chicken is cooking on the grill.

cherry-red, to give the skin a nice crust and let the fat liquify and escape. Your timing should allow the meat to be cooked thoroughly, but still be moist, while the skin is crackly-crisp and brown and the layer of fat between skin and flesh has disappeared completely. Today's battery-raised chickens tend to be overfat, and these should be cooked for longer periods over medium-dark coals than you'd cook a fat-free broiling-sized chicken.

Timing chickens on a grill or spit is a judgment call at best. Ten minutes or so per side is about right for a small broiler, but if the bird's marinated or you've gotten hold of a big, fat hen, extend the cooking time. Start cooking cut-up chicken with the bone side down, for the heated bones contribute to cooking the center of a breast or back until the flesh is tender and thoroughly cooked without being unpleasantly dry.

For grilling fish, consult the recipes in Chapter 15; there are so many different kinds and sizes of fish that averaging timing to cover all of them just isn't possible.

Vegetables cooked on the grill over direct heat and without a pot should be placed at the very edge of the grill and rotated and turned frequently. Because their moisture content and sizes vary so greatly, there aren't any rules of thumb that will help you in timing vegetables. You can test them by poking into the cen-

Chicken is such an outdoor favorite because numerous sauces can be used for basting, each sauce giving its own unique flavor while at the same time preventing the meat from burning.

ter with a thin skewer to determine when they're done.

Spit-cooking and cooking *en brochette,* which is what most of us loosely call shish kebabs, are two different things and we'll go into them separately. As cooking *en brochette* can be covered quite briefly, let's consider it first.

KEBABS

Let's get the names straight first. Food cooked on skewers is a style of cooking strongly associated with the Near East. In most Arabic languages, the word for lamb is "shish," and that for meat cubes is "kebab." Thus, the precise meaning of the Near East's popular dish of cubed lamb cooked on skewers has been corrupted into a genetic description of all foods cooked this way.

By whatever name you call it, this style of cooking applies to small cubes of meat interspersed with small vegetables or chunks of vegetables, impaled on a skewer, cooked over coals. Popular ingredients include cubed beef and lamb, pieces of kidney or sweetbreads, sections of sausage, oysters, mussels, shrimp, or lobster, the latter being the only crustaceans with flesh firm enough to be held on a thin skewer. The layered nature of the flesh of chicken, crab, and most fish makes them unsuitable for skewering.

Spaced between the meats on the skewer are vegetables or chunks of vegetables: cherry tomatoes, mushrooms, cubed eggplant, green pepper, Brussels sprouts, pearl onions, sometimes bits of fruit such as pineapple.

Skewered foods such as those mentioned are usually basted with oil or butter as they cook quickly over bright coals. They are usually served on the skewers. No detailed recipes are really needed for preparing this patio specialty, so let's get back to spit-cooking.

SPIT-COOKING

Spit-cooking requires coals a trifle duller than bright cherry-red, for most spit-cooked meats are thick—roasts or whole birds. This, of course, means slower cooking for a longer time, with the spit 14 to 18 inches above the coals. Rotating the spit regularly distributes the heat more evenly and in effect retards cooking slightly. Remember that a spit doesn't have to be turned constantly. A quarter-turn about every 15 minutes does the job very well.

Proper spit rotation also produces that special thin crust which is one of the real treats offered by meats cooked this way. The crust is, of course, the result of heat drying the juices that ooze to the meat's surface, and seals their flavor in. This crusty rim on a slice taken from a spit-cut roast is in itself a treat. If the spit is placed over too-high heat, though, the crust thickens too deeply, and if the spit is

not turned evenly the crust will be too thick in some places and thin in others.

For spit-cooking, I like boneless beef roasts of 4 to 6 pounds. If I can't get a Pike's Peak cut, which is a single piece taken from the rump, I'll have the butcher make up a roll roast of the desired weight. Incidentally, you don't need to worry about the butcher's cord used in tying meats burning away; the juices from the meat keep it moist enough to prevent this. I really prefer to cook a rib roast on the grill, because there are a lot of times when it's the devil's own job trying to balance a rib cut on a spit.

Major roasts cook best when boned and spit-cooked, and the details of making a large spit for camp cookery are given in Chapter 1. If you don't have a spit and don't feel like making one, just grind a sharp point on a 4-foot length of iron rod, suspend it between forked branches driven into the ground, and hold it with a pot holder or cloth pad when turning it.

Basting spit-cooked meat with its drippings is integral to this kind of cookery, so you'll need a drip-pan to place under the spit. The pans used in bakeries to produce "Pullman" loaves are ideal; you can get one at a bakery supply house, or perhaps a local bakery will sell you a used one. Another alternative is a cam cover used on automobile engines. Buy a new one at a parts house, use washers and screws to close the holes it will have. Wash it well with boiling water before using.

Heat from the coals will flow around the sides and ends of the drip-pan and do a very satisfactory job of cooking the meat, which doesn't have to be suspended directly above coals for it to cook, though the narrower the drip-pan used the better. The simplest spit setup described will also handle poultry and turkeys. You will have to attach the chickens with wire twists if you cook more than one at a time, but the turkey can be held by the fork.

In addition to the variables already detailed in earlier paragraphs, cooking large cuts of meat involves another factor which must be considered. The factor is the inner temperature of the roast or bird.

If the roast or fowl you are cooking on a spit comes from the camp cooler immediately before being impaled on the spit, it's going to take longer to cook than would be the case if it is at ambient air temperature. There are two ways to do this, and the easiest way to assure that the meat will cook evenly is to take it from refrigeration long enough before cooking to allow its temperature to equalize.

In case this isn't practical, do as many other chefs do and start the roast cooking 8 to 10 inches higher above the coals than you would normally. Cook it at this height for about 10 minutes, until its temperature is uniform, then lower it to the more usual height of 14 to 18 inches.

When spit-roasting beef, allow 12 to 15 minutes per pound for meat that's crisp on the outside and rare in the center, add 4 to 5 minutes per pound if your objective is medium meat, and 6 to 7 minutes if you want the roast well-done. Pork roasts should always be well-done, so cook a pork roast about 20 minutes per pound. Timing for lamb is the same as beef, but I like to bard lamb, which tends to be dry when spit-roasted.

This is as good a place as any to explain that barding meat of any kind simply means encasing it in a thin covering of pork fat. If you have a friendly butcher who gets his pork by the half-carcass, get him to trim sheets of the fat from the carcass instead of waiting until the butchering is finished and trimming the cuts that will go into his display counter. If your butcher doesn't feel inclined to help you, go to another butcher shop and buy a chunk of salt pork, cut it on the long dimension into thin slices, trim off the salt edges, and blanch it by dipping it into boiling water for a couple of minutes.

Poultry and game birds can also be barded.

Don't mistake barding for *larding,* which means threading thin strips of pork fat through a cut of meat with a special larding needle. The needle is hollow, and when withdrawn the pork strips are left in the meat. If desired, the pork strips can be rolled in herb seasonings before being inserted to spread flavor through the roast. Game, which tends to be dry, is the meat most commonly larded, and small game birds are the food most commonly barded.

When cooking stuffed fowl, you do not need to extend cooking time to be sure the stuffing is cooked, though spit-roasting a stuffed bird isn't common. Try putting into the cavity of any bird you spit-cook a rib or two of celery, including the leaves, some chunks of onion or a shallot or two, and to rub the cavity well with seasonings. When ducks or geese are the fowl on the spit, apple quarters are traditionally put into the cavity. These internal fixings aren't eaten, of course.

Timing fowl being spit-roasted is a bit trickier than timing solid chunks of red meat, but it's really not all that hard. If the meat is commercially raised chicken, allow 8 to 10 minutes per pound for small birds, and keep the coals bright. If the bird weighs more than 2 or 3 pounds, add a minute or so. Turkeys should be spit-cooked over medium-bright coals, with the spit a bit higher than the level used for chickens—say 6 to 8 inches. Time a 10-

pound turkey at 4 to 6 minutes per pound, add or subtract 2 minutes per pound for heavier or lighter birds. Game birds are dealt with in a later chapter.

One small suggestion. Don't be too much of a fanatic about following timing suggestions to the split second. I recall an experience of many years ago, when with a couple of long-standing fishing buddies I went up to Chiquita Lake, which lies just outside the southwestern boundary of Yosemite National Park in the Sierra Nevadas. We'd started long before daybreak and eaten lightly late in the morning; shortly after noon, when we'd finished setting up camp where the vestigial road ended a half-mile from the lake, we were starved. But, as eager as we were to eat, we were even more eager to fish.

One of us—not me, but a chum of Italian descent who'd been promising us his own version of chicken cacciatore for supper that evening—urged me and the third man to go on and hike up to the lake and fish while he cooked supper. While we argued, he was making his preparations. This was to be spit-cooked chicken cacciatore, a dish in which neither of us noncookers believed.

We stuck around long enough to see the volunteer chef well along with his job, then hiked on up to the lake. The fish were hitting on almost any fly at just about every cast, so we forgot about supper. We fished until dark, a matter of three hours or so, and stumbled down the steep trail back to camp.

There on a spit over a bed of embers were the chickens, stuffed with the traditional ingredients of green pepper, tomato chunks, onions, mushrooms, and a tiny dab of garlic, their breasts gleaming with olive oil. There was no sign of our companion, but in a moment we heard snores coming from the tent.

"Holy cow!" the volunteer cook exclaimed when we roused him. "I put those chickens on to cook four hours ago, and they weren't supposed to cook more than an hour! They'll be ruined!"

But they weren't. In fact, the chicken cacciatore was about the best I'd ever tasted. And after that experience, I've never worried too much about overcooking anything spitted over coals.

POT-COOKING TECHNIQUES

Pan- and pot-cooking are much the same, whether the utensil is resting on coals or the burner of a stove. Timing and seasoning dishes cooked outdoors in a pan or pot differ not a bit from what you'd do in your own kitchen; you can observe and taste just as usual. Later, in the recipes chapters, you'll find included the seasonings customarily used in the dishes they cover, but do feel free to modify any that you don't really relish after you've tasted them.

Dutch-oven cooking falls in a separate category, and in this section it can't be safely assumed that you can easily transpose to outdoor use the skills you've acquired at home. Dutch-oven cooking can't be practiced indoors, because no matter how high you turn your oven it still won't heat the oven the way it's heated when buried in coals.

There's no point in giving you estimated timing for foods cooked in a pot or pan, as you can easily tell by stirring, looking, and tasting how the cooking is progressing and make any adjustments necessary by moving the pan to a fresh spot on the coals when you want to speed up the cooking, or placing it at the edge of the coals to slow it down.

Perhaps the most important thing for you to keep in mind when you put a pot or pan directly on coals is that its weight will keep a full flow of oxygen from reaching the area the pot covers, and in a relatively short time the coals on which the pot rests will die. The heat reaching the food diminishes as the coals die and the cooking process is slowed, often to the point of stopping almost completely.

Here, in my double skillet, a beef pot roast cooks in the large bottom half. All that's necessary is to sear the meat in a bit of hot oil, add a cup of water, cover with the lid and let the works slow-simmer to perfection for one hour.

Steady high heat under a pan is very important when you're pan-frying on coals, less important when you happen to be using a stew pot or making soup. When boiling something, a great deal of heat is retained by the food itself, and you have plenty of time in which to move it to a spot where the coals are glowing. When you do this, by the way, the coals in the area where the pot had been sitting will quite likely regain their life.

If you'll look back on the history of cooking and cooking utensils to the day when all cooking, indoor and out, was done over the coals of a wood or coal fire, you'll discover that cooks used a *spider* for sautéing. If you're not acquainted with this utensil, a spider is a type of cast-iron skillet with tripod legs 6 or 7 inches long which hold the pan just above the coals.

Pioneer cooks liked to use spiders, especially when cooking in fireplaces where hearth room was limited. The spider's three legs insured that the coals under it wouldn't be smothered by the weight of the pan, and made easy the job of replenishing dying coals with fresh ones. The waning coals were simply scraped away from between the legs and fresh, glowing coals pushed under the bottom, thus saving the cook from having to move the pan.

How much time will be required for a bed of coals to darken and lose efficiency when weighted down and partly smothered by the bottom of a pot depends largely on the kind of wood which created the coals. We'll get to that in a minute, but the point here is that a pot sitting on a bed of smothered coals is cooking at steadily diminishing efficiency. So, the thing to do is to move the pot from time to time to keep it on fresh coals.

DUTCH-OVEN COOKING

Dutch-oven cooking is the exception to this routine procedure. A Dutch oven doesn't have to be moved, though if you're cooking some dish that requires several hours, the coals are generally renewed at midpoint of the cooking. A 2- to 3-hour cooking time, such as might be needed to cook a stew or pot of beans, will generally require one fresh batch of coals around the pot; but after that one renewal the oven can be left several hours, even overnight, without the quality of the food being impaired. It's virtually impossible to overcook or to burn foods when cooking in a Dutch oven.

In later chapters devoted to recipes you'll get very well acquainted with Dutch-oven cooking, and if you haven't yet begun using one, you should. Use is the only way you can discover why camp cooks usually have a soft spot in their hearts for these versatile and virtually indispensable camp cooking utensils.

A Dutch oven cooks foods in what the technicians of today refer to as a "closed environment," and Dutch ovens were producing this environment several centuries before the technicians or the phrase they coined came into being.

Be sure to distinguish between a closed and a sealed environment. When foods are cooked in a closed environment, their flavors are commingled and recirculated to a point of saturation which no other method of cooking achieves. In a sealed environment, superheated live steam is released into sealed retorts containing the foods to be cooked. The steam penetrates the solid portions of the foods and cooks them quickly, then the steam precipitates and becomes water. When this water is drained from the cooking retort, it takes with it much of the flavor of the food.

Food canneries and large institutions such as prisons and hospitals, where immense quantities of food must be prepared in a short time, cook in steam kettles, which is the chief reason why canned foods and the meals served in big institutions are so generally blah. When camp cooks use a Dutch oven for stewing or roasting meat—or baking bread, for that matter—their dishes please the palate instead of insulting it.

Dutch oven baking (biscuits or camp breads) requires bright coals in fairly large quantities, and usually the coals need not be renewed. In all Dutch-oven cooking, coals should be heaped on top of the lid as well as being pushed high around the sides.

This is why Dutch ovens have a high lip or collar around their lids, why their lids are flat and have high handles. There is no such thing as a dome-topped Dutch oven, and the glass-topped cast-iron pots advertised as being Dutch ovens are to be laughed at rather than used.

In the recipes chapter which follows this one, you'll find detailed ingredients lists and procedures for cooking in Dutch ovens, pots, and skillets, so there's no real reason to go into a lot of dos and don'ts here. One big don't, though. Don't overlook the Dutch oven. It's one of the most versatile utensils in a camp cook's battery. Use it for pot roasts, stewing, and baking, to give variety to meals, and to save a lot of the time that spit- and grill-cooking call for.

DUTCH-OVEN ROAST

Below-ground Dutch-oven cooking is an exciting eating experience. While coals are burning down, sear a venison or beef roast in the oven, then add potatoes, carrots, and other vegetables of your choice, followed by one cup of water.

Next, dig a pit 2 feet deep. Shovel into the pit one-third of your coals and lower the oven on top.

Now shovel the remaining two-thirds of the coals on top, followed by a layer of dirt for insulation. Be careful you don't add too much dirt or you'll smother the coals. Your meal can slow-cook all day while you're hunting and still not burn, although it's ready to eat in two hours.

A whiskbroom is handy for sweeping away ashes before serving the meal.

Dutch ovens are more versatile than most people suspect. For example, if you don't want to take along a skillet, simply use the inverted lid of your oven, placed directly on the coals, to fry foods.

SEASONING

While there's little argument about seasoning foods being cooked in a pot or pan, there are two schools of thought regarding seasoning meats that are cooked on a grill or spit. One school holds that no camp cook worthy of the name would season meat before starting it to cook, the other avers stoutly that seasoning is seasoning no matter at what point in cooking it's applied or added.

Specifically, the don't-season-before-cooking school upholds its stance by pointing out that salt draws the juices, and thus the flavor, from raw meat.

Those in the other corner maintain that several pounds of salt applied in a crust 2 or 3 inches thick would be needed to draw *all* the juices from a piece of meat the size of a roast and add quickly that preseasoning encourages spit- or grill-cooked meats to form the crusty exterior coating which is such a welcome addition to meats cooked by these methods.

Being by nature a peace-loving individual, I try to avoid partisanship on either side. Sometimes I go with one group, and sometimes with the other. Quite frankly, I never have been able to detect much difference in the results achieved by adherents of either school. However, I'm not an advocate of using large quantities of straight salt.

What I prefer as a precooking seasoning for meats that are to be grill- or spit-cooked is a mixture of finely ground herbs to which a bit of salt has been added. I like to pulverize a tiny pinch of dried herbs in a mortar along with a pinch of salt and a very, very tiny amount of either sweet Hungarian paprika or cayenne or chili molido. The herbs vary; they might be basil, oregano, summer savory, dried parsley, or celery tops, or a combination of two or more. If the spirit moves me to do so, I'll often substitute garlic salt or onion salt for plain salt.

Being welded to a single kind of seasoning is as monotonous and unrewarding as watching television repeats or serving vanilla ice cream for dessert 365 days a year. Certainly with the variety of seasonings you can create with a minimum of trouble or effort, you'll be able to find not one, but several combinations that will please you.

CLEANING UP

Let the firepit do a lot of cleaning up for you when a meal has been finished. Toss on a couple of fresh logs—real or the pressed variety—or lay strips of corrugated cardboard on the coals to get a quick, hot flame that will burn plate scrapings and paper napkins, bones, and other after-meal debris. If you're in wild animal country, this is especially important. Fire will devour the fat, and the smell of fat is the main thing that draws carnivores to a campsite.

Let the firepit help with the dishes, too. Put a dishpan of water on the dying coals after a meal's cooked and have hot dishwater when cleanup time begins. Have a teakettle on the boil on the coals for scalding and let dishes air-dry instead of using a dishtowel. Cutlery and cooking tools should be dried, though. Fill emptied cooking pots with water and put them on dying coals to boil, this will cut in half the job of scouring them.

Don't empty dishwater, rinse water, or any cooking debris into a lake or stream, and don't pour it on the ground close to your firepit, tent, or other sleeping area, or to one of the places you use for recreation. Go some distance from camp and dig a hole 8 inches to a foot deep. Pour the used water in this hole and then fill the hole and tread the filled earth firm.

This isn't just in the interest of sanitation, though that is part of the reason. The noses of carnivorous animals are much keener than you might imagine, and both dishwater and rinse water will retain just enough of a food odor to draw them if emptied on the ground. This is very important if you're in bear country, as you'll know if you've ever seen the devastation a bear can wreak in search of food. They'll tear up not just tents, but sturdy cabins, and I've seen the container of a sealed canned ham that a bear had ripped apart

It's inevitable that after every meal someone must wash dishes. When it's your turn, make the job quick and easy by securing dishes in a nylon mesh bag, then sloshing the bag around in boiling water. To save still additional time, don't bother drying the dishes. Simply hang the mesh bags from nearby tree branches and the dishes will quickly drip-dry.

with claws and teeth to get to the morsel inside. A can opener might have done a neater job, but certainly not one that was more efficient. The can looked like its contents had exploded.

Bears aren't really common today, but smaller animals such as raccoons and foxes and coyotes can be real pesky if they come investigating your campsite in the dead of night. One of the most miserably disturbed nights I can remember spending in a semicivilized camp was in a cabin where a trio of chipmunks persisted in mining the floor under my bed for peanuts that an earlier occupant had apparently dropped and that I'd missed in my moving-in cleanup.

If your camps are like most, the chances are you've had a busy day, and need your sleep. It can be downright disconcerting to be waked up by a wild visitor, even if the animal doesn't mean any harm to you.

Now, with all the precautionary preliminaries out of the way, we can at least get down to the actual cooking in our next chapter.

By this time you should have a pretty good idea of the precooking steps and most of the actual cooking details important to the outdoor chef. Actually, with nothing more than the steps detailed in this chapter, you should be able to do a pretty good job of cooking almost anything over a bed of coals, whether or not you have a specific recipe to follow. Oh, there are a lot of traditional recipes that you'll want to use from time to time, and a large number of these will be found in later chapters.

Basically, though, it's up to you to take it from here.

5 RECIPES FOR CAMPGROUND COOKING

Camp cooks really shouldn't feel bound to follow rigidly another cook's listing of ingredients and seasonings. Whether camp-style meals are cooked over charcoal or a firepit in a patio, on a grill or spit or in a Dutch oven or skillet in a wilderness camp, it's the cook's improvisational touch that gives them that extra dimension of goodness. Of course, it helps that those who share outdoor meals are usually as hungry as bears after a day spent outdoors, but even on the occasions when the cook's inspirations don't quite come off as planned, everybody around the cooking fire still enjoys the meal.

So, don't feel obliged to follow these recipes as though they were rules set down by the Internal Revenue Service. Follow your instincts instead. If a recipe calls for thyme and you're fresh out of thyme, use basil or marjoram or rosemary. Who knows? You might like the substitute better than you would have liked the original.

On the rare occasions when there really isn't any adequate substitute for an ingredient, this will be stated clearly in the recipes that follow. You won't find very many recipes where it's necessary to use exactly the ingredients specified, but there are a few.

Look on this chapter as a sampler, not as containing all the foods or food combinations you might enjoy. The recipes were generally chosen because they provide guideposts that can be used in preparing other combinations of ingredients in about the same style. Most of the recipes in this chapter can be infinitely varied with ingredients other than those listed, not because they are necessarily superior to a similar one which specifies another kind of meat or a different combination of seasonings, but because in camp cooking the cook, not the recipe, is king.

What I've tried to do here is to offer a group of dishes in the major spectrum of camp cooking. There's a little bit of beef and a little bit of pork, some steaks, some roasts, some fish, a number of grilled foods, some spit-cooking recipes, some for Dutch ovens and skillets. In later chapters, such as the one on camp baking, you'll encounter some pretty positive do's and don'ts. Baking is a bit more demanding in terms of ingredients and timing than are main dishes.

All the recipes included here have been tested and proved in my own camps, but that doesn't mean you can't improve on them, or that they're infallible. They're subject to the same cook's devils that haunt home kitchens: meat that's tough in spite of a butcher's assurances that it's not, slipups in measuring or in adjusting seasoning, or injudicious substitutions that insert an ingredient alien to the balance of the dish. But, try them. I think you'll like most of them.

MEAT

BEEF POT ROAST

3- to 4-pound beef pot roast
2 Tbsp flour
1½ tsp salt
½ tsp freshly ground pepper
1 small bay leaf, powdered as finely as possible
3 medium-sized onions, peeled and quartered
1 large clove garlic, mashed
6 carrots, peeled, quartered lengthwise or cut into 1-inch-long chunks
4 celery ribs, cut into 1- to 2-inch sections, the big bottom ends split lengthwise
6 small potatoes, halved or quartered
Water to cover, or better yet, a mixture of half water and half beef stock

Wipe the meat well with a cloth or paper towel. Mix the flour, salt, and pepper and rub into the roast. Have a Dutch oven on the coals and hot, its interior oiled. Sear the roast well on all sides. Add the solid ingredients and pour in the liquid; cover the Dutch oven and bury in coals. Cook 2 to 2½ hours. No pot-watching is needed, but the coals should be renewed at about the midpoint in cooking. Serves 6.

SPIT-COOKED BEEF ROAST

6- to 8-pound roast of beef, prefer-
    ably a boneless rump or rolled
    roast

If the roast is a rolled one, be sure
the butcher's prepared it properly, with
the fat on the outside. Put the roast on the
spit, but before placing it over the coals,
rub it with the following:

3 Tbsp butter (don't substitute)
½ Tbsp salad oil
4 to 6 crushed white peppercorns
    or ¼ tsp freshly ground black
    pepper
¼ tsp salt

After the roast has been turned one
complete revolution on a hand-spit, or has
been on a slow-speed power spit for 3 to 4
minutes, begin basting with the following
mixture:

¼ pound butter (not a substitute)
4 crushed white peppercorns or
    ¼ tsp freshly ground black pep-
    per
¼ cup salad oil
¼ tsp salt
⅓ cup red wine vinegar

Cream the butter with the salad oil, mixing in the pepper and salt. Warm the vinegar slightly and combine it with the butter mixture. If you wish, add herbs for
additional seasoning. Stir the basting
sauce well just before brushing it on the
meat.

Revolve a hand-spit about one-quarter turn every 6 to 10 minutes, turning less
often as the coals darken. Cook 14 to 16
minutes per pound for rare meat, 25 minutes per pound for medium, 30 per pound
for well-done. Let the roast rest at the
edge of the firepit for about 10 minutes
before carving. Serves 10–12.

MARINATED STEAK

BEEF ROLLS

Make a marinade by mixing:

⅓ cup dry red wine
¼ cup light cooking oil
¼ cup minced sweet onion
1 small clove mashed garlic
⅓ tsp salt
⅛ tsp freshly ground pepper

Use the loaf pan that serves as your drip-pan to mix the marinade in. When the marinade is ready, put in:

1½ to 2 pounds of beef steak—
flank, round, arm, or chuck—
cut into individual servings
about ½ inch thick (this recipe
isn't for choice cuts such as T-
bone or filet mignon; use one of
the secondary steak cuts)

Marinate the meat for at least 2 hours, moving the pieces now and then so that each gets its fair share of contact with the marinade liquid. (For details on marinating, see Chapter 17).

When ready to cook, grill the steaks over medium coals 20 to 25 minutes, turning them three or four times with tongs and brushing with the marinade each time they're turned.

Leftover marinade can be used as a salad dressing, sprinkled sparsely over lettuce or sliced tomatoes. Serves 4.

2 to 2¼ pounds round steak, cut
about ⅛ inch thick
8 to 10 large mushrooms
½ cup melted butter
4 cups fine breadcrumbs (no
squoosh bread, please; use a
firm bread that won't dissolve
into an unpleasant gooey paste
when moistened)
½ cup minced sweet onion
¾ cup minced parsley
1 large clove garlic, mashed
1 tsp salt
¼ tsp freshly ground pepper
Water
½ cup cooking oil

Pound the steak to thin it still further with a blunt utensil such as the flat side of a heavy cleaver rather than the serrated-face meat hammers which tear up the meat fibers. Cut the steak into pieces about 4 by 6 inches and set aside.

Cut the stems from the mushrooms, reserve the caps. Mince the stems coarsely, combine them with the butter, breadcrumbs, onion, and seasonings. If the mixture is too dry and crumbly to handle easily, add additional melted butter, a dash of the cooking oil, or even a bit of water. Divide this mixture equally between the pieces of steak, roll the meat around the filling, hold with small skewers or cocktail picks.

Heat the oil in a skillet over medium coals, add the rolls and cook 20 to 25 minutes, turning them to prevent excessive browning.

About 10 minutes before the rolls are to be served, brush the mushroom caps with butter and broil them to serve with the meat. Serves 6.

4. Finally, slowly cook in just a bit of hot oil until the meat is tender.

1. With the flat side of a knife or cleaver, tenderize the meat by flattening it. Then cut it into rectangles (save the scraps for soup the next day).

2. Coarsely chop onions, then remove caps from mushrooms and mince the stems.

5. Served with the sautéed mushrooms and fresh biscuits, this is a hearty meal that will delight any camper.

3. After making stuffing, roll it up inside the beef and secure with toothpicks.

BEEF SHORT RIBS

4 to 6 pounds beef short ribs, cut in serving sections
¼ cup flour
1 Tbsp cooking oil (more or less)
½ tsp salt
¼ tsp dried crushed basil
1 cup apple cider

**6 sweet gherkins minced fine, or
2 Tbsp sweet pickle relish, well
drained**

Wipe the short ribs well with a cloth or
paper towel and rub them with the flour
to coat thinly. Over medium-bright coals,
heat the oil in a Dutch oven; use only
enough oil to coat the pan and keep the
ribs from sticking; short ribs tend to be
fatty and excess grease should be avoided.
When the fat is smoking-hot brown the
pieces of ribs a few at a time. When all
pieces are browned, return them to the
Dutch oven, place it on coals, heap coals
around its sides, but do not put coals on
the lid. Cook 30 minutes.

Combine all remaining ingredients;
open the Dutch oven, stir the ribs as
needed to cure unevenly cooked areas,
and drain the pot of excess fat.

Distribute the sauce over the ribs,
being sure all pieces are well coated.
Cover the oven, set on fresh coals, heap
coals around the sides and on the top.
Cook 1 to 1½ hours. Renew coals as
needed. Serves 6–8.

CAMP CHILI

There's nothing better than good camp-
cooked chili, and sadly there's no dish
which has undergone more wanton tin-
kering than has chili con carne, if you
want to give the dish its true name, which
translates as "pepper and meat."

There isn't space enough here for me
to list all the reasons why most of the alterations to chili are phony, so please take
my word that tomatoes, paprika, sour
cream, lime juice, catsup, red wine, Tabasco sauce, soy sauce, butter, or beans of
any kind but especially kidney beans,
have no place whatever in chili con carne.
The following recipe is for genuine chili,
and if you want to serve beans with it,
fine, as long as they're pinto beans. But
don't cook them with the chili itself.

Now, if you feel like embroidering
the recipe that follows, do so by all means.
But if you do so, don't call it chili—call
your version of the dish what it really is, a
meat stew seasoned with red peppers.

**3 to 4 pounds of beef flank,
shank, or arm meat, the least
desirable, leanest, and toughest
you can find**
**¼ to ½ pound beef suet—use the
fat trimmed off the beef bought
for the chili**
1½ tsp cumin seeds (cominos)
**2 Tbsp ground chili powder—its
correct name is chili molido**
1½ tsp salt
1½ cups coarsely chopped onion
**2 cloves finely minced garlic
Water**

Trim all suet off the beef and cut it into
pieces no bigger than the first thumb
joint. Crush the cumin seeds and mix
them with the chili powder and salt. Have
a Dutch oven or a deep, heavy pot very
hot, and in it sear the suet until it is deep
brown. Remove the solid pieces and discard them, leaving a pan of smoking-hot

fat. Add the beef to the pan a handful at a time, stirring as added, and sprinkling with the chili powder, cumin seeds, and salt mixture.

When all the beef has been added and seared, pour off the hot fat, then put in the onion and garlic and stir well. Add cold water to cover, plus 1 inch. Cover the pot; if it's a Dutch oven, bury it in coals; if it's a regular stew pot, put it over medium-bright coals and move as necessary to keep the mixture bubbling gently. Cook for 1 to 1½ hours or longer. No pot-watching is called for, though you may want to stir in a bit more water when you renew the coals at about the midpoint of cooking. Once it's in the pot, there's nothing you can do to hurt a batch of chili or to improve it.

Traditionally, chili con carne is served with well-drained pinto beans and plain boiled rice. Serves 6–8.

2. Fry beef suet until there is a film of hot oil in the bottom of skillet or Dutch oven.

3. Brown beef chunks on all sides. Drain off hot grease, add the remaining ingredients, and slowly simmer for 1 to 1½ hours or longer.

1. To make chili, a special favorite of outdoorsmen, use a tough piece of flank meat, sliced in large cubes.

4. Chili should be ready to eat in 1 to 2 hours, but this is one dish that improves with each additional hour on the coals.

ROAST PORK LOIN

SMOTHERED PORK CHOPS

5- to 6-pound pork loin roast (have the butcher cut the chine-bone between each rib)
1 tsp salt
½ tsp freshly ground pepper
⅛ tsp garlic powder

Mix the seasonings and rub into the roast; put the meat on the grill bone-side-down, over medium-bright coals. Use a drip-pan under the meat. Cook 10 to 15 minutes, until the underside begins to brown.

While the roast is browning, mix the basting sauce. Two are given here, one slightly sweet, the other tarty:

Basting sauce #1—sweetish:
¼ cup dry sherry
2 Tbsp soy sauce
2 Tbsp clover honey
¼ tsp ground ginger

Basting sauce #2—on the tart side:
½ cup tomato paste
2 Tbsp cider vinegar
½ tsp dry powdered basil
¼ tsp dry powdered oregano

Mix ingredients thoroughly. Brush on pork each time it is turned. When sauce is exhausted, baste from the drip-pan. Cooking time, approximately 1 to 1½ hours.

8 thinly cut pork chops or 4 pork steaks
1 Tbsp flour
½ tsp freshly ground pepper
Tiny pinch of powdered cumin seeds
1 tsp cooking oil (more or less)
2 ancho peppers, seeded and cut in chunks (ancho peppers are long and green, thin-fleshed, and slightly hot; if you can't find them, use bell peppers and a double pinch of cumin)
3 small potatoes, peeled and quartered
2 onions, coarsely chopped
2 cups beef stock, or use canned beef broth, or even double the amount of water specified below
2 cups water

Wipe the chops with cloth or paper towel. Combine flour, pepper, and cumin seeds; rub the meat well with this mixture and brown lightly in the cooking oil; use only enough oil to film the bottom of a Dutch oven or covered skillet.

Layer the chops on the bottom of the pan, add remaining ingredients. Cook over medium-bright coals until the liquid begins to bubble, cover the pan, and let cook 45 minutes to 1 hour. Move pan to fresh coals as necessary.

PORK AND SAUSAGE STEW

Trim all visible fat from meat. Mix flour, caraway seeds, and salt and dredge the meat. Have the oil in the Dutch oven very hot and brown the meat lightly. Cut the sausages in 1-inch lengths and add them; then put in the remaining solid ingredients, stirring to mix them with the meats. Finally, mix the liquid ingredients and pour over the meat. Close the Dutch oven and bury it in coals. Cook 1¾ to 2 hours. No pot-watching is required, but when renewing the coals at midpoint of cooking, you might open the pot and stir it well. Serves 6.

GRILLED SPARERIBS

3 pounds pork, cubed about 1 inch, or use small pork chops
¼ cup flour
2 tsp caraway seeds
2 to 3 Tbsp cooking oil—the smallest quantity needed to put a thin film on the bottom of a Dutch oven
1½ tsp salt
1 pound knackwurst, bratwurst, chorizo, or Polish sausage; any firm uncooked sausage will do, but avoid frankfurters
4 or 5 medium-sized carrots, cut in large chunks
½ head cabbage, shredded coarsely
2 small onions, quartered
½ cup water
½ cup dry white wine
2 Tbsp tomato paste

3 to 4 pounds pork spareribs (allow roughly a pound per serving)

Basting sauce:
1 cup tomato juice
¼ cup cider vinegar
½ cup tomato catsup
2 Tbsp. Worcestershire sauce
2 Tbsp scraped onion pulp (use a serrated steak knife to speed the scraping)
1 clove garlic, mashed
  Pinch powdered basil
  Pinch powdered oregano

Trim all visible fat off ribs. Cut them into two pieces for easy handling. Combine the remaining ingredients in a bowl. Put the ribs over bright coals with a drip-pan under them and cook 10 minutes per side before beginning to baste. Continue cooking for 45 minutes to 1 hour, turning the ribs often and basting them with the sauce each time they are turned. When all the basting sauce has been used, baste with liquid from the drip-pan. Before serving, cut the ribs into individual pieces. Serves 4.

Spare ribs are ideal for cooking over coals. Buy whole rib plates, then slice them so there are two ribs in each portion.

Traditionally, ribs are basted with some type of sauce or marinade, usually one that has a spicy tomato base. Over the years, camp cooks have created hundreds of recipes.

GRILLED PORK CHOPS

4 large or 8 small chops, about ½ inch thick

Basting sauce:
- ¾ cup warm beer
- 1 Tbsp lemon juice
- 1 Tbsp Worcestershire or Picka-peppa sauce
- 1 tsp dry mustard or ¾ tsp prepared mustard
- ½ tsp onion salt or 2 Tbsp scraped onion pulp
- ⅛ tsp freshly ground pepper

Trim excess fat from chops; put them on the grill over bright coals, over a drip-pan. Let cook 5 minutes per side before beginning to baste. Cook 30 to 40 minutes, turning every 10 minutes and basting each time the chops are turned. When the sauce is exhausted, baste from the drip-pan. Serves 4.

GRILLED HERBED LAMB OR VEAL CHOPS

2 lamb chops or 1 large veal chop

per serving, the chops cut about ½ inch thick
- 2 Tbsp soft butter
- 1 tsp salt
- ½ tsp freshly ground pepper

Cream together the butter and seasonings and rub the chops well with the mixture before starting to grill them.

Basting sauce:
- 2½ cups soft butter
- 1 Tbsp freshly chopped parsley
- ½ tsp powdered thyme
- ¾ tsp crushed marjoram
- 1 tsp lemon juice

Combine the sauce ingredients and warm them so they can be brushed on easily.

Grill the chops 5 minutes per side over medium-bright coals and begin basting the second time they are turned; total cooking time is about 30 minutes.

SPIT-ROAST LEG OF LAMB

- 1 bone-in leg of lamb, 5 to 6 pounds
- 2 cloves garlic
- ⅓ to ½ cup butter
- 1 tsp powdered rosemary
- 1 tsp salt
- Dash of pepper

Make small incisions in the meat, cut the garlic lengthwise into thin slivers, and insert them in the slits. Balance the leg on the spit; usually this can be done most easily by following the bone with the point of the spit. Combine butter, rosemary, salt, and pepper and rub meat with a portion of the mixture, using the remainder to baste with while cooking. The meat should be 8 to 10 inches above medium-bright coals. Give spit one-quarter turn every 15 to 20 minutes. Cooking time will be approximately 1¼ to 1½ hours. Serves 6–8.

GRILLED CHICKEN

2 frying-sized chickens, quartered

Marinade:
½ cup light cooking oil or olive oil
⅓ cup fresh lemon juice
2 Tbsp scraped onion pulp
1 tsp chopped fresh tarragon or ¾ tsp dried powdered tarragon
1 Tbsp freshly chopped parsley
½ tsp salt
2 dashes Tabasco sauce

Wipe the chicken pieces well with cloth or paper towel. Combine the marinade ingredients; marinate the chicken pieces for a minimum of 2 hours—4 is better—moving them in the pan and stirring the marinade occasionally. Drain well and put on the grill over medium-bright coals, using a drip-pan. Cook 1 to 1¼ hours, turning the pieces about every 10 to 15 minutes and basting with the marinade when turned. Serves 4–6.

CHICKEN CACCIATORE

This is the Italian classic, Hunter's Style Chicken. There is also a spit-cooked version, which you'll find in Part III.

1 large chicken, roasting-size, or two small ones, disjointed
¼ cup olive oil
½ cup dry red wine—Chianti is traditional, but a Barolo or Barbera is equally good

1 **large sweet onion, coarsely
    chopped**
1 **clove garlic, minced very fine**
1 **medium-sized bell pepper, cut
    in strips**
6 **cherry tomatoes, halved, or 1
    large tomato cut in thumb-sized
    chunks; be sure to add the juice**
6 **large fresh mushrooms,
    coarsely chopped**
1 **tsp salt**

Brown the chicken pieces lightly in a
small quantity of the oil in the Dutch
oven. Put all the pieces in the pot, mixing
the vegetables with them. Mix the oil and
wine and pour over the chicken-vegetable
mix. Cover the Dutch oven, bury in coals,
not overlooking a layer of coals on the lid.
Cook 1½ to 2 hours. No pot-opening is required, but when you renew the coals on
the lid you might feel like opening the pot
and stirring a bit. Serves 4–6.

ARROZ CON POLLO

Spain's answer to Chicken Cacciatore is
Chicken with Rice, and although fairly
complicated to prepare, is a fine dish if facilities are ample.

1 **large chicken, about 3 pounds,
    cut up**

¼ **tsp saffron**
1 **onion**
1½ **tsp salt**

Put the chicken's back and wingtips into a
pot with 3 cups of water, the onion, saffron, and salt. Boil briskly for 30 to 40
minutes. Strain the stock and reserve 2½
cups.

1 **Tbsp flour**
½ **tsp salt**
¼ **cup fine olive oil**
¼ **lb lean ham or Canadian bacon,
    diced**
6 **small green onions, including
    tops**
2 **Tbsp minced parsley**
1 **small can diced pimientos, well
    drained**
1 **powdered bay leaf**
1½ **cups long-grain rice**
1 **level tsp salt**
¾ **cup pitted ripe olives, well
    drained**

Rub the chicken pieces with flour and salt.
In a deep skillet with a cover, sauté in the
oil over medium-dark coals until lightly
browned and tender. As the chicken
begins to brown, add the onions. Remove
chicken and keep warm. Add ham, parsley, and pimientos to skillet; cook 5 minutes over dark coals. Add the chicken
stock and move the pan to bright coals;
bring it to a boil, add the rice and bay leaf,
and cook 10 minutes, until the rice is
tender. Return the chicken to the pan,
add the olives, cover the pan, and place
over dark coals 20 to 25 minutes, until the
rice has absorbed all the liquid.

DUTCH OVEN TURKEY DRUMSTICKS

2 **large or 3 medium-sized turkey drumsticks (allow half a drumstick per serving; if cooking in larger quantities, simply increase all drumsticks)**
1 **bay leaf**
1 **small onion, minced**
½ **tsp salt**
¼ **tsp freshly ground pepper**
¾ **cup warm beer**
¼ **cup bottled chili sauce**
1 **Tbsp prepared mustard**
2 **Tbsp cooking oil**

Lay the drumsticks on the bottom of the Dutch oven with as much space as possible between them. Add the bay leaf, sprinkle on the minced onions, dust with the salt and pepper. Combine remaining ingredients and pour over the drumsticks. Cover the Dutch oven, bury in coals, cook 1¼ to 1½ hours.

FRESHWATER FISH

Many a camp cook gets in his or her best licks on a fishing trip, especially after they've found out how delicious really fresh fish taste. Now, a campfire isn't the place to do a lot of fancy cooking, so we'll save the fancy fish dishes until later and give you a few very simple ones here.

Although trout seem to predominate in this section, remember that recipes for preparing freshwater fish can almost always be interchanged to accommodate any species. When substitution of one species for another can't be made, a warning will be included in the recipe.

DUTCH OVEN TROUT

6 **8-inch trout**
12 **slices bacon**
1 **tsp ground pepper**

After cleaning the trout, remove the heads and split them along the backbone. Push the flesh on each side of the cut away from the spines of the trout to expose the juncture of backbone and ribs. With the tip of a very sharp knife, cut the ribs free from the backbone. Remove the heads and all fins, including the caudal, or tail fin.

Lay three slices of bacon on the bottom of a Dutch oven, put a half-trout, flesh-side-down, on each slice. Sprinkle pepper lightly over the upper sides of the trout. Arrange a second layer of bacon slices and trout at right angles to the first, and continue to arrange other layers, each at right angles to the one below it, until all the trout halves are in the pot.

Cover the Dutch oven, bury in coals, cook for 35 to 40 minutes. Serve a slice of bacon with each half-trout. Serves 3.

If you cook bass this way, they should be skinned.

TROUT BAKED IN COALS

1 8-inch trout per serving
6 to 8 fresh green cornhusks per trout
1 tsp butter per trout
   Salt, pepper

If no green cornhusks are available, use dry cornhusks; many grocery stores which stock ethnic foods now carry these in small bundles, ready for use. If dry husks are used, soak them in water for 2 hours before.

Rub each trout lightly with butter; put the remaining butter into the cavities. Dust the fish very lightly with salt and pepper. Wrap each trout separately in 5 or 6 layers of cornhusks, overlapping as

needed to enclose them fully. Use light wire wrapped loosely around the husks to secure the parcel.

Bury the parcels (and do not add foil to them as an outer covering) in coals and cook 25 to 30 minutes for 8-inch fish; the cooking time can be shortened or extended a few minutes for smaller or larger fish.

GRILLED TROUT

6 to 8 trout, a bit larger than pan-size, 8 inches or more
   Butter
   Salt and pepper
6 to 8 thin slices of lemon

Wipe the fish inside and out with cloth or paper towels. Rub them inside and out with butter; dust with salt and pepper. Put a slice of lemon cut into halves into the cavity of each fish and grill over medium coals, about 5 to 6 minutes per side.

Old-time woodsmen, to whom salt was an expensive and scarce commodity, used to grill freshly caught trout without seasoning, just tossing them on the coals and letting them cook until the skins charred black. I tried this once, when I was fishing a tiny spring-fed lake on an isolated mountain ridge that was very tough to climb. The fish were hitting on every cast, and the joy of taking and releasing them kept me so engrossed that dusk got there before I was ready for it. Not wanting to risk climbing down the steep ridge in the dark, I decided to stay the night. I had no utensils, but there were enough windfall branches for a fire. I cooked the fish on the raw coals, and sure enough, the charred skin did give them a sort of seasoning. But later, when repeating the trick at a time when it wasn't necessary, the trout charred black without seasoning didn't taste nearly as good as I remembered.

POACHED TROUT

1 10- to 12-inch trout for each two servings

Court-bouillon:
  6 cups water
  1 tsp salt
  ½ lemon
  1 carrot, peeled and chopped coarsely
  ½ medium-sized onion, chopped coarsely
    Sprig of parsley
    Sprig of fresh thyme or ½ tsp powdered thyme
  ½ bay leaf
  2 or 3 peppercorns

Boil the bouillon 30 to 45 minutes and strain through cloth into a large deep skillet. Remove the heads and tails from the fish so they'll fit the pan. Put them in the bouillon; if it does not cover the fish com-

pletely, add water. Cook over medium-bright coals 10 to 12 minutes.

This recipe adapts itself nicely to small trout or fillets, but there's no point in filleting a trout less than 12 inches long. If it's properly cooked, the skin can be slit along the spine and the top layer of flesh lifted free of the bones; then the bones can be lifted off the bottom half.

PANFISH PAN-FRIED

Allow 4 to 6 large panfish, 8 to 10 small ones, per serving.

18 to 20 perch, bluegill, or other panfish
    Butter or other cooking fat as needed
  2 cups well-crushed cracker crumbs
    Salt, pepper

After the fish have been cleaned and scaled, wipe them with a cloth dipped in lightly salted water—about 1 teaspoon salt per quart. Heat fat or cooking oil in skillet; the fat should be no more than ⅛ to ¼ inch deep in the pan. Sprinkle a dash of salt in the fat. While the fat heats, rub the fish inside and out with fat, sprinkle with salt and pepper, roll in the crumbs.

When the fat is hot enough to brown a cube of bread in 2 minutes, begin cooking the fish. The number you cook at one time will depend on the size of the skillet used; just don't overcrowd it. Cook about 3 to 4 minutes per side, until nicely browned; turn and cook until other side browns. Drain on papers before transferring to plates, or eat them out of hand while waiting for the next batch to cook.

In Chapters 14 and 15, you'll find tips on handling freshwater fish, preparing them for cooking, and more recipes. The only information lacking is how to catch the fish when they're not biting. This isn't included, because I don't have any sure-fire recipes for catching fish, and if you do, or know of anyone who does, you should broadcast this news to the fishing world. But life would be dull, wouldn't it, if you had no challenges at all?

SALTWATER FISH

There's only one difference between cooking freshwater and saltwater fish: the latter tend to contain a higher percentage of oil in their flesh. To compensate for this difference, saltwater fish are usually prepared in ways which allow these oils to escape during cooking, and by adding a slightly larger proportion of acidic ingredients such as wine and lemon juice to recipes used in preparing them.

As a general rule, any recipe for the cooking of freshwater fish except those involving pan-frying is suitable for use with saltwater fish. Because there are a number of recipes for saltwater fish in later chapters, only a few are included here, to provide you with some basic guidelines.

As a rule, saltwater fish should be filleted or cut into steaks. Cook fillets on the grill with the skin side down; brush with fat as they cook. Turn fish steaks only once, using a pancake turner; handle gently to keep the flesh from separating. And remember in all saltwater fish cookery, use a light hand when adding butter or other cooking fat.

Use your own judgment about seasonings, but lean largely on lemon juice, white wine, and the less-pungent herbs such as thyme and parsley and rosemary. Usually, the least seasoning put on a freshly caught fish is the best.

One of the best methods to use in preparing saltwater fish is to plank them. This is the traditional method of cooking shad by the seashore or on the banks of one of the streams up which they migrate on their spawning runs. The recipe that follows will give you the basic procedures for planking fish. It's an easy way to cook outdoors, and it saves a lot of time in preparation and pot-watching as well as after-supper cleanup. Here's how it's done.

PLANKED SALMON

If you plan to plank-cook a fish on a seashore camping-fishing trip, carry along a wide board—solid wood, not plywood, which will blister and buckle—and the necessary black or blued roofing nails. *Do not use galvanized nails.* In Chapter 13 you'll find details of cleaning a fish for planking and how to cut fillets, which are also suitable for plank-cooking.

12- to 15-pound salmon, cleaned from the backbone or cut into fillets with the skin left on
Salt, pepper, lemon juice

Flatten the fish or fillets and nail with the skin side to the board. Prop the board 20 to 30 inches away from a bed of red coals, using rocks or stakes to hold it in place. The fish should be nailed to the middle of the board.

A 12- to 15-pound salmon will cook in about 45 minutes, fillets in about 30 minutes. The plank should be turned once, end over end, at the midpoint of cooking. When you can slip a blunt knife easily between skin and flesh, the fish is ready to eat. Do not season until the fish is cooked, then season lightly with salt, pepper, and lemon juice. Serves 12-15.

GRILLED STRIPED BASS, FISHERMAN-STYLE

8 fillets about 3 by 6 inches and ½ inch thick
2 Tbsp light cooking oil

2 small sweet onions
3 ripe tomatoes
1 bell pepper
1 cup dry white wine
12 to 14 stuffed green olives

Grill the fillets over bright coals 4 to 6 minutes per side. While they cook, prepare the sauce in a big skillet set on the coals. Heat the oil; cut the onions and tomatoes into chunks, the pepper into strips. Sauté in the oil until the pepper begins to soften, then add the wine. Slide the fillets in the sauce; drain the olives thoroughly and add them. Serve a portion of the sauce with each pair of fillets to 4 hungry campers.

VEGETABLES

Almost all fresh vegetables can be grilled. They should be cooked around the edge of the grill, not directly over a bed of glowing coals, and rotated from time to time. Potatoes, squash, onions, eggplant, corn, turnips, carrots, beets, cabbage, green tomatoes, mushrooms, parsnips come to mind at once. Most of these can also be cooked buried in coals, though most of them need to be wrapped up to keep them from charring.

Please—forget about foil when you cook vegetables buried in coals. Foil forms a sealed package which traps and holds the vapors driven by heat from the food it encloses, and what you get is soggy, watery vegetables cooked as though they'd been steamed to death in one of the mass-production vats in a hospital or prison. If you *like* steamed vegetables, that's fine, but you'll find their flavor is improved if you wrap the vegetables in cornhusks or some brown paper sacks or newspapers wetted thoroughly and applied in 6 or 8 layers. The outer layers will char, but the inner wrapping will stay intact, and paper, unlike foil, will let the steam escape.

In some places, old-timers like to talk about the days when everything they ate was cooked over a firepit or in the coals encased in clay. Well, it sounds fine, but when you wrap food in clay you're still going to trap most of the steam, and vegetables don't need this kind of treatment.

One more thing comes to mind: If you plan to use clay around any food that will be buried in coals to cook, be sure that you're expert enough to choose a real clay instead of just plain mud. There are relatively few places where you'll find true clay soils, and when you encase food to cook in mud, the mud bakes into dust and your food comes out as charcoal.

For other vegetables, beans and peas and suchlike, use the Dutch oven or a plain cooking pot. Vegetables don't really need the steaming they get in a Dutch oven, nor do they need the long unwatched cooking time that is the Dutch oven's chief claim to a place in the camp cook's battery.

As for seasoning vegetables, you can't go very far wrong if you stick to butter and herbs, with a dash of salt. By doing so, you can always be sure that the flavor of the vegetables will be compatible with or contrast with that of the meat in the main course, and whether you choose compatibility or contrast comes under the heading of cook's choice.

Now, here are a couple of "made" dishes that to my way of thinking fall into the vegetable category, though the first one is really husky enough for a one-dish meal.

VEGETABLE STEW

3 slices lean salt pork
3 yellow turnips (or rutabagas)
2 large potatoes
3 medium-sized white onions
3 firm but ripe medium-sized tomatoes
1 cup fresh green peas or green beans or both
3 Tbsp minced parsley
2 cloves garlic, mashed
½ tsp crushed cumin seeds
½ tsp minced fresh ginger root or large pinch of powdered ginger
1 tsp salt
    Generous dash of freshly ground white pepper
    Water

Cut the salt pork into chunks and blanch by dropping the pieces in boiling water for a moment, then draining well.

Peel turnips, potatoes, and onions and cut them into chunks about an inch in each dimension. Chop the tomatoes coarsely.

Cook the salt pork in a large stew pot until it begins to brown. Add the pieces of turnip, potato, and onion and stir them in with the pork and pork fat for a couple of minutes, not long enough for them to brown, just enough to allow them to absorb a bit of flavor from the pork fat. Add peas and/or beans. Combine the seasonings; the garlic enables you to form them into a paste. Add the paste to the pan and stir the vegetables while it transfers its flavorings to them. Add water to cover and cook over medium-high coals at a simmer for 30 to 40 minutes, until the turnips are easily pierced with a fork. Serves 6.

FRIJOLES BORRACHOS

What do you do in the arid country along the Texas-Mexican border when you're short of water but have plenty of beer? You cook your beans in beer, of course.

2 or 3 thin (⅛ inch) slices salt pork
2 to 2½ cups dry pinto beans
1 small onion, peeled and chopped coarsely
1 clove garlic, mashed
2 dried hot red peppers or 4 mild ones
3 ripe tomatoes chopped fine or one #2 can tomatoes

1½ to 2 bottles warm beer
1½ tsp salt

Cut the salt pork into cubes; boil water in a small skillet and drop the pork pieces in about 2 minutes, to blanch them and remove excess salt; pour off the water and fry the pork pieces until crisp. Discard the fat unless needed for other cooking. Put all remaining ingredients into pot, adding beer to cover, and simmer until the beans are soft. Covering the pot will usually speed the cooking, but cook covered or uncovered, according to your wishes and the limitations of your cooking pots.

Timing will depend on your altitude; at high altitudes 3 to 4 hours may be required. Keep the liquid covering the beans by adding more beer as needed. If you have water to spare, soaking the beans for an hour before cooking will reduce cooking time. The soaking water should be discarded. When the beans are soft, use a big heavy spoon to mash them to a pulp, stirring the pulp into the pot liquid. Serves 6.

CORN PUDDING

Not a dessert, in spite of its name, but an old-fashioned main vegetable dish.

3 cups fresh corn, just cut from the cob.

2 cups warm milk
3 Tbsp butter
3 fresh eggs, lightly beaten
1½ tsps salt
¼ tsp freshly ground white pepper

2 large potatoes, peeled and cubed
4 carrots, peeled and cut into chunks
2 bay leaves
2 small dry red peppers
2 Tbsp salt
Water to cover

Put the corn into a Dutch oven or a deep skillet that has a tightly fitting cover. Stir the butter into the milk until it melts, add beaten eggs and seasonings, stir to blend, pour over the corn. Cover the Dutch oven and place on medium-bright coals; heap coals up the sides and on the lid. Cook 45 minutes to 1 hour. Fresh coals need not be added. When serving, be sure that a portion of the crust that has formed on the bottom and sides of the pan is included with each helping. Serves 4.

Combine all ingredients in a deep pot or Dutch oven and simmer until the beans are soft. This will take 1½ to 4 hours depending on the altitude. As noted earlier, cooking times vary with altitudes, and covering a pot when preparing any recipe involving boiling reduces cooking time at any altitude. Serves 6–8.

We're not through with recipes yet; there'll be others later on, but these are all fairly basic dishes that can be modified as you choose. If you're an expert camp cook using this book as a refresher course, you might know most or all of them, but if you're just getting started, they'll give you some useful guidelines to timing, seasoning, and general cooking procedures.

Remember, too, that they'll work just as well in a patio firepit or grill as they will in the bigger outdoors.

BEANS AND PORK

Please distinguish between this and the glutinous contents of cans labeled "Pork & Beans."

2½ to 3 cups dried beans—any kind
1 pound raw pork or parboiled well-drained salt pork
2 medium-sized onions, peeled and cut into chunks

6 CAMP-COOKED BREADS

A variety of breads extending beyond pancakes and biscuits should certainly be a part of your campground cooking skills. If you're in a wilderness or semiwilderness camp, they'll bridge the bread gap for your party. Even if you're camping somewhere close enough to civilization to allow for trips to a store to buy fresh bread, there's a difference in camp-cooked breads that adds extra enjoyment to a meal eaten outdoors.

A lot of otherwise experienced camp cooks don't include any kinds of breads in their repertoire because they think that a conventional oven, like that of the kitchen range, is necessary in preparing them. Not so. Dutch ovens do a very good job of camp baking, and even a heavy cast-iron skillet with a tight-fitting cover will do a very satisfactory job of turning out a batch of biscuits or a round of cornbread cooked on the coals.

For use over camp stoves there are accessory ovens which fit over one burner. These will turn out a good batch of biscuits, and bread can also be baked in them, but these attachments have limits imposed by the fact that baking risen breads requires that you provide the fairly considerable amount of extra fuel required for the accessory oven's prolonged use. To get the maximum good with the least fuel consumption from this type oven, you must also carry an extra pan or two, the thinnest possible aluminum baking tins, for the camp stove auxiliary ovens don't have the capacity to heat a thick cooking utensil quickly.

There are other kinds of ovens or oven substitutes available for camp cooking. One is the reflector oven. I do not admire reflector ovens, probably because as a novice camper I never did succeed in finding one that functioned satisfactorily. Though I tried three or four different kinds, I was never really satisfied with the results I got.

Your success in cooking camp breads depends on two things: the pan used, and the coals on which that pan rests or is buried. Don't take this remark as downgrading the skill of the cook who mixed

More and more camp-
ers are making bread
and biscuits in camp.
It's not as difficult as
many think. Here, a
camper is about to
bake biscuits in a col-
lapsible oven that fits
on top of a camp stove
burner.

the dough or batter. Even the best, most experienced camp cook can't turn out good bread without the right kind of pan and the right kind of coals.

You cannot make good bread in a pan that develops hot spots or one that warps and buckles and allows the cooking fat to form puddles in places, leaving other areas bare of even a film of fat to prevent the dough from burning or stick-ing. No pan that performs so unevenly will turn out good camp bread, regardless of the skill applied and the care taken by the cook.

Nor can you cook camp bread over coals that are too hot. A bed of coals suit-able for baking should emit the bright cherry-red hue described in an earlier chapter. As the coals fade to dull red and then to embers they will give your camp-baked bread the same treatment some-

times prescribed for kitchen ovens. Some bread recipes you'll encounter call for a reduction of oven heat during the final stages of baking.

If you haven't yet invested in a Dutch oven or cast-iron skillet, keep bak-ing in mind and buy a bigger one than you think you'll need. They're better than a reflector oven. Even if you never use either one for baking, the day will come when you'll want to cook a lot of some-thing, but your pan won't stretch. You can cook small quantities of food in a big pan, but there's no way to crowd a double batch of biscuits or a big quantity of any-thing else into a pan that's too small.

A #2 size Dutch oven, which is about 9 inches in diameter, will turn out enough biscuits for four hungry campers, but if you're going to bake for more than four go up to a larger size. When you

choose a cast-iron skillet that will on occasion double as a baking pan, look for at
least a 10-inch size, and a 12-inch job isn't
a bit too small. The deeper the skillet is,
the more useful it will be. Cast-iron utensils have in recent years surged back into
popularity, and you no longer have to
scour second-hand stores or antique shops
to find them.

To repeat an earlier caution, don't
buy any cast-iron utensil with a glass lid.
It's a bit laughable to see cast-iron pans
with glass lids advertised as Dutch ovens
or camp utensils, but it's no laughing matter when you try to cook in coals in one of
these hybrids. Any cast-iron utensil that
you buy for camp use should naturally
have a metal lid so that it can be buried in
coals for baking.

If it's new, your bread-making skillet
or Dutch oven must be seasoned; if it's an
older utensil that's been scoured with a
harsh-acting cleanser, reseasoning will be
required. Seasoning a cast-iron utensil
simply means renewing its inner patina,
the coating acquired through use, which
keeps foods from sticking to a cast-iron
pan's sides and bottom. The method was
described fully in Chapter 1.

As has already been mentioned
briefly, your coals need to be a bright
cherry-red when you're baking. If they're
too bright, your bread will burn; if they're
not bright enough to begin with, heat will
not penetrate quickly enough to the center of the dough, nor will the bread brown
properly. It will come out of the pan a pale
tan on the outside and soggy inside. Rake
or renew the coals you use for baking to
make a bed about 2 or 3 inches deep and a
couple of inches greater in diameter than
the size of the pan you're using. This is
adequate for the 20 to 50 minutes most

baking of this kind requires. When following a recipe that calls for burying the
utensil, the coals on top may need to be
renewed midway of the cooking time.

Finally, a few ground rules for ingredients. Rule one: An all-purpose flour produces the best results. Most flours today
are milled from soft wheat, and this isn't
the very best baking flour, but it's adequate. If you want to go first-class and
produce really superior breads, look
around for a flour made from hard durum
wheat. A number of small mills grind this
kind of wheat, and your search for it will
be rewarded by the exceptional quality of
your breads. If your regular supermarket
doesn't stock hard wheat flour, try a natural foods or health food store.

Rule two: Don't try to use bacon
drippings in bread dough, or for oiling a
cooking pan when baking. A lot of old recipes call for drippings, but they came into
being before the degradation of bacon already described in an earlier chapter. The
fat from the chemically pickled bacon
produced by major meat packers today is
useless for cooking. Use cooking oil, solid
shortening, or plain old-fashioned lard
produced from hog fat.

Now let's look at the several kinds of
breads you can bake in your cast-iron
skillet or Dutch oven over a bed of coals.
To begin with, we'll take the most famous
of all camp breads, sourdough. Even
though sourdough baking can be a real
challenge to the camp cook, it retains its
top position after having been in use for
several centuries. You'll see why, when
you've gone through the recipe, and you'll
agree the trouble's well worthwhile when
you've baked and eaten real sourdough
bread.

SOURDOUGH BREAD AND BISCUITS

In order to qualify as a sourdough cook, you need to understand a bit of the chemistry of bread-making. For the benefit of those who aren't familiar with baking, let's start at the very beginning. The fluffiness and texture as well as the flavor of bread are the work of leavening, a gaseous process. The gas which leavens bread is produced by a fungus, a living organism, which produces a gas when heated. In one form or another, this fungus is found in nature in many warm environments. In most of these environments, the fungus cannot be easily controlled.

All starches contain this fungus, which is killed by both too high or too low a temperature, which allows its activity to be controlled. Controlling the degree of activity to which the fungus is aroused by warmth and killing it by heating its starchy host to a degree of heat in which the fungus cannot survive is the basic chemistry of all bread-making.

Yeast is a host in which the fungus is highly concentrated, but in the form the fungus takes in yeast it will be killed by even a very low degree of heat, as well as by age. Yeast must be kept mildly refrigerated; if yeast gets either too warm or too cold the gas-producing fungus dies. Before the days of portable refrigerators, yeast could not be stored by travelers or campers or settlers, who had no refrigeration to keep it alive on hot days and no way to keep it from freezing on winter nights.

History doesn't record who discovered that potatoes stored a fungus that made an excellent yeast substitute, and history is equally hazy about when the discovery was made several centuries ago. Potatoes are hardy and storable, and for several centuries they have been the main source of the yeast used in leavening sourdough bread. Your yeast, called the *starter,* begins with potatoes, flour, and water:

SOURDOUGH STARKER

---

3 medium-sized potatoes, 2 to 2½ inches in diameter
3½ cups water
3 Tbsp all-purpose flour—do not use cake flour or any other specialty flour (if you shop around a bit at health food stores you will find a good hard flour made from durum wheat; this is the best flour to use for the starter)

Peel and quarter two of the potatoes and boil in the 3½ cups water until they are very soft. Sterilize a cup and a jar by filling both with boiling water; let them stand filled for a few moments, then empty them. Pour 2 cups of the water in which the potatoes cooked into the sterilized jar. It must stand until it is lukewarm.

Peel the third potato and scrape off 2 level tablespoons of pulp from it with a sterilized spoon. Add the pulp to the lukewarm water in the jar. Stir in the flour. Cover the jar, but do not seal it. Put it in a warm place to stand.

Between 36 and 48 hours later, depending on the temperature, the mixture in the jar will ferment. As fermentation progresses, the solids and liquids will separate. Pour off the liquid, reserving 3 tablespoonfuls. Return the 3 tablespoons of liquid to the solids that remain in the jar. Let stand 2 to 3 hours.

What is in the jar has now become a form of yeast, your sourdough *starter.* You will know it is good if the starter is a pure white and has a sharp "yeasty" smell; it should be filled with tiny bubbles about the size of rice grains. If the contents of the jar are grayish or tinged with yellow, if it does not contain bubbles, the flour you used is too soft and you must discard it and start over from the beginning.

Your starter is used for all sourdough baking: bread, rolls, biscuits, or pancakes. Each time you use the starter, at the proper stage in the preparation of the "sponge"—the mixture that will become your baking dough—you must remove a portion of the sponge and put it in a sterilized jar. The reserved portion then becomes the starter for your next baking.

You need not add anything to the portion of sponge that you reserve. It will keep three to four days without refrigeration, up to three months in a refrigerator, and as long as six months in the freezer. Starter that has been cooled or frozen must be brought to a temperature of about 70 degrees before use; if necessary, put its container into a pan of lukewarm water to do this.

Nobody really knows how long a sourdough starter will last. San Francisco is the spiritual home of sourdough baking, and in the 1950s, when we lived in the San Francisco Bay area there was a restaurant which claimed that its sourdough starter had been in constant use since the 1849 gold rush. We've been able to keep a starter alive for as long as six years, but this was during a period when baking was done at least weekly. It seems that constant use is the secret of keeping a sourdough starter viable.

SOURDOUGH BREAD

1 full batch sourdough starter
3 cups lukewarm water
7 to 8 cups flour, preferably the same kind used in making the starter
3 eggs
1 cup fresh or diluted evaporated milk
½ tsp baking soda
3 Tbsp sugar
4 Tbsp liquid fat, either cooking oil or melted solid shortening
1 tsp salt

Put the entire starter into a mixing bowl and slowly stir in the water. Add 3 cups of the flour. Stir well, with a spoon; cover the bowl with a cloth and let stand 4 hours at a 70-degree temperature. *This is a guideline; if the temperature is higher, the fermenting time will be shorter, if lower, the time will be longer.* When the surface of the starter is covered with small bubbles about the size of beans which form and burst slowly, then you're ready to go to the next operation.

Remove 1 cupful of the sponge and put it in a sterilized crock or jar. This is your next starter. It can be stored as described in the starter recipe. Each time you bake, you must at this stage put aside this cupful of sponge or make a fresh batch of starter the next time you bake.

Beat together the eggs, milk, salt, sugar, soda, and fat. When these are thoroughly blended, mix them into the remainder of the sponge. Blend well, then by hand combine with this mixture the remaining flour. Add only a small handful of flour at a time and be sure it's incorporated thoroughly before adding more. You may need to use a bit more or less flour than the remaining 4 cups to get a firm, very resilient dough. When the dough is firm enough to resist your efforts to blend it further, you're ready to go ahead.

On a very lightly floured breadboard (a scrap of plywood is fine), turn out the dough and knead until its surface takes on a satiny sheen and the dough no longer wants to stick to your hands or the kneading board. Test the dough by lifting it; the doughball should not sag or string. At this point, put the doughball into a lightly greased bowl, cover with a towel, and let stand until it doubles in bulk. Ideally, when the temperature is 70 degrees, this should take between 2 and 4 hours. If the doubling takes place in less than 2 hours, your bread will be coarse and porous; if longer, it will be solid and soggy.

Turn the risen dough onto a lightly floured board and knead just enough to remove the bubbles created when it rose. Divide the dough into 2 or 3 balls, depending on the size of the pan in which baking will be done. (The quantity of dough formed by this recipe will fit a 3-quart Dutch oven, or will make a somewhat flatter loaf in a 10- or an 8-inch cast-iron skillet. If you're baking at home, it will make three loaves in standard-sized pans or two French-style loaves on a baking sheet or in a tube.)

Let the doughballs rise in the pan until they double in bulk. In the Dutch oven, baking time will be 50 to 60 minutes; in skillets, 40 to 50 minutes; in a home oven at 350 degrees, 35 to 40 minutes.

SOURDOUGH ROLLS

Use the same procedure as in baking bread, forming the dough into balls. In a Dutch oven, baking time will be 35 to 40 minutes; in a home oven at 350 degrees, 15 to 20 minutes.

SOURDOUGH BISCUITS

To make 20 to 24 biscuits, follow the bread recipe to the point where the starter is taken from the sponge. After that, use the same ingredients specified in the bread recipe, but halve the quantities. Follow the bread recipe to the first kneading, and let the kneaded dough rise.

Turn out the risen dough on a lightly floured surface and knead just enough to remove bubbles; then pat the doughball to a thickness of ¼ to ½ inch.

Cut the biscuits, or make pinch-offs and form them in your hands. Put the biscuits in a lightly greased Dutch oven, al-

lowing room for them to rise, and let rise until doubled in bulk.

In the Dutch oven, baking time is 30 to 35 minutes; in a shallow skillet, 25 to 30 minutes; in a home oven, on a baking sheet or in thin baking tins, 18 to 20 minutes at 350 degrees.

SOURDOUGH PANCAKES

Caution: Sourdough pancake batter must be started 12 hours before cooking.

  1 cup sourdough starter
  2 cups lukewarm water
  2 cups all-purpose flour, prefera-
     bly the same kind that was
     used in the starter

Mix starter, water, and flour; let stand 12 hours in a covered mixing bowl. Before adding the remaining ingredients, remove 1 cup of the mixture and add it to the starter remaining in the crock or jar.

  2 eggs
  1½ Tbsp sugar
  2 Tbsp liquid fat
  ⅓ cup lukewarm milk or water
  1 tsp baking soda
  1 cup flour, as above

Combine above ingredients, adding the solids and fat in the order listed to the lightly beaten eggs. Blend this mixture with the starter; let stand 15 to 20 minutes. It can stand longer, up to 45 minutes or an hour, without harming the resulting pancakes.

OTHER WHEAT BREADS

DUTCH OVEN BISCUITS

2 cups flour
½ tsp salt
3 tsp baking powder
4 Tbsp solid shortening
1 cup milk (diluted evaporated milk is OK)

Blend the flour, salt, and baking powder together, mash in the shortening with a fork until a crumbly mixture is formed, add the milk, and stir until the dough sags down into the trough left by the spoon as it moves around the bowl.

Turn the dough out on a floured mixing surface, knead for 30 seconds, pat out the dough gently until it is ½ inch thick. Cut the biscuits with a round cutter, or pinch off dough and form by hand.

Put biscuits into a greased Dutch oven, cover, and bury in bright coals for 5 to 10 minutes, or until golden brown.

Cook on a very lightly greased griddle or in a heavy skillet that is heated to the point where a few drops of water spattered on it dance and vanish in a minute or less. Cook cakes until browned on one side; turn and brown the second side.

Makes 20 to 24 chewy pancakes 3 to 4 inches in diameter. Sourdough pancakes make a good substitute for bread in lunch sandwiches, as they don't get mushy or soggy.

BAKING DUTCH-OVEN BISCUITS

1. Blend dry ingredients in a bowl and mash in shortening with a fork. Then add milk and stir.

2. After kneading the dough for 30 seconds, pat it flat and cut out the biscuits with a round cutter (a small cup works fine), or pinch off dough and form by hand.

3. In go the biscuits. Careful, don't crowd them.

4. Place one-third of the coals underneath the oven, the remaining two-thirds on top of the lid.

5. Don't go far away! Your biscuits will be golden brown and fluffy in 5 to 10 minutes. Use a piece of wire coat hanger to lift the lid. If the biscuits aren't quite ready, simply lower the lid and allow them to bake longer.

SKILLET BISCUITS

To produce 20 to 24 biscuits, 2 to 2½ inches in diameter:

1¾ cups flour
3½ tsp baking powder
 1 tsp salt
 ½ cup solid shortening
 1 cup milk plus or minus 1 tsp (this is an inexact quantity; the precise amount of milk required depends on the kind of flour used; diluted evaporated milk is OK)
 1 or 2 Tbsp flour to cover the kneading board

Combine flour, baking powder, and salt by stirring, shaking, or sifting them together. Using your fingertips, work the shortening into the flour mixture, pinching it in about a tablespoon's worth at a time until you have a crumbly mixture. Stir in the milk to produce a dough that is neither runny nor solid.

Turn the dough out onto a floured kneading surface and knead it very gently, no more than three or four times. Pat the dough flat, do not roll, into a sheet about ¼ inch thick. Cut the biscuits with a round cutter or into squares with a knife; don't slice, just press the knife straight down into the sheet of dough to form squares.

Rub the skillet with fat and bring it to a medium-high, not a smoking heat. Put in the biscuits a few at a time; don't overcrowd the pan. Let them brown on the bottom; turn once to brown the other side. About 4 to 5 minutes per side is the right timing. As they cook, the biscuits will puff up until they're about ¾ inch thick. They're light and delicate, and can be reheated.

Incidentally, if you're going to be camping for just a short time and want to speed up your cooking, you can premix a batch of skillet biscuit dough at home. Combine the dry ingredients with the fat, and carry it in a tightly closed jar to camp. Keep the jar as cool as possible. Then, add the milk and cook.

BANNOCK

This is the traditional camp bread of the Canadian rivermen, the *voyageurs,* who carried the trappers and fur traders up and down the northern rivers. It's still cooked by rivermen in the northern wilds. In its native habitat, bannock is cooked in a deep, narrow pan with curved ends, somewhat like an elongated loaf pan, but it can be cooked equally satisfactorily in a skillet or Dutch oven.

3 cups unsifted flour
1 Tbsp baking powder
   Large pinch of salt
3 Tbsp milk (fresh or diluted evaporated)
2 Tbsp liquid shortening
1¾ cups water
 ½ tsp fat for greasing pan

Combine the dry ingredients, combine the milk and shortening separately, and stir the milk-shortening mixture into the flour mixture to form a smooth thick paste. Add water slowly to form a smooth dough, thicker than pancake batter but thinner than biscuit dough.

Grease the cooking pan and pour the dough into it, place it at the edge of the firepit, but not on the coals, and let stand for 20 to 25 minutes until the dough rises, turning the pan occasionally. In cold weather, the rising may take longer.

Cover the skillet or Dutch oven, bury in coals, cook 25 to 30 minutes. Test by slipping a straw or a knife-blade into the center; when straw or blade come free without sticking, the bannock's done.

If you want a crusty loaf, let the dough rise in its own pan and put about ¼ inch of cooking oil into the loaf pan. Get this fat bubbling hot when the dough has risen and pour the dough into the fat, then cover and bake as above. The loaf will be a bit flatter, but it'll have crusty sides and bottom.

You can also make pones of bannock dough and cook them in an uncovered skillet. Cooking time is about 8 to 10 minutes per side. Turn only once.

You can make a mix for bannock dough by combining enough of the dry ingredients to make several batches, dividing the mix into amounts needed for a single batch and sealing the divided mix in press-to-seal bags. When ready to cook, just add the quantity of liquids required.

SWEET OR CAKE BANNOCK

Bannock is often cooked as a sweet bread for breakfast or dessert. Some *voyageur* guides use the same dough for both types, simply adding fruit, but you'll find the following more satisfactory for Cake Bannock:

 3 **cups flour**
1¾ **Tbsp baking powder**
   Large pinch salt
 3 **Tbsp milk (fresh or diluted evaporated)**
 2 **Tbsp shortening**
1¾ **cups water**
1½ **cups brown sugar or 1½ cups brown and white sugar mixed in equal parts or 1¼ cups white sugar**
 1 **cup raisins or seeded chopped dry prunes or chopped dried apples, peaches, or pears, or ¾ cup of any firm fresh fruit**
 ½ **tsp oil or fat for rubbing the pan**

Follow the preparation procedure given for regular bannock, adding the dried fruit and sugar by stirring it in gently just before putting the dough to rise. Be sure not to use big pieces of fruit, for if you do they'll settle down to the bottom of the loaf during cooking.

PUEBLO INDIAN SQUAW BREAD

Virtually all North American Indian tribes had breads of one kind or another. Some of the tribes who did not grow maize or corn gathered acorns and ground them into a meal for bread-making, but my experience is that acorn-meal bread is a taste you must acquire in childhood. At least one prehistoric Plains tribe had a kind of primitive wheat which they cultivated, but the history of this tribe of wheat-growers has been lost in the mist of many centuries. Later Plains tribes ground the beans of mesquite trees into flour and made a flat bread baked on hot stones, but like acorn-meal bread, this is a taste that must be acquired early. The Pueblo people had a very advanced corn culture, and baked a type of cornmeal bread in beehive ovens. These ovens are still used in a few pueblos, but today their bread is generally made from flour. The thin flat Pueblo loaves can't really be duplicated without the beehive oven, but try Squaw Bread.

  3 cups flour
  1 tsp salt
  2 Tbsp baking powder
1½ Tbsp solid shortening (lard is
     the usual kind)
  2 cups lukewarm water
  3 to 4 cups cooking oil or fat,
     enough to fill the pot or pan to
     a depth of ¾ to 1 inch

Combine the dry ingredients; cut in the shortening with a knife or the edge of a spoon. Add the water while stirring to make a dough about the consistency of biscuit dough. Roll dough on a lightly floured board to a thickness of about ½ inch; cut the dough into 3-inch squares. Push your thumb through the center of each square to form a hole.

Cook the bread in very hot, bubbling fat, about 3 to 4 minutes per side, and drain it on papers before eating.

That hole you poke with your thumb in each piece of dough before cooking is very important. Forget it, and you'll have a small wad of raw, soggy dough in the middle of each piece.

SKILLET CORNBREADS

Wheat flour was scarce and expensive during the early days of North American settlement. Cornbreads abounded, and as the tide of settlement moved, these breads took on regional forms and names, though all of them were basically the same.

Corn pones were the most common. In the Northeast they were called johnny-cake, a corruption of "journey cake"; in the South, they got the name hoecake because field hands cooked the pones on the blades of the hoes they used to grub out the fields. Ashcakes were corn pones baked in the ashes of the hearth; crackling

BEER BREAD

1. Undoubtedly the easiest—and one of the tastiest—camp breads you can make is beer bread. In a bowl, mix together 3 cups self-rising flour, 3 tablespoons sugar, ¼ teaspoon salt, 1 can of beer, 1 teaspoon dill seed, and 1 tablespoon dried onion. Then knead the dough on a floured surface.

2. Swab the inside of Dutch oven with cooking oil.

4. Baking time will vary in accordance with heat generated by coals, but it averages 15 to 25 minutes. After about 10 minutes, begin checking bread's progress. If you thump it with your finger it should give a hollow sound when done. Or, insert a sliver of wood; when it comes out clean, the bread is done.

3. Lay the bread in the oven. Place one-third of the coals beneath the oven, and the remaining two-thirds on top of the lid.

5. Absolutely delicious! You can't taste the beer, as it is used only as a leavening agent and evaporates during the baking.

bread was made by adding crisp, finely chopped fried pork cracklings to the corn-pone dough. Shortening bread, also called eggbread, was still the basic corn pone, lightened by the addition of fat and an egg to the dough.

All these call for much the same ingredients, and all of them are skillet-cooked. You can make a basic mix that will serve for any of them, and modify the mix to produce different kinds of corn-breads simply by adding the additional ingredients required just before cooking. Use either white or yellow cornmeal; for all practical purposes in cooking they are interchangeable. Prepare the mix in a large enough quantity to serve your needs before leaving home, divide it into batch quantities, and carry it in press-to-seal plastic bags, using a bagful as needed.

CORNBREAD MIX

For each cup of mix, combine by stirring:

    1 cup cornmeal
    1 tsp salt
    ¼ tsp baking powder

This mix saves a little bit of time and trouble when you're cooking in camp. There are times when you'll need to add more salt or baking powder or produce a lighter type of cornbread than the mix generally yields, but these adjustments to the mix are all noted in the recipes that follow.

CORN PONES

    1¼ cup cornmeal mix
    1   tsp salt
    2   cups boiling water
        Cooking oil or fat

Combine cornmeal and salt. Pour boiling water into the mixture very slowly while stirring to form a stiff dough. You may use a bit more or a bit less water, depending on the cornmeal.

Shape the dough into oval pones by squeezing about 2 tablespoons of it between your palms. Cook in a well-greased skillet over medium-bright coals, about 8 to 10 minutes per side.

CRACKLING BREAD

    3 cups cornmeal mix
    3 to 4 Tbsp fine-chopped pork fat,
       fried very crisp
    2 cups boiling water

Stir cracklings into the mix, adding water slowly while stirring. Form into pones and cook in a lightly greased skillet. Drain on paper while cooling.

SHORTENING BREAD

4 cups cornmeal mix
1 tsp baking powder
3 Tbsp melted butter
3 cups boiling water
1 egg

Combine the dry ingredients. Stir the melted butter into the hot water and pour this into the cornmeal mixture while stirring to make a smooth heavy batter—not a dough. When the batter is formed, beat in the egg.

Drop the batter by tablespoonfuls onto a hot, well-greased skillet. Cook about 6 to 8 minutes per side, turning once after the pones are nicely browned on the bottom.

CORNCAKES

2 cups cornmeal mix
1 tsp baking powder
1½ cups milk (fresh or diluted evaporated milk)
1 egg
1 cup fresh corn kernels or well-drained canned whole-kernel corn
Fat for cooking

Add baking powder to mix, combine milk with egg, stir into the dry ingredients, add the corn, and stir well. Drop 2 to 3 tablespoonfuls batter per cake into a hot greased skillet, cook on one side until nicely browned, turn and cook to brown second side. These are not pancakes, but a skillet bread served with meals.

PANCAKES

Without any question, the best pancake cook among the many whose works I've sampled was a crusty old ex-lumberjack named Joe O'Donnell. Joe's skill as a pancake cook was matched only by his adeptness as a steelhead fisherman, and he was one of the best with whom I've ever fished. Joe was just about as proud of one accomplishment as he was of the other.

Joe's territory was the upper reaches of California's Klamath River, where he lived in a little cabin near the town of Orleans. A dozen or so steelhead addicts turned Joe's cabin into a sort of informal fly fisherman's headquarters, and for several years I was a more or less regular member of the group.

While all of us bugged Joe good-naturedly about his secretiveness concerning his pancake recipe, he steadfastly refused to pass it on. He maintained that he really didn't have a recipe, that he adjusted each batch of batter as he mixed it to allow for such variables as the kind of flour he was using, the state of the eggs, the effect of atmospheric conditions and temperature on the batter, and how he happened to be feeling on the morning he mixed up the batter.

Of course, Joe had some advantages most of us lack. His eggs came from his own flock of chickens, his woodstove was fueled with chunks he'd split himself from trees that he'd felled at just the time when their wood had dried precisely enough to burn evenly. He used a soapstone griddle over the firebox of his ancient wood-burning kitchen range, a griddle on which nothing except pancakes was ever cooked. After all the years he'd used the griddle, Joe could gauge its surface temperature to the tiniest fraction of a degree. It's no wonder that his pancakes were always perfectly and uniformly brown on both sides, tender yet chewy, always the same.

All of us who stayed at Joe's cabin used to watch him while he mixed pancake batter, and most of us wound up with a pretty good idea of the proportions of ingredients he used. None of us ever quite succeeded at matching his work, though. As tasty as our pancakes at home might be, they'd still fall short. Maybe the mountain spring water or the hand-chosen wood chunks had something to do with the difference.

JOE O'DONNELL'S PANCAKES

4 cups all-purpose flour
3½ tsp baking powder
½ tsp salt
3 tsp sugar
3½ cups lukewarm water
2 fresh eggs

Stir the dry ingredients together in a bowl, add the water slowly while stirring, finally stir in the eggs. Beat the batter vigorously for 5 minutes. The batter should be a bit thicker than rich fresh cream just before it reaches the clotting stage.

Have the pan hot, but below the smoking point; drops of water sprinkled on its surface should not dance, but should sizzle and vanish in about 30 seconds. Pour the batter on to make cakes about 6 inches in diameter. Once a cake has formed, never add more batter or try to spread thinner the batter poured. When the very first bubbles form on the top of the batter, turn the cake and cook until the second side is tanned.

Using the quantities given, you'll get 12 to 14 big pancakes—big meaning about 6 inches in diameter. The recipe can be halved if you're cooking for only a few, or you can increase the yield to 16 or 18 cakes by making 4-inch cakes.

Oddly, the runner-up to Joe as a pancake chef was also a Klamath River steelhead addict, though Elmer Meyers claimed the lower stretches of that magnificent river as his own. As fishermen, their skills were very much the same, though Joe used only flies and Elmer stuck with lures. At the time about which I'm writing, Elmer built a temporary camp each summer just a dozen steps from the Klamath's rushing water. He'd picked a spot in the middle of a 20-mile stretch of the river which had no access roads leading to it.

Each year, winter high-water washed away the camp's only building, a big shedlike shanty made of green lumber, erected within a few steps of the water's edge. At the beginning of each summer a bunch of us went upriver with Elmer, towing a fresh load of lumber, and spent a couple of days building a new shanty for the camp. Above and below the camp, the Klamath was a big water with very few wadable gravel bars or riffles, so most of our fishing at Elmer's camp was done from boats.

Elmer scorned such niceties as griddles and skillets. He cooked his pancakes directly on the top of the sheepherder stove which was hauled up to his camp each summer, as soon as the spring flooding period ended, and hauled back downstream when the camp was closed before the winter floods began. (If you recall, in Chapter 1 sheepherder stoves are described in detail.)

Pancake time at Elmer's camp began by giving the top of the sheepherder stove a good scrubbing as it heated up each morning. While one or two of the other campers scrubbed the stove top, Elmer stirred up the batter; and when the scrubbing job was finished, he swabbed the top with grease and took over. The top of that particular stove held about 30 pancakes, and from start to finish, the

cooking of a batch never took longer than about 20 or 30 minutes.

While the first batch was being eaten, Elmer stood by the stove flipping the second batch between bites of his own breakfast. There was very little time lost in mixing a batch of fresh batter, for Elmer made up his own mix—in a day long before packaged mixes were found in supermarkets—and stored the mix in big 2-gallon pickle jars in his home refrigerator. Elmer's pancakes were a bit chewier than Joe O'Donnell's, but were about equally tasty. There's never been anything like a good pancake breakfast to give a fisherman the stamina that'll carry him through a long morning of fishing.

ELMER MEYERS'S PANCAKE MIX

1   **quart unbleached, unsifted white flour**
½   **cup sugar**
1   **heaping tsp baking powder**
1   **tsp salt**

Combine by stirring well; store in a tightly closed jar under refrigeration until ready to use.

When ready to make pancakes, measure the mix by cupfuls into a bowl. Each cupful of the dry mix will produce 3 to 4 cakes about 4 inches in diameter. For each cupful of mix, add:

¼ cup undiluted evaporated milk
¼ cup lukewarm water

Combine the milk and water and stir into the dry ingredients to make a creamy, smooth batter. Let the batter stand about 10 minutes, then beat vigorously for a minute or two. Pour enough batter to form cakes 3 to 4 inches in diameter into a greased hot pan, turn when bubbles form on top, cook the second side until brown.

Over the years, I've used Elmer's pancake mix many times, but even when I cooked them on a sheepherder stove they never tasted quite like his did. Even so, the pancakes were good. But just as Joe O'Donnell's pancakes were never as good when cooked by somebody else away from Joe's cabin, Elmer's pancakes lacked some mystic ingredient they seemed to get when cooked and eaten in that raw wood shanty on the Klamath's banks.

Still, these recipes produce pancakes far superior to those made from commercial mixes, and if you should ever tire of eating pancakes made from either recipe, here are a few more ideas.

1 teaspoon salt
4 teaspoons baking powder

Let the mixed ingredients stand overnight in a covered bowl. On getting up the next morning, mix the following liquid items:

2 cups milk (diluted evaporated milk is OK)
1 Tbsp honey
1 egg, beaten before adding to other ingredients
⅓ cup liquid shortening or melted solid shortening

Beat the mixed dry ingredients into the liquid ingredients, let stand 10 to 15 minutes, and beat again. Cook on a very lightly greased griddle or in an ungreased, well-seasoned cast-iron skillet.

You'll get 8 to 10 pancakes, 4 to 5 inches in diameter, using the quantities given in the recipe. The batter does not keep well, so for fewer cakes use half the quantities given, or double them if you're cooking for a crowd.

NIGHT-BEFORE BUCKWHEAT CAKES

Before going to bed, blend the following dry ingredients:

1 cup white flour
1 cup buckwheat flour

FRUITED PANCAKES

3 eggs
2 Tbsp sifted flour
¼ cup scalded milk, fresh or diluted condensed
1 Tbsp cold water
   Small pinch of salt
1 cup fruit: raisins, prunes,

apples, apricots, etc., minced quite fine; well-drained canned fruits can be used

Scald the milk by sitting it in a small pan at the edge of the firepit until bubbles form all around the line where the milk meets the pan; be careful not to let the milk boil. Remove the milk from the heat, let it cool, strain through a cloth.

While the milk is cooling, beat the eggs until frothy, adding about a teaspoonful of flour at a time while continuing to beat. Mix the scalded milk with the water and salt; pour into the batter while beating. You want a mixture somewhat thinner than regular pancake batter, and depending on the flour used, a bit more or less may be required.

Pour enough batter into the skillet to make 2 or 3 pancakes and quickly sprinkle the batter with the fruit. The instant the first bubbles appear, turn the cakes to cook on the topside. These cakes will always be a bit pale, so don't worry if yours look a bit too light. The cakes are also a bit delicate and should be turned carefully. Make yours about 3 inches in diameter; the recipe will yield 10 to 12 this size.

LUNCH PANCAKES

Make pancakes according to any of the preceding recipes, but to the batter add bits of precooked shredded meat, crumbled well-drained precooked sausage, or slivers of firm cheese instead of fruits. Let the cooked pancakes cool; roll them up and wrap them in waxed paper for a filling, easily carried lunch for a long hike when you don't want to be burdened with a load of gear. A half-dozen rolled pancakes can easily be carried in a pocket.

7 TRADITIONAL COOKOUTS

Until relatively recent years, anyone wanting to enjoy one of the three great traditional regional cookouts had to be in the region where they originated. The three most noteworthy cookouts to which I'm referring are the Down East clambake, the Southern fish fry, and the Western barbecue.

Now, make no mistake about one thing. To get the fullest flavor of these three feasts, it's almost necessary to enjoy them on their home grounds. You can duplicate the food anywhere, but it's not as easy to duplicate the climate or the surroundings.

A clambake tastes more like a clambake when it's held on a raw evening with tendrils of fog beginning to creep in from the darkening Atlantic, the scene around the feast made bright by a fire that gives off in its smoke the pungent unmistakable aroma of saltwater driftwood.

A fish fry is more like a fish fry on a bright, hot afternoon on the banks of a greenish river lazily flowing down to the Gulf, with loblolly pines or perhaps a few bright pink camellia bushes or some snowy flowering magnolias adding their scent to the resinous smoke of the logs under the cooking pot.

A barbecue seems more like a barbecue if it takes place within the sound of a herd of cattle blatting in the distance, a well-bleached cowchip or two merging with the dry ground. A horse corral should be visible as well as a few clumps of sagebrush in the background, while a big pot of coffee bubbles over a small crackling fire of mesquite twigs.

To be sure, none of these traditional backgrounds is absolutely essential for the separate feasts. You'll need the real ingredients, of course, and to preserve as much of the flavor of these ingredients as they'd have on their home grounds, they must be prepared the traditional way.

Thanks to technologies unknown and undreamed of in the days when each of these outdoor feasts evolved, the ingredients are available almost anywhere today. All you need is the energy to assemble them and to cook them as they would be cooked if you were actually where any of the three great cookouts were born.

You want to stage a large cookout, but your patio grill won't provide enough food for those expected to attend. The best solution is to improvise a cooking pit by stacking two courses of concrete blocks to form a rectangular cooking area. Tie a long, rectangular strip of wire mesh to several lengths of discarded pipe and lay the works on top. Throw five or six bags of charcoal into the pit; when glowing coals are ready, you'll be able to grill as much food as you need.

HOW TO ROAST CORN

No cookout is complete without sweet corn roasted right in their own husks. Begin by carefully pulling back the husks and removing the silk.

Now pull the husk back over the corn as it originally was and tie the loose end with cotton string.

Soak the ears in cold water for about 5 minutes, turning them occasionally.

Lay the sweet corn on a grill over coals and continue roasting them until their outer husks are charred black. Turn the ears frequently. The average roasting time will take about 40 minutes, depending upon the quantity of coals you have laid.

Even though the outside husks of roasting ears are charred black the inside portions of the husks are still moist and green. Sweet corn prepared in this manner is so delectable you'll probably never want it served any other way.

CLAMBAKES

Clambakes call for more than just un-shucked clams. You'll also need a few lob-sters and some ears of corn and a few po-tatoes. Some veteran clambakers include onions; others don't.

For the cooking, there must be a seashore area where you can dig a pit in ocean-washed sand; stones with which to line the pit, big bunches of seaweed—though inlanders must depend on lettuce leaves soaked in salt water as a substi-tute—a tarpaulin to cover the pit, and a sizeable stack of firewood.

If you're starting with freshly dug clams, which can be cherrystones, little-necks, quahogs, butters, or razors, they will have been dug 24 hours before they are to be cooked and kept overnight in a tub of salt water to which about a quar-ter-cup of cornmeal per quart of clams has been added. This overnight isolation is to allow the clams to purge themselves of the sand they ingest as they eat. Don't try to shorten the purging period, unless you like the feel of grit between your teeth while you're chewing.

Allow about a quart of unshucked clams and half a lobster per person, as well as two potatoes, two ears of un-husked corn, and one onion, if you're an onion fancier. An incredible quantity of butter is essential, so is a lot of salt and pepper, which is best provided in small in-dividual shakers. Beer is the traditional beverage, with coffee as a top-off after eating.

How big a firepit you dig will depend on the number of people you'll be feeding. To serve a dozen, your pit would be roughly 6 feet long, 3 feet wide, 18 to 20 inches deep. In the soft sand of a seashore, you'd need a bigger pit than would be re-quired for the firm earth of an inland site. If you're cooking on a small scale, for four people, sink a washtub into the ground and forget about a big pit.

Line the pit—or tub—with stones, and build a blazing fire on the stones. Three to four hours of burning, and the stones will have absorbed enough heat to do their job. Shovel out the coals, but don't extinguish them; you'll use them later.

Build up a layer of seaweed (or the lettuce leaves if you're inland) on the hot stones and on this put a layer of well-scrubbed clams. Add another layer of sea-weed and the lobsters; a third seaweed layer and the corn, potatoes, and onions. The ears of corn will have been stripped of all but about three or four layers of husks and the silk removed, the potatoes washed so they can be eaten, peel and all, out of hand. Top the vegetables with an-other seaweed layer into which the still-glowing coals are shoveled.

Put a final thick layer of seaweed over the coals and spread a tarpaulin over the pit, then shovel sand around its edges to seal in the steam that's already begin-ning to rise. Go away and leave things alone for 3 to 4 hours. Three hours is the minimum, and if you allow 4½ or 5 hours, nobody's going to know the difference.

When the pit is opened, spread the tarpaulin to serve as a table. Provide thick gloves or some rags with which to shield hands from the hot shells of the clams and lobsters, and if you want to be fancy, fur-nish the eaters with plates. Plates aren't really necessary, though. Part of the fun of a clambake is watching the way each individual handles the hot shellfish, and trying to discover the easiest way to handle your own.

If you're on a public beach, you'll want to shovel the dead coals and stones out of the way, and remove your shells and litter to leave a clean site for the next clambakers, of course.

Inlanders who can't dig their own clams or drop in at a fish market can usually get unshucked clams and live lobsters from the specialty shippers who supply restaurants with seafoods. You'll probably pay for them by the pound instead of the quarts quoted in the recipes. Just remember the old adage, "A pint's a pound the world around," and you'll be all right.

A SOUTHERN FISH FRY

Fish fries are to the South what the fried-chicken picnic is to the rolling Midwestern farm country, the clambake to the denizens of the northern Atlantic seaboard, and the barbecue to the West. In the beginning, fish fries were usually held in connection with an all-day prayer meeting or streamside baptism, or with a day of political speechmaking. The rule was that the deacons of the church or the office-seekers provided the fish. But fish fries weren't always public affairs. Quite often a big fish fry was a family event on holidays or a gathering to celebrate a reunion or a wedding or christening service.

In prerefrigeration days, cooked foods kept badly in the hot, moist atmosphere of the region, and its residents learned quickly that the safest foods to eat were those that the locale itself provided, cooked on the scene.

There was a general scarcity of game in the area, but its multitude of streams provided a large variety of panfish that could be harvested by seines, and the catfish which abounded in most Southern waters were easily caught with a worm-baited hook and a line tied to a thin branch. A few hours of fishing in the early morning, done by the youths when it was a family affair, would generally provide enough to feed a sizeable crowd.

Panfish were cooked whole; catfish were skinned and cut into chunks, the chunks rolled in salted cornmeal. The cooking fat in the big cast-iron cauldron was almost invariably lard; the fuel was for the most part pine-tree saplings, also easily come by in the South's earlier days. Hush puppies, corn pones deep-fried in the same fat in which the fish had been cooked, were the bread. Everyone who's ever read a book about Southern cooking or Southern customs knows that hush puppies got their name by being tossed to the dogs that had tagged along to the fish fry, to quiet their begging whines while the people ate.

A fish-fry menu was simplicity itself: fried fish, fried hush puppies, onion slices soaked in salted water, and dill pickles. The meal was topped off with whatever fruit was plentiful at the time, or perhaps cookies, cakes, or pies brought from home. In areas where yams or sweet potatoes were grown, the tubers left from last fall might be parboiled, sliced, and fried and sprinkled generously with brown sugar to

Fish frys sometimes draw enormous crowds. Although they originated in the South, they're now popular almost everywhere. Here, huge wire baskets of fish are being lowered into hot oil while eager onlookers patiently wait.

serve as a dessert. Every bit of food served at a fish fry was what today we call finger food. Plates were never used; even the gentle flowers of Southern womanhood ate with their fingers.

You need no recipe for fish cooked fish-fry style. The only advice I have to offer is an easy way to judge the temperature of the frying fat. Consider it ready when a 1-inch cube of bread tossed into the bubbling pot turns a rich deep tan color in 30 seconds. Coat the fish by rolling them in a mixture of cornmeal and salt, about 1½ teaspoons of salt per pound of meal. Add pepper if you wish, but remember that in the South when fish frys began, pepper was a scarce and costly spice.

Even in Canada, no fishing trip is complete without a noontime fish fry, except that throughout the provinces the pastime is more commonly called shore lunch.

Panfish and panfish-sized chunks of catfish are done when their cornmeal coating is a crisp light brown. Put in only a few at a time to keep the grease at an even temperature. Use whatever kind of long-handled strainer or scoop is handy to lift them from the bubbling fat and drain them on brown paper sacks or several folds of newspaper.

Hush puppies are made from the following dough:

2 cups cornmeal
1 tsp salt
2 Tbsp lard
1½ cups boiling water

Mix the cornmeal and salt; cream the lard into it with a spoon. Stir in the boiling water (and it must be boiling) a bit at a time to make a thick dough.

Drop the dough into the cooking fat by tablespoonfuls, or form the moist dough into pones by compressing a tablespoon of dough between cupped palms. As the blobs of dough bob around, turn them so they will cook evenly, fish them out, and let them drain for a few moments on papers.

This recipe will yield 26 to 30 hush puppies, and can be halved, doubled, or tripled.

In later days, cooks generally have come to add an egg to the hush-puppy dough. This makes a lighter pone, but the old-fashioned traditional hush puppy was always eggless. I suppose it's possible to make hush puppies from one of the prepared cornbread mixes that abound on supermarket shelves, but have never tried it. The original recipe is so simple that it seems a waste of money to use a packaged mix. Feel free to experiment, if you like, of course.

BARBECUE

Having gotten this far along in the book, you will have noted by now that in outdoor cooking I tend to be a traditionalist. This is especially true where barbecue is concerned.

The term "barbecue" originally applied to a method of cooking sauced, oversized pieces of meat in a tightly closed earthen pit over expiring coals. Today the term is used to describe almost any type of cookout or even outdoor cooking device. In this chapter, I am using "barbecue" in its original sense.

In my youth, a skilled barbecue cook in the average Southwestern community occupied a position far above that of the town's mayor; a really expert barbecue cook was looked on with the respect that in those days was accorded only to such exalted individuals as members of the President's Cabinet or the Supreme Court. People took barbecuing seriously, then.

A good barbecue cook was noted for his sauce as much as for his skill in judging the quality of coals and the time that must lapse between the closing of the pit and its opening. Usually, this ranged from 16 to 24 hours, depending on whether the meat in the pit was the entire hindquarter of a tough old range-run steer or a set of ribs from such a steer, or whether it was a boned-out haunch cut into two or three pieces. Whatever form the beef might take, it was always wrapped in several layers of sauce-soaked burlap, salvaged from feed bags, and held around the meat with twists of wire.

According to the most believable legends, barbecue originated in the Caribbean islands in the days of the buccaneers. Now, the word "buccaneer" is a corruption of *boucainer,* and the original word came from *boucan,* which in the patois of the islands meant a raw steer-hide, or *boucaine,* meaning smoked beef. Most of the sailing bands of hide-sellers stole the cattle they skinned, so *boucainer* came to mean "cattle-thief," and gradually came to be applied to all the Caribbean pirates, pirates who preyed on humans instead of cattle.

Tradition has it that when the original *boucainers* beached their vessels to eat on shore, they would slaughter a steer from the cargo. The animal was gutted, its cavity filled with a mixture of peppers and tomatoes, then without being skinned the steer was cooked by being buried in a pit of burning coals. It was, in the local corruption of mixed Spanish and English, *barbecocido,* or "cooked with the hair on."

As time went on, the *boucainers* extended their looting forays further westward and pushed deeper inland, raiding the big ranches that in the 17th and 18th centuries filled the land between the Rio Grande and the Yucatán Peninsula. The buccaneers' style of cooking whole steers supposedly migrated from Mexico into Texas and California, the technique changing over the years as the art of pit-cooking moved north. Nobody really knows, but that's the legend.

Whether the story of its origin is true or false, the main features of this legendary method of cooking beef were still being observed when I got acquainted with barbecue. It was then strictly a regional style of cooking. Easterners coming to Texas had more often than not heard the term, but had no idea what to expect in the way of taste.

Cattle drives, which began in the early 1700s between Texas and California, carried the cooking style west along the cattle trails, and when the trails shifted to the north, in the mid-1800s, barbecue went with them. But barbecuing was not practiced on the trails; the long cooking time required precluded that. A barbecue was usually the highlight of a trail-end blowout, a final fling after the herd was safe at railhead before the trail crew broke up.

Beef, then, was the original barbecue meat in North America, though in China pork had been cooked in a form of barbecuing for centuries, and in the South Seas, fish and fowl had been wrapped in leaves or encased in clay and cooked with coals in earthen pits.

There's no real difference between barbecuing beef and pork, but no self-respecting barbecue cook will barbecue a chicken. Actually, the only difference in barbecuing different kinds of meat is the timing and the saucing. In traditional barbecuing, these are the only ways by which the flavor of the meat being cooked can be changed.

Let's dispose of technique first, then go on to sauces.

Any wood, but preferably a hardwood or semihardwood, can be used to prepare a bed of coals in a barbecue pit. By the time the coals are ready for use, all the resins and aromatics in any wood in common use will have been dissipated. The only exception I can think of is eucalyptus wood, which even when reduced to ashes never seems to lose its characteristic odor.

Let the size of the pit be determined by the size of the pieces being barbecued.

A small pit, 3 feet deep by 2 feet wide by 4 feet long will serve quite well for the barbecuing of two 10-pound chunks of beef, or two fresh pork hams. For ribs an even smaller pit will usually serve. The pit should never be less than one-third full of glowing coals, and half-full is even better. The fire is built in the pit and stoked generously until the required quantity of coals remains and there are no big tongues of flame left.

Barbecue sauce (recipes follow) should be mixed by the tub or bucketful, as you will need enough sauce in which to dip the meat before wrapping it. You'll also need some double-thick brown wrapping paper, or if you're barbecuing small chunks of beef, a supply of brown paper bags, and several burlap sacks. Feed dealers almost always have burlap sacks for sale; so do many seed dealers. Wash the sacks before using them.

Don't prepare the meat until the pit is ready. A barbecue can't be hurried along. You'll have lots of waiting to do, for each time wood's added to the pit you'll have to give it time to burn down into coals before replenishing the fire. Use these periods of waiting to prepare the barbecue sauce and to bundle up the chunks of meat.

A word of caution about one of the ingredients in the sauce. Use sugar-free canned tomatoes or tomato puree when preparing barbecue sauce. Most major brands now include a line of sugar-free fruits and vegetables, and European-packed tomato paste in tubes is also now widely available. The tube-packed pastes are sugar-free, and the contents of one 5½-ounce tube, diluted with ⅓ cup of warm water is equal to an 8-ounce can of tomato puree.

BARBECUE SAUCE FOR 5-POUND PIECE OF BEEF

2   cups light cooking oil
4   Tbsp white vinegar
6   #2 cans (or one #10 can) Italian plum tomatoes, put through a sieve or mashed very fine (plum tomatoes are usually canned with a bit of basil and oregano and seldom contain added sugar)
3   cans tomato puree
6   large onions, ground, grated, or scraped
2   cloves garlic, mashed
2   tsp powdered oregano
2   Tbsp chili molido (chili powder)
1   tsp brown sugar
2½ tsp salt
1   tsp freshly ground white pepper

Combine the liquid ingredients; consider the mashed tomatoes a liquid, as you should mash the solids into the juice that the can contains. Stir in the remaining ingredients. Bring to a boil, stir well, let cool. The resulting mixture should be somewhere between a puree and a liquid. When cooked, insert a spoon vertically into the sauce, remove it, and let the liquid drip off its tip. The sauce should cling well rather than dripping off rapidly. If it is too thin, add more mashed tomato solids; if too thick, dilute with water.

While you've been preparing the sauce, you've also been replenishing the bed of coals in the pit. By now, it should be filled one-third or halfway from the bottom with glowing coals. The time has come to begin barbecuing.

Anoint the meat with the sauce, and wrap each chunk well in brown paper or put each piece of meat in a paper sack. Using an inner wrapping of paper is a modern touch; originally, the meat was simply wrapped in burlap and the finished package dipped in the sauce. Wrap each chunk of meat separately, covering it with four or five layers of burlap. Secure the wrapping by crisscrossing the bundles with medium-gauge stove wire.

Do not use galvanized or any other coated wire; some coatings used on wire emit noxious, even poisonous fumes when heated. Stovepipe wire is black and very pliable.

After securing the wrappings, dip the packages of meat in a tub of water, then lay the pieces of meat right on the coals and close the barbecue pit at once. The burlap will not burn, as will be explained later on.

Cover the pit with a single piece of sheet metal or smaller pieces overlapped 6 to 8 inches and extending at least a foot beyond the edges of the pit on all sides. If galvanized corrugated sheet metal is used as a pit cover, it's a wise precaution to expose it to heat first, to remove all traces of the galvanizing compound.

Shovel the dirt removed when the pit was dug over the cover. The dirt should extend beyond the edges of the metal cover and be tamped firmly to seal the pit.

Now, go away and let the coals do their job. Do not open the pit until 8 hours have passed if you are cooking beef in 5-pound chunks; 12 hours if the chunks are 10 pounds; 16 to 18 hours for chunks up to 20 pounds. For beef short ribs, 5 to 6 hours should be adequate unless the ribs are quite fat; if this is the case, cook an extra hour to let the fat drain away.

At the end of the cooking time, uncover the pit and use ice tongs to lift out the meat. Clip the wires and cut away the burlap wrappings, and cut the meat in chunks to serve it. Have the remaining sauce at hand in a bowl so those who want more can spoon some over their plates.

In the Southwest, the traditional barbecue side dishes are pinto beans boiled with whole onions, sliced raw onions, and sour pickles, with beer as the go-with beverage and coffee later on.

Another tradition that has come down from the past years is to serve canned peach halves right from the can as dessert. Back in the beginning days of food preservation, peaches were among the first fruits canned in the new "air-tights." They were very expensive, but the cowhands, who had few sweet foods, didn't mind the cost.

Now, a sampling of other barbecue sauces.

BARBECUE SAUCE FOR PORK

1 quart tomato puree
1 cup lemon juice (fresh or fresh-frozen; do not use one of the re-

constituted lemon juices, as
they contain chemicals which
when heated in a barbecue pit
react with heat to produce an
unhappy flavor)

¾ **cup molasses**
1½ **cups grated, ground, or scraped
onion**
1 **tsp powdered marjoram**
½ **tsp powdered sage**
2 **tsp salt**
1 **tsp freshly ground black pepper**
3 **or 4 drops Tabasco sauce**

Combine the liquids, stirring to mix the
molasses thoroughly. Do not allow to boil.
Add the remaining ingredients and mix
well. If the mixture is too thin to cling well
to a spoon, add a bit more tomato puree; if
too thick, dilute carefully by adding small
amounts of water until the sauce is neither runny nor too thick to spread easily.

Soak the burlap in the sauce, wrap
the meat, and wire in place with uncoated
stove wire. Put the wrapped meat on the
coals, cover the barbecue pit with sheet
iron or sheet tin, and shovel the dirt taken
from the pit over the covering, paying
special attention to the edges, which must
be tamped firmly to seal the pit.

Cook ribs 4 to 6 hours, loin roasts up
to 8 pounds for 8 to 10 hours, whole fresh
pork hams 12 hours or longer. Do not
open the pit while the meat is cooking.

Now, to answer a few questions that
are probably bugging new barbecue cooks.
The burlap wrapping will not burn even
after it has dried from the heat. When
first put on the coals, the liquid in the
burlap will form a dead spot which keeps
it from bursting into flames. By the time
the burlap has dried, there is not enough
oxygen left in the sealed pit to support a
flame.

No, the barbecued meat will not
form a thick crust as will a roast cooked in
an oven. The sauce moisturizes the meat
and the diminishing heat from the coals
will not sear or harden the exterior of
even a big piece of meat during an extended period of cooking. There will probably be a layer of fairly dry, firm meat on
the bottom of each piece, where it's rested
on the coals, but even this section won't
be crusty.

How can you be sure the meat will
be completely cooked within the indicated
cooking times? You can't, but it will be. If
you have any doubts, leave the pit closed
an extra half-hour or hour. It's impossible
to overcook or to burn barbecue.

No, you should not try to carve barbecued meats into neat slices. It will
usually be too tender for proper slicing.
Cut it off in chunks the size of a lemon and
let those who're eating it reduce it to bite-
size bits.

A small-scale barbecue can be prepared with a 5-
pound piece of beef. Douse the beef in sauce, wrap it
in brown paper and burlap, and secure it with wire.
Lower the bundle into a deep pit where enough
wood has been burned to produce a bed of coals 12
to 14 inches deep. Cover the pit well. The coals will
not be extinguished, but will no longer flame when
the dirt covering deprives them of oxygen. Leave
the meat in the pit for 8 to 10 hours before uncov-
ering it to serve.

8 FOOD FOR PATIOS AND PICNICS

In an all-embracing and generally tolerant world, there's certainly room to accommodate the three groups of people for whom this chapter is intended.

In group one are the individuals who don't care for camping but enjoy cooking outdoors. Group two includes those who like to cook and like the flavor of foods cooked outdoor-style, but who have no desire to take up the art of cooking outdoors. In the third group we find those who don't enjoy either camping or outdoor cooking, but simply like to carry food cooked at home to the nearest open space and enjoy a picnic under the summer sky.

"All outdoors" is a very embracing phrase, and surely it's broad enough to include these three culinary preferences.

If we look at both the warm and the cold facts of life, we just might discover that the "I like to cook outdoors but I don't care for camping," the "I like the taste of outdoor-style food but I don't enjoy doing outdoor cooking," and the "I like to eat outdoors, but I'll prepare my food at home" contingents outnumber the campers, hikers, hunters, fishermen, and other nature-lovers who both cook and eat in the open as a secondary pleasure while pursuing another outdoor interest.

This may be the reason why the plans of so many homes, even those of modest size and cost, include patios which offer the facilities for at-home outdoor cooking. It might also explain why an increasingly large number of kitchen ranges now provide accessories that make possible range-top spit-cooking and grilling, to give kitchen-cooked food an outdoor touch.

A number of kitchen ranges and drop-in countertop stoves are available now which do a very good job of simulating the cooking results of outdoor grills, and these are appearing in more and more home kitchens. Most of these offer both grilling and spit-cooking facilities, combining conventional gas burners or electric elements with permanent heat-reflectors such as actual beds of lava stone and

For those who like an outdoor flavor to enhance foods cooked indoors, various types of ranges now incorporate special grills. Lava stones beneath the grating give foods a slight charcoal flavor, and unique exhaust systems suck away all traces of smoke in an instant.

Range-oven combinations are also popular. This model is particularly versatile because when you need additional burners the grillwork assembly lifts right out and a two-burner unit slips into its place in less than 30 seconds.

heavy cast-iron plates which create in a home kitchen the intense heat once possible to get only with actual coals of burning wood or charcoal.

What we're seeing when we look at cooking outdoor-style without going outside the home kitchen is not a diminishing number of outdoor cooking or outdoor eating enthusiasts. Nor is it a contradiction in terms when we speak of cooking outdoor-style without going outdoors.

What we're really looking at is a growing number of people enthusiastic about outdoor cooking or enjoying the distinctive flavors of foods cooked outdoor-style. In an era of two-job families and increasing travel costs, these enthusiasts are willing to invest a substantial amount of money in facilities that allow them to extend the outdoor cooking season across the entire year. They've also found a solution that allows them to share outdoor cooking pleasures when they are too involved in work to travel readily; they've found a way to put a bit more money in their menus than into the gasoline tank of the family car or into rail, bus, or airline tickets.

It's also possible to prepare foods in a patio or kitchen setting that are a bit difficult to cook in a wilderness camp, which results in expanded menus. Food cooked on skewers, for example, usually requires constant turning, and this is more readily done with an electric rotisserie attachment over a patio grill than by hand over a firepit, or even a small grill, in camp where electricity isn't available.

Some dishes contain ingredients which are not practical to carry to a camp because they require refrigerated storage until they are cooked; ground meat and fresh chicken livers come at once to mind as two of many such foods. Using the kitchen, or just having a kitchen handy to a patio, expands the number of options open to you.

Nor has the old-fashioned picnic ever lost its appeal. For every outdoor excursion that involves cooking there are perhaps two or three picnics at which the traditional sandwiches and finger foods served have been brought from the home kitchen.

No book on outdoor cooking would be complete without covering all the ways possible to achieve desired goals, so in this chapter we'll look in turn at patio and outdoor-style kitchen cooking and then at picnics. The options you have available in equipment make as good a starting place as any.

Gas-fired patio grills are extremely popular nowadays. One small tank of propane should last a year. On this model, an overhead hood can be lowered if long, slow cooking is preferred over broiling.

PATIO GRILLS

Patio grills can be divided into two kinds, movable and permanent. Movable grills, as opposed to the portable kind which we look at in Chapter 1 of this section, are too bulky or heavy to be easily transported to a distant campsite; if you'll recall, this disadvantage was mentioned in connection with the sheepherder stove and the oil drum grill.

Some movable grills also use gas or electricity, which generally removes them from the strictly portable category. Most such grills, though, can be shifted short distances in a backyard or patio to take advantage of changing conditions of shade and shelter.

Permanent grills are usually built of fieldstone or brick, cast concrete or concrete blocks. Today, these grills, too, often use gas or electricity. Both movable and permanent grills range from the very simple and inexpensive to the costly and elaborate, and many of the simpler kinds can be made by home craftsmen. Unlike the complex job of erecting a brick building, small-scale bricklaying such as that involved in erecting a simple patio grill is a craft that is quite easy to learn.

A fixed-position grill may be simply a brick box topped with a grid, or it may be built around a metal firebox or oven. Large grills of this kind are often quite literally outdoor kitchens. Many such grills include warming ovens; a few have ovens that are usable for baking.

Permanent backyard grills can be simple, homemade affairs like this. Note the absence of mortar joints, and the handy slab-stone work surface.

If you have the time and confidence in your skill and are willing to settle for one of the simpler kind, you can build your own fixed-position grill, even if you're a total stranger to the fine art of bricklaying. The amount of work, time, and skill required to build a simple brick grill are all quite small, and there are a number of do-it-yourself books devoted entirely to the subject of patio grills that give you all the necessary instructions. Spit-cooking and rotisserie attachments for fixed-position grills are available in a variety of styles and sizes, so your cooking options are virtually unlimited.

One grill that falls between being fixed and movable is the oil drum grill illustrated. Its construction is simple, and

even if you aren't a skilled metalworker or lack the necessary tools, a metalworking shop's charges for converting an oil drum into a grill of this kind should be quite reasonable.

Any of the portable grills which were pictured and discussed in Chapter 1 can of course be set up on a porch or lawn or patio.

Hibachis are extremely popular as patio grills, and some charcoal-cooking enthusiasts bring hibachis inside and cook on them at the dining table. Now, charcoal is a very fine fuel for cooking, but it has one insidious characteristic. When burned in a tightly closed room, even in small quantities, charcoal not only consumes oxygen at an alarmingly fast rate,

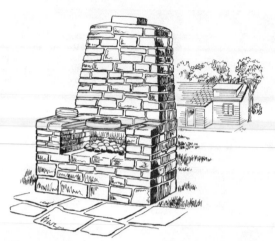

Permanent backyard grills can be made as elaborate as you like, but for a professional job you'll probably have to hire a mason.

As the accompanying illustrations show, movable outdoor grills go from basic to elaborate in several steps. Each step, each added feature, will cost just a bit more, of course. The simpler types of artificial-fuel grills will be much like the portable charcoal grills at which we looked in Chapter 1.

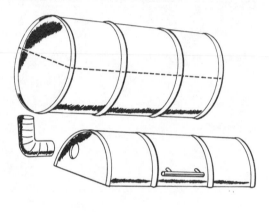

but produces fumes which can make those inhaling them quite ill and can even result in death.

If you insist on using charcoal for indoor cooking, be sure that your hibachi or grill is used only in a fireplace, where its fumes will escape up a chimney, and provide adequate ventilation by leaving the windows open.

Vertical drum grills are very practical and efficient. Many of them can use wood or be converted to use either natural or LP gas. When you wish to use one of these grills as a smoke, you must of course use charcoal as your fuel, and sprinkle hickory chips over the meat being smoked to provide the smoky flavor.

With a grid placed over the bottom half, a vertical drum will serve for all outdoor cooking needs with one exception: It lacks enough capacity to allow you to cook food buried in coals. Some of these grills are fitted for a small spit, but none of them is large enough to accommodate a drip-pan.

Simple to make, but pretty well anchored in a permanent position by its weight and bulk is the oil-drum grill. Open, the grill becomes a traditional surface cooker, and closed it can be used for smoking. This grill provides so much surface-cooking room, you can prepare food for as many as 25 people if need be.

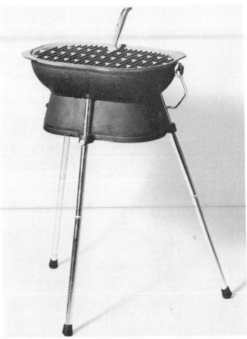

Much smaller, and still easier to make, is this nifty beer-keg grill. Have a metal-working shop cut the keg in half lengthwise with an acetylene torch, then reunite the two halves with hinges. Next, mount the unit on a framework made of aluminum angle bolted in place where appropriate.

Hibachis are popular for patio cooking. This type comes with detachable legs that raise the grill to a comfortable height for cooking. If you use a hibachi indoors, be sure to place it in a fireplace so the fumes will escape up the chimney.

You can cut an old oven rack to size with a hacksaw to fit the inside of the beer-keg grill. This unit provides ample cooking room for four people.

Perhaps the most widely sold grill is this inexpensive sheet-metal model. If you decide to buy one, make sure the brand you select has a feature that allows you to adjust the grill to different height levels. Also, if you line the inside of the pan with foil, you'll receive more heat output from lesser quantities of charcoal, and as an extra bonus the grill will last much longer.

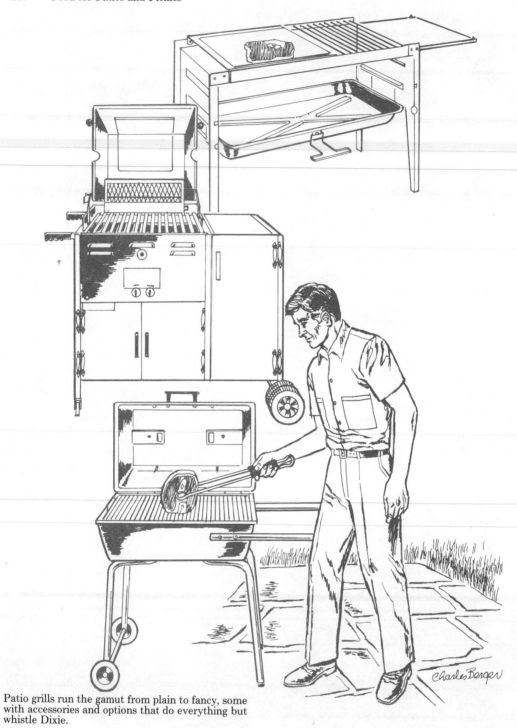

Patio grills run the gamut from plain to fancy, some
with accessories and options that do everything but
whistle Dixie.

On the elaborate side of the artificial fuel models is this top-of-the line Ducane grill, which is fueled by either liquid propane gas or natural gas, with self-cleaning lava rocks used as a heat distributor. The vertical heat source at the back of the grill provides the flow of superheated air that is necessary in rotissiere and spit-roasting. A rock-maple cutting board is provided in this model, and when its top is closed the grill functions as a smoker or oven.

Usually, the simplest of these grills will be light enough in weight to be lifted easily when you want to move one of them from place to place. They may or may not have provisions for attaching such accessories as a spit or a skewer-type rotisserie. They will be rather small in size, which limits the quantity of food that can be prepared on them at one time.

At the other end of the scale are the cabinet-type grills, such as the Ducane Grill shown. The largest of these take up quite a bit of space, and are usually mounted on wheels so they can be moved from point to point. Some will have tightly fitted arched tops that allow them to be used as smokers, and for the most elaborate models there are available such accessories as a cutting surface, as well as electrically powered spit and rotisserie attachments.

INDOOR FACILITIES

In recent years a lot of thought and ingenuity have been devoted to providing outdoor-style cooking facilities to be used in the house. Not all of them are planned for the kitchen, as you will see as you scan the following brief summary of what's new and currently available in this area.

FIREPLACE GRILLS

In the beginning days of Colonial America, all homes stood on the frontier,

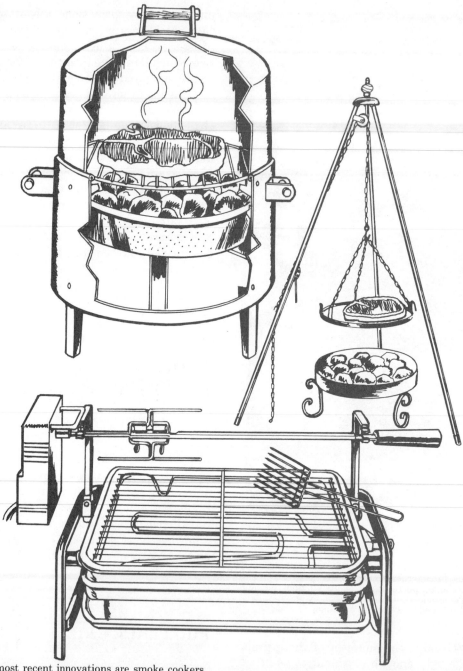

Three most recent innovations are smoke cookers, tripod grills, and combination units incorporating griddles, grills, and rotissieres.

and most of them followed the familiar pattern of settlers' dwellings everywhere. They were simply one big room which served as parlor, bedroom, dining room, and kitchen. Cooking was done in the fireplace, using cast-iron utensils. These included the familiar Dutch oven, which served for stewing, soup-making, and baking. Spiders, skillets on legs that raised them above the coals for slower cooking, were a commonplace. So were cast-iron skillets and deep pots and kettles.

Fireplace grills were once commonplace but slowly fell into obscurity. They're now making a comeback, due largely to the energy crunch and also the renewed popularity of fireplaces themselves. You can obtain other cooking equipment for use in fireplaces, such as vertical rods from which you can hang bean pots and assorted kettles.

With fireplaces being restored to prominence because of high fossil fuel prices, fireplace cooking is enjoying a revival today and several manufacturers now offer cranes, which support kettles and stew pots over the coals. Several new types of grills have appeared on the market, some of them offering as many as three tiers on which foods can be grilled, and while these grills are specifically designed for use in indoor fireplaces, they will function equally well in a patio. The accompanying drawing shows you one of these.

In Chapter 1 you saw the Qwick-Cook Grill, which can be used in a fireplace as well as outdoors.

SPECIALTIES OF THE PATIO

Most of the recipes that follow can be cooked over a camp as well as a patio grill. They were not included in earlier chapters because some of them call for ingredients which require a degree of refrigeration difficult to attain during a prolonged trip to a remote campsite. Others have steps in their preparation which are a bit too elaborate unless you have a kitchen close by. Still others are for skewer-cooked foods that require constant turning, which in camp is a somewhat demanding routine, but which is easy when you can plug into a patio electrical outlet a motor-driven rotisserie attachment.

You will notice that frankfurters are conspicuous by their absence in the recipes that follow. The reason for this omission has already been touched on in an earlier chapter, but let me refresh your memory in as few words as possible.

Frankfurters were originally made from scalded beef trimmings with all but a small quantity of the suet removed. The beef was very lightly seasoned and packed into an edible casing. The frankfurter could both transmit and absorb flavor, and thus it was a valid ingredient in any dish in which it was used.

Today's frankfurter is made from tripes, stomachs, lungs, and other slaughterhouse leftovers. By law, they may contain up to 30 percent fat, and such other fillers as soybean meal or unspecified cereals. They are highly seasoned to compensate for the fact that their ingredients have no flavor in themselves, and are completely cooked. Consequently, the modern frankfurter can neither transmit nor absorb flavor to or from any of the ingredients used in a recipe. It is as inert and unappetizing as a chunk of stone.

To franks, then, I say thank you, but no thanks. It's less trouble and more rewarding to cook real meat.

STEAKS

In spite of the constantly rising cost of prime-cut meats, steak remains the most popular with most outdoor chefs, whether they cook in the patio or over a fireplace grill, or in a camp. Steak also is—or should be—the easiest of all cuts of meat to cook. However, two pitfalls await the outdoor chef. The first is beginning a thick steak over coals that are too bright, the second is cooking with the grid too near the coals. Both result in a thick steak being charred on the surface before the inside portion is cooked.

Charcoal, the chief fuel used in patio grills, produces a deceptive amount of heat. A charcoal fire that's glowing bright cherry-red should be used only when cooking thin cuts of steak or chops no thicker than ½ inch. If you're cooking prime-cut steaks an inch or more thick, let the charcoal darken to a medium red and put the steaks on the grill only when the coals begin to grow dark at the edges.

Patio grills which use gas for fuel and have a firepit lined with ceramic or lava stones or a mass of cast iron to simulate glowing coals aren't subject to the vagaries of natural fuels. I'm sure the manufacturers of this equipment have done adequate research to give their units cooking characteristics that closely resemble those of natural fuels.

My experience with the gas-fueled Ducane grill, which uses lava stones, and the Jenn-Air electric range, which has a thick cast-iron slab in the bottom of its grill unit, indicates that the cooking times on both of these correspond very closely to the heat of natural coals when used at a medium-high setting and to charcoal briquettes when a high setting is used.

You must keep in mind the variables which form pitfalls for the outdoor cook. The most common of these is the wind. Currents so tiny that they are barely noticeable will fan a bed of coals to a deceptively high heat and overcook a steak while the chef is chatting with guests. Another variable is the time when you salt a steak; this should be done after cooking rather than before or during cooking. Salt pulls juices from meat, and when salted before cooking the heat accelerates the salt's action. A dry, tough steak is the result.

Still another variable is the difference in meat quality. There are really two kinds of beef sold at retail butcher stores and supermarkets today: feedlot beef and range-fed beef. You can safely assume that the meat you buy from a supermarket or run-of-the-mill butcher shop was "finished" on a feedlot. Range-fed beef is very scarce, and most of it goes to deluxe restaurants and specialty butcher shops, where it commands a premium price. The butcher from whom you buy the beef should know the difference and be able to tell you what you're buying.

Feedlot beef is fatter than range-run beef, and the fat is not concentrated in a rim around the skin-edge of a cut, but is distributed in tiny pockets throughout the meat itself. Feedlot beef also has much softer tissues than beef from a steer which has grown up free to wander in search of graze. Feedlot beef is more predictably uniform than range-fed beef, and the grill-to-coals spacing given in a later paragraph is for feedlot beef.

Feedlot beef should be cooked at a lower temperature for a longer time than beef from range-run cattle. The longer cooking will liquify much of the fat in this kind of beef and allow it to drain out of the meat. If you know you're going to be cooking range-fed beef, drop your grill an inch or two closer to the coals, which will cook the meat a bit faster.

With the grill 4 to 6 inches above the coals of a patio grill, a thin-cut steak will suit most tastes when cooked 4 to 7 minutes per side over bright coals and turned only once. Most thin cuts are very easily overcooked, and a thin overcooked steak belongs in a shoemaker's shop instead of on a dining table.

Steaks more than an inch thick should be cooked on a grill 6 to 8 inches above medium-red coals. Sear both surfaces by cooking 4 to 6 minutes per side, then turn the meat and cook 6 to 8 minutes per side to produce a rare steak. If a medium-rare or medium steak is your ob-

jective, cook as above, then turn the meat a second time and cook each side an additional 3 to 5 minutes.

A very thin line divides a well-done steak from one that is overdone, and when you pass the two or three minutes that result in a medium-cooked steak, you run the risk of overcooking. No chef worthy of his high bonnet and apron will overcook beef. When overcooked, the finest beef becomes dry and tasteless, and even well-done steaks should have a small blush of pink in the center when served.

Now, let's take a look at lesser cuts of steak, which you'll find discussed in some detail as to origin in Chapter 4. These steaks benefit from being marinated for an hour or two in a mild mixture of acid liquid which will soften up the grained tissues and tame the tough connective tissues which are in most of them.

Marinating does not equate with sprinkling the meat with one of the commercial tenderizers. Most of these contain an enzyme synthesized to imitate that in papaya fruits, which is extremely active and attacks all meat tissues indiscriminately. The result is mushy meat. Use one of the several marinades given elsewhere in this book to mitigate the inherent toughness of the lesser steaks and cook them over brighter coals, as indicated earlier, to preserve their natural juices.

CHOPS

When we say "chops," we generally mean lamb or pork. Lamb chops are inherently dry, and need to be cooked the shortest time possible: 3 to 4 minutes per side over bright coals. If you have the courage to do so, forget about salting lamb chops. Instead, sprinkle them with a bit of lemon juice, squeezed from a genuine lemon, and dust them very very lightly indeed with white pepper to give grilled lamb chops a new dimension of flavor.

Pork chops should be trimmed of excess fat before going to the grill; a quarter-inch rim is plenty. Cook the chops over medium-bright coals, for they need slow cooking to remove all traces of redness while still leaving them juicy. Turn half-inch-thick chops three times, leaving them on each side for 3 minutes. Salt after cooking, but if you want to titilate jaded taste buds, omit the usual salt and pepper. In a small mortar, or by rubbing between your fingers, reduce to a fine powder equal parts of dry rosemary and dry thyme and sprinkle this on the meat very sparsely before grilling.

Above all, remember that cooking on a grill over coals is not an exact science. Experience is still your best teacher, and all that can be done in a book of this kind is to give you guidelines that are reasonably accurate for most situations.

Lamb, veal, or beef make equally good kebabs, and they can be considered as interchangeable in the following groups of recipes for skewer-cooked meats. All meat used in kebab cookery is customarily marinated anywhere from a few hours to a day or more.

After having been marinated, most meats used in kebab cooking can be cooked with approximately the same timing. Cut the meat into 1-inch cubes and marinate 6 hours, stirring occasionally. The marinating time may be extended up to two days if the bowl in which the marinating is being done is kept in the refrigerator.

Before cooking, drain the cubes and put them on skewers, alternating the meat cubes with small fresh vegetables such as cherry tomatoes, pieces of sweet green or red pepper, zucchini, small onions, mushrooms, cucumber, celery chunks, etc. You can also use olives, gherkins, tiny pickled beets, and so on between the pieces of meat for greater variety. Grilling time varies from 5 to 10 or 12 minutes.

SKEWER COOKING

As has already been noted, not all small chunks of meat cooked on skewers are shish kebabs. In the Middle East, where this style of cooking is most common, "shish" is the word for lamb or mutton, and kebabs (or kabobs, if you prefer) are identified as "dana kebabi" for veal and "sigir kebabi" for beef. You will not find pork cooked in this region, for Moslem dietary laws classify pork as unclean.

KEBAB MARINADES

#1

  ¾ cup olive oil
  ½ cup vinegar
  2 Tbsp grated or scraped onion
  ¼ tsp ground coriander
  ¼ tsp freshly ground black pepper

GRILLING A SUMPTUOUS
SHISH KEBAB

1. Delicious combination of meats, vegetables, and fruits for a shish kebab: sirloin steak, bermuda onions, bacon, green peppers, hot banana peppers, and apples. Cut them into large chunks, then alternate them on skewers.

2. Youngsters love to make shish kebab, and there's no way they can make a mistake, so let this be one of their first outdoor cooking experiences.

3. When your skewered kebabs are prepared, let them sit in a marinating solution for 20 minutes. Turn them so all sides absorb the marinade.

4. Now lay kebabs on grill over a bed of bright coals. Cooking time will take about 40 minutes. Turn the kebabs every 5 minutes, and baste every 10 minutes with remaining marinade from your pan.

⅛ tsp turmeric
Large pinch freshly grated ginger root

Stir the oil and vinegar together; add onions and seasonings. Marinate the meat under refrigeration, stirring now and then.

#2

½ cup olive oil
2 Tbsp Worcestershire sauce
¼ cup broth (canned or use the beef stock recipe given in an earlier chapter)
2 cloves garlic, mashed
⅛ tsp cayenne
½ tsp ground thyme

Stir liquids together; add spices. Marinate the meat under refrigeration, stirring occasionally.

#3

½ cup olive oil
¼ cup fresh or frozen lemon juice
¼ cup grated or scraped onion
¼ tsp freshly ground white pepper
1 Tbsp minced parsley
1 tsp ground marjoram

Stir liquids together; add spices. Marinate the meat under refrigeration, stirring occasionally.

#4

½ cup olive oil
¼ cup white wine vinegar
2 Tbsp fresh or frozen lemon juice
1 clove garlic, mashed
¼ tsp ground oregano
½ tsp ground cumin seeds
½ tsp grated fresh ginger root
Large pinch freshly grated nutmeg

Stir liquids together; add spices. Marinate meat under refrigeration, stirring occasionally.

BASQUE-STYLE CHICKEN THIGHS

2 chicken thighs per serving
¼ pound butter
½ cup dry white wine (Chablis, Pinot blanc, etc.)
2 Tbsp tomato paste
2 Tbsp finely minced shallots
2 cloves garlic, minced
1 Tbsp minced parsley
1 tsp ground thyme
Small cherry tomatoes or plum tomatoes
Small white onions
2 sweet red peppers, cut in strips
3 Tbsp minced parsley

1 **clove garlic, minced very fine**
1 **Tbsp capers, drained and
    rinsed**

Bone and skin the chicken thighs, rub sparsely with part of the butter, set aside. Melt remaining butter, combine with it the wine, tomato paste, shallots, 2 cloves garlic, 1 tablespoon parsley, thyme. Keep warm.

Place the chicken pieces on skewers, alternating with cherry or plum tomatoes, onions, and pieces of red pepper. Grill 6 to 10 minutes, turning often, and basting with the butter-wine sauce occasionally.

Combine remaining parsley, garlic, and capers and sprinkle this mixture on the grilled thighs as a garnish just before serving.

SKEWERED CHICKEN WINGS

3 **to 4 chicken wings per serving,
    depending on size**
½ **cup chicken broth (see instruc-
    tions below)**
1 **cup soy sauce**
2 **Tbsp brown sugar**
½ **cup butter**
1 **tsp dry mustard**
  **Pineapple chunks or slices, well
    drained**

Remove tip sections from chicken wings; boil tips briskly for 10 minutes in water to cover, remove tips, and reduce broth to ½ cup by boiling.

Combine hot broth, soy sauce, sugar, butter, mustard; marinate in this sauce for 2 to 3 hours. Do not refrigerate while marinating.

Put chicken wings on skewers, with a pineapple chunk between each wing and a chunk in the vee of the wing joint. Grill 6 to 10 minutes, turning often, brushing with marinade while cooking.

SAUCED CHICKEN LIVERS

2 **pounds fresh chicken livers**
½ **pound button mushrooms**
½ **cup melted butter**
½ **Tbsp Worcestershire sauce**
⅛ **tsp freshly ground white pep-
    per**

Drain and wipe chicken livers thoroughly. Put livers on skewers, alternating with button mushrooms.

Combine butter, Worcestershire sauce, and pepper. Brush this sauce on the livers and mushrooms before beginning to grill them, and brush frequently while grilling for 5 to 7 minutes. Turn the skewers often as the livers grill. Serves 4-6.

MORE PATIO SPECIALTIES

SYRIAN-STYLE LAMB

1 small lamb cutlet or 2 chops per serving
½ pound fresh button mushrooms
1 cup dry cider (though Moslem dietary laws forbid the use of alcohol, ale or beer is sometimes used instead of cider)
1 Tbsp butter
1 tsp chopped chives
1 tsp paprika
½ tsp salt
  Large pinch freshly ground white pepper

Combine cider, butter, chives, paprika, salt, and pepper over low heat. Marinate the cutlets or chops and mushrooms 1 to 2 hours at room temperature. Drain chops well.

Grill cutlets or chops on one side for 5 minutes. Brush with the sauce once or twice before turning. Turn chops, cover them with the mushrooms, grill for 5 to 7 minutes, until done. Serve on a bed of rice and green peas.

GRILLED SPARE RIBS, CANTON STYLE

4 to 6 pounds pork spareribs, cut into serving portions
1 cup Olorosa (sweet) sherry
4 crushed cloves
½ tsp cinnamon
1 Tbsp cornstarch
3 Tbsp finely minced sweet onion
¼ tsp cayenne

Lay the rib sections on the grill and cook each side 5 minutes. While the ribs cook, combine in a small saucepan on the edge of a grill the sherry, cloves, and cinnamon. When the mixture is warm but not boiling, stir in the cornstarch moistened with a tablespoon of cold water and blend until smooth and slightly thick. Add the onion and stir well. Keep the mixture warm, but do not allow it to boil.

Turn the rib sections a second time and dust sparingly with the cayenne, then brush generously with the sauce. Cook 5 to 8 minutes; turn again and brush with the sauce once more while the ribs cook another 5 to 8 minutes, until they are done.

Transfer the ribs to serving plates and brush again with the sauce before serving. Serves 4-6.

DEVILLED CHICKEN BREASTS

4 boned chicken breasts, the skin left on
½ cup deviled ham (canned)
1 tsp dry mustard
2 tsp chopped parsley
3 or 4 drops Tabasco
¼ cup fine dry breadcrumbs
½ stick butter

Gently pound and press the chicken breasts until they are quite thin. Spread a film of butter over the sides of the breasts.

Combine the ham, mustard, parsley, Tabasco, and breadcrumbs and spread this mixture on the insides of the breasts, roll the breasts up, secure with short skewers. Brush with butter.

Grill the breasts, turning often, and brushing with butter as they brown. Cooking time is about 10 minutes; this will depend on the intensity of your coals and the distance of the grill from the coals.

Allow one breast per serving. If more than four are to be served, increase the quantity of the ham mixture in ratio to the number of additional breasts.

APPLE-GLAZED GRILLED PORK CHOPS

4 large pork chops, about ¼ inch thick
1 large clove garlic
1 tsp salt
1 cup calvados or applejack
1 cup finely grated apple pulp
¼ tsp powdered cloves
   Large pinch salt

Trim the chops of excess fat, leaving only a thin rim around the fatty edge. Sliver the garlic toothpick-thin and with the point of a knife make tiny slits in the chops, inserting a sliver of garlic into each slit. Rub the chops very sparingly with salt and start them on the grill; cook 3 to 4 minutes per side.

In a small saucepan on the edge of the grill, combine the calvados (an apple brandy from Normandy) or applejack with the apple pulp, cloves, and salt. Stir until blended; keep warm, but do not boil.

Before the chops are turned for the second time, brush their upper surfaces with the basting liquid, using a brush or swab. After turning, brush the upper surfaces of each chop while cooking for about 5 to 8 minutes; turn and cook until done, another 5 to 8 minutes. Total cooking time will depend on the intensity of the coals and the distance from coals to grill. Test by inserting the tip of a knife along the bone; when no pink shows in the juices, the chops are done.

Allow one chop per serving. If more than four are to be prepared, increase the volume of the sauce in ratio to the total number of chops being cooked.

DILLED BURGERS

1 pound ground beef (most supermarkets offer three grades of ground meat; the top grade, which has the lowest ratio of suet to lean is the most desirable for grilling)
½ cup chopped sweet onion
2 large dill pickles
1 tsp powdered dillweed
⅛ tsp (about 4 dashes) Tabasco sauce
1 tsp salt

Break up the ground beef and spread it in small loose pieces on a working surface.

Sprinkle the chopped onions over the meat; chop the pickles medium-fine, drain them thoroughly by pressing them between several thicknesses of paper towels, and add them to the meat; sprinkle on the dillweed, salt, and Tabasco and work the meat mixture together until the added ingredients are well distributed in it. Form into patties and grill 10 to 15 minutes per side over bright coals. Serve on buns as finger food, or on plates.

TERIYAKI HAMBURGER

2 pounds lean ground beef
¼ cup teriyaki sauce (bottled)
2 Tbsp minced fresh parsley
1 tsp salt
¼ tsp freshly ground white pepper
8 fresh small green onions, minced, including tops

Combine 2 tablespoons of the teriyaki sauce, the parsley, salt, pepper, and onions with the ground beef and form into patties about ½ inch thick. Grill 4 to 6 minutes on one side; brush with the teriyaki sauce after the patties have cooked 2 or 3 minutes. Turn patties, brush with the remaining sauce, and grill 4 to 6 minutes, or until done as you prefer, with slightly pink centers or well cooked. Serves 6-8.

MOCK CUTLETS

1½ cups very dry, very fine bread-
    crumbs (please don't use
    squoosh bread; if no real bread
    is available, use unsalted
    cracker crumbs)
½ cup fresh milk (or undiluted
    evaporated milk)
¾ cup grated or scraped onion
1½ tsp salt
¼ tsp freshly ground white pep-
    per
 2 pounds lean ground beef
½ cup undiluted evaporated milk

Soak the crumbs in the milk until they
have absorbed all of the liquid. Combine
all remaining ingredients except the undiluted evaporated milk with the meat and
form into patties about ½ inch thick. Grill
3 to 4 minutes on one side, turn, and brush
the tops of the patties with the undiluted
evaporated milk; grill 3 to 4 minutes, turn,
and brush the tops of the patties again,
and repeat the turning and brushing process once more before serving. Serves 6-8.

VEGETABLES

Here are a few suggestions to start your
imagination working on ways to get double duty out of your patio grill. It's by no
means a complete list of the vegetables—
and fruits as well—that can be cooked
along the edges of a grill while the center
section is occupied with the meat course.

Small white potatoes, very thin
yams, well-scrubed carrots, baby eggplant, large mushroom caps, bell peppers,
zucchini and other squash, unpeeled
onions, all respond well to grilling. Serve
them with butter or sour cream.

Peel small pearl onions, rub them
with butter, roll them in breadcrumbs,
roll them into a cylinder in foil, and let
them cook along the edge of the grill.
Onions are among the very few vegetables
that can be successfully grilled in foil.

Cut small zucchini in halves lengthwise, grill for a very few minutes—no
more than three—with the cut side down,
and after turning the pieces, baste the cut
surfaces with butter and sprinkle with a
mixture of grated Parmesan cheese and a
dash of cayenne.

Cut baby eggplant in half; grill cut-
side-down for a few moments. Turn, and
while the eggplant continues to cook,
brush the cut side with a very light olive
oil into which has been stirred a pinch of
salt and a dash of Tabasco; dust with a
few gratings of parboiled garlic.

Start big mushroom caps—stems removed—with the stem side down. Grill 3
or 4 minutes, turn, and fill the stem side of
the cups with butter into which you've
blended finely minced chives, salt, and
freshly ground pepper; continue grilling
until the butter melts.

One of the nicest things you can do
with button mushrooms is to pickle them.
They will then keep for several weeks in a
tightly closed jar in a corner of the refrigerator to be served as a relish or garnish.

While steaks, chops, burgers, and chicken are the mainstay foods of backyard cooking, vary your routine by including wild game, sausage, and especially the numerous vegetables that are adaptable to cooking over coals. Here, stir-fried vegetables will soon accompany smoked bratwurst.

PICKLED MUSHROOMS

1 **pound fresh button mushrooms**
1 **cup white wine vinegar**
¼ **tsp salt**
2 **small sweet onions (or 2 cloves garlic)**
¾ **cup white wine vinegar**
⅓ **cup fine light olive oil**

After cleaning the mushrooms, drain them well. Add the 1 cup vinegar to 1 cup water and bring to a rolling boil; add salt, and drop the mushrooms into the boiling liquid a few at a time. Boil about 2 minutes, remove from heat, drain thoroughly, first in colander, then on paper towels.

Slice the onions quite thin, discarding the stem and root ends. Separate the slices into rings, removing the thin membrane that is between the onion's layers. Put the ¾ cup vinegar and the olive oil in a jar and combine by shaking thoroughly. Put the mushrooms and onion slices in with the oil-vinegar mixture; if it does not cover them, add a bit of vinegar and shake to combine it with the liquid in the jar. Let stand at least 48 hours before using; the longer they stand, the better they'll be.

BREAD ON THE GRILL

While cooking other foods on a grill, bread for the meal can be heated by buttering on both sides the slices of an entire loaf and sprinkling them lightly with garlic salt and freshly minced parsley, or any other herb. Wrap in foil, leaving a vent-hole for steam to escape, and place at one side of the grill.

PARMESAN BREAD

1 **loaf good crusty French or Italian bread**
¼ **to ½ pound butter**
⅓ **to ½ cup grated Parmesan cheese**
2 **Tbsp fresh parsley, minced**

Slice bread diagonally to, but not through, the bottom crust. Combine butter, cheese, and parsley; spread the sides of each slice. Heat on the grill, turning often, until the butter penetrates the soft inner portion and the crust is crisply browned. Other herbs can be added to the parsley, or used in place of it.

PICNIC FOODS

When picnics were in their finest flower, almost every Sunday and all holidays ex-cept Thanksgiving and Christmas were picnic days. Fried chicken was almost inevitably the mainstay of a picnic meal, with ham sandwiches running a close second. There were always hard-boiled eggs in the shell, and sometimes deviled eggs as well, stuffed with the mashed yolks combined with mustard and chopped pickles or relish.

There were few packaged treats such as potato chips or the cornmeal-based puff with artificial cheese flavors that are so commonplace today, but there were always crisp homemade pickles to be crunched with the sandwiches or chicken.

No picnic meal was complete without a freezer of ice cream, frozen on the spot from a mix made at home, to which fresh fruits were added just before the freezer was closed. The ice might have been brought from home, swathed in thick layers of burlap, or bought at the icehouse nearest the picnic grounds. A freezer of ice cream was a long time in the making, with the men taking turns chipping the ice and adding rock salt, and grinding away at the constantly slowing crank, while the youngsters hung around waiting to join in scraping the dasher.

Today's picnics tend to be a bit more elaborate, which may or may not be a good thing. Perhaps in losing the simplicity of those old-time picnics the picnic isn't very different today from a meal at home.

Picnickers need to be a bit more careful today, especially in the matter of keeping foods refrigerated during the trip to the picnic grounds and while the foods wait to be eaten, for manufactured products such as mayonnaise tend to spoil more rapidly than did the simpler foods of the past. Almost everything except pre-packaged bakery foods today requires refrigeration after their vacuum-sealed jars or cans have been opened.

There are foods which can be prepared at home, finger foods of various kinds, which don't need a great deal of special care on even the warmest summer days. Some are sauces or dressings that contain no vulnerable mayonnaise, but can be safely kept in a jar and mixed with ready-cut boiled potatoes to make a salad or used as a spread for sandwiches. Others are vegetable dishes that can be carried in jars or plastic snap-shut refrigerator containers and served on paper plates to be eaten with disposable utensils. A few bread treatments are also included, as well as a suggestion or two for desserts.

DRESSINGS AND SPREADS

Any of these dressings can be combined with cubed boiled potatoes or green vegetables to make a salad. For a salad that is a one-dish meal, add strips of precooked meats and a few chunks of cheddar or Edam or one of the firm cheeses.

YOGHURT GARLIC DRESSING

  1 **cup low-fat yoghurt**
  1 **tsp fresh lemon juice**
  ½ **tsp grated lemon peel**
  ½ **clove garlic, mashed**

  2 **Tbsp fresh chopped parsley**
  1 **Tbsp chopped chives**
  ½ **tsp white pepper**

Beat ingredients lightly together. Use as a dressing for a potato or chef's or green salad, or crumble with yolks of hard-cooked eggs when preparing stuffed eggs.

TOMATO DRESSING

  ½ **cup tomato puree**
  2 **Tbsp cider vinegar or white wine vinegar**
  ½ **cup grated or scraped onion**
  2 **tsp minced fresh parsley**
  ¼ **tsp powdered thyme**
  ¼ **tsp salt**
     Large pinch of freshly ground pepper

Stir all ingredients together. Use as a dressing for a green salad or mix with minced cooked beef or pork to make sandwich filling.

MUSHROOM DRESSING

1 cup chopped fresh mushrooms (mushroom stems are fine; save the caps for other uses)
1¼ cups light salad oil
¾ cup fresh or frozen lemon juice
1 tsp salt
¼ tsp freshly ground white pepper
½ tsp powdered basil
½ tsp powdered marjoram
¼ tsp powdered oregano

Fresh herbs, finely minced, can be used in place of dried herbs. Combine all ingredients by stirring. Use as a dressing for a green salad or to pour over thick slices of ripe tomatoes.

POPPY SEED DRESSING

1 cup low-fat yoghurt
½ cup low-fat cottage cheese, drained
1 tsp sour cream
½ tsp salt
1 small cucumber, peeled and grated
2 tsp minced chives
1 Tbsp poppy seeds

Combine all ingredients by stirring or with a chef's whip. Use as a dressing for potato or green salad, as a sauce for baked potatoes, or combine with grated mild cheese (Monterey jack, Samsoe, etc.) to make a sandwich spread or dip.

CUCUMBER CRISPS

2 large cucumbers, peeled and sliced or cut lengthwise into strips
½ cup light oil
1 cup low-fat yoghurt
1 Tbsp canned hot green chili peppers, seeded and mashed
¼ tsp salt

Bury the cucumbers in crushed ice to crisp them. Combine other ingredients in a bowl or jar. Immediately before serving, remove and drain the cucumbers, pour the dressing over them, and stir well. Use cocktail picks to fish out the cucumber pieces.

PARSLIED CAULIFLOWER

1 small cauliflower (about 1½ lbs)
1 hard-cooked egg

3 Tbsp finely minced fresh parsley
1 Tbsp light oil (sesame seed is
fine)
1 tsp salt
¼ tsp freshly ground white pepper

Parboil the cauliflower, but do not cook it until it is soft. Separate it into finger-sized flowerets; drain well. Sieve the hard-cooked egg and reserve it. Combine parsley, oil, and seasonings, stir into the cauliflower until each floweret is well coated, sprinkle with the sieved egg.

GLAZED RADISHES

2 Tbsp butter
½ cup minced shallots
2 bunches radishes (about 15 to
20), cleaned
1 cup water
2 Tbsp white wine vinegar or
cider vinegar

Melt 1 tablespoon butter in a skillet and sauté the shallots until soft; add the radishes, water, and vinegar, bring to a fast boil, and cook 8 to 10 minutes. Drain radishes well, add the remaining butter, keep over low heat while stirring the radishes to coat them. Drain excess butter. Chill the radishes on waxed paper; carry in a jar or refrigerator container to the picnic.

CARROT CRISPS

8 to 10 large carrots, peeled or
scraped
Water to cover
1 tsp salt
1 small onion, sliced very thin
1 cup tarragon vinegar
1 Tbsp sugar
¼ tsp salt
⅓ cup light oil

Slice the carrots thinly on an acutely slanted diagonal to produce oval pieces. Bring water to a boil, drop in the carrot slices, add salt. Cook 4 to 5 minutes; drain at once. Put carrot slices and onion slices in a china or glass bowl. Heat vinegar, sugar, salt, and oil until sugar dissolves; pour over carrots and onions. Cover the bowl; marinate overnight, stirring once or twice. Drain off liquid in strainer; put carrots and onions in a covered refrigerator dish or jar to carry to picnic.

AVOCADO SPREAD

2 large or 3 small dead-ripe avo-
cados

1 clove garlic, mashed
3 Tbsp minced white onion
2 or 3 dashes Tabasco sauce
1 large dead-ripe tomato,
   skinned, seeded, and pureed or
   2 tbsp canned tomato puree
1 tsp salt
3 Tbsp vodka

Peel, seed, and mash the avocado. Add all other ingredients except the vodka, blending them with the mashed avocado. Add the vodka a bit at a time until the mixture reaches a smooth, spreadable consistency. It should not be at all runny. Let stand in a covered container under refrigeration for several hours or overnight. Serve with crisp crackers or toast.

CHEESE SPREAD

½ pound cream cheese
½ pound Roquefort or blue cheese
¼ cup good brandy or cognac
¼ cup sesame seed

Combine cheeses by mashing together, add brandy until the mixture reaches a spreadable consistency, add the sesame seeds and blend into the cheese mixture. Serve on crackers or thin crisp toast.

LIVER PATÉ SPREAD

¾ pound fresh chicken livers
¼ cup unsalted butter or washed
   butter
1 clove garlic, minced
½ tsp salt
4 oz cream cheese
6 drops Tabasco sauce
¼ cup good brandy or cognac

Wash, drain, and dry the chicken livers. Melt unsalted butter over low heat. If no unsalted butter is available, let the best butter available soften to room temperature and wash it by beating it in a bowl with 2 to 3 tablespoons cool water, changing the water three or four times. Drain the water off. Sauté the chicken livers and garlic in the butter over low heat until the livers are very tender. Do not allow them to brown. When done, let the livers cool in the butter.

With a pestle or the bowl of a heavy spoon, mash the livers and garlic to a paste in a bowl. Add the salt, cream cheese, and Tabasco and blend into a smooth paste. Add brandy a teaspoon at a time until the paste reaches a spreadable consistency. A bit more or less brandy than indicated may be required.

Form the paste into a mound on a plate for immediate serving, or put it in a wide-mouth jar for transportation. Keep under refrigeration when possible.

STUFFED EDAM CHEESE

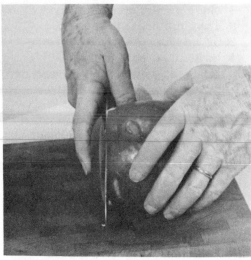

1. Slice off one end of the Edam cheese.

1½-to 2-pound whole Edam cheese
¾ cup sliced or slivered almonds
1 Tbsp butter
¾ cup pitted green olives,
       drained, washed well, and
       minced
¼ cup grated or scraped onion
6 to 8 drops Tabasco sauce
2 to 3 Tbsp brandy or cognac

Have the cheese at room temperature. Cut a ½-inch-thick slice off the top, without removing the wax coating. Score carefully with a knife, then with a spoon scoop out the inside of the cheese, leaving a shell ¾ to 1 inch thick.

Sauté the almonds in the butter over low heat until they are a light tan, drain on a paper towel, and chop them coarsely. Chop the green olives coarsely. Grate the pieces taken from the inside of the cheese. Combine grated cheese, almonds, olives, and onions, adding the Tabasco. Add as much of the brandy as needed to make a smooth mixture.

Return the cheese mixture to the inside of the cheese, packing it as firmly as possible without breaking the crust. Chill until firm. Remove the wax coating before serving. This is a serve-yourself dish; provide butter knives or the equivalent to enable diners to help themselves from the cheese.

2. Scoop out the interior of the cheese, leaving about ½ inch of cheese as a wall.

3. Dice stuffing ingredients medium-fine.

5. When the stuffing is blended, pack it firmly into the cheese shell and chill to firm up.

4. Use a Mouli grater or an electric food processor to grind the cheese taken from inside.

6. Mound the stuffing. Leave the red rind on the cheese, removing it from the segments sliced for serving portions.

II

TRAIL COOKING

9 SHORT HIKES

We're talking now about a hike that's a bit more than a casual stroll of a mile or two and back to camp. For an extended stroll, a granola bar or a packet of trail nibbles will do quite well, and if the outing's going to last longer than three or four hours, perhaps a sandwich or some other prepared food might be included. On a hike of this kind, of course, it's self-defeating to carry anything except precooked, ready-to-eat food.

In this chapter's frame of reference, though, a hike is an all-day affair, leaving camp early and getting back late. You want enough to eat to keep you at a high peak of energy through a long active day, and that means more than a sandwich or two. What you'll want to carry is probably more than your pockets will hold, but you don't want to burden yourself with anything that isn't necessary.

If your hike is extended to an overnight affair, out one day and back the next, you'll need some kind of sleeping gear, which adds still more weight. When you're camping even for one night, filling that night with strength-restoring sleep is as important as filling your stomach with good, nourishing food. As fond as I am of eating, I'm not so sure that a full night's sleep doesn't take precedence over a full meal.

There was a time, and it was not long ago, when in order to eat even a single hot meal on an all-day hike, the hiker had to tote a fairly heavy load. Today's condensed and instant foods were still a promise that lay in the future. The only options available were fresh foods to be cooked, or cans of food that had to be heated to be at all palatable. Either option meant a pot or pan of some kind in which to cook or heat food, perhaps a coffeepot; in some kinds of country a belt-axe to provide firewood and a canteen of water added to the load.

About the lightest that I'd like to go in the food department on a long day's hike or an overnight safari is a soup mix of my own devising. It was originated before

A short hike may mean hitting the trail at dawn and returning to your car before dark. Or, it may mean sleeping under the stars and returning the following day. In either case, you'll have to plan meals and food choices carefully because you'll be expending far more energy than at home.

the space age brought us today's wealth of dehydrated and freeze-dried foods, and I still like it because of its very low salt content. Foods heavy in salt and sugar are stomach-cheaters and thirst-provokers. The hiker can do much better without them than with them, and some of the trail foods so widely available today are unduly heavy in both salt and sugar. But here's my hiker's soup mix:

HIKERS' SOUP MIX

To make four portions:

4 **thick slices roast beef**
1 **#2 can green peas**
4 **tsp unsalted broken cashew nuts**
4 **pieces celery stalk tops, including leaves**
½ **of white of hard-cooked egg**
1 **small bottle capers**

Chill the beef well and shave each piece into the thinnest possible strips; cut the strips into quarters or thirds. Drain the peas well, first in a strainer, then between pieces of paper towel. Use only the top 3 inches of the celery stalk; chop both stalk and leaves coarsely. Chop the egg white half coarsely. Drain the capers in a sieve and then between pieces of paper towel.

Divide the ingredients into four equal portions and put each portion in a press-to-seal plastic bag. To reconstitute, empty a bag into a large metal cup or small pan, add water to cover, and heat, stirring occasionally. To speed the process, use hot water; if the water added is boiling, all that needs to be done is to stir until the soup is cool enough to eat.

This mix will hold without refrigeration for two days in a reasonably warm climate and up to four days in cooler weather. It not only provides balanced nutrition, but the meat, cashews, and egg white provide different degrees of chewiness which have the psychological effect of convincing those eating the soup that they've really enjoyed a hearty meal. Its chief advantage over prepared mixes is that it requires only a minimum amount of heat and no soaking time at all to prepare.

Since World War II, which gave us the dubious blessings of Spam, the original instant coffee, which freeze-drying quickly made obsolete, and the world's worst pemmican as emergency and survival foods, a great deal of progress has been made in food concentration. This makes the logistics of extended backpacking trips much simpler today than formerly.

To a very large extent, of course, the type of country over which you're hiking will dictate what you carry with you. Common sense dictates planning in advance, whether your hike is starting from a base camp in a wild or semiwild area, or from a roadside. Your starting point sets the requirements for the food you take, almost as much as does the season and the terrain.

If you're setting up camp in a national park or forest, you will probably be required to check in at the office nearest your entry point and get a campfire permit and a booklet or leaflet that outlines restrictions and requirements. In such cases, a few minutes spent chatting with a park or forest ranger will be more helpful than even the most detailed map.

About this time you might be asking yourself what all this has to do with cooking. The connection may be more direct than it seems at first glance. If you don't know whether you'll be able to build an open fire to provide your cooking coals, you'd better take along some kind of camp stove and leave your axe behind. If you don't know the location of drinking water, you're really up a tree. The list could be extended, but the point's been made.

Let's go on with the preliminaries, and very soon we'll get back to foods and cooking. Suppose we begin with the premise that you're starting from camp to explore an area you haven't visited before. You're in a temperate climate at a moderate altitude, and your map shows that most of the terrain over which you plan to hike will be level and not really very challenging. You intend to start right after breakfast, and be back in camp for supper. You're going into strange country, though, and your map doesn't show too much detail as to the existence or location of streams or springs.

On the plus side, the map doesn't show that you'll be doing a lot of climbing or scrambling over very rough terrain. At the same time, you haven't been doing much hiking recently, and you know you're not in peak physical condition. You need to keep the body stoked up so that · you won't suffer from hunger exhaustion.

You and only you can evaluate the different factors going into the equations which contribute to the sum of your needs on a short hike, for no two situations are quite the same. The answer you come up with will—or should—be reflected in the preparations best suited to your individual needs, not necessarily to mine or those of your next-door neighbor. All that can be done in a book of this sort is to flash warning signals and point out pitfalls, to be sure you haven't overlooked something.

Terrain, climate, and season must be considered, of course. At moderate altitudes in a temperature climate such as late spring or early autumn, your options are much wider than they'd be if your pack-trip is going to be made in the dead heat of summer over desert or semiarid country. Conversely, in winter, the pack you'd put together would be different from either of these. In both cases, the quantity of nonedible gear you'd be taking will limit you in your menu selections.

It's also necessary to consider the season. Again, carbohydrate intake should be increased, but not in huge amounts at any one time. Prepackaged trail foods fill the bill here, because you can nibble on them all day long.

If you're going to be making even a day-long hike during a season of the year at an altitude when the weather can be treacherous, part of the weight of your

Also during late-season hikes, you'll want to increase your protein intake to help your body produce heat. Therefore, combination high protein/ high carbohydrate meals are the best bet.

pack must be devoted to a slicker or other protective clothing. If it's a hunting or fishing trip, some kinds of heavy or bulky foods may have to be sacrificed in favor of the gun or tackle you'll carry.

In winter, on skis or snowshoes, common sense demands that you carry some kind of emergency shelter in the event you're caught by an unexpected storm. At the other end of the scale, on a summer hike in desert country, you will need to carry enough water to insure your safety.

In most situations, the best practice is to travel light, because every ounce you add to the weight of your own body and clothing—a camera, for instance, to record your outing—will seem to double in weight by the time you're halfway back to camp. At the same time, you should be prepared for the unexpected, so that you can be sure of getting safely back to camp in spite of some unforeseen mishap.

A one-day hike presupposes that you'll need food for only one meal, but make that meal a nutritious one. You

should also carry nibbles of some sort that can be eaten during a rest stop, and will constantly replenish your energy. Call it persnicketiness if you want to, but I don't like to hike when my pockets are overloaded and bulging with food. Being carried in pockets doesn't do the food any favors, either, for exposure to your body heat will erode its freshness.

There are three easy and economical solutions. One is the little fanny pack, worn at your belt-line in back; another is much the same, what photographers used to call a gadget bag. The third is simply a small rucksack, often called a day pack.

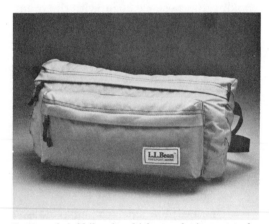

For very brief hikes in which you don't want to be burdened with the weight of a full-size pack, the Fanny Pack is ideal. Each hiker can easily carry enough food for a single day, with room left over for a raincoat or even basic fishing tackle.

All come in too many styles and sizes to list. Some are made of duck or canvas, others of nylon or dacron or plastic. Most of them are waterproof and spillproof. Some can be carried at waist-level by straps or snaps that hold them on your belt and some have shoulder straps. I like the belt-attached style, and have found that a medium-sized bag carried in the small of your back does not interfere in any way with your freedom of movement. Even if you carry a camera in the bag as well as food, a belt-carried pack or bag is far superior to the more conventional knapsack for toting food on short hikes.

Almost all these bags are very light in weight, and most of them are compartmented so that you can separate your food from your photo equipment, if you're also carrying a camera. Put your food into plastic squeeze-to-lock bags; they will do two jobs at once: keep food fresh and protect camera gear from crumbs.

Unless you're absolutely sure that you'll be able to find fresh water on the trail you'll be taking, carry water with you. When you're on a hike, water's more important than food. If there are several hikers going in a group, provide water for the entire party by taking along a shoulder-slung canteen, and let each person carry it in turn for a fixed length of time so that no one gets burdened with it unduly. If it's a very large group, carry two canteens.

In this case, you might consider filling one canteen with water, the other with *unsweetened* tea, made from tea leaves rather than the instant powders. Genuine tea, properly brewed and drunk without sweetening, quenches thirst and satisfies the appetite temporarily, for tea contains as much caffeine as does an equivalent quantity of coffee. The stimulus you receive from it is temporary, of course, but it does tend to help you over a rough spot or to revive you toward the end of a day-long hike.

For only two or three people on a one-day hike, a better alternative than a canteen is for each person to carry a pair

of what have come to be called "commuter cups." Made of tough plastic, these cups have double walls, which provide enough insulation to keep hot liquids hot for three to four hours and cold liquids cool for six to eight hours. Their locking tops prevent spills, and are fitted with spring-actuated spigots that allow you to take sips from the cup without removing the lid.

If each hiker carries two of these cups, all members on a day-long hike will have hot tea, chocolate, or coffee to go with the noon meal as well as a dependable supply of water which will serve for the full day if used sparingly. Even when filled, these cups are lighter than a metal canteen.

Leave your canned colas and similar beverages behind. All of them are thirst-provokers rather than thirst-quenchers. When your water supply is limited, the thirst that is created by both salt and sugar must be avoided. Leave canned beer behind, too. Save it for relaxed suppers at your home camp, where you'll enjoy it more.

Food as well as drinks should be chosen to avoid overly seasoned items or those which generate excessive thirst. This includes the popular junkfood snack items such as potato chips, pretzels, cheese twists, tortilla chips, salted crackers, and similar items. For these, substitute nonsalted water crackers or oyster crackers, which you can modify to make tastier and less thirst-inducing, or make your own herb-seasoned bread croutons, using the recipe given later in this chapter. Both croutons and water crackers will provide a surprising amount of quick energy.

Water crackers and oyster crackers are similar. Both are baked from unleavened doughs and have no shortening or other ingredients in them which would cause them to become rancid. For trail snacks, modify them as follows:

MODIFIED WATER OR OYSTER CRACKERS

1 **package (usually about 10 oz) crackers**
2 **to 3 Tbsp unsalted butter, melted**
   Herb Seasoning mix #1, #2 or #3

Spread the crackers on a baking sheet and brush them very lightly with melted butter; sprinkle with your choice of the Herb Seasoning mixes. Heat lightly; allow to cool. Store in the box the crackers came in, resealing the liner with stickytape.

Other trail snacks will be given later in this chapter, but as the temptation to stay with things that are familiar to us is always present, let's take a quick look at snacks to be avoided.

Steer clear of smoked or cured meats such as ham, bacon, chipped beef, and sausage. As noted earlier, frankfurters can no longer be considered food, since they are now made from packing-house offal such as lungs, tripes, and snouts. Almost without exception, commercial lunch meats are also made largely from offal and are oversalted to conceal their base origin. So is the meat product which today is labeled "jerky." Its name is a sham and a deceit, for the packaged jerky you buy today has nothing at all in common with

that which was the reliable trail food and iron ration of the Indians and pioneers.

JERKY AND OTHER MEATS

Almost every bar and convenience store keeps little glassine packets of something called jerky on their counters, but these products have only a ghostly resemblance to the genuine jerky which helped to win the American West. Commercial jerky is an artificial by-product made from packing-house scraps that have been pickled and baked, then painted with a chemical smoke flavor. Try them if you like, but don't say you weren't warned.

Originally and traditionally, jerky was plain meat, dried in the sun. Its production in the traditional manner is for all practical purposes impossible now for two reasons. First, the meat used in jerky must have an absolute minimum of fat. In an earlier day, jerky was made from the flesh of wild game or from the virtually fat-free meat of range-run cattle, and the overfat flesh of today's feedlot-finished cattle will spoil during the several days required for the sun to remove its moisture.

Second, sun-dried jerky can only be made in places where two conditions prevail: long, warm summer days and nights and pure, unpolluted air. Sadly, there is no place today on the North American continent that provides both these conditions. This does not mean that you must go jerkiless, for there are ways by which you can make your own. If you have a bit of venison, it will make better jerky than will feedlot beef, though if you use the least fatty portions of commercial beef, your homemade jerky will be very close to that made by the traditional method of sun-drying.

Up in Billings, Montana, my friend John Willard makes his own jerky of venison from deer and elk, which like most wild game meats are virtually fat-free. John uses a vertical smoker to make his jerky instead of air-drying it in the old style, seasoning it with salt and pepper well rubbed in on all the meat's surfaces. The only thing you need in the way of a recipe is the admonition John gives, and which I omitted mentioning in earlier paragraphs: Let the strips of venison smoke until they're stone-hard. That's how jerky should be.

2. Season the meat and leave overnight in the refrigerator. Here, we use garlic powder and hickory-smoked salt.

3. Next, arrange jerky strips on a pan and place inside oven. the idea is *not* to cook the jerky but slowly dry it, so set oven at the lowest possible temperature (usually 125 degrees). The drying process may take as long as 3 to 6 hours.

HOW TO MAKE JERKY IN YOUR OVEN

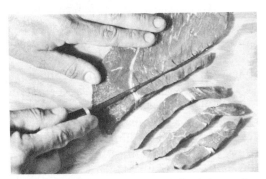

1. Obtain lean beef or venison and slice it into strips about ½ inch thick.

4. The jerky is finished when it has a coal-black appearance, but it is not burned. Nor does it require refrigeration. Stow a plastic bag full in your jacket pocket and enjoy nutritious nibbling all day long. Jerky can be sliced and added to soups and stews. The dried meat absorbs water and returns to its former tender state.

You can also make jerky in a sportsman's home smoker. An electric heating element is inside on the bottom. A pan of hardwood chips sits on the element and begins to smolder, filling the inside of the chamber with smoke.

CHEESE AND EGGS

Cheese is almost as good as meat in that it provides high energy per ounce consumed. However, there are some fake cheese products which you should avoid. You can be sure of getting the maximum food value from cheese if you stick to the aged semihard true cheeses such as cheddar, Mimolette (which is a French version of cheddar), Gouda, Emmenthaler (which we incorrectly call Swiss and which has no relationship to the square slices of flabby white stuff sold in supermarkets), provolone, Samsoe, or longhorn (cheddar's poor relation).

If your taste runs to a softer cheese, choose a domestic Monterey jack, or a Gruyère, or Gouda, Port-Salut (also called Esrom), a domestic Muenster, or an unaged longhorn. These will not have the deep, appetite-satisfying flavor of a semihard aged cheese, but they are genuine cheeses and will not insult your stomach as do the cheese substitutes and imitations which are so prevalent today.

Avoid as you would the plague those little jars of cheese spreads, which you'll discover on examination of the labels are chemicalized imitations of real cheese and contain as much as 40 percent water. You would also do well, if you want the most enjoyable flavor and the maximum nutrition from your trail-lunch cheese, to walk away from the products labeled "pasteurized processed cheese," which is an imitation cheese made largely of chemicals and colored skim milk. Avoid even more carefully the imitations of these imitations which are labeled as "pasteurized processed cheese food," and have a water content up to around 50 percent.

Eggs are also among nature's own high-nutrient-yielding foods. Hard-cook your eggs. The best hard-cooked eggs are those put into a pan of unheated water, brought to a boil, simmered three minutes, then allowed to remain in the water until you can remove them bare-hand without burning your fingers. Take the eggs in their shells to preserve their flavor until you're ready to eat them. Don't use salt and pepper as a seasoning; use one of the herb mixes which you'll find later on. These herb seasonings not only contribute to the flavor of food, but they don't make you thirsty.

SANDWICHES AND SNACKS

For sandwich spreads, use genuine mayonnaise or real butter. These provide both flavor and nourishment, so spread the sandwich bread with them. Incidentally, if you prespread bread slices and put them together with the spread sides facing, the bread won't get soggy. Carry the meat separately, making up the sandwiches just before eating. And do stay away from thirst-creating spreads such as mustard, and the spiced-up chemical mixtures of imitation mayonnaise laced with chopped pickles and peppers and labeled "sandwich spread."

Add flavor to sandwiches by carrying an onion which can be peeled and sliced just before it's eaten in a sandwich. Onion breath? Sure, but who's to complain if everybody eats a slice? Both onion and little cherry tomatoes, which resist squashing better than do full-sized tomatoes, add moisture to your body as well as flavor to your sandwich.

An apple, a pear, or a banana is far superior to candy as a dessert for a hiker's meal. All of these provide moisture and stomach-filling bulk as well as slowly assimilated carbohydrates. Candy, or anything else made with refined sugar, not only creates thirst, but gives you a spurious burst of energy followed by an equally quick letdown.

Beware of some of today's highly advertised granola bars which their makers claim are energy boosters. Read the labels on these products, most of which come from the factories of the food conglomerates, and you'll quickly see that a lot of them are simply candy bars under an assumed name. Several recipes for honest granolas are given later in this chapter, and you'll be better advised to make your own than to rely on advertising claims for the spurious granola products. Under any name and in any disguise, candy is a greatly overrated energy food.

For as-you-hike or rest-stop snacks, carry nibbles such as raisins, *unsalted* nuts, and such edible seeds as sunflower

You needn't always purchase expensive backpacking foods. Many highly nutritious snack items are available in your local grocery or health-food stores at reasonable prices. The beauty of these offerings is not only do they offer instant go-power but can be eaten right from their packages.

or pumpkin. Dates provide high energy and their sweetness comes from a form of sugar called xylose, which has a different chemical structure than do cane, beet, or fruit-derived sugars. Xylose is assimilated by the body more gradually, and its use does not result in the physical letdown caused by fructose- and glucose-based sugars. Further along, you'll find several variations of trailside nibbles.

Still more economical is to prepare your own trail nibbles at home and store them in zip-loc poly bags. Use your own preferred combination of dried fruits, hard candies and different kinds of nuts.

So far, we've been dealing in basics, so let's move on to the specifics dictated by season, altitude, and terrain.

These might be reduced to three axioms: (a) When the weather is hot, eat lightly and drink plentifully. (b) In cold weather, eat plenty of high protein and fatty foods to generate body heat, but slightly reduce fluid intake. (c) At high altitudes (above 5,000 feet) there is progressively less oxygen to metabolize foods, so begin slanting the menu toward those which are high in carbohydrates and therefore easily digestible.

Both these oversimplified rules make sense when considered in the light of the human body's metabolism. In warm climates, digestions tend to be sluggish and need stimulation to handle the heavy foods for which your body clamors during periods of extra muscular activity. Stimulation of the digestion *by natural means* involves seasoning foods with herbs and spices rather than with salt. Salt creates thirst, while heat encourages perspiration. The combination requires a greater liquid intake.

In cold climates, the reverse is true; fats, which take longer to digest than lighter foods, provide fuel for the body over a longer period of time in ratio to their bulk. If you drink a lot of liquid, though, you'll sweat under your clothing even in near-zero weather, and this can make hiking very uncomfortable. You're perfectly safe in cutting your liquid consumption on a cold day; on such days, less liquid is demanded by the human system because less is lost through the evaporation of perspiration, provided you're not engaging in strenuous physical exertion.

Remember, these are *general* rules. Your needs are individual, and you must work out specific diets for yourself within the framework of the generalities. If you feel unable to work out your own diet requirements for the needs of the season during which you'll be hiking or packing, consult a professional.

In this case, the professional would not be your doctor. Medical schools have been paying attention to nutrition for only a short time, and unless your doctor is a recent graduate, he or she will quite probably be a nutritional innocent. Find a professional nutritionist to consult, one who can determine your specific requirements and advise you knowledgeably.

RECIPES FOR SHORT HIKES

In Part I you'll find a number of recipes for meats and breads that go into the finger foods most useful on short hikes. Here, we're going to look at such things as seasonings which you can prepare in advance, at home, to be carried on a camping trip, and such other things as trailside nibbles.

Don't simply assume that the usefulness of either herb seasonings or nibbles is confined to your outdoor cooking. You'll find the seasonings equally tasty in any cooking you might do anywhere. Since there are differences between the herbs marketed by different companies, you may have to do a bit of experimenting to arrive at proportions which best suit your own taste.

Use the nibbles as substitutes for those oversalted junkfood snacks that are so prominent in many diets, and the homemade granola bars are a good replacement for the candies too often handed out indiscriminately to children.

HERB-SEASONED CROUTONS

½ loaf of honest bread
   Oil for deep-frying (use peanut or safflower or sesame seed oil to avoid later rancidity)
   Herb mixture of your choice from the three that follow, or select other herbs and mix your own

Cut the bread into cubes. Bring the oil to a bubbling boil in a deep-frying pot with a basket. Combine the herbs by shaking in a plastic bag. Put a scanty load of bread cubes in the basket and fry until a light golden brown. Drain on several thicknesses of paper toweling. As the cubes begin to drain, sprinkle them very lightly with the mixed herbs. Allow the croutons to cool, store them in a waxed paper packet in the freezer or refrigerator. Do not seal airtight, or condensation will make the croutons soggy. Use within a week.

HERB SEASONING #1

1 tsp dry summer savory
1 tsp dry basil
⅛ tsp dry oregano

Crush the herbs to powder in a mortar or with a rolling-pin on a flat breadboard. Shake to mix well, and keep in a tightly closed container. Sprinkle sparingly on bread to be used in sandwiches, on hard-cooked eggs, or mix with mayonnaise or butter to make a sandwich spread or to dab on pieces of baked potato.

HERB SEASONING #2

1 tsp dry marjoram
1 tsp dry thyme
½ tsp dried parsley flakes

HERB SEASONING #3

1 tsp freeze-dried chives
1 tsp dry rosemary
½ tsp dry chervil

PITA BREAD

1 package dry yeast
2 cups warm water
1 Tbsp solid shortening
6 cups flour
2 tsp salt

Dissolve yeast in the warm water. Work the shortening into the yeast-water mixture with fingers until shortening dissolves. Stir flour and salt together in a mixing bowl; add the yeast mixture to the flour mixture and blend with fingers until the dough loses its stickiness. Transfer dough to a large, lightly greased bowl, cover with a cloth, let the dough rise until it doubles in bulk. This will take 35 to 45 minutes, depending on temperature.

Divide dough into 12 pieces. With floured hands, work each piece on a mixing board until dough is smooth and elastic, then form each piece into a ball. Scrape the mixing board clean, dust lightly with flour; put the 12 doughballs on the board, cover with cloth, let stand 20 to 25 minutes.

In carrying out the next two steps, handle the dough very carefully. Do not stretch, puncture, fold, or crease the doughballs as they are flattened and rolled.

On a flat, lightly floured surface, flatten the doughballs gently, using only hand pressure. Then, gently roll each flattened ball into a round just a bit smaller than the diameter of your Dutch oven or covered skillet.

Preheat the cooking utensil; do not oil or grease its surface. If cooking at home, use baking sheets and preheat oven to 450 degrees. If cooking in camp, preheat ungreased Dutch oven or skillet and test by splashing a few drops of water into it. When the droplets dance and vanish within 15 to 20 seconds, the pan is at the right temperature.

Cook one round at a time, with the Dutch oven or skillet covered. Cook 4 to 5 minutes, until the dough is puffed and set and the bottom lightly browned. Turn with a wide spatula; cook 3 to 4 minutes, until second side is lightly browned. Set the loaves aside until cool.

To use the bread, cut each round in half, split the cut side to form a pocket, fill, and wrap in waxed paper.

GRANOLAS AND NIBBLES

There's no one recipe for granola. The very word itself is new, dating back less than 20 years, and derives from the prefix "grano," which simply means "grain." Today, of course, "granola" can be and is applied to a lot of products as an advertising gimmick, and a lot of the applications can be misleading.

As used by nutritionists, granola describes a mixture of several kinds of grain, though this definition gets stretched a bit out of shape at times. However, for our present purposes, let's assume that granola requires grains as its foundation. Granolas can be cooked or raw; it depends on the whim of their originator. It's much easier to prepare granolas at home than in camp, and all of these will keep well without being refrigerated.

Granola and high-fiber natural grain cereals are perfect for trail use. First, pour the contents of the bulky boxes into plastic bags, then add powdered dry milk. For breakfast, all that's necessary is to stir in water.

There are at present several hundred granola recipes kicking around, as well as a number of commercial recipes manufactured by the same firms that gave us the 65 percent sugar-content breakfast foods, but if you're both wise and economy-minded, you'll ignore these off-the-shelf products and mix your own. Granolas can be pressed into bars or sticks if you care to take the trouble. They can be eaten with milk, cereal-style, or just put into a press-to-seal plastic bag and eaten like you would a snack.

Most of the ingredients called for in the next group of recipes can be bought at grocery stores, but you may have to look in health food stores for a few of them. Perhaps things are changing for the better, for during 1981 the Kellogg Company added to its products a new assortment of flaked grains under the name "Nutri-Grain." Unlike the firm's frosted, sugared foods, the NutriGrain products are free of preservatives, sugars, and other ungrainlike additives. They are available at all supermarkets.

There are a few no-nos to observe in making your granola. If nuts are called for, don't use the salted variety. Don't use sugar in a granola; if you want it sweetened, toss a few dried pitted dates into a blender and use the resulting saucelike goo for a sweetening agent. If dates are included in the recipe, don't add more. Finally, don't feel compelled to use *all* the ingredients a recipe calls for. One of the chief charms of granola is that you can tailor your own to meet your individual liking.

HOW TO MAKE GRANOLA

1. Basic ingredients for granola (there are dozens of recipes) are oats, nuts, molasses, honey, raisins, and assorted spices.

2. After thoroughly mixing everything in a bowl, spread a thick layer into a buttered baking pan and pop into your oven.

3. When the granola has finished baking, press waxed paper into the top, then place in your refrigerator overnight.

4. The next day, slice the granola into bars which can then be stored in their own separate plastic bags for whenever you need a high-energy snack.

BASIC GRAIN GRANOLA

- 2 cups rolled oats
- 2 cups flaked wheat
- 1 cup bran, whole or flaked
- 1½ cup chopped nutmeats (walnuts, peanuts, pecans, almonds, Brazil nuts—whatever you prefer, or if you can't decide, use a mixture)
- 2 Tbsp brewer's yeast
- 2 cups dry milk
- ½ cup honey or molasses
- ½ cup butter or safflower oil
- ¼ tsp powdered ginger
- ¼ tsp powdered allspice
- ¼ tsp powdered cloves
- ½ tsp powdered cinnamon

Combine the dry ingredients, then over low heat, combine the honey or molasses and mix with the dry ingredients. Spread in a thin layer on a baking sheet or shallow pan and bake at 225 degrees for 45 minutes to 1 hour or until brown and crunchy but not burned. If you plan to press the granola into a solid cake to be cut into bars, double the quantity of honey or molasses and bake in a thick layer in a shallow baking pan, cover with waxed paper while still hot, press together with the heels of your hands, allow to cool, chill for 1 hour, and cut into bars or squares with a buttered knife. Wrap the bars in waxed paper and store in the refrigerator until an hour or so before eating.

FRUIT AND NUT GRANOLA

- 1 cup rolled oats
- 1½ cups wheat germ
- 2 Tbsp flaked rye grains
- 3 Tbsp bran
- ½ cup chopped pitted dates
- ½ cup raisins
- ½ cup chopped dried apple
- 3 Tbsp chopped walnuts
- 3 Tbsp chopped raw peanuts
- 3 Tbsp chopped almonds
- 3 Tbsp chopped cashews
- ½ cup sunflower seeds
- ½ cup shelled pumpkin seeds
- 1½ cups dry milk
- ½ cup honey or molasses
- ¼ cup safflower oil or melted butter
- 1 tsp cinnamon
- ½ tsp powdered cloves

Combine the dry and wet ingredients separately. If you wish to omit any of the nuts or seeds, keep the bulk of the mixture constant by increasing the amount of another. Mix dry and wet ingredients thoroughly. Spread in a layer in a shallow, lightly oiled baking pan. If the granola is to be cut into squares or bars, cover the pan with a sheet of waxed paper and press firm with the palms.

Bake in a 225-degree oven for 2 hours. Do not overcook. When cool, cut into squares or bars and wrap separately in waxed paper.

GRANOLA TRAIL NIBBLES

#1

1 cup parched rolled oats
1 cup wheat germ
½ cup chopped dates
½ cup raisins
½ cup pitted dry prunes
½ cup sesame seeds
¼ cup chopped walnuts
½ cup chopped dry-roasted unsalted peanuts
½ cup chopped roasted almonds
   or cashews
½ cup chopped Brazil nuts
¼ cup shelled pumpkin seeds

If you cannot find parched rolled oats, buy regular (not instant) oats and spread them on a baking sheet, bake in a 220-degree oven for 45 minutes to 1 hour, stirring occasionally. Dust the chopped dates, raisins, and prunes lightly with powdered milk to keep them from being sticky and gumming up the mixture.

Combine all ingredients and blend well by shaking in a bag or stirring. Store and carry in press-to-seal plastic bags.

#2

¾ cup carob powder
2½ cups dry milk
½ cup bran
½ cup chopped walnuts
½ cup dry roasted unsalted peanuts
½ cup chopped roasted almonds
½ cup chopped pitted dates
¾ cup raisins
½ cup sunflower seeds
¾ cup shelled pumpkin seeds
¾ cup crushed banana chips or
   banana flakes

Combine the carob powder (available at health food stores and some grocery stores and drugstores) with 1 cup of the dry milk, add just enough water to make a thin paste (about the consistency of warm honey). Stir the bran and nuts into this paste until they are lightly coated. Use about ¼ cup of the milk powder to coat the date and raisin bits.

Stir all ingredients into the remaining milk powder, spread in a shallow baking pan, and bake in a 225-degree oven for 30 to 45 minutes, stirring occasionally. Cool; put in press-to-seal plastic bags. Keep bags in refrigerator for long-term storage, removing quantities as needed. The mixture will keep for three to four weeks without refrigeration.

10 BACKPACK COOKING

From the day the heading of this chapter was added to the outline being prepared for this book, I've found myself wondering from time to time whether yesterday's backpacker was better off than today's or vice versa. Certainly equipment has been vastly improved; most of the backpackers during the era in which I began hiking used World War I surplus packs, mess kits, canteens, and so on, all of which had been designed to fit the needs of military marchers rather than civilian hikers. Adapting the gear was a challenge, not always met successfully. The one bright spot in the 1920s surplus picture was the universal availability of field artillery boots, which were beautifully made and extremely comfortable, and sold widely for around $2.00 to $2.50 a pair.

We're not interested in boots here, of course; our field is food and food-related hardware. Where the foods themselves are concerned, backpackers certainly weren't as well off then as now. I've debated whether to ignore the tried and true standbys that have been around for so many years and concentrate on the new items, but the old war-horses still have a basic validity. Some of them are superior to the new developments that were supposed to replace them. As you'll see when you read on, the decision was to split down the middle and include some of both. Most of the hardware is of the new breed, though.

BACKPACKING HARDWARE

Any backpacking trip which will keep you in the field for more than three or four days is going to require some cookware. You'll also be wise to carry a small stove using artificial fuel, and to take along some kind of device that will insure the purity of the water you drink and use in cooking.

Today's backwoods trails aren't the virgins of yesterday. Aside from the high country of the Rockies and the Sierra Nevada, and some areas along the U.S.-Canadian border west of the Great Lakes, there are few great expanses of unspoiled and virtually untouched land. Pockets of almost-primeval wilderness still exist, but in many of these pockets the operative word has come to be "almost" rather than "primeval."

Backpack cooking becomes far more involved than merely nibbling upon snack items during short hikes or preparing meals in established camps. Your equipment must be greatly scaled down, and your food choices relatively light in weight, because everything must be carried on your back. It's a joyous challenge that thousands gladly accept.

A GALLERY OF
BACKPACKING STOVES

This propane model is ready to cook over at the turn of a dial. The fuel canister unscrews and the legs fold for easy storage. The cups and assorted bagged foods go into the light aluminum coffeepot.

Another lightweight stove comes housed in its own pot/pan case. Made by Optimus, it weighs only 26 ounces and yet with only a ¼-pint fuel supply will burn continuously for 1½ hours.

Optimus gasoline stove is a favorite with ultralight enthusiasts. The stove is housed inside its own protective case, the top of which doubles as a handy pot. That sheet metal gizmo you see at the left is a windscreen, to improve the stove's efficiency in breezy weather. Entire ensemble, including the full fuel tank, weighs only 32 ounces!

The stove of your choice should be dictated primarily by the number of people in the party it must serve. This somewhat larger trail stove by Coleman is suitable for cooking meals for three.

This unique backpacking stove uses kerosene for fuel. It is slightly heavier but kerosene is considered a safer fuel.

Another consideration when selecting a stove is the climate in which it will be used. In cold weather, use a stove with a pressure-pump handle to force-feed additional fuel to the burner head.

Perhaps the best all-around choice for year-round use is a stove that burns gasoline. This Optimus is a good all-weather stove; it has a large burner head and a pressure-pump handle.

Yet another variation of trail stove burns a type of jellied alcohol. This one is made by Sterno. The ring collar extends to provide a burner surface, then retracts for easy storage. For slow simmering foods, this stove is ideal, but it does not produce enough heat for sustained high-temperature cooking.

In earlier times, a backpacker entering a semiwild area could be sure of finding enough deadfalls to provide wood for a cooking fire. Today, several generations of use of some of the most popular backwoods trails has diminished loose deadfalls to a few splinters. Looking for useable wood for a campfire has come to be such a loss of time in so many places that you'll do better by yourself if you take along a small camp cooker. This doesn't

mean a stove, but one of the several types of diminutive one-burner devices that will allow you to prepare a one-dish meal and a pot of coffee in places where no natural fuel is available.

There are several compact one-burner cookers on the market today. Some use propane cylinders, some burn alcohol or fuel gel or unleaded gasoline. All of them are practical, and since there is really little difference between them, which one you select is a matter of personal preference.

It's possible to do without utensils entirely. Some foods can be cooked directly on the coals of a small campfire, and shown here are several ways of improvising grills and spits that eliminate carrying a grill or utensils. Improvising takes time, though, and its success depends to a large extent on having favorable natural features to help you along. If you're unsure of the terrain over which you're going to hike, find someone who does know it and ask about it. Once you know what to expect, you'll know how much gear you must carry with you.

As noted earlier, there are pockets of almost-unspoiled wild country in many places. However, some of these pockets are surrounded by industrial areas from which windborne pollutants are carried. The polluting agents—"acid rain" is the most common term for them—can render what appears to be an unspoiled stream if not marginally safe, at least unpleasant. Other pockets are adjacent to farmlands where drifting aerial sprays have settled on foliage adjacent to clear streams and been washed by rain onto the banks and into the water.

These things are unhappy-making to contemplate, but they have already happened. This is not the place for breast-

Learn how your stove works and you'll have few problems. The most likely difficulty occurs with the pressure pump. Inside the housing, a leather washer must be kept well oiled. If it dries out, the pump will not pressurize the fuel tank. The handle is easily unscrewed from the fuel fount so the dried leather washer inside may be reoiled upon occasion.

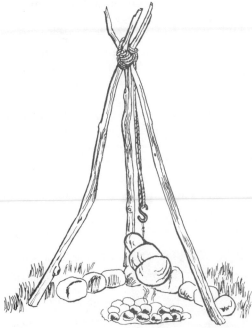

If you can afford the weight of meat in camp, or happen to kill a deer, one unique way to prepare a big roast is by using the gypsy spit. Remember how you wound up a playground swing as a child? The same principle works here. The hanging rope needs to be rewound about every 15 minutes.

Liquid fuels such as unleaded gasoline or kerosene need appropriate containers. They must be safe, leak-free, and lightweight. The one on the left is made from tinned steel and the one on the right from spun aluminum. Both are excellent choices.

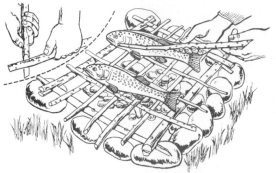

In an emergency, you can grill fish by first cleaning them, then using a split stick to either hold them over a fire or arrange them on a grill of green sticks.

Always use a funnel when filling your stove or microscopic particles of dirt or lint may clog burner orifices. If you spill a bit of fuel, allow it to evaporate completely before attempting to light the stove.

Here are two woodstoves you can make yourself from tin cans. Wood sticks are laid inside the fire door at the bottom and then ignited. These stoves operate like chimneys and become extremely hot.

beating or *mea culpas*; all that can be done here is to recognize that some areas of hazard exist and carry along a water-purifying device when going into territory with which you are unfamiliar or which you suspect might present problems of water purity.

Ironically, the technologies that in some cases created the water problem have also provided the solution. There is now on the market a very compact water filter which in a matter of two or three minutes will remove all pollutants and

Of paramount importance to any trail cook is water. It's needed for drinking, preparing meals, and cleaning up afterward. But, don't trust the water to be safe, even in wilderness regions.

impurities from a quart of water. The device illustrated here is called the H2OK filter. It is almost small enough to be carried in a pocket, weighs only a few ounces, and is quite inexpensive.

There are many ways to purify suspect water. At any pharmacy you can obtain tiny Halazone or iodine tablets intended for the purpose. Follow the instructions carefully and the water will be safe to drink in one-half hour.

When large quantities of clean water are needed for several people in the party, a water purifier such as the lightweight H2OK is handy. It is light in weight due to its plastic construction, and inside is a specially treated filter. Pour suspect water into the top of the H2OK, and it quickly drains out the bottom, ready to drink or use in cooking.

For your backpacking base camp—if one figures in your plan for an extended trip—there's a solar water heater available which can be folded like a handkerchief and weighs very little more. It could relieve fuel problems by supplying heated water for dishwashing, cooking, and people-washing as well.

There are a number of other new items of backpacking hardware that you'll want to investigate which don't fall into the category of cooking. If you're a confirmed backpacker, though, it's very likely that you'll already have found out about them yourself, so let's move along to food.

Much lighter in weight, and designed to serve one person, is the Super Straw, which also is made of plastic and contains a special chemically treated filter inside. Simply sip suspect water through it like an ordinary straw.

Avoid using glass bottles. Instead, transfer loose foods to plastic bags or special bottles designed for backpackers. Small-mouthed bottles should be reserved for liquids, and wide-mouthed bottles used for dry ingredients such as flour.

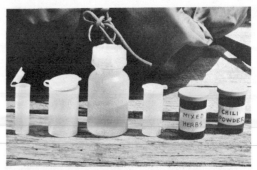

Plastic backpacking containers come in an infinite array of sizes and shapes. These tiny ones are perfect for spices and like foods when embarking upon an ultralight adventure. And don't forget 35mm film canisters with snap-top lids which have many uses.

Cooking kits should likewise be reduced in size, but try to remain with a nested version that is compact. This two-person model weighs only 21 ounces and contains a pot, frypan, bowl, and two dishes.

Each backpacker should have his or her own personal set of utensils. This lightweight combination has a slip-lock rivet so the individual pieces won't get lost in transit.

If you're backpacking and cooking over coals, you won't want a full-size, heavy grill. This tubular-aluminum model is extremely popular because it weighs only 7 ounces. Note also that instead of a heavy shovel or entrenching tool for fireside work, this camper uses a featherweight trowel.

BACKPACKER FOODS

It's not easy for the backpacker of today to realize just how limited the food choices were for his counterparts of yesterday. It's been only a relatively short time, in the neighborhood of 20 years or a bit more, since freeze-drying and packaging a wide variety of foods in impermeable packages of sealed foil became a day-by-day routine.

Before freeze-drying, the backpacker setting out for a long trip had to rely primarily on smoked meats and root vegetables, both of which weighed heavily and took up a lot of space. They also tended to make meals monotonous, so yesterday's backpacker learned to watch for and use the foods of the land over which he traveled to add a welcome touch of variety to his generally spartan menus.

In that earlier day, though, game was more plentiful, fish in the backcountry less wary, and game laws less stringent. A knowledgeable backpacker could live off the country to a certain extent, something which really isn't practical today. However, in Chapter 8 you'll find some data on survival foods that might help you to recognize and use to round out your menu any edible plants that you might encounter.

Later in this chapter, we'll look at the concentrated foods, often called "trail rations" or "pouch foods," that are available for those who want to travel very light indeed. We've already seen the virtual disappearance of many of yesterday's staple foods, which could be carried by a backpacker without spoiling from lack of refrigeration. There are alternatives, which is what we're interested in right now.

CURED MEATS

If you want genuine ham, bacon, and sausages, they are available at a price. My opinion is that if you want them badly enough, you'll do well to meet the price, for one factor of backpacking has not changed. An extended backpacking trip requires physical stamina on a continuing basis, and enjoying such a trip means eating substantial foods. Concentrates do an excellent short-term job of substituting, but they are still substitutes for belly-filling solid foods.

A few small meat-packing plants in widely scattered locations still produce traditionally cured hams and bacon. Unless you're fortunate enough to have such a plant in your immediate vicinity, you'll have to order by mail. An appendix lists some sources, and there are many others that you can find with a minimum of trouble.

A bit of prowling around in the ethnic neighborhoods of almost all cities of any size will generally uncover a few small food stores which can supply you with such hard-cured sausages as Italian *salami,* French *saucissons fumés,* German *knackwurst,* Spanish *chorizos,* and other sausages which require no refrigeration. These can be sliced for noonday sandwiches or eaten out of hand or added to a camp stew to replace fresh meat.

CHEESE

Good solid cheeses are still widely available; most supermarket chains do keep a few on their shelves. If you can't find them in your local stores, a number of reliable mail-order firms are listed in the appendix. The varieties of cheeses named in Chapter 7 can be eaten as snacks or used in sandwiches for a cold lunch, and can also be used in cooking. None of the cheeses mentioned in Chapter 7 will sag into a watery, flavorless goo in a cooked dish, as do most of the process cheeses and processed cheese foods, which you should studiously avoid.

VEGETABLES

Fortunately, dependable vegetables remain in good supply. Some, like tomatoes, have been spoiled by plant geneticists, who in their search for a tomato thick-skinned enough to be machine-harvested have given us a thick-skinned, watery flavorless fruit. The famed Idaho and Maine potatoes have vanished from most stores, and have been replaced by all-purpose potatoes which are reasonably satisfactory, but not superior, as were their predecessors. However, you can still rely on potatoes, yams, onions, carrots, turnips, and a new root vegetable, the *jaicama,* to add bulk and flavor to your camp cooking.

There are some vegetables which you can partially prepare at home and serve on the first evenings of your pack-trip. Those requiring long cooking can be precooked, and carried in your pack in press-to-close plastic bags; they will take up little space and add very slight weight to your load and the empty bags can be disposed of in the coals of your cooking fire. Some of the recipes that follow shortly make use of partly precooked ingredients. Any precooked foods included in these recipes can be counted on to hold for three to four days without requiring refrigeration, so do feel safe in using them.

CANNED FOODS

Nothing has been said about canned foods, because they aren't really a backpacker's dream. Cans are heavy, bulky, and hard to pack easily. They do save a lot of cooking, but the main thrust of all my efforts in planning my own backpack trip meals has been to avoid any kind of glass or metal container because of those twin annoyances of weight and bulk. If you want to use canned foods, by all means do so. In most of the recipes this chapter contains, some canned items can be substituted for fresh or freeze-dried or home precooked ingredients without any alteration of cooking or preparation procedures.

You will naturally work up a meal plan as soon as you know how many hungry hikers must be provided for. This isn't the full extent of your meal-planning, of course. You'll want to consider nutritional balance and variety as well as how many meals will be required, which meals will be cooked and which cold.

By doing a little judicious juggling of menus, you can make sure that readily perishable food will be consumed first.

Then there'll be a second session of revising menus and supply lists as you distribute the food supplies among the packs, trying to hold the weight and bulk of each packer's overall load within reasonable limits. Finally, from your meal plan your shopping list will emerge triumphant and you'll be over the first hurdle.

To help you along the way to that first hurdle, let's look at a few recipes. We'll consider first those which use perishable ingredients, both fresh and precooked. Next will come those dishes which require only ingredients that will hold for a reasonably lengthy period without refrigeration, and finally we'll get to the use of packaged freeze-dried foods and a few concentrates which you can prepare yourself.

HALF-AND-HALF RECIPES FOR BACKPACKERS

I've called these half-and-half because they depend partly on foods that have been cooked or half-cooked at home. The other parts of most of the recipes are either bacon or ham or hard-cured smoked sausage. Though such sausages aren't especially designed to be cooked, they're versatile enough to hold up their heads in these recipes.

HOOSIER PORK CHOPS

(Better make this a first-night supper; pork doesn't keep.)

- 4 **thin-cut pork chops**
- 3 **precooked boiled potatoes, peeled and diced**
- 1 **large sweet onion, peeled and diced**
- 2 **cups precooked carrots, peeled and diced**
- 4 **to 6 cherry tomatoes, quartered Salt and pepper**

Dust the chops with salt and pepper and brown them well on both sides. Add the potatoes, onion, and carrots and cover pan until they are well warmed. Turn the chops, cook 3 to 5 minutes, add the tomatoes. When the juice from the tomatoes boils, dish up. Serves 4.

TOAD IN THE HOLE

Try this old British dish for the first day's breakfast. Per serving:

- 1 **egg**
- 1 **slice bread**

Butter or fresh bacon fat

After the breakfast bacon is cooked and set aside to drain, cut or tear a hole in the center of a slice of bread. Drop the bread slice into the pan; break a fresh egg into the hole. Cook until the egg is set, turn quickly, and cook until yolk is firm. Repeat as needed until all are fed. Serve on paper towels which can be burned to save dishwashing time.

SAUSAGE STEW

1 slice diced bacon
1 large sweet onion, peeled and diced
1 sweet green (bell) pepper, cleaned and diced
2 precooked boiled potatoes, peeled and cubed
2 cups diced hard smoked sausage, cook's choice of kind

Heat the bacon pieces until they begin to brown and have released enough fat to grease the pan. Add the onion and cook until it begins to soften and grow translucent, then add the potatoes and sausage. Cook until the potatoes begin to brown, stirring as necessary. Serves 4.

HOPPING JOHN

2 cups precooked beans (lima, pinto, navy)
1 cup instant rice
2 cups cubed ham or smoked sausage
Water to cover

Combine all ingredients in pot or deep pan and cook until rice is fluffy and ready to eat. Add salt and pepper as needed; quantities of seasonings required will depend on the sausage. Serves 4.

COCIDO

2 slices bacon, chopped coarsely
1 medium-sized onion, chopped fine
8 to 10 cherry tomatoes, cut up fine
2 cups precooked garbanzos (chickpeas)
1 cup precooked carrots, quartered and sliced
1 cup thin-sliced chorizo sausage
1 tsp salt

Cook the bacon until it begins to get crisp. Add onion; cook until the bits begin to become transparent. Add the tomatoes and enough water to cover. Cook about 5 minutes, add remaining ingredients, salt to taste. Simmer 5 to 10 minutes. Serves 4 generously.

BACKPACK COOKING IN FOIL

On brief outings in which only a few meals have to be prepared and heavier than usual foods can be taken along, one of the easiest ways to prepare them is by creating one-pot meals whereby meat, potatoes, and vegetables are wrapped in foil and then buried in coals for 45 minutes.

Foil can be the enemy or the friend of the camp cook seeking to get along with a minimum of utensils, which certainly is the situation in which a backpacking cook finds himself or herself. I seldom use foil as a cooking aid, especially in semiwild country, for one very good reason which has nothing to do with the unhappy things foil does to food cooked in it.

Among my friends are a few game wardens, whom I've met in the course of following my trade. I've gone with them quite a number of times when they've performed autopsies on animals such as dead deer reported by some woods-wanderer, or have performed autopsies on animals brought in to their stations. My game warden friends tell me that in seven out of ten times when they check a dead animal outside of hunting season, foil thoughtlessly discarded by hunters, campers, or hikers has caused these deaths.

There are starvation seasons in the woods, periods when animals are so desperately hungry they'll eat almost anything. Foods cooked in foil leave their odors on it, and even if it's been buried, the sharp noses of hungry wild animals lead them to it, and they'll dig the stuff up and eat it. The foil lacerates their stomachs or intestines or blocks them up, and the animal dies, often quite lingeringly and painfully.

Now, the chances are that half the animals killed by eating foil would have starved anyhow, but I hate to think that I might have been the cause of killing some animal that I didn't stalk while hunting. I have no compunctions about a hunter—myself or any other hunter—bringing down wild game in a matching of skill against the wild instinct of a deer, for instance, but I do have an unhappy feeling when I think how human carelessness can be the cause of any wild animal's accidental death.

So, on the rare occasions when I do use foil for cooking on a backwoods hiking trip, I carry it out with me. Will you do the same? Oh—by the way, fish snap at beer-can caps zigging to the bottom of a lake just like they do at a spinner and some of the fish I've cleaned in busy lakes have yielded a surprisng number of these tabs. If you must drink beer in a boat, which isn't a good idea to begin with, slip the pull-tab into the can and take the can away with you when you leave.

Of course, I seldom use foil or recommend its use, because it's perniciously habit-forming. The outdoor chef who starts using foil soon finds himself hooked on the stuff and uses it to cook all sorts of things, most of which were never intended to be cooked in foil, and few of which respond gracefully to being handled in this fashion.

Foil's fatal flaw (nothing like a bit of alliteration to brighten up a cookbook) is that it *steams* the foods encased in it, and gives them an institutionalized flavor. Bread warmed in foil comes out unpleasantly soggy, so do potatoes baked in it. So do a lot of other things that should be crisp or flaky. But there are a few cases when foil is worth carrying, and a backpack trip is one of them. Just remember to carry it out, because you're the one who carried it in.

The following four recipes require somewhat heavy ingredients that may not be compatible with extended outings. However, on trips of brief duration in which only a few meals have to be planned, or when several partners can share the carrying weight of meal components, they're all excellent foil foods I heartily recommend.

STEAMED ONIONS

4 large sweet white onions
1 tsp Herb Seasoning #1 or #2

Peel the onion and score it at the top in a cross, bringing the cut just past the middle of the onion. Sprinkle the herb seasoning in the cut. Wrap the onion in foil and bury it in coals for 30 to 40 minutes. Serves 4.

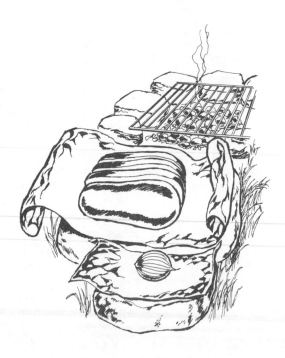

STEAMED EGGPLANT

1 medium-sized eggplant, quartered lengthwise
1½ tsp Herb Seasoning #2

Sprinkle the seasoning on the cut sides of each quarter of the eggplant, reassemble it, and wrap it tightly in three or four layers of foil. At the top, use a toothpick or tip of a knife-blade to make a very small vent hole, or the plant may explode as it begins to give off steam. Bury in coals 40 minutes to 1 hour, depending on the size of the eggplant. Remove, unwrap, eat with a spoon. Serves 4.

STEAMED ORANGES

1 orange per serving
6 or 8 whole cloves per orange

Stud oranges with cloves and wrap them in three or four foil layers. Make a tiny vent hole with a toothpick or knife-blade at the top of each orange to keep them from exploding as they begin to let off steam. Bury in coals for 25 to 30 minutes. Remove, cut into quarters, and eat out of hand.

APFEL-ZWIEBEL

1 firm apple per serving
1 sweet white onion per serving
Butter
Salt

Try to choose apples and onions of the same size. Quarter the apples and cut out the seeds and seed-pocket. Do not peel the apples, but do peel the onions. Quarter the onions. Spread the cut surfaces with butter and salt lightly. Arrange the apple and onion quarters alternately to form complete globes; wrap tightly in several layers of foil. At the top of each packet, make a vent hole with a toothpick or knife-blade. Bury in coals and bake 20 to 30 minutes.

HOMEMADE MIXES

Bread or its equivalent is one of the major problems that must be solved when you plan to travel light on an extended backpacking trip. Ordinary commercial squoosh bread from the mass-production bakeries barely qualifies as real food; it's a thin mixture of chemicals combined with wheat which has been stripped of most of its nutritional value.

Independent bakeries have just about vanished from small communities, but if you live in or near a large city you will be able to find a few which still bake real bread. However, a loaf of bread is a clumsy thing to pack. It is bulky in ratio to its weight and usually gets squashed flat during the first day out. It's soon eaten, and leaves a menu void that can only partly be filled by pancakes and potatoes. Ordinary crackers are too fragile and thirst-provoking to be a viable backpacker's choice, though Bolton Biscuit and Pilot Bread are made and packaged especially for campers and backpackers; for sources, see the appendix.

There are some satisfactory alternatives. The Skillet Biscuits in Chapter 4 can be cooked quickly, and to avoid the need to carry condensed milk, dry milk can be substituted. The Squaw Bread in Chapter 4 is also a recipe which can be used by substituting powder milk for fresh or condensed. And in that chapter you'll find Elmer Meyers's Pancake Mix, which will provide a good bread substitute.

A few more nonbaked breads and bread mixes follow. Remember, there's no real trick to making or using bread mixes. You prepare the mix at home, in advance of your trip, and store it in a big jar in the refrigerator until you're assembling your grub, which is the last step in your pretrip preparation.

Take the mix out, and divide it into portions that will provide the amount of bread or pancakes or biscuits that you'll need for each meal. Put these portions in press-to-seal plastic bags, and toss them into your pack. When ready to use, add water to produce dough or batter of the desired consistency, and cook.

BAKING-POWDER BISCUIT MIX

8½ cups all-purpose flour
1 Tbsp baking powder
1 Tbsp salt
2 tsp cream of tartar
1 tsp baking soda
1½ cups nonfat dry milk
1¼ cups solid vegetable shortening

Sift all the dry ingredients together and blend well. Using a pastry blender, cut in the shortening until it is distributed evenly. At this point, the mix should look like cornmeal. Store in the refrigerator in a tightly closed screw-top jar until ready to package, then divide the mix into batches; about 2 cups of mix will yield enough biscuits for four. Seal each batch in foil until ready to use. If kept reasonably cool, the packets will hold up to 10 days without refrigeration. Reconstitute by adding a little water at a time and stirring into a stiff dough. Makes 6 batches of mix; each batch yields 4 to 6 biscuits, depending on their size.

WHOLE-WHEAT BISCUIT MIX

4½ cups whole wheat flour
4 cups all-purpose white flour
2 Tbsp baking powder
1 Tbsp salt
2 tsp cream of tartar

1 tsp baking soda
1¼ cups nonfat dry milk
2 cups vegetable shortening

Follow directions for mixing, storing, and using given in the preceding recipe.

WHEATCAKE MIX

8 cups wholewheat flour
½ cup granulated sugar
2½ tsp baking powder
4 tsp baking soda
4 tsp salt

Sift all ingredients together; store in a tightly closed screw-cap jar in the refrigerator until ready to use or pack. To pack, divide into 3 or 4 equal portions and seal in foil. The mix will hold about 3 days after being taken from the refrigerator. When ready to use, to each cup of mix add:

1 to 1¼ cups reconstituted nonfat dry milk
1 egg
2 Tbsp salad oil

Stir into a medium-thick batter and cook in a lightly greased pan. Each batch of mix will yield about 8 medium-sized pancakes.

JOHNNYCAKE

This is a type of bread that our ancestors called "journey cake," because it could be made up in advance and lasted almost indefinitely, and because it was very easy to make during a trip.

1 cup regular cornmeal or ¾ cup stone-ground cornmeal
1 tsp salt
2 cups boiling water
Fat for frying

Stir or sift the cornmeal and salt together; add the boiling water a little at a time while stirring into a dough or thick batter that will hold its shape when lightly compressed. Form pones between the palms of your hands; the pones should be no more than ½ inch thick and about 2 by 3 inches in dimension. Cook in hot fat in a skillet, turning when the bottom side browns. Cooking time is usually about 3 to 4 minutes per side. Drain on absorbent paper. Eat hot or cold. Makes 8 to 10 pones.

STICKBREAD

FOOD CONCENTRATES

When backpacking, cut your cooking time by making stickbread instead of biscuits. Divide either of the biscuit mixes given here into equal batches for each member of the party and let each one cook his own.

To cook stickbread, cut reasonably straight branches from a nonresinous tree into 4-foot lengths and clear them of bark and pith. Form the biscuit dough into a single length about 1½ inches wide, and wrap in a spiral on the sticks. Anchor at top by overlapping the first turn and by moistening the bottom end and pressing it into the spiral above it.

Push the end of the stick into the ground about 6 to 8 inches from the fire-pit, at an angle that will hold the dough over the coals. Revolve the stick a quarter-turn about every 4 to 5 minutes while the dough cooks. When the outside of the spiral is a crusty brown, the bread should be ready to eat.

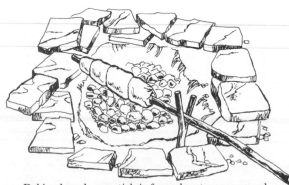

Baking bread on a stick is fun, adventuresome, and fills the need for bread products when you can't tote the weight of a heavy Dutch oven. Just remember to keep turning the stick so all sides of the dough receive even exposure to the heat.

There are two kinds of concentrated foods. One is the ready-to-eat concentrate, which is a kissing cousin to granola. It is eaten as is, and requires no preeating preparation. The other is the concentrate which can be reconstituted by adding hot water, and thus makes a hot meal. Both kinds of these concentrated foods are available from commercial sources, and we'll look at these a few pages further on. However, you can prepare some concentrated mixes at home.

However, because the success of concentrates which can be reconstituted depends primarily on the freeze-drying process, you'll be time and money ahead if you buy this type. Reconstitutable concentrates can be tricky to prepare and require a lot of time in their preparation. Unless you spend an entire summer backpacking, you won't be using these reconstitutable concentrates often enough or in large enough quantities to justify the time and effort required to make them yourself. One recipe is given in this section, in case you'd like to prove this point to your own satisfaction.

As for the ready-to-eat variety, they're quick and easy to mix up. They're not so much a concentrated form of conventional mealtime foods as they are a mixture of high-nourishment, high-energy-producing foods; the concentration is in the ingredients themselves, not in the method of preparation. They're really very little more than the trail nibbles you met in Chapter 7.

HOMEMADE VEGETABLE SOUP CONCENTRATE, OR "LEATHER"

1 **soup bone with a substantial amount of meat on it**
4 **medium-sized potatoes**
6 **large carrots**
2 **large sweet onions**
2 **cups shredded cabbage**
2 **cans tomato paste**

Boil the soupbone in lightly salted water to cover, replenishing the water as needed to maintain its level during the first half-hour of cooking. Skim off and discard scum that rises to the surface as the bone boils. Boiling time, about 1 hour.

Drain the soupbone from the pot, reserving the stock. Remove marrow and meat from the bone; set the meat aside. Strain the stock, return to pot, bring to a boil. Stir in the marrow until it dissolves. Reduce heat to simmer.

Peel and cube the potatoes, scrape the carrots and slice them into rounds, peel and chop the onions coarsely. Add them to the pot, together with the cabbage. Simmer until the potatoes just begin to soften. Do not add additional water; as the vegetables absorb the stock stir them to redistribute them so they will cook evenly. Strain the vegetables from the pot and put on layers of cloth or paper towels to drain.

Bring the stock to a boil and let boil until it is reduced to a thick liquid the consistency of gravy. Scrape the sides and bottom frequently to prevent scorching. When the stock has been reduced, add the tomato paste. Remember that tomatoes in any form have a tendency to scorch easily, so stir often, scraping the sides and bottom of the pot. Cook until the liquid is reduced to a thick paste.

Grease lightly a shallow baking pan and pour the tomato mixture into it. Set oven at its lowest heat; usually this will be 125 or 150 degrees. Put the baking pan in the oven, stirring occasionally, until the paste is reduced to a flexible, semisolid layer. This is called "leather." Using a convection oven will speed up the process of dehydrating the paste until the leather forms. Some health food stores stock leather; for ordering details see the appendix.

At the same time the paste is placed in the oven, spread the vegetables and meat pieces on a lightly oiled baking sheet and put them in the oven. Turn them occasionally. Your object is not to cook these further, but to dehydrate them. When the vegetables and meat are dry, remove them from the oven.

When the leather has reached the proper consistency, it will be firm but flexible, and almost dry. Turn the leather out of the pan onto a sheet of waxed paper or foil. Cool both the leather and meat/vegetable mixture, then refrigerate them uncovered for 12 to 18 hours to draw out any remaining moisture.

Store leather and meat/vegetable mix in the refrigerator in tightly closed containers until ready to pack them. In foil packets or press-to-seal plastic bags,

HOW TO MAKE "LEATHER"

1. Begin by slowly simmering a large beef bone to produce broth, occasionally spooning away the scum that forms on the surface.

2. Meanwhile, cut potatoes, onions, carrots, and cabbage into chunks.

3. After slowly simmering the vegetables in the broth, thoroughly drain them on paper toweling.

4. Now, place the vegetables on a baking sheet and pop into your oven. Mix the broth and tomato paste and pour it into a separate pan. You don't want to cook the tomato puree or the vegetables—merely dehydrate them—so place your oven's temperature dial on its lowest setting, leave the door slightly ajar, and patiently wait. Depending upon your oven, and the quantity of leather you're making, drying time may be completed in as little as 6 hours, or it may take as long as 20 hours.

5. This is the "leather," or dried tomato paste. It's pliable just like leather and needs no refrigeration.

6. Here are the finished, dehydrated vegetables. They, too, require no refrigeration and can be stored in a plastic bag. On the trail, add the dried vegetables and leather to a pot of boiling water and everything will reconstitute into a robust vegetable stew that is absolutely delicious.

they will hold for about four days in moderate temperatures.

To reconstitute, cut the leather into chunks, put it and the vegetables in a pot, cover with water, and simmer, stirring occasionally.

Because there are so many variables of air, moisture, and climate to consider, exact cooking times are impossible to give. You will have to experiment to find out how long it takes to form the leather in your oven; this may be as short a time as five hours or as long as twelve hours. The time required to dehydrate the meat/vegetable mix is equally variable.

Don't be skittish about this recipe, though. The process of making tomato and fruit leathers is an ancient one, going back many centuries. In fact, this is the way tomato paste originated in the days before the paste itself could be canned. In Italian home kitchens, the leather was formed and stored without refrigeration between tomato harvests, and chunks were cut off as needed to be reconstituted with water to make tomato paste.

FRUIT/NUT
TRAIL RATION

GROUP 1—NUTS
    1 cup dry-roast unsalted peanuts
    1 cup slivered roast almonds
    1 cup coarsely chopped walnuts
    1 cup coarsely chopped pecans
    1 cup coarsely chopped Brazil
      nuts

GROUP 2—SEEDS
    ½ cup sunflower seeds
    ¾ cup hulled pumpkin seeds
    ¼ cup sesame seeds

GROUP 3—FRUITS
    1 cup raisins
    1 cup chopped pitted dates, rolled
      in dry milk
    1 cup chopped pitted prunes,
      rolled in dry milk
    ½ cup coconut flakes or shreds
    1 cup dried banana flakes

This is a select-it-yourself mix. Choose any three ingredients from Group 1, any two from Group 2, and three from Group 3, and shake well in a plastic bag to mix. Depending on your choices, the yield will be 5 to 6 cups of mix. Not all people have the same tastes; for instance, I don't like coconut, so I omit it from my mixture. You might not like banana flakes or sunflower seeds or some other ingredient, so feel free to leave out or include whatever you wish. The omission of any of the ingredients will not change the nutritional balance of the mix or substantially alter its balance of minerals, vitamins, and other goodies. This mix needs no refrigeration and holds well.

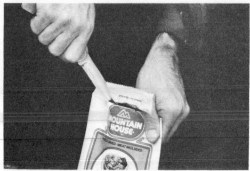

Prepare freeze-dried, or pouch, foods right in their own storage containers. First, of course, open the top of the pouch, being careful not to tear one of the sides.

Next, add one cup of hot water.

Stir thoroughly and wait five minutes. You can then transfer your meal to a plate, but if you're in a hurry and don't want to wash dishes, eat right from the makeshift container.

COMMERCIAL FREEZE-DRIED BACKPACKING FOODS

There are three kinds of backpacking foods on the market: pouch foods, retort foods, and compressed foods. The first two are what we might call boil-in-the-bag foods. They are completely cooked, sealed in heatproof foil or plastic bags, and require boiling water for their preparation.

You can distinguish between them easily. The difference between them is this:

Pouch foods are prepared by placing the unopened bag in boiling water.

Retort foods are prepared by opening a bag or bags, combining their contents, and pouring boiling water into the bag that holds the combined contents.

Compressed foods are reconstituted by opening the bag and placing the small wafers it contains in cool water, and these wafers swell into foods which must then be heated.

In all three products the food is pre-cooked, dehydrated, and flash-frozen. All of them are available in a variety of combinations so that meals in which they're used provide a varied menu. None of them require refrigerated storage, and all of them will remain stable for relatively long periods. Some pouch foods have a limited unrefrigerated storage life due to the ingredients used in their preparation.

These products reached their present development primarily because of military needs and, later, the needs of the space exploration program. They are simply technological extensions of ancient needs; primitive peoples before history began to be recorded had discovered how to preserve meats and fish by salting or brine-pickling as well as by air-drying and smoking. In North America, the Indian tribes had also developed pemmican, which as far as history records is the first condensed ration.

These primitive methods of food preservation and condensing were the result of trial and error based on observation. Science did not enter into food preservation efforts until 1809, when after years of experimenting a French confectioner, Appert, found a way to seal cooked foods into glass jars. Appert's efforts were spurred by an offer of a cash prize by the French government which needed portable, spoilproof foods for Napoleon's armies. The first successful concentrated preserved food was invented by a New Yorker, Gail Borden, who in the 1830s resettled in Texas to publish the first newspaper in the Texas Republic.

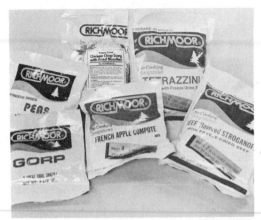

Vegetables, meats, desserts, and complete dinner entrees are now available in lightweight form. Check any store that carries camping/backpacking supplies and the number of enticing food items will be bewildering.

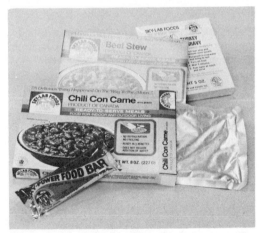

Other types of backpacking foods—even entire meals that are delicious and ready to eat in minutes—come sealed in foil pouches. The entire pouch is submerged in boiling water until the food is cooked. Then the pouch is opened and the food transferred to your plate.

Most experienced backpackers settle on three cardinal rules regarding the use of freeze-dried foods. If the instructions call for hot water, use boiling water. If the instructions call for cold water, the colder the better. And, serving quantities are for the most part greatly exaggerated. If it says "serves four" on the package, the entire meal can probably be devoured by two hungry backpackers in short order.

By 1840, Borden had succeeded in reducing the bulk of milk by boiling and had found that adding sugar to the condensed milk prevented it from souring. Success of his discoveries and their commercial application were closely allied with the development of sealed tin cans, which had been invented in England in the 1820s. Tin quickly replaced fragile, hard-to-seal glass as a container, and "airtights," as the cans were first known, played a large role in opening and settling the American West. The milk canning firm which Gail Borden founded still bears his name today.

Experiments with atomic bombardment as a method of food preservation were made in the early 1950s, but were shelved when no method could be found to keep the foods from becoming radioactive. Returning to dehydration by flash-freezing, foods that could be preserved in sealed pouches reached the military market and later, the space program, in time to be useful in the Viet Nam misadventure and the successful space program.

Their offshoots are seen today in supermarket "bubble packs" of such products as cured meats and partly processed vegetables, but all these depend on being kept refrigerated.

Pouch foods are very big today in institutional foods; they are the backbone of a number of hotel, restaurant, and fast-food chains. Many of these products, however, must be kept frozen or at least refrigerated, until they go into the microwave oven to be heated for serving. Almost 100 percent of the large hotel and motel chains which feature deluxe dining facilities get their fancy dishes in frozen plastic pouches.

Today's backpacker has an ever-increasing choice of both retort, pouch, and compressed foods. For sources of supply, see the appendix.

All that today's backpacker really needs to dine quite well and still travel light is a small camp stove and a cup in which to boil some water. The pictures show you how retort and pouch foods are used.

11 "SURVIVAL" FOODS AND SKILLS

Part 1

To avoid confusion, since we're dealing with two topics that are only peripherally related, this chapter is divided into two parts. The first part describes in words and pictures the wild foods that you can eat with a certainty that they're safe, and gives you a few recipes for cooking them at home. "Survival foods" is the name that still clings to these uncultivated plants because for a span of about two hundred years in the early days of our nation, a lot of explorers and settlers did depend very largely on them for survival.

In today's highly organized society, the prospect that someone will be lost in a wilderness long enough for wild foods to be a major survival factor is relatively remote. People do get lost in wild places today, but they seldom stay lost long enough to be forced to eat wild fruits, berries, and plants in order to stay alive. We'll save further comments on this for Part 2, because the comments it contains will make a lot more sense after you've read and digested Part 1.

Now, the first section of the chapter takes us into an area which I approach with a good deal of caution, and my advice to you is to approach it in the same way. Edible plants that grow uncultivated in wild areas are relatively plentiful, but many of these plants have look-alikes, virtual duplicates, which are not only inedible, but can be downright dangerous.

Our lives have changed with our land through the years that have passed since the Pilgrims were trying to get a toehold on an unexplored continent up on the New England coast, and DeSoto was leading his little band west from Florida along the Gulf coast. These first arrivals were taught to use survival foods by the Indians, and many Indian tribes lived in a state of more or less constant hunger, meeting the challenge of keeping alive by eating almost anything that wasn't instantly toxic.

Today's travelers don't encounter the same conditions that the frontier-makers faced a couple of hundred years ago. When North America was first being explored and settled, travelers needed very desperately to be able to find wild foods as supplements to the limited rations which they were able to carry. Many settlers struggling to get a foothold on a homestead also relied on wild plants to help them survive during the critical period before their first crops could be harvested and even later, in bad years, between crops.

There are many, many wild plants which are edible. Indeed, some experts in the field have estimated that about 65 to 70 percent of all wild plants (except trees) have some portions which can safely be eaten. Old records bear this out. Early explorers and settlers in all parts of North America have written about the foods eaten by those Indian tribes which at that time were nomads or seminomads and did not cultivate the ground. In some cases the uses of plants named in these early accounts have now been almost forgotten by modern members of the tribes.

What today's seeker of wild food must constantly bear in mind is that the mountain men and pioneers who used these foods in years gone by had grown up from childhood with a wilderness which began almost at their doorsteps. Most of them recognized plants as readily as today's city-dweller recognizes streets by reading their names from the signs on the corners.

In today's increasingly urbanized society, even those who live in rural areas spend only a fraction of their time roaming the uncultivated land around them—if indeed there remains any such land around them to roam. The girls who once helped their mothers in the kitchen and who helped harvest the wild foods that grew near rural homesteads now help their mothers harvest the supermarket shelves with a shopping cart. The boys who once learned about wild plants as they wandered through the woodlot on the back forty to a swimming hole on the creek now wander from the schoolroom across the parking lot to a swimming pool in the school gymnasium. Whether we're young or old, few of us today are intimately familiar with raw land where edible plants grow.

During the 1960–70 decades there was a brief revival of interest in wild foods, in what might be called the mystique of living off the land; if you think back a few years you'll remember this as being a popular fantasy during the time of the youth revolution. A few of those who succeeded in turning fantasy into reality and did go to rural areas to live off the land eventually learned which wild plants were safe and which were not.

Those who stuck out the transition gained an insight which was inherited by our ancestors: that nature is both generous and cussed, generous in providing sustenance in the form of wild plants, and cussed in creating a number of plants that are both edible and poisonous at the same time.

This preamble has a point. For emphasis, I'll rephrase the last sentence of the preceding paragraph: *There are a number of plants which have both edible and toxic parts growing from the same root.*

Those of us who aren't oriented toward farming seldom stop to think—indeed, might not know—that two of our most popular and plentiful farm crops are plants which have this characteristic, and which show it in two different aspects. The potato has an edible *root,* but its flowers and vegetation are toxic. The tomato has an edible *fruit,* but its vegetation is toxic. Not all plants having this duality are fatally poisonous, of course, but the very existence of the phenomenon should be enough to cause anyone to think twice before eating any part of a plant before firmly establishing its safety.

Awareness of the fact that certain portions of a wild plant may be edible and other portions toxic leads experts in the field to agree on one thing: There is no positive way to identify by description or by pictures *all* the wild plants which are safe to eat as opposed to those which are dangerous. Even selecting for use plants which you've seen eaten by birds or animals is not a sure guide. Many plants which are safe for birds or animals to eat are not necessarily safe for human consumption.

Those two statements lead me to echo here a bit more of advice from those who are much more knowledgeable about such matters: Unless you are *absolutely sure* a wild plant you are thinking of eating is safe, don't eat it.

the only plants described here. They are by no means all the edible plants, leafy or otherwise, but they are the few which do not have virtual duplicates which might be picked by mistake.

Recognition and cooking of field or forest plants is an area in which I claim no special expertise, though in most of the places where I've lived or camped or hunted, I've found enough wild foods for an occasional sampling. Some of these have been enjoyable, some are better written off as experiments, and others have been terrible. Because no two people have exactly the same tastes, I'm not going to prejudice you by offering my opinion on any of the wild plants we'll be dealing with here. Incidentally, the botanical name of each of the plants is included, so that you can check in a standard botanical reference book to be sure of the identity of any plant you might decide to try.

Suggestions for cooking are included here with the plant's identification characteristics, and a bit further along you'll find a few generic recipes that can be used in preparing most or all of the wild edibles listed.

WILD PLANTS

There are just over a dozen edible leafy wild plants, most of them very widely distributed, which have no toxic look-alikes. Because no other wild plants resemble them, it would be very hard indeed for you to make a mistake in identifying them. For that reason, and because they are representative of their type, these are

Amaranth (*Amaranthus retroflexus; A. hybridus*). Also called careless weed, pigweed, redroot. Most varieties grow to a height of 3 feet or less, but *A. hybridus* may grow as tall as 6 to 8 feet. Cook the tender tips of the leaves as garden greens, preferably in a mixture with such cultivated greens as mustard, spinach, collard, and turnip.

Amaranth

Cattail (*Typha latifolia*). Also called bullrush, but very easily identified, as the plant grows in swampy spots and at the edges of ponds and streams. Cattail roots can be eaten raw, or cooked like asparagus. Cook the tender sprouts and shoots as garden greens; the pollen is used as a flour in baked foods.

Chickweed (*Stellaria media*). Also called starwort and stitchwort. A low-growing, ground-hugging plant; it rarely gets more than 3 or 4 inches above its long underground rootstalk. Serve the leaves raw in a mixed green salad (the taste is like that of green peas) or stir-fry, braise, or steam with other greens as a pot-filler.

Chickweed

Dandelion (*Taraxacum officinale*). No way of mistaking a dandelion because of its early yellow-gold flower and late-season fuzzy, downy seedhead. Dandelion wine, fermented from the young plant, roots, leaves, and flowers, was for many years a rural mainstay. Serve the youngest, tenderest green leaves in a mixed salad; braise the young buds before they flower; braise or steam alone or with cultivated greens. The young root can be boiled as a vegetable.

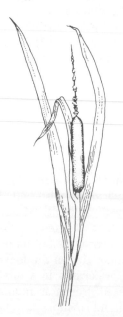

Cattail

Dandelion

Dock (*Rumex crispus; R. orbiculatus; R. patientia*). In sequence with the botanical names, varieties are curly, common, narrow, sour, and yellow dock; water or great water dock; patience, spinach, or passion dock. Of the different kinds, narrow dock is the most desirable. Gather young leaves in early spring and cook with cultivated or other wild greens.

Fiddlehead Fern

Dock

High Mallow (*Malva rotundifolia*). A migrant from Egypt that reached Europe and Asia around the 14th century and was brought by settlers to North America. The round leaves are sometimes called cheeses. Grows to a normal height of 6 to 12 inches. Braise or serve the leaves raw in a mixed salad. The seeds are roasted and salted to be eaten as a snack.

High Mallow

Fiddlehead Fern (*Pteridium aquilinum; Osmunda cinnamomea; Matteuccia struthiopteris*). Common names of these ferns, in the sequence of their botanical names, are bracken, cinnamon fern, and ostrich fern, but all share the fiddlehead name because of the similarity of their coiled heads which vaguely resemble the contours of a violin's neck as they open. Snap off the heads when the root-plant is no more than 6 inches high. The heads must be defuzzed before cooking; then they can be served raw as a salad ingredient, cooked as a vegetable, or pickled. No other part of the plant is edible.

Lamb's Quarters (*Chenopodium album*). Also known as goosefoot and wild spinach. The latter name gives you an idea of how to serve it, as you would cultivated spinach. In fall, the seeds can be gathered and roasted for a snack-food.

Lamb's Quarters

Milkweed (*Asclepsis syriaca*). Called silkweed, and in the West, antelope horn. If stalks are to be used they must be gathered very early, before the plants are 8 inches tall. Steam them like asparagus. Gather leaves in early summer, before they reach a length of 6 inches and cook as garden greens. Pick buds in late summer, before they fill with milk. They should feel firm and solid when squeezed. Milkweed is too bitter to be eaten raw and is tedious to cook. It must be parboiled in three or four changes of constantly boiling water, to remove all its bitterness, before finally being cooked to serve.

Milkweed

Poke (*Phytolacca americana*). Also called poke greens, poke salad, pokeberry, and pigeonberry. Next to dandelions, poke is probably the most generally used wild green. It appears early and is best when gathered before the stalk emerges from the soil. Poke when young needs no special treatment other than parboiling; the water is then discarded and the leaves cooked in fresh water. After the plant stalks and heads, poke should be avoided, and its berries, which appear soon after stalking occurs, should never be eaten—though they are relished by birds.

Poke

Purslane (*Portulaca oleracea*). Also called pursley or pussley. It grows low, the plants rarely reaching a height of more than 4 or 5 inches. It should be picked and used young, before its flowers develop. The leaves are thick and slightly sour, and when cooked exude a mucus much like that in okra. Braise or cook with other greens, or pickle the leaves and tender stems.

Purslane

Sorrel (*Rumex acetosella; R. Acetosa*). Again in sequence with the botanical names, the common names of the subspecies are red and common sorrel; garden, green, and French sorrel. All are often referred to as sheep sorrel or sourgrass. *R. acetosella* is much more widely distributed; it is a small plant, usually under a foot high, with long arrow-shaped leaves ending in two spurs at their base. The leaves of *R. acetosa* are shaped like regular arrowheads, without spurs; it is often cultivated, and you'll find its seeds listed in garden catalogs. Early spring is the best time to pick, though plants which grow in shady places are often quite small and their leaves are palatable through summer. Both sorrels are high in acidity, but a few leaves brighten up a salad, and add tang to such bland garden greens as spinach.

Sorrel

Sow Thistle (*Sonchus arvensis; S. asper; S. oleraceus*). A family which, once more in sequence with the botanical names, has a number of members: field sow thistle and perennial sow thistle; annual sow thistle and common sow thistle; spiny sow thistle. The different varieties grow to different sizes, but all have readily recognizable characteristics: straight spikelike stems with elongated leaves that coil around the stems at their base, and yellow flowers with petals that grow from a bulbous bud. Only the leaves are edible. They should be picked while small and when cooked should be parboiled, the water discarded, and then boiled again in fresh water. The leaves are not eaten raw.

Sow Thistle

Winter Cress (*Barbarea vulgaris*). Also known as yellow rocket, spring cress, and upland cress. This plant, like its kin, watercress, favors damp shaded places. Only the leaves are eaten; they are quite tart and should be parboiled and the water changed for a final cooking. However, a few leaves in a green salad will add zest to its flavor.

Winter Cress

In addition to these plants, there are quite a number which have been tamed and become garden or commercial plants. There is a wild asparagus, as easily recognized as its tamed cousin, and not duplicated by any toxic plant. There are several varieties of wild mint, all having elongated leaves shaped like spearheads and all exuding an unmistakably minty aroma when you pinch or crush a leaf.

There are wild onions and garlic, leeks and chives which cannot be mistaken for anything except what they are because they taste and smell just like their garden-grown relatives. There are cresses which are indistinguishable from the commercially cultivated varieties, quite probably because they are direct ancestors of the cultivated kinds. The flowers of wild violets, another unmistakable, can be candied or used as a mild spice in tea, just as can those of the violets in your garden.

One final caution: If you plan to do any intensive investigating of edible wild plants, you should invest in a good botany text, one having colored plates, to guide you in your searching.

MUSHROOMS

Over the years, field or meadow mushrooms have been the wild food which I've enjoyed the most, and consequently the one with which I've become most familiar.

There are two tests, taught me by a lifelong student of mycology, which I've come to look on as a very reliable guide to the edibility of a mushroom. Neither of these is the spore test, which is considered by experts to be infallible. To carry out the spore test, place the mushroom caps with their gills down on pieces of clean paper. Cover the mushrooms with a piece of clean cloth, or upend a large pan over them. After three to four hours enough mushroom spores will drop from the gills to make a print on the paper. This is much like fingerprinting a human for identification; each variety of mushroom, no matter how much alike two species look, has different spore prints.

Unfortunately for amateur mycologists, the fingerprint analogy holds true in identifying the prints. They must be evaluated by an expert, someone who's made a study of mushrooms. Spore prints are reproduced in many standard texts on botany, and there are books on mushrooms which contain them. One of the best of them, Louis Krieger's *The Mushroom Handbook,* published by the Dover Company in softcover, contains enough pictures and other details to get you started if you wish to study the subject.

Unlike the spore test, the two tests on which I rely for testing meadow or field mushrooms can be made by anyone. The first test is to look at the mushroom's gills; they should be a vibrant, almost living shade that ranges from light rose to dark brown. The second test is to stroke the mushroom's cap with the fingertips, and if the surface has the feel of live human skin, the probability that the mushroom is edible is 99.99 percent positive.

Solely on the basis of these two tests, I've eaten far too many thousands of wild meadow mushrooms to count and have never had a stomach qualm from eating them. However, the mushroom must pass *both* tests before I'll eat it.

Meadow Mushroom

A mushroom's gills darken very quickly, often in an hour or two, but this has no effect on their edibility and very little on their flavor. The best time to cook a meadow mushroom is before the gills get too dark, but they're safe to eat even when the gills have become almost black. They're at their very peak when you can cook them while the tender membrane between the bottom rim of the cap and the skin is just breaking open.

While mushrooms add greatly to the flavor of many dishes, I think the best way to enjoy them is to plunge them for three or four minutes into lightly salted boiling water and then sauté them gently in sweet fresh butter over low heat, turning them often. When serving, pour the pan juices over the mushrooms and the dish they will accompany.

Mushrooms push through the ground quickly. Often, when on a mushroom-gathering expedition in familiar territory I've found mushrooms 4 to 6 inches in diameter, still surrounded by the broken earth from which they grew, while returning along a trail that I passed over in the opposite direction less than a quarter-hour earlier. Within that quarter-hour, the mushrooms had pushed up fully grown from their underground incubation.

Morels, both the meadow and forest variety, have no gills to speak of, but the morel's spongelike pitted body and pronounced conical form make identification easy. However, there is a "false morel" that looks almost identical and is dangerous to eat.

Morel

Chanterelles, with their varicolored caps, and Judas's ears, which also vary in color, are both types of mushrooms which I hesitate to judge for myself. Before cooking and eating them, I find someone whose judgment about mushrooms I trust and get a second opinion.

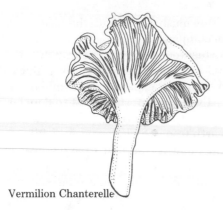

Vermilion Chanterelle

Mushrooms which should generally be avoided by any except experts are those with dead-white gills and those which have caps that feel at all slimy or rough and papery. The most notorious of the white-gilled mushrooms is the amanita, which is quite deadly and if handled extensively can even transmit toxic spores to the hands. Not all white-gilled mushrooms are amanitas, of course, and not all mushrooms with white or varicolored gills are toxic by any means.

Oyster Mushroom

Edible varieties such as chanterelles, Judas's ears, oyster mushrooms, sulfur shelves, and a number of tree mushrooms vary in color from pale yellow to bright orange and some have rough or uneven caps. However, these characteristics also appear on other fungi which should not be eaten. If you do not know mushrooms thoroughly, avoid those fitting the descriptions just outlined.

For example, oyster mushrooms and sulfur shelves, which grow on the trunks of trees and decaying logs, are quite common in two of the Western areas where I've spent much time camping, hunting, and fishing. I've encountered these fungi frequently in the Sierra Nevada and in the densely forested Pacific Northwest.

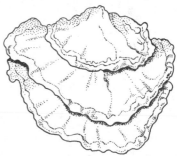

Sulfur Shelf

Some of the mushrooms of these species will pass the test of the fingertip caress, but have white gills. Others feel moist, even slimy, but have attractively colored gills. Though I'm *reasonably* sure they are quite safe, I find a local expert in wild mushrooms and get a better-informed judgment as to their edibility before picking.

Puffballs are commonplace in many uncultivated areas, and are generally edible, but their dead-white color, or lack of color, makes them unattractive to me.

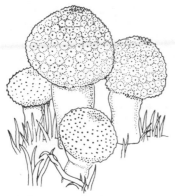

Small Puffball

WILD FOODS FROM BUSHES, VINES, AND TREES

Growing in wild places are a number of berries and fruits that you're quite safe in harvesting and eating.

Depending on the section of the country you're in, you'll find black haws, elderberry shrubs, and blueberry bushes. Along Southeastern streams you can still find a few maypops, and in the Southwest there are sandplum and mesquite bushes.

Sandplums bush along watercourses, but mesquite grows everywhere. The sandplums yield a sweet small fruit which is eaten raw and made into jam and jelly. The mesquite's yield is in the form of beans, which hang from the shrub's low branches in long pods. Indians sun-dried the beans and cooked them into a stew with buffalo meat and pounded them into a powder to be used in making pemmican. The beans are edible, but not appetizing just as they come from the pod.

Perhaps one of the reasons for this is that the highly toxic amanita in its first stage of growth forms a white ball much like a small puffball. There is a test by which you can identify the amanita and distinguish it from a puffball, but even the test involves a certain amount of risk, and I would urge you to avoid puffballs unless you are absolutely positive that you know how to protect yourself from the danger of confusing one of them with an amanita.

Giant Puffball

Even though I've been assured that puffballs are quite safe and very fine eating, because of their association with the amanita, I've never been able to bring myself to try one.

Blueberry

Blackberry

When you set out to go berry-picking, you're on very safe ground. Wild berries are not as far apart from cultivated berries as are some wild leafy plants. A strawberry is always a strawberry, a huckleberry a huckleberry, and a grape is still a grape, indistinguishable except by its deeper color from the commercially grown varieties sold in stores. Wild cherries grow on vines instead of trees; they are a deep red, almost black. To the best of my knowledge—admittedly scanty in this instance—there are no more wild cranberries, all the bogs in which they grow now being reserved for commercial harvesting.

Go berrying with an easy mind and a light heart. Just watch out for bears if you're in the Pacific Northwest, for bears have a notorious sweet tooth and enjoy berries perhaps even more than do humans, as bears have no stores from which to buy such treats.

Nuts are not the only edibles that grow on trees. There are persimmons and somewhere there may still be a few wild pawpaw trees. Mayapples are considered edible, but I'd approach these with caution, for they have a slightly laxative effect on some individuals; you'd probably be safe eating no more than one or two. These are all soft fruits, best harvested late in the season. Traditionally, persim-

mons are not plucked for eating before they've been touched by a frost. There are also wild mulberries, but these tree-grown berries are really unworthy of notice; they have little flavor and wild mulberries are generally insect-ridden even before they ripen for picking.

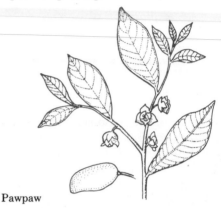

Pawpaw

Any nut which you choose to harvest in the wild is safely edible, of course, though the great stands of hickory and walnut vanished long ago. In the mountainous Southwest there are piñon nuts, and in the South a few wild pecans are to be found. I'm sure there are a number of butternut trees left, and a few of the tiny chinquapins which are all that remain to remind us of the once-plentiful chestnut trees.

Even the ubiquitous acorn is edible, if you want to take the trouble to debitter. The method of doing this is to crack the shells and boil the acorns in 5 or 6 changes of water. You can then dry them, which takes a day or two. Once dry, the acorns can be roasted to be eaten out of hand, or you can grind them up to make an acorn meal for use in bread, crackers, or cookies. The meal should be mixed with flour, for even after debittering the nut of the acorn is slightly acidic.

CACTI AND THEIR KIN

Cacti grow profusely—and are about the only plants that do grow in vast sections of uncultivated land in the desert Southwest. This huge area is loosely called desert, but in only a few places will you encounter the utterly vegetationless shifting sands that characterize the Sahara. The Great American Desert, as it was marked on early maps, is centered around the Sonoran Desert, which has its midpoint in southern Arizona and extends south deep into Mexico. To the north and east, it takes in the southern portions of Nevada and Utah, most of Arizona and western New Mexico, and a good-sized chunk of southwest Texas.

This is cactus country. In the central portion of the desert, you'll find the tall saguaro and the stubby hogshead-shaped barrel cactus, a few prickly pear, and even fewer stands of the thin spiny ocotillo. There is a variety of saguaro cacti, the pitahaya, that bears a sweet, juicy applelike fruit which is edible and is also a good source of liquid, which is needed in desert country. The barrel cacti store water in the interior, and have been the salvation of more than a few desert travelers.

Before you begin searching for these cacti, though, please note that they are close to being endangered species. cacti-rustlers, uprooting them for sale as picturesque patio and yard plants, have drastically reduced their numbers. There are stiff fines imposed now for mutilating or uprooting saguaro cacti, so unless your need for water is very real, admire them, but don't remove the fruits which contain the seeds, and don't cut into a barrel cactus just to find out if it really does hold water.

Prickly pears are another thing entirely. They aren't all that common in the central desert, but grow prolifically in a wide belt along its eastern edge, in Texas and southern New Mexico. The reddish fruit of the prickly pear is edible if you have the courage and patience to remove its spines; it's not very sweet, but does have a faint and delicate flavor. Its flat leaves yield a drinkable liquid, bitter but wet. A candy is made from the pulp of prickly pear, but the pulp itself is only a vehicle to carry the sugar used in the candy-making. Unadorned, the pulp is tarty and has little nourishment.

A close relative of cacti is the yucca, which grows very prolifically in from central Texas west to California, and north through Colorado and Wyoming, and easterly into Kansas. Only the flowers and seeds of the yucca are edible. The flower's petals can be fried or braised; the seeds are cooked vegetable-style.

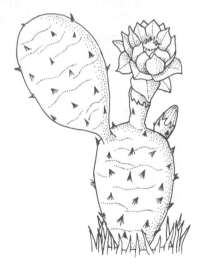

Prickly Pear

COOKING WILD FOODS

MIXED GREENS AU GRATIN

There are as many ways to cook wild greens as there are to cook the commercially grown or garden-grown kind. These few recipes are intended for home use after an outing and are given as generic methods which you can alter to suit your own taste, changing the types of greens, seasonings, or anything else that doesn't suit your fancy.

By following the cooking suggestions given with the descriptions of wild foods in the foregoing sections, you can easily determine which wild foods are suitable for camp cooking.

Wild mushrooms, asparagus, and fiddleheads require very little preparation. Mushrooms, for example, need to be parboiled very briefly, drained well, and sautéd gently in butter. Asparagus and fiddleheads are simply boiled in salted water, and fiddleheads can be eaten raw or in a salad. Chickweed, mallow, dandelion, and flavor-accenting plants such as wild onions, garlic, leeks, and chives, can be added to other dishes or to salads.

Wild greens which require a substantial amount of preparation, such as milkweed and others which are quite tarty, respond best to cooking at home, where you can mix them with greens that are a bit on the bland side, such as spinach or beet tops. Some of the more pungently flavored wild greens also need to be parboiled in several changes of water, to make them really palatable to modern palates.

To serve four, you will need four to five tightly packed cups of mixed greens, the mixture being your choice.

4 to 5 cups greens, cleaned, parboiled if necessary, and coarsely chopped
1 to 2 cups water
1 tsp salt
4 Tbsp butter
2 cups milk
2 to 3 Tbsp flour
½ tsp salt
1½ cup sharp cheddar cheese, grated coarsely
¾ cup fine cracker or dry bread crumbs
2 Tbsp butter

Put the greens in a tightly closed pot, mix water and salt, pour over the greens, and precook 10 to 15 minutes over very low heat.

Use a portion of the 4 tablespoons butter to grease a baking dish.

Melt the remaining butter in a small saucepan, blend in the flour and salt, adding the flour a bit at a time while stirring.

Drain the greens well in a colander; place them in layers on the greased baking dish, sprinkling each layer with a scant tablespoon of cheese. Reserve at least 1 cup of the cheese for the topping.

Pour the milk-flour sauce over the greens when the baking dish is filled.

Combine the remaining cheese with the crumbs and spread over the top layer of greens. Dot the top with butter. Bake in a 325-degree oven for 35 to 40 minutes.

STIR-FRIED MIXED GREENS

You can stir-fry successfully in any large skillet; a wok is not necessary, just traditional. The secret of successful stir-frying is having all ingredients ready, the sauces premixed, and the pan at a high temperature.

3 to 4 cups (packed) mixed greens
½ cup peanut oil (or other light neutral oil)
2 tsp cornstarch
1 Tbsp dry sherry
1 clove garlic
1 small slice ginger root
1 Tbsp cornstarch
2 Tbsp water
½ cup chicken or beef stock

Precooking preparations: Drain the greens thoroughly and slice them into strips about ½ to ¾ inch wide and 3 to 4 inches long. Combine the 2 teaspoons cornstarch and the 1 tablespoon sherry. Mince the garlic and ginger root. Combine the 1 tablespoon cornstarch and the 2 tablespoons water. Preheat the stock and cooking pan.

Put half the peanut oil in the heated pan, tilting the pan to cover its bottom thoroughly. Add the greens; pour over them at once the cornstarch-sherry mixture while stirring them with a wide spatula, preferably a wooden one. Cook 2 to 3 minutes.

Pull the greens to the sides of the pan, put the remaining oil in, add the garlic and ginger root. Stir-fry the greens 3 to 5 minutes more, adding the cornstarch-water mixture.

Add the stock and stir-fry 2 minutes. Remove from heat, cover the pan for 1 to 2 minutes, and serve at once.

BRAISED MIXED GREENS

As in the two preceding recipes, use any wild greens you might have, or mix several kinds for a blending of flavors.

4 to 5 cups (packed) coarsely chopped mixed greens
2 or 3 slices salt pork or bacon
1 small onion, chopped coarsely
¼ to ½ cup beef stock
   Small pinch of powdered ginger
1 to 1½ tsp salt

Prepare the greens by cleaning, parboiling if needed, and drain them on paper towels after chopping. Trim rind off the salt pork and cut it into small dice.

Sauté the pork until it is lightly browned, then add the greens a handful at a time, stirring after each addition. Add the onion. Add enough of the beef stock— about 2 tablespoons—to moisten the greens. Cover the pan and reduce heat to low. Cook 3 to 4 minutes, add more beef stock and the ginger, stir well, close the pan, and cook 3 to 4 minutes.

Taste a small piece of the greens, and add salt as needed. Because the flavor of wild greens varies so greatly in intensity at different seasons and their tenderness is never quite alike, tasting is the best and safest way to test for both salting and cooking time.

After tasting and salting, cook the greens further if necessary and serve. Hot cornbread or corn pones make a good go-with.

CATTAIL POLLEN CAKE

Cattail pollen gathers on the long spike that extends from its bulbous brownish fruit. To gather it, bend the stalk over a pan or box and shake the fruit or brush the pollen off the spike.

2 cups cattail pollen
2 cups all-purpose flour
4 tsp baking powder
1 tsp salt
2 eggs
½ cup evaporated milk
1½ cups water
1 Tbsp honey

Combine pollen, flour, baking powder, and salt. Beat the eggs lightly, combine with milk, water, and honey. Beat the dry and liquid ingredients together very gently. Pour into well-greased baking tins, bake in a preheated 400-degree oven 15 to 20 minutes.

Part 2
SURVIVAL TACTICS

It's very hard indeed today to get lost in what remains of the great American wilderness. Only on the fringes of seasonal weather changes, and only in Alaska or the Sonoran Desert country of the Southwest is there a real chance that a lost person will go unfound for longer than a few days, or in normal weather will run any great risk during the period when he or she is missing.

Portable point-to-point communications equipment, coordinated air searches, plus the increasing spread of civilization have made the individual or group lost for an extended time virtually a phenomenon of the past. Even an injured lost person is usually quite easily found. Injury is always a danger, of course. So is foul weather, especially in mountainous terrain in the late part of the summer, when unexpected storms can blow in.

When you go out on your own in strange country or during a season where sudden weather changes might take place, or bad weather is possible, carry some kind of condensed food with you. In the distant past, pemmican and jerky were the only food that could be depended on to stay edible over a long period of being carried in a pack or saddlebag. Today there are numerous ready-to-eat freeze-dried foods in foil pouches that add little weight or bulk to your load. Many of the items listed in Chapter 8 can be used as survival foods.

If you want to stick to tradition and carry pemmican, here's how to make one of several types:

PEMMICAN

2 **pounds dried venison. Put slices of venison roast in your freezer unwrapped and let the cold draw the moisture from the meat; the venison will be covered with frosty rime after a day or two, and when this rime is brushed off you will have the dried venison you need**

1 **cup seeded raisins**

1 **Tbsp honey**

2 **Tbsp chunk-style natural peanut butter (get one of the brands specifying on the label that the product's only ingredients are peanuts and salt; if this isn't on the label, the peanut butter may be as much as 20 percent lard)**

Grind the dried meat fine; pulp the raisins in a mortar or food processor. Combine meat, raisins, honey, and peanut butter. Store in plastic press-to-seal pouches. No refrigeration is needed; the pemmican should keep for 8 months to a year.

Let's assume, though, that you've gone off without tucking into your pocket any kind of emergency rations. Perhaps you started off for a short hike and got hopelessly lost. You don't know where you are, no familiar landmarks are in sight, night's coming on. You have no food, no water, and you're hungry as that proverbial bear that we met at the beginning of this chapter. What do you do about supper?

Perhaps the smartest thing you can do about supper that first night is to make up your mind to go without.

If that sounds like an unkind and unsympathetic suggestion, it really isn't. You're more interested in your predicament than your stomach, and this may make you unwary enough to eat a wild plant that could be harmful. Besides, in your present situation, water is a lot more important than food. Make eating your second priority.

Going without supper isn't going to put you on the brink of starvation. Find water first, then find a place as close to the water as you can in which you can curl up during the hour of darkness. With dark coming on, and your mind preoccupied with your predicament, you're likely to make a mistaken identification and eat something that will harm instead of nourish you.

Let's carry our fictional scenario a step further. Luck is with you, and you find a creek. In the gathering darkness, the water looks clean and safe to drink, but you can see only a short distance upstream. Before you drink, filter.

Filter? With no tools and nothing to strain the water through except a pocket handkerchief or your shirttail?

Certainly. Nature's provided the best improvised filter you can use: a foot or two of earth between you and the bed of the creek. Before it gets too dark, find a stretch of clear soil that extends 5 or 6 feet away from the bank of the stream. Dig a hole a foot or so from the water's edge, using the stub of a wind-felled branch, or loosening the soil with your knife if necessary and scooping it out with your hands.

You don't have to make a major excavation, just a hole 6 or 8 inches in diameter and deep enough to be a few inches below the level of the creek's surface. Wait a few minutes, and the hole will slowly fill with water. It'll be muddy, but be patient. Within ten or fifteen minutes the water in the hole will clear as the loose soil your digging disturbed settles to the bottom of the hole. Now you can scoop out a drink with your cupped hands. You've taken care of your first need.

In the morning, see what nature's provided for you in the way of food. There are a half-dozen wild plants that can be eaten raw. The leafy plants include chickweed, fiddleback fern, high mallow, and winter cress, or one of the other wild cresses. Just take your time in looking, examine each plant carefully, and be sure you've chosen one of the edibles. There may also be mushrooms around, and they can be eaten raw. So can nuts and berries.

One more word about tactics. If the area along the creek where you stopped for the night provides enough wild forage to sustain you for a few days, stay there. If it doesn't, move on downstream. But stay close to the creek. If searchers go out looking for you, at least one party is going to follow that creek upstream, and you'll want to be close by when rescuers arrive.

If searchers don't reach you in the first day or so, the creek will lead you to a larger stream, ultimately to a river, which in turn will lead you to civilization. But staying close to water is the best way to assure yourself that you'll have the strength to keep moving. The best picking of wild food will usually be near water, and the water itself is the one thing you can't be without too long.

Lack of water is the chief hazard to being stranded in desert country, of course. The best thing you can do is to find a sliver of shade, put out a marker—any bright-colored piece of gear or cloth that will stand out in sharp contrast to its surroundings—to guide air searchers to you. Then, get back to your sliver of shade and lie still. At dusk, when the air begins to cool, investigate any cacti in the vicinity, especially those species listed earlier as being sources of moisture.

There is a hazard to some ponds in the desert Southwest; the hazard is alkali. Although most of these poison ponds have long ago been found and marked, if you stumble onto a pond which has no foliage growing around it, don't drink the water. Alkali is as unfriendly to plant life as it is to people and animals. Most wild animals can identify alkali water, so don't look for skeletal remains to help you in identifying these ponds.

A desert pond which has safe water will nine times out of ten have some kind of vegetation in or around it. This may be in the form of a scummy unappetizing moss on and in the water, but as unappetizing as it is, the moss is a sign of safety. So are the droppings of birds and animals around the waterhole. In some parts of the Western desert country these safe-water ponds are called wells, but don't expect them to look like a well of old oaken-bucket fame. Wells generally won't have much vegetation growing near them, for most of these waterholes are in rock formations which won't support plant life.

Desert-wise travelers know how to make solar stills, and many whose business takes them into the desert carry the needed equipment with them.

There's no trick to making such a still. You need a doubled 3-by-3-foot square of plastic film; preferably it will be the dense black polyethylene film widely used in agriculture. Before sundown, dig a 2-foot-square hole about 8 inches deep,

and spread the plastic, doubled, over the hole. Use rocks or sand to weight down the edges. In the morning, a small amount of water will have been condensed on the bottom side of the upper piece of plastic and will have drained into the bottom piece. A still of this kind won't yield much water, but it will provide enough to keep you from getting totally dehydrated.

Whether you're stranded in the mountains, in a forest, or on the desert, always follow the basic survival rules: Move as little as possible. Stay close to a source of water; you can live two weeks without food, but only two or three days without water. Above all, keep calm. Somebody will find you a lot sooner than you think.

III

COOKING FISH AND GAME

12 EQUIPMENT AND UTENSILS

In this section, we won't be talking about camp cooking, but about preparing in the familiar surroundings of your home kitchen the trophies of your hunts or your harvests of the waters. When you cook a meal in camp and it falls short of your expectations, you can always blame a wind-blown bed of coals or a falling barometer or some other vagary of nature. On your own home grounds, you want everything to be perfect.

Coming right down to the bare bones of the matter, cooking game at home gives you a built-in advantage, whether the game is furred or feathered. The advantage is that the meat being cooked has been allowed to age for at least a few days, and the table-flavor of every wild animal or bird with which I'm familiar improves with aging.

Fish aren't included in this sweeping generalization, of course. The perfect way to handle a fish destined for the table is to wrench the hook out of its mouth, clean it while running as fast as you can to a wait-ing bed of coals, and pop the fish into the pan while it's still wriggling. A bit further along we'll get to the specifics of aging game birds and animals and keeping fish fresh for cooking. Right now, we've gotten off the trail of our discussion of kitchen equipment suited for or required for game and fish cooking, so perhaps we'd better get with it.

POTS, PANS, AND KITCHEN RANGES

If you have an average selection of good-quality cooking utensils, you quite probably have just about everything you need to handle any type of game cooking. A little bit of improvising might be required for some dishes, depending on the kind of

216

game or fish you're going to cook, or the style in which you want to prepare it, but improvising is a challenge in itself.

A fish poacher, for example, is a fairly expensive and quite specialized piece of equipment which will only gather dust and take up space unless you cook a lot of fish. Improvise a poacher by using a roasting pan with a row of small pieces of tableware, forks, or spoons, to hold the fish above the bottom of the pan.

Your basic needs for game cooking are the same as those for any other kind of dishes. You need a couple of good skillets, large and small roasting pans, and two or three saucepans of different sizes. A shallow roasting pan which will accommodate a haunch of venison or a lineup of such small game as squirrels or rabbits or quail will come in handy. So will a big stockpot, in which a massive stew can be prepared. Covers should certainly be provided for all utensils, as one of the secrets of game cookery is slow moist sautéing or roasting in a closed pan at low heat.

This battery of cast-iron utensils does a splendid job with virtually any type of fish or game. The Dutch oven, of course, is just the ticket for preparing soups, stews, chowders, roasts, or fowl. The skillet is a never-ending friend when it comes to frying fish or preparing steaks or chops. The long cast-iron tanker is ideal for deep-frying fish, but it also can be used for poaching or baking.

Using a basket or holder of this kind simplifies the job of cooking fish on a grill. Oil the basket before putting in the fish, then merely lay it on the grill. These gadgets allow you to turn the fish without having them stick to the grill rods.

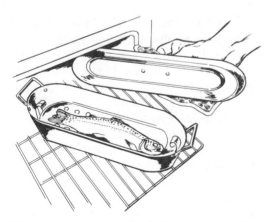

Fish poachers are generally made of copper, stainless steel, and sometimes aluminum. The one you select should have a lid, heavy-duty handles at each end, and an insert rack for lowering fish into the cauldron and then lifting them back out again.

There are a number of fancy earthenware utensils that have been widely promoted for game cookery, but in my experience, single-purpose utensils for game and fish cookery don't really earn their storage space. They're used perhaps four or five times a year, game laws and limits being what they are today. You're better off with an all-purpose casserole that has a well-fitted cover than with a baking dish moulded to accept only a duck or a rabbit carcass.

You will want a mixing bowl or two, and some little oddments such as storage containers that can be sealed tightly. But for the most part, the same utensils that serve you well every day are just as suitable for cooking game as they are for other foods. More to the point, you'll feel more at home with well-used utensils than you would if you reserve special pots and pans for game and use them only rarely.

Becoming intimately acquainted with the characteristics of a piece of kitchen equipment is a matter of using it over a long period of time. Everyone who cooks has acquired strong preferences for certain types of utensils and other kitchen tools. In the past few years there's been a veritable Mount St. Helens eruption of new cookware, but that doesn't mean your familiar old standbys must be tosed away in favor of something new.

So far, the eruption of new products hasn't produced any new items which are superior to tin-lined or aluminum-lined copperware, solid cast aluminum (not *pressed* aluminum, which warps), stainless steel, colorful and practical enamelware utensils such as those made by Le Cruset and Dansk, and plain old-time ugly unadorned cast iron. All these materials are time-tested and dependable, as are stoneware, tempered glass, porcelain, and other vitreous or earthenware baking utensils. In cooking game as well as in cooking anything else, it's not so much *what* you use as it is how familiar you are with the characteristics of the cookware you select for a given dish.

Heavy-duty kettles like this are chiefly designed for making boiled fish or "poor man's lobster," neither names justifying the excellent eating. But you can also put a trout kettle to many other uses as well, such as preparing copious amounts of fish chowder. The inset pan at the top even allows you to steam crabs and other shellfish.

Remember that the axiom of familiarity also applies to such utensils as electric skillets and crock pots. It even extends to the kitchen range, though the heat source is not a matter of primary concern. No single heat source—electricity, gas, coal, wood—is the key to good cooking. Your instant understanding of what a range does at a given temperature setting is what counts.

Long before I ever had a thought of doing any cooking myself one of the finest cooks at whose table I've ever eaten made a remark which I've always remembered. Mrs. Kate Wagenfehr was brought up in Germany and carried old-country ways to the kitchen of the boardinghouse she ran. Her huge kitchen had two ranges, one a massive wood-burner which was used in winter, the other a gas range for use in the hot days of a South Texas summer.

During the transition period between the seasons, cooking was shifted from one range to the other, depending on the day's temperature. During this transition time, I heard one of the kitchen helpers complain about the wood-burner, calling it an old-fashioned, lazy stove. "No," Mrs. Wagenfehr replied in her soft voice which still retained a trace of her native tongue. "Such a thing as a lazy stove there is not. Is only lazy cooks."

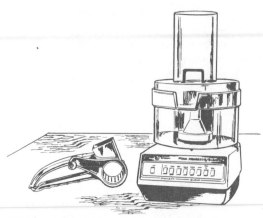

When cooking outdoor-style at home, a food processor can perform an infinite variety of tasks.

APPLIANCES AND ACCESSORIES

When the kitchen-sized food processor appeared a few years ago, more than the old hand-cranked meat grinder bit the dust. Of course, grinder attachments had long been available for most full-sized power mixers, but for the most part they were difficult to attach and troublesome to clean. The food processor's versatility, streamlined components, and the ease of storing and cleaning them had instant appeal.

Now, with blender attachments appearing for some food processors, and with more powerful hand-held mixers appearing, it seems that in most kitchens the number of electrical helpers of this kind can be safely reduced to two.

To me, a food processor-blender combination and a hand-held mixer with enough power to turn dough hooks are all the electric-powered helpers any kitchen needs.

In terms of game cookery, the processor makes easy the preparation of pâtés and terrines, both of which provide a salutary end-use for awkward scraps resulting from butchering. Pâtés and terrines are very nice game dishes in their own right and also stretch the limited quantity of wild meats far beyond the conventional roast and chops and rack.

Similarly, the hand-held mixer with dough hooks—the only one with which I'm personally acquainted is the Mouli, but I'm sure there are others—allows the quick composition in small quantities of the doughs and pastes which are a traditional part of many game dishes.

This doesn't mean I'm suggesting that you dash out and buy either of these appliances, if you don't already own them. Anything you do with either can be done as well by hand. Of course, preparing the dishes will take a bit more time, and you'll be using your own muscles in their preparation instead of adding to the profits of your friendly local power monopoly. Even so, if you do have such appliances, don't let them sit idle. Use them.

KITCHEN TOOLS

Let's dispose quickly of the tools other than knives and leave them for the last. Game and fish cookery do not require a troublesome clutter of kitchen gadgets. Heading the list is a meat thermometer, followed by a siphon-type baster.

As already noted, the flesh of game birds and animals is dry and close-grained, and even small game animals such as squirrels need a bit of aging before they are cooked. So do game birds. While aging softens the tissues of game meats, the process also removes more of the scant supply of moisture they contain.

An overdone roast or steak cut from soft feedlot-fattened beef is edible, even if not especially enjoyable, but overcooking game is a cardinal sin. Remember, the cooking times with which you're most familiar are based on your everyday cooking, and the timing which works for beef doesn't apply to game. The only sure way to cook game is by using a meat thermometer.

Basting, which also keeps game meats moist and flavorful, is also essential to the cooking process. Basting with a spoon is time-consuming and inefficient. If

you don't have a syphon baster, get one and use it. Be sure to get one of the better models, with a bulb of long-lasting synthetic rubber and a tube of glass or stainless steel, and be sure that bulb and tube can be separated easily for quick, effortless cleaning. Use the baster when cooking roasts and all small game animals cooked whole, such as squirrels and rabbits, and any type of game bird which is cooked whole.

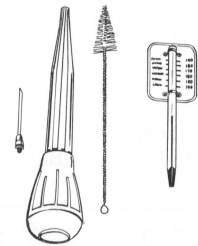

A meat thermometer and a siphon-type baster are two accessories that are almost indispensable to preparing game in the kitchen. Baster has a cleaning brush and a needle for injecting flavorings deep into a roast or bird.

When preparing sauces and gravies, your indispensable tool is the chef's whisk. It is in many cases better to use a whisk in blending a sauce than to use a power mixer or blender. In some recipes, a sauce is quite literally beaten to death by a power mixer.

A whisk is an oblong wire gadget which resembles an elongated birdcage. They range in size from enormous to tiny, and something in the mid-range is your best bet. Whisks are inexpensive, and it's a good idea to have two or three of them, the small 6-inch size, an intermediate 8-inch size, and a larger 12-inch model. With the three, you'll be ready to handle any whipping-up job from a single egg to a huge cauldron of wild turkey gravy.

Whisks are handy for whipping up batters, sauces, basting mixes. Since they're so versatile, and so inexpensive, every cook should have several sizes.

You'll need a kitchen fork and spoon. The fork needs to be sturdy, something which you can slide into the cavity of a bird as big as a turkey and lift it out of the pan, and at the same time its tines should be delicate enough to anchor small pieces of raw meat while a stew is being prepared. The spoon, in addition to being used for tasting, may be immersed in hot gravy or sauce for a long period of stirring,

so look for one with an insulated handle, or get a good wooden spoon or two.

While on the subject of wooden kitchenware, there's another handy piece of gear that you might like to know about, one easier for most people to handle than a wooden mallet, yet equally necessary when the meat from a tough old buck or a boar-bear must be tenderized by beating.

Salmon fishermen and deep-sea anglers call the tool a "priest." How the priest earned its name is lost in very ancient angling lore, but the priest is simply a billy club or small baseball bat. Those used by salmon fishermen are 8 to 10 inches long and about 1¼ inches in diameter at the head; the saltwater version is 12 to 14 inches long and about 2 inches in diameter at the head. The priest is traditionally used to give a big, flopping fish the coup de grace, but it's also a superior meat tenderizer.

Today's most popular tenderizing mallet is made from cast aluminum, with one smooth face and one corrugated face. I don't recommend the use of this metal mallet, for no matter which face of the head is used, it tears the meat fibers rather than just spreading and softening them. The result is that the small amount of moisture which wild meats contain is lost at once when cooking begins, instead of remaining trapped in the flesh.

It's this natural moisture that not only contributes a great deal to the meat's flavor, but keeps it from cooking into a dry hard slab about as appetizing as a cedar shingle. If you insist on using a mallet, use one with a wooden head. However, I'd suggest that you get a priest, for it weighs much less than a mallet, which makes it much easier to wield, and when using it you can't strike hard enough to tear and mangle the meat.

A good substitute for a priest is a European-style wooden rolling pin. You'll need a rolling pin anyway, and for the small quantities of dough that game dishes call for, the European style is fine. In game cookery, about the biggest quantity of dough you'll encounter will be that used to cover a terrine, or for a batch of noodles. The small-diameter European-style rolling pin isn't really the most efficient tool for general baking, because for rolling out a large quantity of dough you need a pin with a bigger diameter.

A pair of kitchen shears will pay their way many times over, so invest in a good pair with sturdy 6-inch corrugated blades. At times you'll run into snipping jobs that defeat a knife. Finally, be a big spender when it comes to stocking up on skewers of all sizes. These aren't the kind of skewers you use for cooking *en brochette,* but the small kinds used in trussing. No kitchen where game is cooked ever had enough skewers of assorted sizes. Get some in each length, 3, 5, and 8 inches and a roll of stout lintless twine to use with them.

KNIVES

Now we've come to the subject of knives. Over the years, I've used just about every kind of knife there is, from hunting knives with hand-forged and tempered blades that I've made myself on through pocketknives and penknives to kitchen knives with blades of a half-dozen different kinds of steel in all the traditional contours and a few that were anything but orthodox.

Perhaps the most valuable advice I can pass on to you about kitchen knives is to shun those which you see advertised as being of a new shape or design which is the biggest boon to cooking since steel met whetstone.

Knives have been used since the Stone Age, a matter of 600,000 to 700,000 years ago, give or take a century or two. In such a span of time, certainly every shape of blade that the fertile human imagination can create has been used, at least experimentally. The shapes that have proved most efficient have survived, and they are the traditional shapes we use today. Those new shapes so often touted are generally nothing more than the rediscovery of a shape first used in the Dark Ages or Middle Ages and abandoned because it wasn't as practical as the half-dozen traditional blade contours which have survived almost unchanged through the centuries.

Since stainless steel first began to be used for blades, a continuing argument has been going on as to its virtues relative to high carbon steel. If you've missed the discussions, they can be summarized in one long sentence. Stainless steel includes in its composition a quantity of nickel, which is classed as a soft metal, in comparison to high carbon steel. Consequently, knives with stainless blades do not take as keen an edge or hold it as long as do those of carbon steel.

When used in connection with knives, "stainless" is really a misleading term, for some stainless steels do stain and rust, while a well-used blade of carbon steel soon acquires a patina that makes it both stain- and rust-resistant after a short period of use. Carbon-steel knives might not look as pretty as those having stainless-steel blades, but they cut a lot better and need sharpening less frequently.

Steel's ability to take and hold an edge is measured on the Rockwell Scale, abbreviated "R." For purposes of comparison, surgeon's scalpels are made of stainless steel with an R-rating of 60–64. Files and other metal-cutting tools are R-rated in the 60–63 range. The finest woodworking edge tools such as the blades of carpenter's planes and wood chisels also rate R60–63. However, metals with such high ratings are brittle, and a knife-blade must be flexible. A good carbon steel knife normally rates R56–58, and the best stainless blades should match this rating.

Don't be bashful in asking about the Rockwell rating of any knife you're thinking of buying. Because the R-rating of the best carbon-steel knives has been in the R56–58 range for many, many years, knives of this metal don't usually carry a manufacturer's rating. Stainless blades of such high quality are fairly new, and their manufacturers generally advertise the fact that their products can meet R56–58 standards.

Leading European cutlery-makers are Henckel, Twin-Werke, and Sabatier. There are others, but I mention these because knives of this manufacture which I've been using since the 1940s are still in my kitchen knife rack today. The handles are worn a bit, but the blades still take and hold a fine edge. What's more important, I know exactly what they'll do—they fit my hand.

Most knives designed for the kitchen, though, are a bit too delicate for use in camp. In most camps, knives are borrowed and loaned pretty freely, and one of the best investments in camp gear that you can make is a set of knives that will stand up to rough use. The camp knives in my necessary box were made by Old Hickory, and the newest has been used for a bit over 20 years.

There are many special-purpose knives, used in carving and in professional butcher shops. However, for home kitchen use, you can limit your needs to four; the butcher knife, the utility knife, the chef's knife, and the paring knife. In a pinch, you can even sacrifice the butcher knife, though in game cookery where some butcher-cuts are almost always required, a butcher knife is a handy tool to have.

Butcher knives have blades which widen to an abrupt semicircular arc at the tip. They have heavy backbones, which keep the blades rigidly straight when you're cutting chops from a rack of ribs or steaks from a haunch of venison. They also have tips that can handle better than other knives such jobs as disjointing and prying up sinews. A good butcher knife has enough weight and heft to be used as a cleaver, but we'll get into cleavers a bit later, for even the best butcher knife won't do a cleaver's work. Butcher knives are available in lengths from 8 to 12 inches. An 8-inch knife will handle the jobs encountered in the average kitchen.

A utility knife is as important in any kitchen as the knives designed for specific jobs. It's the kitchen's Mr. Handy. The utility knife should have a gently curved blade and a rigid back so that it can do duty as a butcher knife in a pinch; it should be short and flexible enough to be used as a boning knife; narrow enough in the blade to be used as a filleting knife; light enough to substitute for a paring knife. The utility knives illustrated are made by Henckel and Old Hickory, and some shops may classify them as boning knives. If I was allowed to have only one

Don't scrimp when it comes to cutlery. Buy the best you can afford and it will not only last a lifetime but provide superior performance all the while.

knife in my kitchen, this would be the one I'd choose.

Next comes the chef's knife. Its blade is triangular, a gently curving taper. It will handle slicing and trimming jobs and a few others as well, but its chief usefulness is in dicing, cubing meats, and similar tasks. Chef's knives range in length from 6 inches, which is too short, to 12 inches and even 14-inch monsters, which are too long and too heavy for use in any but a professional's hands. An 8-inch blade is about right for a home kitchen.

Finally, there's the cook's friend in tight places, the paring knife. Unlike the other three essential kitchen knives, a paring knife's blade may have any of several shapes, for this is the most personal of any of the quartet. While the paring knife's name describes its primary function, which is removing peels or rinds from fruits and vegetables, there are also

a number of other jobs for which it is used.

Coring such fruits as apples, slitting orange skins to produce zest, nipping out deeply set eyes from potatoes, parting the twine on a rolled roast, removing membranes from such meats as kidneys and liver, separating the flesh from the bones of poultry, scoring the lead collar on the neck of a wine bottle—these are just a few of the dozens of small kitchen chores which a paring knife does better than any other.

Consequently, a paring knife may have a blade in any of several different shapes. Some paring knives have blades quite similar to utility knives, only scaled down to a length of 2 or 3 inches. Others may have blades only ¾ to 1 inch long, with contours which vary from oval-shape to a miniature version of the blade of a chef's knife. The paring knife is one which you may want to duplicate in your kitchen battery, to provide a variety of blades, each of which performs different jobs superbly well, saving you a great deal of time and effort.

Winding up your battery of kitchen cutlery is the cleaver. Use it for heavy chopping jobs unsuited to even the heaviest of your knives, such as splitting the backbone of a duck or pheasant and cracking the bones of animals to reach their marrow. Use the side of the blade instead of a priest or a mallet to flatten out pieces of meat which are to be rolled, or to break down tough fibers and tenderize the flesh of large game animals. Incidentally, because cleavers must not be in the least brittle, don't look for them to have high R-ratings; something in the range of 48–50 is very good indeed.

A butcher's steel or its equivalent is essential to keep knives in peak condition. Keep your steel handy and use it often, for it will save muscles and avoid the need to resort to the whetstone oftener than once every six months or so. Fairly new on the cutlery market are ceramic rods and rods impregnated with diamond dust which will keep a knife in just as keen cutting condition as does the heavy steel, which some find difficult to use. These miniature edgers are especially handy for keeping the edges of small knives in cutting trim.

Don't keep your knives loose in a drawer. Provide a slotted holder or a magnetic bar for storage, so that the edges you've worked so hard to give them won't be dulled by the utensils with which they come into contact when stored in a drawer.

A BASIC PANTRY

To make another large generalization, you should need very little more than you would normally carry as basic kitchen supplies to fill your needs for fish and game cookery.

In my cookbook, basic means such kitchen indispensables as all-purpose flour, cornmeal, liquid and solid shortenings, baking powder, baking soda, vinegar (including wine vinegars), salt, pepper. The list would also include a good assortment of herbs and spices and a few liquid seasoning sauces—soy and Worcestershire and Tabasco.

To be a bit more specific in the area of herbs and spices, fish and game cookery lay a heavier stress on some kinds that you may not encounter frequently enough in everyday recipes to justify keeping them on hand. For example, juniper berries are often called for in game dishes, though rarely in those you might be called on to prepare at other times. The more assertive flavors such as oregano, dill, and a few others are also specified with greater frequency than you might expect, so as a precaution, be sure to check your seasoning shelf against your recipe's requirements before you start cooking.

Because successful fish and game cookery depend on wine both as a tenderizing and flavoring agent, you'll want to have on hand a reasonably complete assortment of both white and red wines as well as the fortified wines, sherry, port, and Madeira.

Let's be clear on one point before getting into a brief discussion of wines used in cooking. By this, I most certainly am not referring to the few wines labeled "Cooking Wine," which still can be seen occasionally on grocery store shelves. These are the last of Carrie Nation's chickens, spawned in a long-dead and almost forgotten time when a handful of well-meaning but misguided reformers stampeded a nation into what we now somewhat abashedly call the Prohibition Era.

Wines carrying this label are simply regular wines to which salt has been added to make them unpalatable for drinking. They will make your game dishes taste terrible if you try to use them. If you by any chance happen to have a bottle of this kind of wine on hand, carry it gently to the nearest bathroom and flush its sins away. You will be giving it better treatment than it deserves.

There was a time before inflation became a constant factor in even small everyday matters when the pleasant custom and accepted cooking practice was to use in a dish being prepared the same wine with which it would be served. Today, even modest varietal wines have risen to prices few ever thought they would reach; even current vintage wines are quite expensive and wines bearing great vintage labels have gone up astronomically.

Given the cost of varietal and vintage wines, the custom of cooking a dish with the wine that will be served to accompany it at dinner can be followed only if you have a bank account that is inexhaustible or share the private pipeline to the U.S. Treasury enjoyed by members of Congress and the federal bureaucracy.

Fortunately, U.S. vintners began improving the quality of their jug wines at about the time the cost of living index began its upward spiral. The chemicalized, off-flavored horrors that once filled so many jugs have all but vanished; you will rarely encounter a bad jug wine today as long as you stay with the products of the better domestic wineries, which I'll list in alphabetical order to avoid favoritism: Almaden, Beaulieu, Beringer, Inglenook, Italian Swiss, Paul Masson, Mondavi, Rossi, Taylor.

All these houses have basic or generic jug wines: burgundy, rhine, chablis, chianti. Most of them also have varietal vintage bottlings which match closely enough the character of their jug wines to give you adequate elbow room to follow the old axiom of serving at table the same wine used in cooking. In actual fact, you're better off using sound domestic wines rather than the cheap and widely televised imports, which are quite often of a quality inferior to the better domestic jug wines.

If your recipe calls for such fortified wines as sherry, port, Madeira, or Malaga, you'll have to look to the imports. Although a few of the domestic sherries and ports are of good quality, they do not yet match the depth of flavor of the older European labels. This is true also of brandies and cognacs. Jersey applejack does not equal calvados, nor does domestic brandy equate with cognac. If a recipe requires a liqueur, you'll do well to use the liqueur specified instead of trying to locate a less costly domestic substitute.

For the most part, though, unless you are entertaining a certified cordon bleu chef or a registered gourmet, use jug wine in your cooking and save those vintage bottles for the table.

13 PREPARING FISH FOR THE TABLE

At the beginning of Chapter 10, you might remember having read this: "The perfect way to handle a fish destined for the table is to wrench the hook out of its mouth, clean it while running as fast as you can to a waiting bed of coals, and drop the fish into the pan while it's still wriggling."

That was not a misguided effort to be humorous. Please take the admonition to heart, for it's the best advice I can give you about handling your catch. The quicker you cook a fish after it leaves the water, the better that fish will taste.

Unfortunately, it's seldom possible to get fish into the pan as quickly as I've suggested, even when you're camped close to your favorite fishing hole. When you want to save your catch to cook at home, you've obviously got to clean and preserve the fish for a few hours, perhaps even a few days. It's axiomatic that the better job you do in handling the fish after they come out of the water, the better they'll taste when they're cooked.

There are some simple things you can and should do to lessen the adverse impact of that time lag between water and table. Some of these things should be done to them at the time you land a fish; others have to do with its treatment in preparation for cooking. You probably know the steps required to keep your catch in the best possible shape during that transition time from fish to food, but there are a lot of fishermen who don't, so that's why this chapter's included.

FRESHWATER FISH

First, keep your fish alive just as long as it's possible to do so. If you're fishing from the bank or from a boat, the best way to do this is to use a live-basket. A live-basket is a telescoping container made of wire mesh and fitted with a snap top. These baskets collapse for carrying into a flat circle that takes up very little more space in your gear than a pie pan.

By tying a length of rope on the handle, you can submerge a live-basket in the water where you're bank-fishing or hang one over the side of a boat if you're afloat. Fish will live in a live-basket as long as you don't tow it behind a fast-moving boat or leave it out of the water for more than a few minutes at a time. It's impossible to tell you the precise safety margin you have, because each time you lift a live-basket out of the water you'll be facing a different set of circumstances. The species of fish, the water and air temperatures, heat of the day, all play a part in setting the safety margin.

An alternative to a live-basket is a snap-locking stringer. These are made by attaching snap-locking hooks to a short length of chain or rope. When you put a fish on this type of stringer, be sure to hook it only through the lower lip so the fish's gills will keep functioning normally. If you pass the snap-hook through both lips, the fish can't work its gills to breathe and will suffocate very quickly.

Fish will also suffocate if you drag the stringer behind a fast-moving boat, so when changing location the stringer should be pulled into the boat and tossed back over the side as soon as you've stopped. What's true of a live-basket is also true of a stringer; you can leave a stringer of fish out of the water for a limited time and they'll stay alive. But the same factors that determine the safety margin for a live-basket apply to fish on a stringer; the length of time they can be kept out of the water and live depends on water and air temperature and heat.

The most popular interim fish-storage methods (before the catch goes into your camping cooler or refrigerator) are stringers, creels, and wire fish baskets. When stringing fish, secure a snap through the lower jaw only. When using a creel, add a handful of damp moss or ferns so breezes will cause evaporation and render a cooling effect. Wire fish baskets are usually hung over the side of a boat, or from a dock or pier; when you bring in a fish, merely drop it through the wide-mouth opening at the top. To remove fish from the basket, open the lid at the very bottom.

If you're fishing while wading a stream or the shallows at the edge of a lake, the best way to carry fish and keep them in good condition—alive, that is—is to sling a creel over your shoulder and carry your fish in it.

If at all possible, keep the bottom two-thirds of the creel submerged most of the time. Fish will stay alive in a creel if it isn't kept out of water longer than 5 to 10 minutes at a stretch and if the fish aren't crowded in too closely. After a creel of fish has been out of the water, the fish must be allowed time to restore their oxygen supply. This means keeping two-thirds of the creel submerged for several minutes between the times when it's lifted out of the water, in the shallows, or when you change position.

We're talking now about the traditional creel, a stiff, curved basket made from willow twigs. There are newer basket-type creels made of plastic molded to imitate willow shoots, and these are about as satisfactory as those made from willow if there are spaces in the sides and bottom that will allow water to enter the creel freely when it's dunked.

Please don't confuse the rigid-sided creel with the floppy plastic bags that are called creels today, for the plastic bag and a genuine creel have nothing at all in common except that both will contain fish. Sheet-plastic bags are impervious to air and water alike and should never even be looked at, much less used. Nor should a built-in plastic-lined pouch in the lower back of a fishing jacket be considered as a creel.

Using either of these is the easiest way I can think of to ruin your catch. A live fish transferred from its cool aquatic home into a tightly closed plastic container on either a hot or very warm day will die within minutes. If you leave an ungutted fish in such a container—sometimes for as little as an hour—you'll almost certainly have a spoiled fish on your hands. Even if you've taken the precaution of cleaning the fish before dropping it in the bag, you run the risk that the fish will begin to spoil before it can be cooked.

Both types of these misnamed creels suffocate fish quickly, so the kindest thing to do is to kill any fish you intend to put into one of these junior-grade abominations. A quick blow at the base of the fish's head with the butt of your fishing knife will do the job, or you can tap the same spot with a stone, or hold the fish by the bottom of its body and whap the base of its head across a boulder.

Both freshwater and saltwater fish have the fastest-working digestive systems nature has yet devised. Unlike human digestive systems, which convert food to nourishment and distribute that nourishment to the body from the stomach, a fish's digestive system converts food to liquid in the stomach and distributes the nourishment contained in the liquid from the fish's intestines. A fish's digestive juices are so brutally efficient that when the normal digestive cycle is stopped by death, the digestive juices left in the stomach will digest its walls.

As long as the fish is alive, it is immune to its own digestive juices, but that immunity ends the instant it dies. Within a matter of minutes, those juices begin to work on the fish's innards. Fecal matter in the stomach and intestines are carried with the leaking digestive acids into the flesh of the fish as soon as even a tiny opening has been eaten in the stomach wall. Result: an inedible fish. If it'll make you feel any better, small fish spoil faster than big ones.

Fishy story? No, indeed. Before I learned better, I've had it happen to fish I was carrying in my creel. More than once I've seen this happen to fish allowed to lie on the bank waiting to be cleaned. At different times and places when fishing from the bank, I've watched anglers next to me bring in a fish and toss it on the bank and leave it unattended too long. They'd let the fish stay there while they lighted a cigarette and had a beer and visited with their friends along the shore before baiting up and making their next cast.

By the time all this had taken place, they'd gotten used to the fish lying on the bank by them. The fish, of course, had stopped flopping and breathed its last long ago, and I'm sure the fishermen believed they didn't have to worry about it lying there. After all, the fish was dead; it wasn't going to get away. No need to clean it until later. What they were really doing, of course, was letting the fish self-destruct.

Each time I had this happen, I'd wait a few minutes before asking my streamside neighbor if he intended to clean the fish before it spoiled. Each time I was either ignored or got a short and snappy reply, to the effect that they'd clean the fish when they got around to it.

Now, another man's fish isn't really my concern, so I'd look now and then at the fish, and sure enough, the belly would begin to wrinkle and a dark spot would appear on it, growing steadily bigger while the fish was digesting itself. I never could really feel sorry for the knuckle-headed angler who let this happen; all I could think about was the wasted, inedible fish.

Don't keep freshly caught fish in a bucket or tub filled with water, either, unless you're willing to aerate the water regularly. Just dip out a bucketful, and pour in a bucketful of fresh water while you hold the bucket high enough to agitate the water in the tub. Fish get oxygen from the water just as humans do from the air. A human will live only a short time in a completely air-tight room, and a fish can't live after it's exhausted all the oxygen from the water in a pail or tub in which it's being kept.

To repeat: if you don't have a way to keep your fish alive, kill and clean them the instant they come out of the water.

In cool country, you can safely keep fish overnight in a willow creel hung up on a tree limb where the cool night breeze will blow through it. Of course, fish being carried in or kept in any kind of container should be cleaned first.

Don't wash them after cleaning, though. Dry them with a cloth or paper towel after they've been cleaned, or with a handful of clean dry grass. Live fish have a coating similar to mucus over their bodies. This coating dries quickly when a fish dies, then if water touches the fish the mucus returns and forms a slick coating on the dead fish, making them hard to handle.

If you're bank-fishing, you can carry a small refrigerator bag, one of the type insulated with lightweight fiberglass. Carry a small piece of dry ice in the bag, and your fish will stay cold and fresh while you carry them home. This kind of carrier is equally useful to boat or wading fishermen. Be sure the dry ice is wrapped, by the way, for if it comes into direct contact with fish for even a short time it will burn their flesh.

Even more efficient than a refrigerator bag is a small camp ice chest. A relatively small piece of dry ice will keep a good string of fish fresh for several days, if you keep the chest closed. I've carried fish for a week in just such a chest, across the hot Southwestern desert country, and when cooked they tasted as though they'd just come out of the water. Even regular ice will keep fish fresh for several days, as long as it's replenished regularly.

Lacking either a refrigerator bag or chest, if you're camping out on a fishing trip, and want to carry some fish home, use your sleeping bag or blankets to insulate them. Wrap the fish in several layers of paper and if possible wrap the paper in foil or plastic wrapping that won't let dampness seep through to your bedding. Keep the bundle containing the fish in the passenger compartment of your car, never in the trunk, and try to keep it out of the sun as you travel.

Cleaning your fish as soon as possible guarantees their freshness. In warm weather, don't even wait until you get home; clean your fish right at the lake, remembering of course to properly dispose of the cleanings rather than leaving them laying on the shoreline.

SALTWATER FISH

Saltwater fish seem to me to be much less prone to spoil quickly when stranded in the air than do freshwater species. Let me add immediately that I'm not presenting this little nugget of information as a scientific fact. To be perfectly truthful, this thought just occurred to me while thinking back over my own experiences in keeping the saltwater fish I've taken in prime eating condition. I haven't yet had a chance to discuss it in detail with an aquatic biologist, but my memory is pretty good where fishing is concerned.

Luckily, I had good teachers when I began ocean fishing. A number of the men who were generous in sharing their knowledge with a saltwater novice had fished offshore commercially, and most of them

Saltwater fish are not quite so susceptible to quick spoilage as freshwater species, but it's nevertheless wise to kill them, clean them, and ice them as soon as possible.

still preferred fish to steak. As a matter of routine they kept their catches in good eating condition. What I learned was to kill a keeper at once and get it into the shade, if we were in the middle of a good run. Later, when activity slacked off, the fish would be cleaned, but scaling was always deferred until the fish had been dead for a couple of hours. I can't recall ever having had a fish spoil, even after several hours lying in a boat.

After convincing myself that my memory hadn't been playing tricks, the thought occurred to me that saltwater fish must run the risk of being stranded by tidal activity, and that because of this nature has provided them with a built-in protection which allows them to survive out of the water longer than will their freshwater cousins.

This may or may not be the reason. It might be that saltwater fish stay alive out of water longer because they're usually bigger and more rugged than most freshwater types. Whatever the reason, you can count on saltwater fish to stay in better condition out of their environment than do the freshwater species. But they do need to be cleaned fairly soon, though their deterioration is measured in hours rather than minutes.

When you're fishing offshore in a party boat, you'll notice that if the boat doesn't have a live-well, crewmen will kill and gut keeper fish as soon as they're brought in and put them in the coolest spot available. If you're in your own boat, you've probably learned to carry a tarp with which to cover the fish you bring in, and to clean them as soon as possible after they're off the gaff or out of the landing net.

Some saltwater fish—tuna, for instance—have very small stomachs in relation to their size, and their intestines are virtually a straight line that discharges at once what isn't assimilated by the fish's body. Fish with this kind of straight-line digestive system empty their stomachs so fast that they don't begin to spoil as quickly as those which have slow-working stomachs and a sizeable intestinal tract.

If you're wondering how commercial fishermen keep their catches fresh, the answer's quite simple. First, like the newer party boats, the newer commercial offshore fishing boats have good refrigeration facilities. On older boats, when a netful of fish is brought up from the cold depths and dumped into the hold, the huge mass of fish quickly chills the air below decks. In effect, the fish themselves provide refrigeration adequate to keep the hold cold during the short time before the boat gets back to port. Even so, a fish that you buy from a market never tastes quite as good as one that's been out of the water for less than the time taken in moving the fish from boat to wholesale dealer to retailer.

One advantage the saltwater angler has over his freshwater counterpart is that offshore fishing boats usually leave from a port where flash-freezing can be done the instant their catch is unloaded. Freshwater fishermen don't often have this service, and with the growing scarcity of local ice-making plants, the freshwater angler must use other methods of keeping in fresh condition the fish he wants to take home.

A portable ice chest will do a good job of keeping fish in good condition for a day. Many auto service stations and all hotels and motels of any size have ice-making machines and can provide cubes to fill the ice chest if the ice you brought

When using a cooler for onboard fish storage, always lay fish on top of the ice and periodically open the cooler's draincock. This way, fish won't soak in meltwater and have their flavor ruined.

To transport fish home by car, clean them and freeze them solidly in meal-size portions. Then stack them tightly in a styrofoam cooler surrounded by shredded newspaper. Fish packed this way will remain frozen for 18 to 24 hours, depending upon the air temperature.

from home has melted. The fish should be cleaned the instant they're out of the water, of course.

If home is a long way off, and you have enough good fish to justify a stop of a few hours, any home refrigerator to which you can get access will freeze your catch. Service stations, hotels, motels, commercial campgrounds will usually have a home-sized refrigerator or freezer that you can use, maybe for a small fee, but usually for free.

If you can't find a refrigerator at one of the places named, do what I've done a couple of times. Look around in the first town you reach for an appliance dealer who can be expected to have a few used refrigerators or freezers that he's taken in trade for new ones and arrange to rent or borrow the use of one of these trade-ins long enough to freeze your keepers. All that you need in addition to the fish and a way to freeze them is a roll of heavy-duty aluminum foil.

When using commercial transportation such as the airlines, pack your fish as previously described, with these two exceptions. Right in the middle of your fish packages, place a two pound chunk of dry ice wrapped in newspaper. And, thoroughly wrap the exterior of the cooler with heavy duty duct tape. Now, your catch can be transported right along with your other luggage. The dry ice should keep everything solidly frozen for 36 hours. If you have a day or two lay-over between flight connections, ask your hotel manager to place your entire cooler in their restaurant freezer. It's a common practice, usually without charge.

To prevent the dehydration that accompanies slow freezing, you must freeze each fish separately into a block of ice, because any fish worth carrying home will be too big to fit into a standard-sized ice-cube tray. Following the pictured procedures, bend the foil into an open traylike receptacle in which you'll lay your fish. Then fill the tray with water and put it into the freezer. Freezing will require from 6 to 12 hours, and you must not thaw the fish until you're ready to cook it, for it will get unpleasantly soft if allowed to stand even a short time after being thawed.

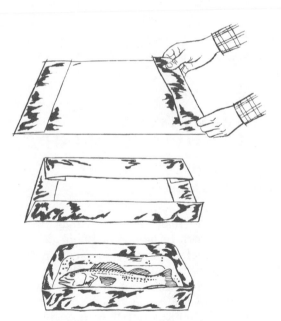

You can bend heavy-duty aluminum foil into a satisfactory freezing tray. First, double each edge, then form the sides. Don't worry about the sides bowing outward when you begin making the end folds as the foil will straighten out when you get to the last step. Finally, bend the vees formed by the corners, pulling the vees up to straighten the sides. Then, crimp the folded vees.

Now, I'm well aware that this type of freezing isn't the procedure recommended by authorities on freezing. I'm also aware that these authorities for the most part are professionally dedicated to what is known in the refrigerating trade as "flash-freezing." Proponents of flash-freezing look on anything else as a heinous offense and classify it as a gross indecency that comes close to endangering public morals.

There's no question about the commercial flash-freezing process being a lot easier and less complicated than freezing fish in blocks of ice in a home refrigerator or freezer. A flash-frozen fish can sit for an hour or two waiting to be cooked, though interestingly enough, the authorities who recommend cooking procedures suggest that flash-frozen foods be cooked before they thaw completely. Just by coincidence, this is the same recommendation made for cooking fish frozen in an ice shroud.

Now, I learned to freeze fish in blocks of ice quite some years before the flash-freeze process was in use. I don't remember how many fish I've preserved this way, but the number is reasonably large, and I've never been disappointed with the flavor of a fish preserved in this style.

Lacking any freezing facilities at all for your saltwater catch, the best thing you can do to get it home in cooking condition is to chill it by whatever means are at your disposal—such as letting it sit for an hour or so in the coldest water available—dry it thoroughly inside and out, and then get it home and cook it without wasting time.

PRELIMINARY TIPS

Before getting into the major jobs of making a fish ready for cooking, jobs such as cleaning and filleting and skinning, there are a few things you'll need to keep in mind if you want to make the later chores easier. I'll try to cover them in as few words as possible.

Never wash a dead fish. If cleaning is required, wipe it clean. Water put on a fish after it's dead brings out a thin slick coating that makes the fish hard to handle. If a fish you've landed on the bank gets dirty, hook your fingers through one side of its gills and wash it before it dies.

If a fish must be scaled, wait until it's been dead a short time and scrape from the tail to the head. If you've taken the fish home, or if you're at a fishing resort where a hose is available, you can scale a fish quickly by playing the hose with the tightest jet possible along the fish's body. Work from tail to head, using a side-to-side motion; clear one side, then the other. If you're at home, do this on the lawn and let the scales work down to the grass roots. They're fine fertilizer.

When you're handling a large fish in a boat or while wading, there's a spot in the lower jaw that if pressed hard will cause the fish to stop wriggling and flopping. Put two fingers into the fish's mouth (and remember large fish have sharp teeth) and press on the under-jaw with your thumb until you find the spot. Of course, this isn't something you should try with a feral fish such as a shark or barracuda.

If a fish has been cleaned and frozen for transporting, cook it immediately after it's thawed and do not refreeze. Fish tend to deteriorate very rapidly when thawed, and if left to warm up slowly may develop bacteria that can cause diarrhea.

There are a lot of recipes current which are based on the Japanese *sushi* or the Mexican *ceviche*, both of which serve raw fish with sauces as a premeal appetizer. Many of these recipes omit the most important feature, which is a warning to use only *saltwater* fish in these raw fish dishes. Not all freshwater fish can safely be eaten raw. Some of them contain in their flesh bacteria which can cause stomach upsets. Cooking destroys these bacteria. Just to be on the safe side, use only saltwater fish if you prepare either *sushi* or *ceviche*.

CLEANING FRESHWATER FISH

Believe it or not, there are a few fishermen who really enjoy cleaning fish. I don't happen to be one of them, so wipe that cynical smile off your face. I'm not going to try to con you into believing that cleaning a mess of fish will give you as much pleasure as catching them, but I'll give you a routine to follow that will ease the trauma of cleaning your catch, if you're among the majority of anglers who consider this particular job to be one that takes some of the pleasure out of fishing.

Cleaning a fish easily really starts with the knife you use. I keep a special knife for the job, one that goes along on every fishing trip I take. It's not a fancy knife in any way. In fact, its blade looks as though it had met with a near-fatal accident from which it never quite recovered. The grip is of plain black hard rubber, and it has a thin 5-inch blade, which over the years has been honed and stoned so many times that it's now a full half-inch narrower than it was when the knife was new.

What makes the knife special is its point. Not the point itself, but the little V-shaped notch that I ground in the curve a bit less than a half-inch from the tip. Like the blade itself, this notch is kept razor-sharp. It allows me to slide the tip of the knife right up a fish's belly from its vestibule to its vent without going deeply enough to snag on intestines, stomach, or gullet. Later in the job, it makes quick work of opening the blood-gorged membrane along the fish's spine.

To clean a fish—or any game bird or animal, for that matter—you need to know a little bit about its anatomy. A fish has a single interconnected internal structure. Tongue, gullet, gills, and intestines are a single unit. Since the unit starts at the fish's mouth, that's the point where you want to start. Most anglers cleaning a fish begin at the vent, and consequently make the cleaning job harder by working backward.

CLEANING FISH FROM THE BELLY

Start by opening the fish's mouth. At the very top of the yawning mouth you'll see a thin strip of gristle that holds its gills to its skull. Slip the knife into the open mouth and cut this strip free.

Go now to the gills. Just behind the gill plates you can see a bony ridge, and behind this ridge is a thin membrane. Put the point of your knife-blade through this membrane at the top and cut through it along the bony ridge to the tip of the lower jaw. Repeat the cut on the other side of the fish's head.

Give your attention now to the tip of the jaw inside the fish's mouth. There's another strip of gristle here which connects the tongue and jawbone. Cut through this strip.

Holding the fish belly-up in your left hand, push the tip of your knife into what would be the fish's throat, if fish had throats. The blade should go in at the gill-line. Keeping your cut shallow, slit along the full length of the belly to the anal orifice. Don't cut any deeper than is necessary to part the thin belly-flesh or you'll be in trouble later. This is where that V-notch in the tip of the knife helps. It allows you to hold the knife parallel to the fish's body while you're slitting. Without the V to guide you, your knife will try to penetrate too deeply.

Holding the fish upright by the head, hook your fingers through the gill-cut under the jaws to circle and grasp the fish's tongue and give one quick, sharp tug. Unless you've made the belly-cut too deep, the pectoral fins, gill rakers, gills, tongue, gullet, stomach, and intestines will come out through the belly-slit in one clean cluster.

Cut around the anal orifice to free the innards and discard them. Then run your knife-tip along the backbone at the top of the blood-filled venous cavity, which is actually a fish's main artery, and make a straight cut to sever the mem-

Cut off the dorsal fin or fins, cut around the anal fins, and pull them away; do another quick job of wiping to get the cavity absolutely clean, and you're home free.

If you want to take the head off before you cook the fish, do so. I like to leave the heads of large trout and salmon on the body, though, to get those little nuggets of sweet flesh at the top of the head just behind the eyes.

CLEANING FISH FROM THE BACK

There are times when you'll want to clean a fish from the back in order to stuff it or smoke it or cook it on a plank over a bed of coals. The reason for cleaning a fish from the back is to allow it to be spread flat, which is impossible to do if it has been cleaned from the belly, because the heavy layer of flesh on a fish's back simply can't be compressed enough to allow the fish to be flattened.

Now, there aren't any shortcuts or tricks to this kind of cleaning job. It's going to take a few minutes, and you're going to get your hands bloody because you'll be working downward into the venous cavity and intestines.

Start by making a cut from the back of the head to the tail. Insert the tip of your knife just behind the gills and cut along the backbone. Make a second cut paralleling the first, but cut on the opposite side of the dorsal fin or fins.

Now you'll have to use both your muscle and a sharp knife; if the fish is a large one, you might have to saw with the

If you plan to cook your fish whole with the head on, it's necessary first to remove the gill rakers and then the entrails. Make these cuts, as described in the text, and you should then be able to grab the freed gill rakers, pull downward and have everything come out all at once. Note the notch I've cut in the tip of my knife to facilitate this operation.

brane. Run your thumb along the backbone to clear the cavity. If the fish is a very large one, you might find it easier to use a teaspoon or even a tablespoon to clear away the congealed blood. Wipe the cavity clean; pull away the strips of membrane on each side of the backbone.

This is the preferred method for filleting very large fish such as saltwater species. The first cut should be to one side of the spinal column, all the way from the head to the tail. This cut creates a flap of thick meat you can then begin pulling down and away as you make additional cuts around the rib cage. The result should be two boneless fillets, but if you see any remaining bones, pull them out with pliers.

knife a bit, for you'll be cutting the fish's ribs away from the backbone. Spread the flesh back from the first cut so you can see what you're doing, and sever each rib until you reach a point above and just behind the vent.

Repeat the cut, on the other side. If you're working on a big fish, you might have to use kitchen shears or poultry shears or even a set of duckbill tinsnips to cut the ribs free.

Now, go back to the head and make the first three cuts described in the belly-cleaning method, those cuts which free the gills at the top of the head, the membrane behind the gills, and at the bottom tip of the jaw.

Cut through the membrane of the venous cavity, pull the gill rakers, gills, tongue, and intestinal cluster free and cut around the anal orifice to remove them completely.

All that's left now is cleanup. Cut through the backbone at front and back, remove it and the dorsal fins. Cut off the pectoral and anal fins, wipe the cavity clean, and pull away the membrane left from the venous cavity. Wipe again, and you have a fish ready for planking or smoking or stuffing.

FILLETING FISH

A fish from which you intend to take only the fillets does not need to be cleaned or scaled. The filleting job is more easily done if the fish is fresh from the water, killed just before you start your filleting cuts. You will need a flat, solid working surface—the top of a table or, if you're afield, a piece of plank at least 8 to 10 inches wide. Your filleting knife is the key to making sure, fast cuts. The ideal filleting knife has a narrow, slightly curved flat blade. It must be scalpel-sharp at all times. If you have a number of fish to fil-

FILLETING A FISH

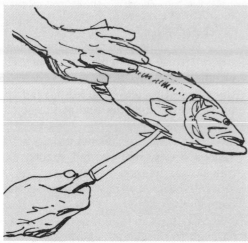

1. Using just the tip of your knife blade, cut from the vent to the base of the gills.

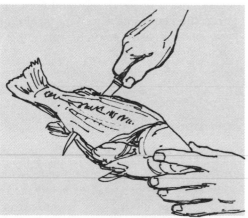

3. Now turn blade flat against spinal column and slice all the way to the base of the tail. Do not cut the fillet free when you reach the base of the tail.

Never try to use a conventional hunting knife or kitchen knife for filleting fish. What you want is a special fillet knife such as the type shown here. These are different from other knife designs in that they have very thin, flexible, stainless steel blades which enable them to easily be guided around and through a fish's anatomy without wasting meat or tearing flesh.

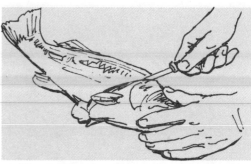

2. Slice downward as indicated until you feel the edge of the blade stop against the spinal column.

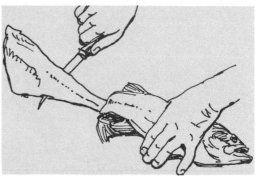

4. Flop the fillet over so it is fleshside up. Since it is still attached like a hinge to the remainder of the fish, you have a handy handle to hold onto for the next operation of removing the skin. Cut down through the flesh until you almost reach the skin, then turn the knife blade flat and with a gentle back and forth sawing motion guide the fillet knife along to separate the skin from the meat.

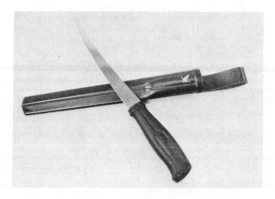

CLEANING PANFISH

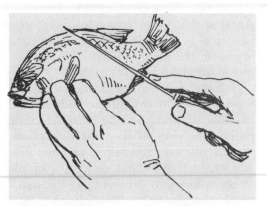

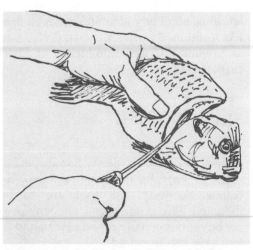

1. To clean small species such as panfish, in order to cook them whole, first scale the fish by briskly scraping your knife blade from tail to head.

2. Remove entire head and gill assembly by propping the fish up on its belly and slicing downward as indicated. Note how this cut curves, to retain the large portion of thick meat just behind the head.

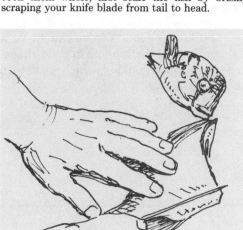

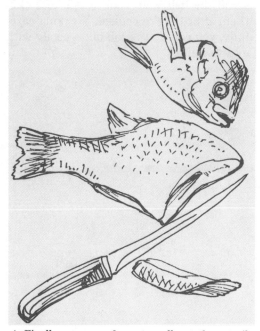

3. Lay fish on its side and make this cut, which removes the vent and anal fin (the pelvic and pectoral fins came away in the previous step).

4. Finally, use your finger to pull out the entrails. Most like to fry fish in this state, leaving the tail and dorsal fin intact. When crispy brown, the tail tastes like a potato chip, and when the fish is cooked you can easily pull the entire dorsal fin right out with your fingertips.

let, use a steel or whetstone between fish. (As mentioned earlier, my own preference or prejudice is for knife-blades of high-carbon steel.)

SKINNING FISH

Unless you have to, don't. Some species, such as catfish, must be skinned, of course. So must fish that are to be mounted. This is one reason so many people buy commercially raised catfish and so few have fish mounted.

Seriously, skinning a large fish isn't really all that bad a job, but if you take small fish from clean water it's easier to scrub the fish well, cook them, and skin them after they're cooked. Working carefully, you can do the job quite easily with a table knife.

However, the skinning technique is much the same as that described in filleting—by cutting with short sawing strokes. Another, but more time-consuming procedure is to clean the fish, cut it at right angles to the body in slices of the thickness desired, and skin the slices.

Small fish may be skinned whole by scoring the skin around the body behind the gills, trimming an edge loose, and then pulling the skin off in strips with pliers.

If you are addicted to skinned fish, you might think about making a simple skinning-board by driving a nail through a plank, sharpening the protruding end, and impaling the fish by the head on the nail to leave both hands free for skinning.

So far, so good. You've caught your fish and gotten them home in good shape. It's time to start cooking, which we'll do in the next chapter.

14 BASIC FISH COOKERY

Since the journey of a thousand miles begins with a single step, that first step is pretty important. Here, the first step is to become acquainted with the six basic ways in which fish are cooked, and the variations in those six ways. It's possible that you know all six methods by heart, and what this chapter contains might be merely a repetition of something with which you're thoroughly familiar, but please don't skip it. There just may be something in it that will be new to you. After all, there's not any way to avoid taking that first step. In spite of all our technological advances, we've got to walk to the car or the plane, and even to the rocket that lifts us off to the moon.

By whatever method you cook your fish, keep in mind the objective of all fish cookery: to cook only long enough to coagulate the juices. If a fish was shaped like a slab, this wouldn't be difficult. However, since fish taper from thick to thin, we must seek a happy medium. Take your fish off the fire while the thickest part is still quite moist. Cooking will continue by retained heat for several moments after you transfer the fish from the pan to a warmed plate or platter. In actual practice, cooking should be completed during the time required to take the fish out of the pan, put it on a plate, and carry it to the table—usually, a matter of 3 or 4 minutes. If you err in timing, it is better to undercook than to overcook.

Your clues to the point at which a fish is done are the condition of its skin and the amount of moisture at its dorsal fin. When cooking is completed, the skin will slip easily from the flesh. Usually, the side that is up will show a few large air bubbles between skin and flesh. The slipping quality of the skin can be tested at the slit cut for cleaning, or where the dorsal fin has been trimmed along the back. Test with a knife-tip or the tines of a fork, and if the skin lifts readily, the fish is done.

Use a knife or fork to make the dorsal fin test, too. Slip the utensil into the skinless line left where the fin was cut off. Twist the blade or tines gently to separate the flesh; if no liquid flows, but the flesh has a moist appearance, cooking is complete. By the time you've taken the fish off the broiler rack or grill, or out of the skillet, and laid it on a hot plate, it should be possible to tweak out the dorsal spines. Usually you can do this with your fingers, pinching the spines through a folded cloth to protect your fingers and give you a better grip. Stubbornly rooted spines, especially in big fish, may have to be pulled out with pliers.

To divide the flesh of a large cooked fish into halves, like big fillets, the skin should be removed first. Then, insert a dull knife at the thickest part of the body, behind the head, and cut along the dorsal line, with the tip of the knife touching the backbone. Work the edge of a turner or metal spatula into the cut and push and lift very gently, keeping the edge of the tool against the ribs and inching along the backbone from head to tail with the spatula while pushing the slab of flesh toward the belly. By working slowly and carefully, you can remove the slab of flesh in one piece, after which it is a simple matter to lift out the exposed backbone with the ribs attached. A few ribs may stick in the bottom half, but they can be loosened with a nick of the knife; if they break, they can be tweaked out.

Your success in doing this depends to a large extent on the fish having been cooked properly; if it is overdone and dry, even a light touch will cause the flesh to separate and break. And don't try this method of separation with exceedingly bony fish such as carp, shad, and pike. It's far better to serve them whole or in sections cut at right angles to the body, and let each diner remove the bones from his own portion.

One more generality. As different as the families of fish are, they have more similarities than differences. As a result, they are largely interchangeable in pan or pot. Although the bulk of this chapter is divided into sections dealing with the principal families of fish, different species can be quite freely interchanged. There are only a few recipes in which substitution of one kind of fish for another is either impossible or ill-advised, and when this is the case, a word of caution will be given.

Now, cook and enjoy. If Allah does not deduct from man's alloted life span the time he spends at fishing, the moments devoted to cooking the fish should be equally exempt.

PAN-FRYING OR SAUTÉING

This is the only method of cooking fish that many people know of or use. The name "pan-frying" is given to this style of cooking to distinguish it from true frying, which is done in a deep pot with the food totally immersed in hot fat. Technically, we are talking in this section about sautéing, which does not mean plopping a fish into a pan half-filled with fat and browning the outside in the shortest possible time over the highest possible heat.

Do that and your fish will have a tooth-shattering crust surrounding a half-raw interior. Use moderate heat, and coat the fish with an ingredient or combination of ingredients that hold it off the bottom of the pan so the fat can get underneath it. Cook it long enough to allow the heat to penetrate even the thickest part and you'll serve up an evenly cooked morsel.

methods given on pages 243-244. Drain the fish for a moment on cloth or paper towels before serving, and do not salt until cooking is completed.

AMERICAN STYLE SAUTÉING

CAMP STYLE SAUTÉING

Whole fish no thicker than 2 to 2½ inches at the thickest part, or fillets
Cooking fat: oil, bacon dripping, butter, solid margarine, lard, as you prefer
Breading ingredients: cornmeal, fine dry breadcrumbs, or fine unsalted cracker crumbs in quantity depending on the number of fish to be cooked

Have enough fat to cover the bottom of the skillet to a depth of ¼ inch to ½ inch for whole fish, and to a depth of no more than ¹⁄₁₆ inch to ⅛ inch for fillets. The fat should be well below the smoking point, the heat moderate. Roll the fish in the breading ingredient, covering its outside surfaces thoroughly. Cook whole fish 2 to 4 minutes per side, depending upon thickness; reduce heat and extend cooking time for thick-bodied fish. Test for doneness by

Whole fish no thicker than 2 to 2½ inches at the thickest part, or fillets
Cooking fat: oil, bacon dripping, butter, solid margarine, lard, as you prefer
Milk or evaporated milk diluted with equal parts of water; the quantity will depend on the number of fish being cooked
Flour; the quantity will depend on the number of fish being cooked

Have enough fat to cover the bottom of the skillet to a depth of ¼ inch to ½ inch for whole fish, and to a depth of no more than ¹⁄₁₆ inch to ⅛ inch for fillets. The fat should be well below the smoking point, the heat moderate. Dip the fish in milk, drain for a moment, then roll in flour. Shake off any excess flour, but be sure all outside surfaces of the fish are covered. Cook whole fish 2 to 4 minutes per side, depending upon thickness; fillets, 2 minutes per side. Use lower heat and extend cooking time for thick-bodied fish. Test for doneness. Drain the fish on cloth or paper towels before serving. Do not season until after cooking.

ENGLISH STYLE SAUTÉING

Whole fish no thicker than 2 to 2½ inches at the thickest part, or fillets

Cooking fat: oil, bacon dripping, butter, solid margarine, lard, as you prefer

Flour; the quantity will depend on the number of fish being cooked

Coating: 1 egg, 1 tablespoon milk, 1 tablespoon cooking oil, ½ teaspoon salt; this will handle a half-dozen panfish, four fillets, or two 8-inch whole fish. Mix any quantity needed, using the ratio given above.

Fine dry breadcrumbs; the quantity will depend on the number of fish being cooked

Have enough fat to cover the bottom of the skillet to a depth of ¼ to ½ inch for whole fish, and to a depth of no more than ¹⁄₁₆ inch to ⅛ inch for fillets. The fat should be well below the smoking point, the heat moderate to low. Whole fish cooked this style are often "crimped," that is, slashed across the body on each side with three or four deep cuts; this is supposed to keep the fish from curling in the pan while cooking, but whether you follow the custom or not is up to you. Wipe the fish with a damp cloth and roll in flour, rubbing it in well. Dip the fish in the coating liquid and let it drain for a moment; then roll in breadcrumbs, covering the outside surfaces thoroughly. Cook whole fish 4 to 7 minutes per side, depending upon thickness; cook fillets about 4 minutes per side. Use lower heat and extend cooking time for large fish. Drain on cloth or paper towels for a moment before serving.

DEEP-FAT FRYING

We turn now to true frying, which is done in a deep pan with the fish completely immersed in hot fat. The process is best suited to small fish cooked whole, or to large fish that have been cut into pieces of approximately equal size. The pieces or the small whole fish should not be seasoned before being cooked unless the seasoning is included in a breading or coating. The coating may be any of those given in the preceding recipes for sautéing, although you will find the plain coating of cornmeal or fine dried breadcrumbs to be the most satisfactory.

There are three keys to success in this style of cooking. The first is the composition of the fat used; ⅓ solid shortening to ⅔ cooking oil is the preferred ratio. The second is the temperature of the cooking fat; if you have a cooking thermometer, 370 to 380 degrees is the ideal. At this temperature the inside of small whole fish or pieces about 1 inch to 1¼ inch large will be completely cooked and the outside crisply browned in 5 minutes. The third secret is to add the fish or pieces a few at a time to keep the temperature of the cooking fat constant.

Use a large pan and do not overcrowd it. Bring the fat to smoking temperature, if you have no cooking thermometer, then reduce heat until the

Deep-frying varies from conventional pan-frying in that a wire basket is used to submerge fish in a pot of hot oil.

smoking stops. Put in and remove the fish or pieces with tongs. Drain the cooked fish on cloth or paper towels for a moment before serving.

BROILING AND GRILLING

To be technical for a moment, broiling is done with the fish or fillets on a rack placed in a shallow pan with the heat source above the fish; heat reflected from the bottom of the broiling pan will generally cook the bottom side so that the fish need not be turned. Grilling is done with the fish on a rack or grill with the heat source beneath it; the heat is usually from live coals, and the fish must be turned at half the cooking time.

When broiling, the broiler as well as the rack and pan should be preheated for at least 5 minutes. Each broiler is unique. Even kitchen ranges manufactured on a production line, using identical components, will vary slightly. Thermostatic devices designed to maintain heat at a uniform level will show similar variation. This is as true of gas broilers as it is of electric broilers. A good rule of thumb is to use three-quarters heat with gas, full heat with electricity. Cook the fish with its top surface 6 to 7 inches from the heat source; the approximate cooking time for a fish 1½ to 2 inches thick at the thickest part will be about 10 minutes.

There are even more variables in grilling. Air currents, depth of the coals, distance of the grill rack from them, all play a part in altering your timing. In this style of cooking, about the only advice I can offer is to have a deep bed of coals, dark red rather than yellow-hot.

Fish broiled or grilled should be basted. Individual recipes will give specific basting mixtures, but a good all-purpose basting liquid can be made by mixing 2 parts oil or drawn butter with 1 part lemon or lime juice.

When cooking pieces of fish on a skewer, what is commonly called kebabing or shish-kebabing, or cooking *en brochette,* marinate the pieces in lemon or lime juice for 45 minutes to 1 hour before cooking. This firms the flesh and makes it less likely to flake into pieces and fall off the skewers as cooking progresses. Fish of any kind, because of the layerlike formation of its flesh, is a poor candidate at best for this kind of cooking. Skewer-cook fish only when you are forced to do so; there are too many other kinds of meats better suited to this style of preparation.

BAKING

For baking whole, choose fish ranging in size from 4 or 5 pounds on up to about 10 or 12 pounds. These are really too small to yield steaks and too big to pan-fry; they should be baked, either stuffed or plain, or poached. Also good for baking are center cuts from fish ranging between 12 and 30 pounds, the roasts cut from giants such as the sturgeon.

Individual recipes for baking fish will give you the specific cooking time, since there will be a variation depending on the type of stuffing or dressing used. For plain, unadorned baked fish, cooked in a pre-heated 350-degree oven in an open pan, the rule of thumb is 7 minutes per inch of thickness at the thickest part; in a closed pan, 10 minutes per inch. This will be accurate within a minute either way, if your oven's thermostat is accurate.

In open-pan baking, fish are generally basted, using the liquid given with individual recipes or the general-purpose basting liquid used for broiling. Fat fish should always be cooked on a rack that will hold them ½ inch to ¾ inch from the bottom of the baking pan. Juices from the pan should not be used for basting.

POACHING

This is what some call "boiling." Except for the traditional outdoor fish boils indigenous to the upper Midwest, fish should never really be boiled. They should be poached in a fish stock or in a *court-bouillon*; the recipes for both of these follow.

Baking is another popular way of preparing fish. Here a stuffing has been placed inside the fish and the body cavity is being closed with cotton string. No matter what the species, the rule of thumb is to bake fish for 10 minutes per inch of thickness, measured at the thickest part of the fish, in an oven preheated to 375 degrees.

FISH STOCK

2 pounds fish trimmings: heads, bones with bits of flesh
2 medium-sized sweet onions sliced thin
5 or 6 large sprigs parsley
4 to 6 peppercorns, nicked or cracked
1½ pints cold water
1½ pints dry white wine
1 teaspoon salt

Rub a deep saucepan very lightly with cooking oil. Put in all the solid ingredients, cover the pan tightly, and cook 15 to 20 minutes over very low heat. Add liquids and salt, bring to a boil, reduce to a simmer, and cook 45 minutes with the pan uncovered. Strain or clarify before putting into container with a well-fitting top for storage in refrigerator; the stock will keep for about 8 weeks. Makes 2 quarts.

COURT-BOUILLON

1 **quart dry white wine**
2 **quarts cold water**
1½ **cups minced sweet onion**
1 **cup peeled minced carrots**
Bouquet garni **composed of:**
    4 **pieces celery tops with leaves left on**
    6 **sprigs parsley**
    1 **bay leaf**
    1 **sprig fresh thyme or 2 sprigs dried thyme**
    8 **peppercorns, cracked or nicked with a knife blade**

Put all ingredients except the peppercorns into a deep saucepan and bring to a brisk rolling boil. Reduce heat until the liquid simmers and cook 40 minutes, adding the peppercorns during the last 10 minutes. (If cooked too long in a thin liquid, peppercorns make it bitter.) Strain or clarify before putting into a container with a well-fitting top for storage in refrigerator; the liquid will keep for about 8 weeks. Makes 2½ quarts.

To Clarify Stock or Court-Bouillon

For each quart of liquid, beat 1 egg white until stiff and break clean eggshell into large pieces. Heat the liquid, stir in the egg whites and shell, bring to a boil, remove from heat, and let stand 10 minutes. Strain into a clean container through a dampened, closely woven cloth; flannel is best.

When poaching fish, it is usually desirable to start the cooking in a cool or lukewarm liquid, although there will be some variation in individual recipes. If you are using a poaching pan, simply put the fish on the rack and lower it into the liquid, which should cover it completely. If you do not own a special pan for poaching, use any container of suitable size, and wrap the fish loosely in 3 or 4 layers of cheesecloth, leaving the ends long enough to use in lifting the fish from the pan when done.

After putting in the fish, bring the liquid to a boil. Then reduce heat until it barely simmers on the surface, the slowest simmering heat of which your stove is capable. Length of poaching time will vary with the size of the fish; a 4-pounder will require about 25 minutes from the time boiling stops. As a rule of thumb, cook 3 to 4 minutes for each pound over 4 pounds.

One more word about the liquids used in poaching. There is no substitute for *court-bouillon,* but you can use canned clam juice diluted with water as a substitute for fish stock. Keep in mind that there are two liquids canned from clams: juice and broth. The juice can be diluted with 3 parts water, the broth with 1½ to 2 parts water.

15 FISH RECIPES

While many of the basics of fish cookery have been covered in earlier chapters, there are a few points that have not yet been made clear. We haven't dealt with shellfish and crustaceans, but will in this chapter. More importantly, though, we haven't yet touched on the basic problem that faces everyone who cooks fish: categorizing the fish properly.

Let's dispose of the category question first. Imagine yourself to be a relatively inexperienced fish cook–elect who's facing a fish that's been acquired either by your own angling skill or the efforts of a fisherman friend. You are not really knowledgeable about fish cookery, but you have a lot of recipes you'd like to try out, and the fish at which you're looking gives you a good opportunity to experiment with something new.

Take stock first of what you know about the fish that sits on your kitchen cabinet or waits in your refrigerator for the moment of truth. Your eyes will tell you whether it's a large or a small one.

Your fingers, or if you're unfortunate, your nose, can tell you whether the fish is fresh enough to cook or is a candidate for the garbage pail. You usually know whether the fish came from fresh or salt water, and you'll probably know one of the several names by which the fish is called.

If fish were criminals, they'd drive the FBI crazy trying to keep straight the multitude of names by which each variety is known. Of course, every fish has been classified and given a definitive Latin name by aquatic biologists, but very few people outside of academic or technical circles know these names. In a few cases, even the scientists themselves can't agree on a single definitive Latin tag for some subspecies.

But in this case, you do have a name for the fish and you know its size and condition and whether it's from fresh or salt water. Even this is not enough information. In your capacity as cook-elect, you lack the one key bit of data that will enable you to make a knowledgeable choice of the best recipe out of perhaps a dozen that you believe are suitable. You should know *from the standpoint of the recipe by which it will be prepared* whether the fish is classed as "fat" or "lean."

This is not the incredible scenario it might seem to be. The bounty of the oceans and lakes and streams is almost infinite. Between them they yield so many different species of fish that are called by so many different names in different geographical areas that you as a cook must be reasonably sure whether the fish belongs in the "lean" or the "fat" category before you even think about choosing a recipe.

It's true that interchangeability is the rule rather than the exception in fish cookery. It's a rare recipe that won't be equally well suited to a half-dozen kinds of fish, but the point is that there *are* exceptions to the interchangeability rule.

A lean recipe is one which subjects a fish to a preliminary treatment designed to reduce the quantity of fat in its body tissues. The treatment might be poaching, or a brief period of baking or broiling. A fat recipe is one which tends to add fats to those already in the fish. You can place many recipes in a different category by the preliminary preparation of the fish you are cooking, for you can precook to add fat to the fish's tissues with an oily marinade just as you can reduce the fat with a precooking designed to remove fat.

This is important, for a lean fish cooked by a lean recipe may come to the table too dry or with stringy, unpleasant

Fatty fish are much better when broiled or baked. One of the simplest methods is merely to dot them with small pieces of butter, then slip into an oven preheated to 375 degrees until the flesh flakes easily. For a special treat, place a slice of onion on top of each fillet during the final 5 minutes of cooking time.

flesh. A fat fish cooked by a fat recipe may turn out bloated, watery, and mushy. This being the case, it's a wise fish cook who knows how to honor the rules and to take full advantage of the exceptions and alterations.

So, to help you match fish to recipe, here's a little list:

Fat Freshwater Fish
Bass, black and rock
Eels, all varieties
Grayling
Herring, also known as Taylor shad and sawbellies
Salmon*
Shad*
Smelt*
Steelhead*
Sturgeon*
Trout
Whitebait
Whitefish

Lean Freshwater Fish
Bass, white, also known as lake bass
Blackfish, aka bowfin, mudfish, and grindle
Bluegill, aka bream, brim, blue perch, dollardee, etc.
Carp, aka buffalo fish
Catfish, aka bullheads and by several other names
Drum, aka sheepshead, gaspergou, and crocus
Muskellunge, aka Ohio pike, salmon pike, etc.
Perch, all 11 varieties which share 21 names
Pickerel, aka jackfish, snakefish, etc.
Sheepshead, aka freshwater drum

Suckers
Sunfish, all 38 varieties which share 69 names

Fat Saltwater Fish
Barracuda
Bass, striped*
Bluefish
Cavalla, aka crevalle, jack crevalle, etc.
Eels, all varieties
Halibut
Herring
Lote, aka eelpout
Mackerel, all varieties
Mariposa, aka moonfish and Jerusalem haddock
Marlin
Mullet
Pompano
Porgie
Redfish
Salmon*
Sardines
Shad*
Smelt
Snapper
Sole, aka dab, lemon sole, etc.
Sturgeon*
Swordfish
Tuna
Turbot
Whitebait
Whiting

* These are anadromous fish, which migrate from salt to fresh water. Where names are duplicated on the freshwater and saltwater lists the species are usually different but are applied to fish that have strong resemblances to one another.

Lean Saltwater Fish

Bass, aka sea, channel, black sea bass, etc.
Bonito
Cobia, aka jewfish
Codfish, aka red cod, scrod, green cod, etc.
Drumfish, aka redfish, channel bass, etc.
Flounder, aka fluke
Grouper, all varieties
Grunt, all varieties
Guacaimia, aka parrotfish, lauia, paluha-
  luha
Haddock
Hake, aka codling, merluche
Kingfish, aka pintado, cerdo
Perch, all varieties
Pollock, aka green cod
Sheepshead
Skate
Weakfish, aka seatrout, speckled trout

There are a few fish on the list which are not commonly considered edible, but quite a few people do eat such fish as bowfin and suckers. For many years, I carried suckers on my list of trash fish and considered them inedible. Then I got acquainted with the late Chief Ranger Forest Townsley of Yosemite National Park, who proved that I was wrong with his singular contribution to the art of fish cookery.

As would be expected in one of his experience and position, Forest held impeccable credentials as an outdoorsman. He was the first Park Ranger in the U.S., having been appointed by President Theodore Roosevelt when the National Park Service was established. In the late 1930s and early 1940s, when I was fishing Yosemite's waters regularly, Forest fished for suckers while the rest of us were fish-ing for trout. In his cabin, he'd clean the suckers, grind them up (bones and all), season them with unrevealed herbs of his own selection, and deep-fry them. The patties he called suckerburgers were very good indeed.

In deep-frying his suckerburgers, Forest followed the rule of thumb which all good fish cooks should. The rule: Cook lean fish wet, cook fat fish dry.

When you're interchanging fish in recipes, then, match or modify the recipe to the *category* of fish it calls for if you want to disregard the exact kind specified, and you'll rarely produce a bad dish.

As most of the preliminary groundwork to successful fish cookery has been covered in earlier chapters, there's no point in repeating it here. Following the section devoted to fish recipes you'll find the sections dealing with shellfish and crustaceans. Unless otherwise indicated, all recipes serve four.

Sail on, then, into the world of fish cookery.

FRESHWATER FISH

TROUT AMANDINE

SKILLET-COOKED TROUT

4   trout, 10 to 12 inches, cleaned and wiped dry
1   cup unsalted almonds, skins removed
¼   pound butter
2   Tbsp lemon juice
½   to ¾ cup all-purpose flour
½   tsp salt
¼   cup olive or vegetable oil

4   trout, 8 to 10 inches, cleaned and wiped dry
⅓   pound butter (you can of course substitute your own favorite cooking oil, such as peanut oil or any other, but today's bacon being so highly chemicalized, it really isn't suitable to be used as a cooking fat)
½   tsp salt
    Optional: flour or cornmeal with which to rub the fish

A flour or cornmeal coating is made optional because neither contributes to the flavor of the trout. If you use either, rub the fish well with the flour or cornmeal before they go into the pan. Heat the butter over high heat until it begins to turn brown; while it heats, dust the trouts' cavities lightly with salt. Cook 4 to 6 minutes per side, shaking the pan now and then to keep the fish from sticking.

Before cooking the trout, chop the almonds coarsely. In a skillet large enough to accommodate the trout, sauté the almonds over low heat in one-third of the butter until they are golden brown. Stir frequently. Add the lemon juice to the almonds as they begin to turn brown. Drain the almonds from the pan and set aside.

Combine the flour and salt and rub on the trout. Heat the remaining butter and oil until it froths; poach the trout about 5 minutes per side. Shake the skillet occasionally to keep the fish from sticking. When the trout are done, pour the almonds over them and stir just long enough for them to reheat. Serve at once.

A light Rhine or Moselle wine goes well with this dish.

1. After dressing the fish, coarsely chop almonds as your fire is burning down to coals. (This sequence shows trout amandine being prepared outdoors.)

2. Brown the almonds in a skillet containing melted butter, then set them aside to drain.

3. Thoroughly dredge trout in flour.

4. Add a bit more butter and the olive oil to the same skillet the almonds were
browned in and cook until crispy brown.

5. Sprinkle the almonds over the trout and serve. (Lemon juice can be omitted if you
don't have it in camp.)

LEMON TROUT

POACHED TROUT

4	10-inch trout
2	Tbsp butter or light cooking oil
½	tsp salt
⅛	tsp freshly ground white pepper
½	tsp paprika
2	large lemons

Wipe the trout well; mix the salt, pepper, and ¼ teaspoon paprika together and rub one side of each trout with the mixture. Lay the trout seasoned-side-down in a shallow broiling pan that has been rubbed with just enough of the butter or oil to keep the fish from sticking. Broil 4 to 5 minutes without turning.

While the trout broil, grate the rind of one lemon, peel off the white pith, and peel rind and pith from the second. Slice both lemons thinly, removing the seeds.

Remove the pan from heat and turn the trout. Sprinkle them with the remaining seasonings and arrange the lemon slices over them; return to broiler and cook 3 to 4 minutes, until the flesh of the fish separates easily when tested with a fork.

1	large trout—12 to 14 inches (if it's possible, leave the fish's head on; it adds flavor)
1	stalk celery, with leaves
1	shallot, minced coarsely
3	or 4 crushed peppercorns
¼	bay leaf
¼	tsp salt
1	slice lemon, ½ inch thick, peel left on
2	cups dry white wine (Chablis, Semillion) Water

Chop the celery and shallot coarsely (a heaping teaspoon of chopped sweet white onion can be substituted for the shallot) and put these into the fish's cavity together with the peppercorns, bay leaf, lemon slice, and salt. If you don't have a fish poacher, you'll find the method of improvising one in Chapter 12. Put the fish in the poacher; mix the wine with enough water to cover the trout. If you're using an improvised poacher, and the quantity of water required is more than twice the amount of wine, use a bit more wine to keep the proportions about half-water, half-wine. Bring the pot-liquid to a quick boil on a surface burner while heating the oven to 225 degrees. When boiling begins, transfer the pan to the oven and cook 20 to 25 minutes.

TROUT FILLETS SUPREME

4 8- to 10-inch trout
1 to 1½ cups fish or chicken
   bouillon or stock (but don't use
   bouillon cubes, they're mostly
   salt)
2 tsp gelatine
½ cup milk
¾ cup finely chopped watercress
¼ cup tiny fresh scallions, minced
   (white ends only, no tops)
½ tsp salt
   Generous dash freshly ground
   white pepper

Trim heads, tails, and fins from trout and poach them in the boullion until completely cooked, about 12 to 14 minutes. Skin and lift flesh from bones, keeping each fillet intact. Put the fillets on waxed paper and refrigerate while completing the dish. At the same time, put into the refrigerator the platter or plates on which the dish will be served.

Heat ½ cup of the bouillon used for poaching and dissolve the gelatin in it. Stir the milk into the bouillon. Combine the cress and scallions by shaking them together in a plastic bag, add half the mixture plus the salt and pepper to the milk, stir to blend. Cool the solution by sitting its container in a pan of cold but not iced water.

Pour a small quantity of the gelatine/milk solution into the platter or serving plates, just enough to form a thin film. Arrange the fish fillets and pour over them the remaining gelatine solution. Chill until set. Just before serving, sprinkle the remaining watercress-scallion mixture over the platter or plates. If you wish, add additional garnish such as lemon quarters, sprigs of cress, etc.

TROUT BERCY

4 trout of about ¾ pound each
½ teaspoon salt
   Dash of freshly ground white
   pepper
3 Tbsp butter or solid margarine
2 Tbsp chopped shallots
1 cup fish stock
1 cup dry white wine

After cleaning, remove heads and fins from fish, trim tails, and sprinkle very lightly with salt and pepper.

Melt 1 tablespoon butter in a shallow ovenproof dish, spread the shallots on its bottom, and put the trout on the shallots.

Reduce the fish stock to half its volume by boiling briskly, let it cool, and add the wine.

Dot the trout with the remaining butter in pea-sized bits, and pour the wine-stock mixture over the fish. Cook uncovered in a preheated 325-degree oven for 12 to 15 minutes. Serves 4.

baking dish and lay the fish in it. Put a slice of ham or two slices of Canadian bacon on top of each trout.

Cook covered in a preheated 350-degree oven for 10 minutes, then pour the cream over the fish and return to the oven uncovered for an additional 8 to 10 minutes. Sprinkle with the chopped chives just before taking the trout to the table. Serves 4.

TROUT IN CREAM

4 **trout of about ¾ pound each**
1 **tsp salt**
⅛ **tsp freshly-ground white pepper**
3 **Tbsp butter or solid margarine**
¼ **cup brandy**
1 **cup heavy cream or evaporated milk, diluted 2 parts milk to 1 part water**

After cleaning the trout, trim tails and fins and dust them lightly inside and out with salt and pepper.

Over gentle heat, sauté the fish in the butter, cooking 3 to 4 minutes per side. Heat the brandy, ignite it, and pour it immediately over the fish in the pan. When the flames die down, pour the cream over the fish and cook without boiling for 5 minutes. Divide the pan juices over the fish on warmed serving plates or a platter. Serves 4.

TROUT LORRAINE

4 **trout of about ¾ pound each**
1 **tsp salt**
   Large dash of freshly ground white pepper
1 **tsp butter or solid margarine**
4 **thin slices uncooked ham or 8 slices Canadian bacon**
4 **tsp heavy cream or undiluted evaporated milk**
2 **tsp chopped fresh chives**

After cleaning and trimming off heads, tails and fins, dust the fish inside and out with salt and pepper. Butter a shallow

TROUT SPANISH STYLE

4 trout of about ¾ pound each
4 to 6 Tbsp olive oil
2 Tbsp flour
½ clove garlic, minced or mashed
¾ cup warm fish stock
¾ cup dry white wine
1 sprig fresh thyme
1 bay leaf
3 or 4 sprigs parsley

After cleaning the trout, trim off the tails and fins. Heat 1 to 1½ tablespoons of the oil in a skillet—use only enough to cover the pan's bottom with a thin film—and sauté the trout 2 minutes per side, over moderate heat. Transfer the fish to a lightly-oiled, shallow baking dish.

Put 4 tablespoons of oil in the skillet, and over low heat stir the flour into it to make a smooth paste. Add the garlic, and let both flour and garlic cook until they are golden tan. Stir occasionally to keep from scorching.

Combine the fish stock and wine and pour into the pan while stirring to keep lumps from forming. Put in the thyme and other herbs, allow the mixture to bubble 20 minutes without actually boiling, and stir just often enough to avoid scorching. Take out the tied herbs, pour the sauce over the trout, and cook covered in a pre-heated 350-degree oven for 10 minutes. Serves 4.

CRISPED PANFISH

12 to 16 cleaned panfish
    Large bowl or bucket of fine cracked ice
 2 eggs, lightly beaten
¾ cup cornmeal
¾ cup flour
1½ teaspoons salt
    Large dash pepper
½ to ¾ cup cooking oil or fat

Bury the cleaned fish in ice for 30 minutes before cooking. Beat the eggs in a shallow bowl. Combine cornmeal, flour, and seasonings in a small plastic bag and shake to mix. Put enough cooking fat in a heavy skillet to cover the bottom to a depth of about ½ inch and bring it to medium-high heat. Take the fish from the ice a few at a time and wipe them dry. Dip them in the beaten egg and roll them in the seasoned cornmeal-flour mixture until they are well coated. Drop the fish into the hot fat a few at a time; don't overcrowd the pan. Cook 2 minutes on each side. Drain well on paper towels or cloth. Keep the level of fat in the pan constant by adding more as needed, and keep the temperature of the fat even.

BLUEGILL IN BEER BATTER

20 to 24 bluegill, cleaned, heads and fins removed
¼ cup cornstarch
¼ cup all-purpose flour
¼ cup beer
2 egg whites
Fat or oil for deep-frying

Sift together the cornstarch and flour; mix the beer in to form a light batter. Beat the egg whites stiff and fold into the batter just before using. Dip the bluegill in the batter, drain for a moment or two, pop one at a time into the bubbling fat. If the fish are added at too-short intervals, the fat will be cooled and will not do its job properly. When each fish is nicely browned, remove and drain on paper for a few moments.

Don't confine the use of Edith McCaig's delicious beer batter to bluegill,

though. It's equally good for cooking any kind of panfish or fish fillets.

PANFISH WITH ZUCCHINI

10 to 12 panfish, pan-fried
3 or 4 zucchini (green Italian squash) no larger than 1-inch in diameter and 4 to 6 inches long
1 canned pimento, drained, wiped dry, cut in 1-inch strips
1 Tbsp cider vinegar

After cooking the fish, put them in a warmed, covered bowl. Drain all but a light film of oil from the skillet. Wash the zucchini, trim off the ends, and slice at a very sharp angle, almost lengthwise, into slices ¼ inch to ½ inch thick. Sauté the zucchini in the oil remaining in the skillet, cooking about 1 minute per side over medium-high heat. Add the pimento strips and the fish, stir, cover the pan and leave it on the heat just long enough to warm the fish. Remove to a heated platter and sprinkle with the vinegar just before serving. (Lemon juice can be used in place of vinegar if you prefer.) Serves 4.

PANFISH IN CIDER

12 to 16 cleaned panfish
1 large sweet onion, peeled and
   sliced very thin
3 carrots, peeled or scraped,
   sliced lengthwise into very thin
   strips
1 stalk celery cut into thin crosswise slices
2 quarts sweet cider
1 tsp salt
2 tsp butter or margarine
2 tsp flour

Put the vegetables into a deep cooking pot, lay the fish on top, and pour the cider over them. Add the salt. Bring to a boil and when boiling begins reduce to a simmer and cook for 5 minutes. At this point the fish should be removed with tongs or a slotted spoon and placed in a heated bowl.

Let the vegetables continue simmering until the carrots are tender; this will be about 5 minutes. Remove the carrots, onions and celery, strain the cider, and return 1 quart to the pan. Boil briskly until it is reduced in volume by one-third, and reduce to a simmer.

Blend butter and flour into a smooth paste and flake it in small bits into the cider, stirring until it dissolves.

Return fish and vegetables to the pot long enough to reheat, about 2 minutes.

Serve in a bowl or individual soup bowls with boiled potatoes or rice as a side dish. Serves 4 to 6.

PANFISH PORTUGUESE STYLE

12 to 16 cleaned panfish
1½ cups fish stock
1 cup canned tomato sauce
1 cup grated sweet onion
1 clove garlic, crushed or minced
   very fine
1 sweet red pepper, cleaned and
   diced fine
2 Tbsp chopped fresh parsley
1 tsp salt
1 cup dry red wine (a California
   Zinfandel is the nearest equivalent to the wine that would be
   used in Portugal)
1 Tbsp butter or margarine

Butter a large ovenproof dish quite generously and lay the fish in it loosely. Combine the stock, tomato sauce, onion, garlic, pepper, parsley, and salt; pour this over the fish. Cook uncovered in a preheated 320-degree oven for 10 minutes. Pour in the wine, flake the butter over the top, and cook 10 minutes longer. Stir before serving. Serves 4 to 6.

PANFISH WITH VEGETABLES

12 to 16 cleaned panfish
    Salt
    Freshly ground white pepper
3 Tbsp butter or margarine
2 large boiled potatoes, peeled,
    cut in julienne strips
2 medium-sized sweet onions,
    peeled, sliced ½-inch thick with
    the slices separated into rings
2 cups green peas, fresh, frozen,
    or canned
½ cup dry white wine
½ cup light cream, or evaporated
    milk diluted ⅔ milk, ⅓ water

Dust the cavities of the fish generously with salt and pepper and set them aside to rest for 10 to 15 minutes before putting into the pot. If fresh green peas are used, they should be parboiled 5 minutes in lightly-salted water. Frozen peas should be dropped in boiling water and left for 3 minutes after they thaw. Canned peas need only be drained.

Melt 2 tablespoons of the butter in a large, deep skillet having a tight-fitting cover. Over medium-high heat, stir and toss the vegetables in the butter until the onions begin to turn a light tan. Spread the vegetables into a layer on the bottom of the pan, lay the fish on them and put a small dot of butter on each. Pour in the wine, cover the pan, reduce heat to its lowest range and cook 15 minutes. Open the pan, pour in the cream, stir well. Close the pan for 5 more minutes of cooking and serve. Serves 4 to 6.

PANFISH WITH SHALLOTS

12 to 16 cleaned panfish
 6 cups *court-bouillon*
¼ cup cider vinegar
 4 shallots, peeled and chopped
    coarsely
¼ pound butter
 2 Tbsp chopped fresh parsley

Have the cold *court-bouillon* in a deep pot, put the fish in and bring to a gentle boil. When boiling begins, reduce at once to a simmer and cook 5 minutes. When simmering begins, take ½ cup of the *court-bouillon* from the pot and put it in a small saucepan, add vinegar and shallots, bring quickly to a brisk boil and cook until the liquid is reduced to half its volume; stir occasionally to avoid scorching the shallots.

When the liquid is reduced, lower heat to simmer and begin adding the butter by tablespoonsful, beating with a wire whisk or an old-style hand eggbeater between each addition to produce a frothy, creamy sauce. Then put the fish on a hot platter and pour the sauce over them; sprinkle with parsley. Serves 4.

PANFISH BORDEAUX STYLE

2 Tbsp butter
3 medium-sized sweet onions, peeled and sliced thin
¾ cup broken or coarsely-chopped walnut meats
1½ cups mushrooms, fresh or canned; if canned mushrooms are used, drain well
12 to 16 cleaned panfish
1½ tsp salt
Large dash freshly ground white pepper
2 cups red wine
1 cup fish stock or bottled clam juice
¾ to 1 cup coarse fresh bread-crumbs
1 Tbsp grated Parmesan cheese
1½ Tbsp melted butter

On top of the stove, sauté the onions in 2 tablespoons butter, using an ovenproof dish that can go to the table later. When the onions begin to turn golden, add the walnuts and mushrooms and stir well. Put the fish on top of the ingredients in the pan, sprinkle with the salt and pepper, combine the wine and fish stock and pour over them.

Close the pan and transfer it to a preheated 300-degree oven. Cook for 20 minutes.

Mix breadcrumbs, cheese and melted butter, open the dish and spread the breadcrumb mixture over the top. Put under the broiler one or two minutes, just long enough to brown the topping to a tasty golden tan. Serves 4 to 6.

PANFISH FRICASSEE

2 Tbsp butter or margarine
2 Tbsp flour
1½ cups fish stock
1 cup dry white wine
¼ cup dry vermouth
1 anchovy fillet, drained and pulped (do not substitute anchovy paste; it is too coarse and too salty)
½ tsp salt
Moderate dash freshly ground white pepper
3 carrots, peeled or scraped, sliced in paper-thin rounds
12 to 16 cleaned panfish

Melt the butter in a deep, heavy skillet. Add the flour by sprinkling it over the butter evenly, then stirring immediately and briskly to form a smooth white paste, or *roux*. Cook over medium heat 3 or 4 minutes, but do let the *roux* brown.

Combine the fish stock, wine, and vermouth and pour into the pan slowly and evenly while stirring to form a smooth sauce. Stir in the pulped anchovy and seasoning; add the carrot and fish.

Close the pan and simmer 10 to 12 minutes. If the sauce thickens too much, stir in a little more stock; you want a sauce just thicker than rich cream. Serves 4 to 6.

CREAMY PANFISH CHOWDER

12 to 16 cleaned panfish
 1 heart of celery with root stub and leaves, minced
 2 small onions, peeled and chopped fine
 1 bay leaf
 2 tsp salt
 3 or 4 peppercorns, cracked or nicked with a knife
 3 large potatoes, peeled and sliced ½ inch thick
 2 thick slices salt pork or fat bacon
 1 cup heavy cream or undiluted evaporated milk
2½ cups milk or evaporated milk diluted with equal parts water
    Oyster crackers

Put the fish in a deep pot and pour in 1½ quarts cold water, more if needed to cover them completely. Add the celery, onions, bayleaf, salt, and peppercorns. Bring to a boil, reduce to a simmer, and cook 5 minutes from the time simmering begins. Strain the broth into a saucepan, put in the potatoes, and bring to a bubbling boil.

While the potatoes cook, remove the fish, skin them and flake the flesh from their bones, and put the flesh in a warmed bowl.

Prepare the salt pork; its rinds should be trimmed off and the pork blanched by plunging it into boiling water for 3 minutes. (Bacon, if used in place of salt pork, need not be blanched.) Dice the salt pork and sauté until crisply browned. As soon as the potatoes become tender, add the pork, fish, milk, and cream to the pot; include the fat from the skillet in which the pork cooked.

When the pot is simmering again, remove from heat and serve in soup bowls with crushed oyster crackers sprinkled on top. Serves 6 to 8.

PANFISH BURGUNDY STYLE

 4 Tbsp butter or margarine
 2 medium-sized sweet onions, peeled and sliced thin
12 to 16 cleaned panfish
    Dash of freshly ground white pepper
1½ cups Burgundy-type wine
 1 Tbsp butter or margarine
 1 Tbsp flour
 1 Tbsp meat extract: Bovril, B. V., etc.

Sauté the onions in 4 tablespoons butter, using a pan that can be put into the oven. Cook until the onions become transparent, then lay the fish on the onions, dust with salt and pepper, and pour in the wine. Cover the pan and cook in a preheated 350-degree oven for 15 to 20 minutes.

Remove the fish to heated serving plates or a platter. Strain the pan liquid into a saucepan. Combine 1 tablespoon butter and 1 tablespoon flour into a smooth paste and flake this into the simmering pan liquid over low heat, stirring each addition until it dissolves. Simmer 3 minutes after adding the last of the butter-flour paste, stir in the meat extract, and divide the sauce over the fish. Serves 4.

HOT PANFISH SALAD

10 to 12 cleaned panfish
1½ to 2 pints *court-bouillon*
¼ cup fine light olive oil
2 medium-sized boiled potatoes, peeled, sliced ¼-inch thick, the slices then quartered
1 large firm-ripe tomato, skinned, sliced very thin
3 hardcooked eggs, sliced
24 pitted ripe olives
1 tsp capers, well-drained
1½ tsp salt
Generous dash freshly ground white pepper
4 or 5 thin slices lemon, seeded

Poach the fish in the *court-bouillon,* starting with the liquid cold. Bring to a boil, and then reduce heat to a simmer; when simmering starts, remove from heat and let stand 5 minutes.

Drain the fish, skin, and flake flesh from bones in large pieces. Heat the oil,

put the fish and potatoes in it to warm, but not to cook. In an ovenproof dish that can go to the table, combine the fish, potatoes, tomatoes, half the olives, and all but a half-dozen center slices of the eggs. Dust the top with salt and pepper, pour over it any oil remaining in the skillet. Cook covered in a preheated 225-degree oven for 10 to 15 minutes. Remove from oven, uncover, quickly dot the top with the reserved egg slices, olives, capers and lemon slices. This is a meal-sized salad; serve it with a dry white wine. Serves 6 to 8.

CATFISH

FRIED CATFISH, WITH HUSHPUPPIES

This is the dish most commonly associated with catfish. Because it is generally served to a crowd, no quantities are given; you can adjust the quantity needed to serve your group by remembering that a half-pound of fish should be allowed per person, and that one cup of cornmeal will coat about three pounds of fish pieces. You will need:

Catfish, skinned and cleaned, cut in fairly uniform pieces

Cornmeal

Salt; allow ½ teaspoon per cup of cornmeal

Pepper; a generous dash per cup of cornmeal

Fat in a big kettle for deep frying; obviously, the size of the kettle determines the quantity of fat required; the level should be maintained at about ¾ full

2 cups white cornmeal
½ tsp salt
½ to ¾ cup boiling water

Stir the ingredients into a thick dough and form the hushpuppies in your hands to make small rounded pones. Drop them into the hot fat a few at a time, and cook for 5 to 8 minutes; strain out with a slotted spoon when nicely brown, or remove with tongs. Drain on cloth or paper towels for a few moments.

Have the fat in the kettle just under smoking-hot—on a cooking thermometer, between 370 and 380 degrees. Mix the cornmeal, salt and pepper together, wipe the pieces of catfish with a damp cloth and roll them in the seasoned cornmeal. Do not overload the kettle; put in the pieces of fish a few at a time so the temperature of the fat will not be lowered suddenly.

Cooking time for pieces roughly 3 inches by 2 inches by 1 inch will be 8 to 10 minutes; by then the outsides will be crisp, and the insides completely cooked. Use tongs or a long-handled, slotted spoon to fish out the cooked pieces; drain them briefly on cloth or paper towels before serving.

Hushpuppies *must* be cooked in the fat in which the fish are fried, otherwise they're nothing but cornpones. The following will give you a hint on how to adjust your ingredients for the quantity required; the quantity given produces 12 to 14 hushpuppies, about 2 inches long by 1 inch in diameter:

BAKED POACHED CATFISH

4 to 5-pound catfish, skinned and cleaned
1½ quarts cold water
1 Tbsp salt
1 Tbsp tarragon vinegar
½ tsp cracked or knife-nicked peppercorns
2 bay leaves
4 or 5 pieces green celery tops with leaves
3 or 4 sprigs fresh parsley
2 whole cloves
1 clove garlic
3 to 4 Tbsp anchovy butter
½ to ¾ cup fine dry breadcrumbs

Put the fish in a deep kettle or fish poacher; if it does not rest on a rack, wrap in cheesecloth so it can be removed without breaking when cooked. Pour in the water and add all other ingredients except anchovy butter and breadcrumbs. Bring to a boil, then reduce to a simmer; cook 5 minutes after simmering starts, remove the pan from heat and let the fish stay in the liquid until it cools. (If desired, the fish can be poached in advance and kept refrigerated until time to be baked.)

Remove fish from liquid, drain well, wipe dry, then divide into two halves and remove backbone and rib bones. Rub the pieces generously with anchovy butter, coating all sides. Lay on a buttered, oven-proof platter; if you wish, reconstitute the fish by arranging the two halves one atop the other.

Cook in a preheated 325-degree oven for 15 minutes, sprinkle with bread-crumbs, put under the broiler for 3 or 4 minutes until the breadcrumbs brown. Serves 4 to 6.

CATFISH IN SOUR CREAM

3- to 4-pound catfish, skinned and cleaned
½ cup flour (approximately)
⅓ cup butter or solid margarine
½ pound fresh mushrooms
1 cup light cream or evaporated milk, diluted
  2½ parts milk to 1 part water
¾ cup dairy sour cream
½ tsp meat extract; BV, Bovril, etc.
½ tsp salt
  Large pinch freshly-ground white pepper
  Small pinch nutmeg
1 tsp paprika
¾ to 1 cup fine dry breadcrumbs

Cut the fish into strips about 1½ to 2 inches long by ½ inch thick and wide. Remove bones while doing this. Roll the strips in flour.

Slice the mushrooms about ¼ inch thick. Sauté the mushrooms in the butter over moderate heat about 1 minute per side; add the pieces of fish and cook 3 to 4 minutes, turning to brown them evenly. The pieces of catfish should be a healthy but light golden tan.

Over very low heat combine the cream, sour cream, meat extract, salt, pepper, and nutmeg. Scrape into this liquid the fish, mushrooms, and any pan juices. Stir well, and then pour into a shallow gratin dish or individual gratin dishes. Combine the paprika and bread-crumbs and sprinkle the top of the dish or dishes generously.

Cook for 10 to 12 minutes in a preheated 325-degree oven and finish under the broiler if necessary to brown the topping to a rich, deep color. Serves 4 generously, 6 in a pinch.

CATFISH SICILIAN STYLE

CAJUN-COOKED CATFISH

3- to 4-pound catfish, skinned and cleaned
½ cup milk or evaporated milk diluted with equal parts water
¼ cup flour
¼ cup olive oil
1 Tbsp minced fresh parsley
1 clove garlic, minced or mashed
½ cup white wine vinegar
¼ cup fish stock
4 large ripe tomatoes, peeled and seeded, with all juices reserved, cut in coarse chunks
1 tsp salt
  Large dash freshly-ground white pepper

Cut the catfish into slices 1 to 1½ inches thick, cutting across the body at right angles. Dip the slices in milk and roll in flour. Wipe off any excess flour; a thin coating is all that's required. Heat the oil in a heavy skillet, and sauté the fish slices 3 minutes per side; they should be a rich brown. Combine all remaining ingredients and pour over the fish in the skillet. Cover and cook 15 to 20 minutes over medium heat. Serve with thick slices of generously-buttered Italian bread. Serves 4 to 6.

In Louisiana's Cajun country, where as a very young tad I learned from my cousins how to fish and shoot alligators for their hides, this was a standard recipe. For all I know, it still is, though it's been years since I sat in a narrow tippy *pirouge* poling through the mysterious black water of the dimly lighted swamps.

4 to 5 pounds of catfish, skinned and sliced across the body into inch-thick slices
½ cup flour
1 tsp salt
¼ tsp coarsely ground pepper
¼ tsp powdered basil
1 egg
½ cup thick milk
¾ cup fine cracker crumbs
1 Tbsp minced parsley
¼ cup cooking oil (bacon dripping was the original fat used for frying; substitute your choice of cooking oils, safflower, peanut, etc.)
2 cloves garlic
½ cup dry white wine

Rub each piece of fish thoroughly with flour. In a shallow bowl, combine salt, pepper, basil, egg, and milk by stirring well with a fork. On a flat work surface, combine cracker crumbs and parsley.

Dip each piece of fish in the egg mixture to coat it well; roll the pieces in the crumb mixture. Heat oil with the garlic in it; remove garlic when it is dark brown.

Sauté the pieces of fish over moderate heat about 3 minutes per side; transfer to oiled baking dish. When all the fish has been sautéd, dash the wine into the fat, stirring well. Pour the mixture over the fish; finish in a 400-degree oven for 20 minutes. Serve over steamed long-grain rice.

BLACK BASS WITH JOHN WILLARD'S SAUCE

2 large or 4 small black bass, preferably taken from very cold fresh water
½ pound fresh mushrooms
1 large clove garlic
½ cup scraped onion pulp or minced green onions
1 tsp salt
¼ tsp freshly ground white pepper
½ tsp powdered dry marjoram or 1 tsp minced fresh marjoram
½ to ¾ cup dry white wine

Prepare the ingredients 30 minutes before cooking and chill the fish in ice water, the sauce in the refrigerator. Split the bass down the back and remove backbone and dorsal fins, but do not try to remove ribs.

Chop the mushrooms coarsely; mince the garlic very fine or mash it; combine mushrooms, garlic, onion, salt, and pepper.

When ready to cook, wipe the bass halves well and lay them skin-side-up in a shallow oiled baking dish and sprinkle with the marjoram. Spread the sauce over the bass; add the wine. Cook under broiler for 20 to 25 minutes, basting with pan juices as required.

BAKED BLACK BASS

3½- to 4-pound black bass, scaled, head, tail, and fins removed as well as the edges of those moss-collecting crevices behind the gills and around the fins
⅓ cup lemon juice
¼ pound butter or margarine
2 egg yolks, lightly beaten
1 tsp capers
½ tsp dill seed
1½ tsp cider vinegar
½ tsp salt

Brush the fish's cavity well with lemon juice; also brush the raw areas where the fins and gills were removed. With the sharp tines of a cooking fork, pierce the thickest sections of the fish and hold the fork at an angle to hold the flesh apart while trickling in a bit of the lemon juice. Do this on both sides and then let the fish rest about 10 minutes before cooking. Bake on a fine-meshed rack in a preheated 375-degree oven 35 to 40 minutes. Baste occasionally with the remaining lemon juice creamed into 1 teaspoon butter.

While the fish is cooking: Cream the remaining butter with the egg yolks and blend into this the capers, dill seed, vinegar, and salt. Have a warmed ovenproof platter ready when the fish comes out of the oven. Slip the skin off the upper side of the fish by inserting a wide spatula along the spine and working it between the flesh and ribs. Transfer this half of the fish to the waiting platter, placing it rib-side-up, and spread with half the butter mixture. Lift out the spine and ribs from the carcass remaining in the pan, and move it with the spatula to the platter; turn it skin-side-up so the remaining half of the skin can be slipped off easily. If the sections of the fish should break when being moved, reform them. After removing the skin spread the upper side of the fish with the remaining butter mixture. Return the fish to the oven for 10 minutes, then serve by cutting slices at right angles to the body.

BLACK BASS WITH WALNUTS

2½ -to 3-pound bass
2 cups fish stock
1 Tbsp butter or solid margarine
¾ cup coarsely chopped or broken walnut meats
1 cup dairy sour cream
⅓ cup lemon juice
Stingy pinch grated horseradish
Small pinch of salt

After cleaning and scaling the fish, remove head and tail; cut out fins and the skin surrounding them. Wrap fish loosely in cheesecloth (the cheesecloth wrapping is only for easy removal of the fish from the poaching liquid; it can be omitted if a poaching pan is used) and poach in the stock by bringing to a boil, then reducing to a simmer. Cooking time will be 20 to 25 minutes after the simmering begins.

Drain fish from stock, transfer to a warmed platter, and slip off skin. If you feel like making the extra effort, divide the fish into two pieces.

Melt the butter over low heat and sauté the walnut meats until crisp but not brown. Combine the sour cream, lemon juice, horseradish, and salt with ½ cup of the hot stock in which the bass was poached. Pour this into the pan with the walnut meats and cook 3 to 4 minutes, just long enough to marry the flavors, before pouring it over the skinned fish on its platter. Serves 4 to 6.

BASS IN BEER

3- to 4-pound black bass
3 tablespoons butter or solid margarine
1½ Tbsp flour
2½ tsp salt
¾ tsp brown sugar
3 or 4 peppercorns, cracked or nicked with a knife
½ tsp nutmeg
1 Tbsp lemon juice

Clean and scale the bass; remove the head, tail, fins, and the skin around them, and divide the fish into slices about 1½ inches thick, cutting at right angles to the body.

Melt butter in a deep skillet over moderate heat, slowly add the flour while stirring until a smooth paste is formed. Cook for 3 to 4 minutes without allowing the paste to brown.

Pour in the beer in a slow, steady stream while stirring briskly with a slotted spoon or whisk to keep lumps from forming. Put in the seasonings, and then add the fish slices. Cover the pan and cook over low heat, the liquid just bubbling gently, for 5 minutes; turn the fish slices, and cook 5 minutes more.

Drain the fish slices from the sauce, letting the liquid return to the pan. Put the slices on a warmed platter or individual service plates, slip off the skin, and remove bones.

Increase heat under the sauce until it thickens to the consistency of a heavy cream, then strain over the fish.

Serve with hot boiled potatoes or thick slices of unbuttered toast for dunking in the sauce. Serves 4 to 6.

BLACK BASS ITALIAN STYLE

4 bass, ¾ to 1 pound each
1 to 1½ teaspoon salt
¾ to 1 teaspoon freshly-ground white pepper
3 Tbsp olive oil
3 Tbsp minced sweet onion
1 clove garlic, threaded on a string
1 cup fish stock
½ cup tomato paste
1 tsp minced fresh basil or 1½ teaspoons crumbled dry or powdered basil

Clean and scale the bass, remove heads, tails, fins, and the skin around them.

Rub the fish lightly inside and out with salt and pepper and sauté in the oil over moderate heat, cooking 5 to 7 minutes per side, depending upon their size.

Remove the fish to a heated service platter or individual plates. Sauté the onion and garlic in the fat remaining in the pan; when the onion is a deep gold in color, fish out the garlic by its string and add the fish stock, tomato paste and basil to the onions in the pan. Stir occcasionally while this simmers 4 to 5 minutes; then pour over the fish. Hot buttered Italian bread or hard rolls go well with this. Serves 4.

BLACK BASS PLANTATION STYLE

4   bass, ¾ to 1 pound each
1½   cups cooked white rice
½   cup grated Parmesan cheese
½   cup grated cheese, longhorn or
     gruyere
½   tsp salt
¼   tsp cayenne pepper
1   egg
4   Tbsp butter or solid margarine
1 to 2 Tbsp flour

Clean and scale the bass, remove fins and the skin around them, trim tails, but leave heads on the fish.

Pound the rice, cold and dry, into a crumbly paste; combine it with the two cheeses, salt and pepper.

Beat the egg lightly and stir into the rice mixture. Stuff the fish with this, closing the openings with small skewers or by sewing.

Rub the outsides of the fish very lightly with butter and roll in flour; shake off any clots of flour that form. Melt the remaining butter in a heavy skillet with a tightly-fitting lid and sauté the fish over low to moderate heat with the pan closed. Cook gently, 7 to 8 minutes per side. Serves 4.

BLACK BASS WITH WHITE GRAPES

4   small bass, ½ to ¾ pound each
3   Tbsp flour
1   tsp salt
¼   tsp freshly ground white pep-
     per
¼   pound butter
¾   cup white wine
1   cup seedless white grapes
3   Tbsp brandy

Clean and scale the fish, remove fins and the skin around them; trim tails, but leave the heads on.

Toss the flour, salt and pepper together in a plastic bag and rub a light, even coating of the seasoned flour over the fish; it may be necessary to wipe them first with a damp cloth to make the coating stick properly.

Sauté the fish gently in the butter over low to moderate heat, cooking 4 to 5 minutes per side, depending upon size. Pour the wine into the pan with the fish, and when it begins to bubble and simmer, remove pan from heat, cover it, and let it stand 5 minutes.

Drain the bass from the pan, letting the liquid flow back into it; put the fish on a warmed platter or individual service plates. Skin the bass at this point, if you feel like it.

Over brisk heat, bring the pan liquid to a boil and cook until it is reduced to half its volume. Put the grapes in a heatproof dish, warm the brandy, pour it over the grapes and ignite it; when the flames die, put the grapes into the pan, scraping the dish to get off all brandy essence. Stir the pan juices once or twice and pour over the fish. Serves 4 delightfully.

BLACK BASS MARYLAND STYLE

5 -pound bass, or two or three
   smaller fish
1 to 1½ tsp salt
¾ to 1 tsp freshly-ground white
   pepper
⅛ pound butter (no substitutes)
1 tsp chopped shallots
½ cup rye whiskey (or Irish whiskey)
1½ cups heavy cream or undiluted
   evaporated milk
2 egg yolks
⅓ cup dry sherry

If you are using a single large fish, cut it into quarters, and skin it; if several small fish, cut them in halves or thirds, depending upon size, and remove skin.

Dust the pieces well with salt and pepper. Melt the butter in a heavy, deep skillet or saucepan with a tightly fitting cover. Put in the shallots and pieces of fish and cook covered, turning the fish so the pieces will cook 3 to 4 minutes per side.

Set aside 3 tablespoons of the whiskey; warm the remainder, pour over the fish in the pan and ignite. When the flames die down, pour in 1 cup of cream, cover the pan, and cook at very low heat for 5 to 7 minutes, depending upon the size of the fish pieces.

When the fish flakes readily, drain the pieces out with a slotted spoon, letting the juices flow back into the pan; put the pieces of fish on a warmed platter.

Beat the egg yolk with the remaining cream, whiskey, and sherry. Pour into the pan and cook 5 minutes without boiling. Strain the sauce over the fish. Serve with plain boiled rice. Serves 6.

BLACK BASS LISBON STYLE

4 small bass, ¾ to 1 pound each
1½ tsp olive oil
2 Tbsp chopped sweet onion
4 large ripe tomatoes, peeled and
   seeded, juices drained, chopped
   coarsely (substitute equivalent
   quantity of canned tomatoes if
   fresh ones not available)
1 clove garlic, minced or crushed
1 Tbsp coarsely chopped parsley
¼ tsp powdered marjoram
½ bay leaf
½ tsp salt
¾ cup dry red wine
½ cup light cream or evaporated

milk diluted 2½ parts milk to 1
part water
1 Tbsp butter or solid margarine
1 Tbsp flour

Clean and scale fish, cut them into 3 or 4
pieces of approximately equal size, discarding heads, tails, fins and the skin
around the fins.

Heat the oil in a heavy skillet that
can go to the oven, and sauté the onion,
tomatoes, garlic, parsley and rosemary
very gently for 5 or 6 minutes. Bury the
bay leaf in the vegetables, and put the
bass pieces on top of them. Combine the
wine and cream and pour into the pan.
Cover pan and cook in a preheated 325-
degree oven for 20 minutes.

Lift out the fish, putting it on a
warmed platter; drain the vegetables from
the pan with a slotted spoon, letting the
juices flow back into the pan. Remove and
discard bay leaf; arrange the vegetables
around the pieces of fish on the platter.

Bring the juices in the pan to a gentle simmer. Knead butter and flour into a
smooth paste and flake into the pan, stirring until each addition dissolves, and letting the juices simmer at least 5 minutes
after the last bit of the paste has been
added. Pour the sauce over the fish pieces
and serve with generous slices of fresh,
crusty bread. Serves 4 to 6.

BASS WITH CELERY STUFFING

3½ to 4-pound bass
 ¾ tsp salt
     Pinch of freshly-ground white
     pepper
  3 Tbsp butter or solid margarine
  2 Tbsp grated sweet onion
 ½ cup celeriac (celery root, some-
     times called celery knob)
     peeled, sliced paper-thin, and
     shredded into slivers the thick-
     ness of toothpicks
  3 sprigs of fresh green celery
     tops with leaves
  1 to 1½ cups coarse fresh bread-
     crumbs
     Juice of 1 fresh lime or 1½ ta-
     blespoons bottled lime juice
  3 Tbsp butter or solid margarine
 ¼ tsp grated Sapsago cheese

Clean and scale the fish, trim tail, and remove fins and the skin around them; leave
the head on. Dust fish sparingly inside
and out with salt and pepper. In 3 tablespoons butter, sauté the onion and celeriac until the onion begins to become
transparent; add the sprigs of celery tops
to the pan when you begin to cook this,
but remove them before adding other ingredients. When the onions begin to clear,
remove the pan from heat, stir in the
breadcrumbs and lime juice, and use this
to stuff the cavity of the fish. Close the
cavity with small skewers or by sewing.
Using about 1 tablespoon butter, grease a

shallow baking pan and put the fish in it. Cook uncovered in a pre-heated 375-degree oven for 35 to 45 minutes, depending upon size of fish. Combine the remaining butter with the Sapsago cheese and brush the fish with the mixture three or four times as it cooks. Serves 4 to 6.

BASS BRANCA

2   bass of about 2 pounds each
2   leeks
1   heart of celery, with leaves
1   sweet red pepper, cleaned and
     seeded, cut in ¼-inch strips
½   teaspoon salt
3   Tbsp olive oil
1   cup mushrooms, sliced about ⅛
     inch
½   cup grated sweet onion
½   clove garlic, minced or mashed
6   red-ripe tomatoes, skinned and
     seeded, or equivalent in well-
     drained canned tomatoes
2   sprigs fresh parsley
1   tsp powdered marjoram
1   bay leaf
1   cup dry white wine
½   teaspoon lemon juice
2   Tbsp chopped fresh parsley

Clean and scale the bass; cut them into 1-inch slices, cutting at right angles to the body, and discard head, tail, fins, and the skin around the fins.

Trim the roots and green tops off the leeks, sliver them and the celery heart into matchstick-sized pieces, combine them with the red pepper, sprinkle with salt, and sauté in 1 tablespoon oil over very low heat until they just begin to soften; do not let them get brown or turn mushy.

In a separate pan, sauté the onion and garlic in 1 tablespoon oil until the onion softens; then add the tomatoes, parsley, marjoram, and bay leaf. Cook until the tomatoes can be pulped easily. Remove parsley and bay leaf, combine the leek-celery-pepper mixture with the onion-tomato mixture, and spread half of it on the bottom of a buttered baking dish. Put the fish on this and cover with the remaining vegetable mixture. Combine the wine and lemon juice and pour into the pan. Cook uncovered in a preheated 350-degree oven for 45 minutes. Sprinkle chopped parsley over the top of the dish before taking it to the table. Serves 4 to 6.

CAMP-STYLE PIKE OR MUSKELLUNGE FILLETS

2   very large or 4 small fillets
8   thick slices of salt pork
2   small sweet onions, peeled and
     sliced ¼ inch thick
     Dash of pepper
2   Tbsp water

2 **Tbsp lemon juice**

Trim rinds from the salt pork and blanch it by plunging it into boiling water for 3 or 4 minutes; drain well. Sauté the pork in a heavy skillet until brown on one side. Turn the pork, cover it with the onion slices, and lay the fillets on top of the onions. Sprinkle with pepper (the pork will still have enough salt in it to flavor the dish). Combine water and lemon juice and pour over the fillets. Cover the pan tightly and cook over moderate heat, 20 minutes for thick fillets, 12 to 15 for small.

fillets to a buttered gratin dish or to individual gratin dishes.

Beat the egg lightly, combine it with the cream, melt the remaining butter with what is left in the pan from cooking the fillets, and stir the melted butter into the egg-cream mixture. Pour this over the fillets and sprinkle the cheddar cheese over the top.

Cook in a preheated 400-degree oven 5 to 6 minutes; if the cheese topping has not browned by that time, put under the broiler for a moment until it becomes a deep tan. Serves 4.

PIKE FILLETS AU GRATIN

4 **large pike fillets**
½ **tsp salt**
   Generous dash freshly ground white pepper
2½ **Tbsp butter or solid margarine**
1½ **cups light cream or evaporated milk diluted 2½ parts milk to 1 part water**
1 **egg**
¾ **cup grated, medium-sharp cheddar cheese**

Dust the fillets very lightly with salt and pepper and sauté them over moderate heat, using 1½ tablespoons of butter and cooking 2 minutes per side. Transfer the

PIKE FILLETS, BRUGGE STYLE

4 **large pike fillets**
¾ **head of curly endive (in some areas this leaf vegetable is called chicory)**
2 **Tbsp chopped shallots**
½ **cup cream or evaporated milk diluted 3 parts milk to 1 part water**
¾ **cup white wine**
4 **thin slices lemon, seeded**
2 **Tbsp butter**
   Scanty pinch of salt
   Small dash of freshly-ground white pepper

Blot the fillets dry. Butter a shallow baking dish and cover the bottom thickly—at least 1 inch deep—with the choice green, leafy portions of endive, discarding the white stalks and center sections of the leaves. Scatter the shallots over the endive and lay the fillets on this green nest. Combine the cream and wine and pour over the fillets.

Cover the pan and cook in a preheated 350-degree oven for 12 to 15 minutes, depending upon the thickness of the fillets. Once or twice while cooking, uncover the pan long enough to baste the fillets lightly with the pan liquid. Place a lemon slice on each fillet and with the pan uncovered, cook 5 minutes longer. Remove each fillet with the endive beneath it to a warmed service plate, letting the pan liquids drain back into the pan.

On top of the stove, over brisk heat, bring the liquid to a seething boil, stir in salt and pepper, taste, and adjust seasoning; avoid over-salting. Divide the sauce over the portions and serve. Serves 4.

POACHED PIKE WITH BUTTER SAUCE

    4- to 5-pound pike
1½ quarts *court-bouillon*
    2 Tbsp chopped shallots
    ¾ cup white wine vinegar
1½ pounds butter
    ½ tsp salt
      Large dash freshly ground
      white pepper

Poach the pike in the *court-bouillon,* bringing the liquid to a boil and then reducing the heat until it simmers very gently. Cook 20 to 25 minutes from the time simmering begins, depending upon the size of the fish.

Drain the pike well, remove to a warm platter, slip its skin off, and flake its flesh from the bones in large pieces.

Over brisk heat, boil 1 tablespoon of the shallots in the vinegar until the liquid is reduced to half its volume; stir to keep the shallots from scorching. Strain the reduced vinegar into a clean saucepan.

Cut 1 pound of butter into small chunks and melt it in the vinegar over very low heat. As soon as the butter has been placed in the pan, begin beating it with a wooden spoon and continue beating as it melts. As soon as the butter starts melting, add the remaining shallots. Beat until the butter and vinegar combine into a creamy, frothy sauce; then cut the remaining butter into small pieces and beat into the sauce to smooth and refine its texture. Spread the sauce over the pieces of pike and serve at once with crusty hard rolls or French bread. Serves 4 generously, 6 adequately.

PIKE FILLETS AMBASSADOR

    4 large pike fillets
      Stingy pinch of salt
      Sparse dash of freshly-ground
      white pepper

1 Tbsp butter (no substitutes)
1 Tbsp finely-minced shallots
1 Tbsp finely-minced fresh parsley
3 Tbsp lemon juice
¾ cup fish stock
¾ cup dry white wine
1½ cups heavy cream or undiluted evaporated milk
2 egg yolks

Dust the fillets very lightly with salt and pepper and place them in a baking dish that has a bare film of butter on its bottom.

Combine the butter, shallots, parsley, and lemon juice, and spread a portion over the top of each fillet. Stir together the fish stock and wine and pour into the pan; it should barely cover the fillets. Cook covered in a preheated 350-degree oven for 12 to 14 minutes.

Remove the fillets to warm serving plates or a platter, letting the cooking liquid drain back into the pan. Strain the liquid into a clean saucepan and boil briskly until it is reduced to half its volume.

Bring cream to the boiling point but remove from heat the instant bubbles begin to form where the cream touches the side of the saucepan. Strain the cream into the reduced pan-liquid and stir briskly; remove at once from heat. Divide the sauce over the fillets. Traditionally, each fillet is garnished with a pair of lightly-sautéed mushroom buttons, put on top of them before saucing. Serves 4.

PIKE FILLETS MEUNIÈRE

4 large pike fillets
1 cup light cream or evaporated milk diluted 2½ parts milk to 1 part water
½ tsp salt
⅛ tsp freshly ground white pepper
1 cup flour (approximately)
3 Tbsp butter (no substitutes)
1 tsp lemon juice
1 tsp chopped fresh parsley
½ tsp chopped fresh chervil or ¾ teaspoon dry chervil
   Parsley sprigs and lemon wedges for garnish

Wipe or blot the fillets dry. Combine cream, salt and pepper. Dip the fillets in this mixture, then roll in the flour; shake off any excess flour that may cling to them in clots.

Sauté the fillets in 2 tablespoons butter over low to moderate heat, cooking about 4 minutes per side, until they are a rich, golden brown. Drain from the pan with a slotted spatula, letting the fat return to the pan, and put on a warmed platter or individual serving plates.

Add the remaining butter to the pan and increase the heat. When it froths, dash in the lemon juice, parsley and chervil, stir quickly and briskly, and pour over the fillets. Garnish with parsley sprigs and lemon wedges. Serves 4.

BAKED PIKE FILLETS

4 large or 8 small pike fillets
4 Tbsp olive oil
1 Tbsp lemon juice
   Large pinch salt
   Small dash freshly ground
   white pepper
¼ cup butter or solid margarine
2 Tbsp minced fresh parsley

Marinate the fillets 30 minutes in a marinade made by mixing the oil, lemon juice, salt, and pepper. Turn once or twice.

Drain the fillets. Rub a thin film of butter on the bottom of a heavy skillet and bring it to high heat. Sear the fillets not more than 20 to 30 seconds per side, then arrange them in a well-buttered baking dish. Melt half the remaining butter, pour over the fillets, and sprinkle them with parsley. Cook uncovered in a preheated 350-degree oven for 15 minutes. Baste with the remaining butter two or three times while the fillets cook. Serves 4.

BOURRIDE OF PIKE

1½ quarts water
¾   tsp salt
2 large, sweet onions, peeled and chopped coarsely
3 red-ripe tomatoes or the equivalent in canned tomatoes, coarsely chopped
2 cloves garlic, peeled and minced or mashed
2 pounds pike fillets cut into ½-inch strips
2 generous dashes orange bitters, or the zest of ½ orange cut into toothpick-sized strips (The zest of citrus fruit is the thin outer peel with all white pith removed.)
2 egg yolks
4 thick slices toasted French or Italian bread

Bring the water containing the salt, onion, tomatoes, and garlic to a boil and cook briskly for 10 minutes. Reduce to a simmer, add the strips of pike and the bitters or orange zest, and cook 5 to 7 minutes, until the fish flakes readily.

Drain the liquid from the pot into a clean saucepan, put the solids in a warmed bowl, and remove the strips of orange zest, if this has been used.

Beat the egg yolks into the liquid in the saucepan over very low heat. With a pastry blender or wire potato masher, quickly reduce the solids to a smooth paste and blend them with the liquid in the saucepan, stirring briskly. Put slices of bread into soup bowls and pour the bourride over them. Serves 4.

BROILED DILLED PICKEREL

4 -pound pickerel, or two fish of
about 2 pounds each
2 Tbsp butter or solid margarine
2 Tbsp lemon juice
½ tsp salt
⅛ tsp cayenne
1 Tbsp dillseed
1 large dill pickle

Cut slits at an angle across the pickerel's body an inch or so apart, on both sides of the fish. Combine the butter and lemon juice, work this into the cuts generously, and rub the entire body of the fish with it, inside and out. Dust the fish, including cavity, with salt and cayenne. Put a big pinch of dillseed and the dill pickle into the cavity; close it with skewers or by sewing. Work the remaining dillseed into the butter mixture packed into the slits, spreading them open to fill generously.

Preheat the broiler 5 minutes. Broil the pickerel 7 to 10 minutes per side, depending upon its size. Serve with a garnish of lemon wedges. (If you cook two small fish instead of one large one, the adjustment of recipe quantities is easy to make; so is the adjustment of cooking time.) Serves 4.

PICKEREL FILLETS, SEVILLE STYLE

4 large pickerel fillets
Stingy sprinkling of salt
Generous dusting of cayenne
1 cup orange juice (fresh juice,
preferably)
4 Tbsp salt
8 slices of sweet onion, about ½-
inch thick
8 slices of firm-ripe (but not soft)
tomato
½ green pepper, cleaned, cut in
matchstick-sized strips
1 Tbsp butter
Large dash orange bitters

Thirty minutes before cooking time, sprinkle the fillets with salt and cayenne and marinate at room temperature in the orange juice. They should be turned once or twice during the marinating period. On a flat surface spread 2 tablespoons salt on waxed paper and press the onion slices into it; sprinkle the remaining 2 tablespoons salt over them.

At cooking time, butter a shallow baking dish. Wash the onion slices under cold running water to remove all salt, and blot them dry. Put the onion slices in the bottom of the pan. Drain the fillets from the orange juice, reserving the juice, and put them on top of the onion slices. Cover the fillets with the tomato slices and strew the slivers of green pepper over the tomatoes. Heat the orange juice, melt the butter in it, add the bitters to the juice, and pour over the fillets. Cook uncovered in a preheated 375-degree oven for 25 minutes, basting occasionally with the pan liquid. Serve with plain boiled rice as a side dish. Serves 4.

BRAISED MUSKELLUNGE FILLETS

4 large muskellunge fillets
  Head, bones, and trimmings of flesh left after filleting the fish
1 quart cold water
3 cups white wine
2 or 3 sprigs parsley
½ tsp shredded fresh thyme or ¾ teaspoon crumbled dry or powdered thyme
2 Tbsp grated sweet onion
½ bay leaf
¼ tsp lemon juice or 1 thick slice lemon
2 Tbsp butter (no substitute)
½ tsp salt
  Dash of cayenne

Put fish head, bones, and trimmings in a saucepan with 1 quart cold water, bring to a boil, and boil for 5 minutes; skim off the froth rising to the surface until no more appears. Reduce heat to simmer, and add wine, parsley, onion, bay leaf, and lemon juice or slice. Simmer for 20 minutes from the time simmering restarts after ingredients are added, and then strain liquid into a clean saucepan through a fine-meshed cloth. Boil until reduced to half its volume.

Butter a shallow baking dish having a tight-fitting cover. Lay the fillets in this, and sprinkle with salt and pepper. Add the remaining butter to the reduced liquid in the saucepan, and pour over the fillets. Close the pan; cook in a preheated 350-degree oven for 25 minutes. Serves 4 very satisfactorily.

BAKED MUSKELLUNGE FILLETS

4 large muskellunge fillets about ½-inch thick
2 tsp salt
½ tsp freshly-ground white pepper
¼ tsp powdered thyme
¼ pound butter or solid margarine
2 Tbsp minced, fresh parsley
2 Tbsp minced shallots
⅓ cup lemon juice
¾ cup white wine

Dry the fillets well; combine the salt, pepper and thyme and rub them well with this mixture. Butter a shallow casserole, put in the fillets, and sprinkle the parsley and shallots over them. Combine lemon juice and wine, and pour over the fillets. Cover the pan and bake in a preheated 325-degree oven for 10 minutes. Open the pan, spread each fillet very thickly with butter, and cook uncovered for 15 minutes longer. Serves 4.

cook 15 to 20 minutes. The red pepper and onion pieces should still be chewy when the stew is ladled into soup bowls with a slice of crisp-crusted Italian or French bread in the bottom. Eat with a spoon. Serves 6 to 8.

DENNY MERCURIO'S ITALIAN-STYLE STRIPED BASS

8- to 10-pound striped bass, cut in
   2-inch chunks, skin removed
   from the pieces
¼ cup olive oil
2 pounds fresh cherry or pear tomatoes (or substitute an equal
   quantity of large tomatoes, cut
   in chunks)
3 sweet white onions, about 2
   inches in diameter, chopped
1 sweet red pepper, cleaned and
   chopped coarsely
2 cloves garlic, peeled and
   minced
¾ pint dry white wine (Chianti,
   preferably)
⅓ cup white wine vinegar (or use
   1 tablespoon cider vinegar)
   Water

Clean and cut up the bass, heat the oil in a large stew pot, and stir the pieces of fish in the hot oil for 3 or 4 minutes. Add the remaining ingredients, increase heat until the pot boils, reduce to a simmer, and

STRIPED BASS STEAKS GENOVESE

2 large steaks 1½ inches thick
   from a large bass, or 4 steaks of
   that thickness taken from a
   smaller fish
½ cup olive oil
4 cloves garlic
½ cup fresh basil or ¾ cup dry
   basil
½ cup fresh parsley leaves, coarse
   stems discarded
½ tsp salt
4 walnut halves
4 mint leaves

Prepare the sauce by pounding together in a mortar ⅓ cup of the oil, the garlic, basil, parsley, salt, walnuts, and mint. Work it into a smooth, creamy paste. If you have a blender, the sauce is easy; just put it in the blender and run at high speed in 10 to 15-second bursts until the desired smoothness is achieved.

Brush the steaks lightly with olive oil and broil them on a rack, about 6 inches from the heat source, for 12 to 15 minutes. (If cooked on the outdoor grill over coals, the timing is 6 minutes per side.) Baste occasionally with fresh oil as the fish cooks—never use the pan drippings to baste with.

Three or four minutes before cooking is completed, remove the steaks, brush both sides thickly with the sauce, and return to the broiler to finish. Serves 4.

SALTWATER FISH

BAKED BLUEFISH

4 bluefish fillets from 6- to 8-pound fish
1 scant tsp salt
  Freshly ground white pepper
½ pound butter
1 cup finely chopped parsley
¼ cup crumbled dry or chopped fresh marjoram

Use a large enameled or porcelainized baking pan; if one is not available, line a metal pan with foil to prevent the fish

from sticking. Butter the bottom of the pan and lay the fillets in it, skin-side-down. Sprinkle the fillets with salt and pepper and dot them generously with teaspoon-sized pieces of butter. Mix the parsley and marjoram together by shaking in a paper bag and spread thickly over the fish. Bake uncovered in a 425-degree oven for 30 minutes, then baste three times at 5-minute intervals with butter from the pan.

BROILED OR GRILLED SALMON

2 large salmon steaks, at least 1 inch thick
⅓ cup drawn butter (see below)
  Salt, pepper, lemon wedges—to be used after cooking

To make drawn (or clarified) butter, heat butter over low heat in a small saucepan until its liquids and solids separate; remove the pan from heat and let stand while the white solids settle to the bottom, and carefully pour off the liquid for use.

Cook the fish on a broiler rack over a pan; preheat rack to keep the salmon from sticking. Rub the steaks well with the drawn butter and cook 6 to 7 inches from the heat source for 10 minutes per side. Baste often with the drawn butter. Remove steaks to warmed plates, and divide into halves by sliding a knife-blade along the backbone and ribs. Serve with seasonings and allow each diner to season his or her own portion.

BROILED WEAKFISH WITH LIME BUTTER

SALMON IN CREAM SAUCE

4 individual serving portions, about 6 by 6 inches, cut from a salmon fillet
⅓ cup drawn butter (see preceding recipe)
¾ pint heavy cream (fresh, not canned milk diluted)
1 cup Rhine wine
½ tsp salt
Large pinch of freshly grated nutmeg

Sauté the salmon pieces over very low heat in the butter, cook 10 minutes per side, remove to warmed plates. While the salmon is cooking, combine cream, wine, salt, and nutmeg and add slowly to the pan after removing the salmon; stir as you add to amalgamate the cream with the butter remaining in the pan. Divide the sauce over the fish portions and serve at once.

2 2½- to 3-pound weakfish, heads removed
¼ pound butter
Juice of 2 limes
Large pinch each of salt and white pepper
⅛ tsp freshly grated nutmeg
¼ tsp finely powdered thyme

Before beginning to broil the fish, simmer the heads for ½ hour in 1 pint water, remove the heads, and reduce the liquid one-half by boiling briskly. Cream together the butter, lime juice, and seasonings. Divide one-fourth of the butter mixture between the cavities of the fish. Brush half the remaining butter mixture over the bodies of the fish. Place the fish on a rack over a broiling pan and broil 5 to 7 minutes per side, basting generously with the remaining butter until it is gone, then baste with the pan juices.

GROUPER FILLETS

BAKED SNAPPER ACAPULCO

4 grouper fillets, about ½ pound
  each
1 tsp paprika
½ cup olive oil or light cooking oil
½ tsp hot pepper sauce (not Tabasco—it's too hot)
1 Tbsp fresh lemon juice
3 or 4 drops onion juice
1 tsp Dijon mustard
¼ cup tomato puree (not catsup, it
  contains too much sugar)
⅓ cup chopped fresh parsley

4 snapper fillets, skinless
¼ cup cooking oil, olive preferred
¼ tsp salt
  Dash freshly ground pepper
1 Tbsp mild chili sauce
1½ Tbsp mashed avocado (or you
  can substitute real mayonnaise—NOT salad dressing)
  Juice of ½ lime (not bottled
  lime juice)
2 Tbsp minced fresh parsley

Rub the fillets on both sides with the paprika. Rub a broiling pan with enough oil
to keep the fillets from sticking.

Combine the remaining oil with the
pepper sauce, lemon and onion juice,
mustard, and tomato puree.

Broil the fillets 4 to 6 minutes at 350
degrees in a preheated oven. Turn when
the tops of the fillets begin to darken and
broil 4 to 6 minutes. Drain fat from the
pan; pour the sauce over the fillets. Reduce oven temperature to 225 degrees and
cook until the sauce begins to bubble.
Serve some of the sauce with each portion
of the fish, and accompany the dish with
crusty French or Italian bread with which
to soak up the sauce.

Combine salt and 1 teaspoon oil; rub this
over the fillets on both sides. Arrange fillets in an oiled shallow baking dish; do not
overlap them or put in layers. Broil in
preheated oven until tops of fillets begin
to brown. Combine chili sauce, avocado,
lime juice, and parsley while fillets are
broiling. Turn fillets and cover each with a
layer of the sauce, dividing it equally between them. Broil 2 to 3 minutes, until
fish flakes easily when tested at edge with
a fork.

SHELLFISH AND CRUSTACEANS

Not all wild foods in these categories come from salt water. Every fisherman who's tried his luck in inland waters is aware of the presence of freshwater mussels, which are edible but tough, and bait fishermen have learned when bottom-fishing to distinguish between the tap-tap of an inquisitive fish and the tiny subtle tugs of a crayfish investigating his bait.

Crayfish can be caught on a hookless line baited with many of the same baits a fish would take, though the best bait is a bit of bacon rind tied to a leader. In some waters these crustaceans reach good size, and are just as edible as their close salt-water cousins, the shrimp. You may call crayfish by one of their other commonly used names—crawfish or crawdad.

Crayfish have a tremendously wide distribution; their eggs are carried on the legs of migrating shorebirds from place to place. You'll find these tasty crustaceans everywhere—I know of one small lake that lies up in the 7,000-foot altitudes of the Sierra Nevadas in which crayfish are so thick you need a spoon to stir the water to make room for your line.

However, unless you live in close proximity to the sea and enjoy beach-combing or skin diving, the shellfish you serve will most probably come from the fish market. But whether you live on the Atlantic or the Pacific or along the Gulf coast, you can make a good harvest from the ocean, its beaches, and its tidal marshes. Of course, in this day of air freight and lightweight refrigeration with dry ice, the fruits of all three coastal areas are readily available to you even in the deepest inland areas.

Along the Atlantic coast, you can harvest mussels from the tidal rocks almost anywhere from Maine to Florida. There are clams to be taken from the beach sands of the northern coast, and from the mid-continent south you'll find crabs offshore in the shallows where the surf begins to break, as well as the ever-present mussels on tidal rocks.

Around the arc of the Gulf coast from Florida to the tip of Texas, crabs of several kinds abound just a stone's throw from the tidal shallows. The warm Gulf waters don't lend themselves to other shellfish life, and though the shrimp which abound in the food-rich areas far from shore grow to huge sizes, they can be taken only by trawlers pulling purse seines through deep water.

From Monterey Bay, which is about half-past California on the Pacific coast, the bounty of the shores increases as you move north to the Canadian border and beyond. Mussels cling to the tide-washed stones; there are clams in the sand at the surf-line; and a bit further north, past San Francisco Bay, the bulbous goeduck buries itself on the beaches well above the low-tide-line. North of Humboldt Bay you'll also find odd brilliant orange sea urchins clinging to tidal stones with the mussels.

Offshore in the depths north of Monterey Bay there are abalone, but these must be harvested by skin diving, which is not a pastime for those who haven't had the training in this skill. Nor is it something you should try unless you know the waters, and unless you have a diving partner along who can help you avoid the hazards and lead you to places where you might find this now-rare and always delicious bivalve.

To suggest that gathering this harvest is your problem, to point out that this book is supposed to tell you how to cook, not catch, would be a craven cop-out. In all fairness, having come this far in titillating your gastric juices, here are the basics you'll need.

GATHERING MUSSELS, CRABS, SEA URCHINS

Gathering mussels is a matter of wading, and you'll need some sort of wide metal pry-bar to get them off the rocks. Work the areas between tidal marks and especially just below the low-tide-line. Tap the shells before you pry the mussels loose. If there's a live mussel inside, the shell will gape open a bit. If you get no response, the shell holds nothing but sand.

Watch the beach as the surf recedes for the dimples made by clams siphoning themselves along under the sand. Get to the spot fast and thrust your hand down to grab the clam before it gets away. Or, you can make a clam box by nailing together four pieces of 1-by-6 inch lumber to form a square and tacking hardware cloth across one side. Scoop up a big load of sand with one side and lift the box to let the sand fall through the hardware cloth, which traps the clam.

On the North Pacific shore the goeduck, called this because of its ducklike neck, must be spotted by the dimple it makes in the sand and dug out with a spade. Taking goeducks is a two-person job. One ducker shoves a hand into the dimple and grabs the clam's long outstretched neck, then holds on while the other digs. Don't try to dig up a goeduck unless you have a partner holding it. A goeduck can dig itself below the reach of your shovel faster than you can dig.

Crabs can be caught with a handline. Bait the working end with a chunk of salt pork as big as your two thumbs and wade out as far as you can, until you're standing waist-deep. Cast the bait into a receding wash of surf and wait until you feel a tiny tug on the line, then v-e-r-y s-l-o-w-l-y bring the crab in, hoping that it will not let go until you've pushed your long-handled dip-net under it.

Or, where the bottom shelves to deep water within wading distance, cover a barrel hoop with chicken wire and fasten three or four chunks of pork to the mesh. Tie a line to the hoop and after flinging it out as far as you can, wait a quarter-hour or so, then drag it to shore slowly, again hoping there'll be a crab or two holding onto your pork pieces. If there are crabs around, your chances of bringing them in this way are good, for crabs seldom let go of a bait.

Sea urchins are taken like mussels, pried from tidal rocks. These bright-orange creatures look like prickly puff-balls and their family name, *Echinus*, means little to anyone but a marine biologist, who knows—or should know—that the word is Greek for "spiny skinned." The sea urchin is related to the starfish and sea hedgehog or cucumber. Sea urchins cling to tidal rocks and subsist on microorganisms washed their way at high tide. During low tides along a rocky coast they are very easy to gather from shoreline rock formations by wading, and when the sea is calm they can be picked from a

pare your catch before we go on to the cooking and eating which is the object of all your endeavors.

PREPARING SHORE FOODS

In the balance of this chapter, we'll treat freshwater crayfish and mussels just as though they came from the ocean, for the way they are prepared and served are the same.

No preparation is needed before cooking freshwater crayfish, but mussels from rivers or lakes should be handled like those from the ocean.

All sorts of seaborne excrescences attach themselves to the rocks where mussels cling, and to the mussel shells, so scrub the shells with a wire brush to remove the barnacles and so on. Both mussels and clams get their food and oxygen by siphoning seawater into their bodies through a set of valves, and the siphons bring in sand as well. It's a good idea to purge crabs, too, as they are bottom-feeders and ingest foreign objects with their food.

To purge the shellfish and crustaceans, put them overnight into a tub of seawater with a layer of cornmeal on the bottom. Allow at least 8 to 10 hours for the purge, and renew the water after 4 or 5 hours.

Goeducks need at least a 12-hour purging, and the longer you purge the less likely you'll be to feel sand gritting over your teeth when you're eating.

Sea urchins need no premeal preparation.

boat off the sides of rocky formations that stand away from the land itself.

A few words of caution to those harvesting the shorelines. Be very sure to check local conditions and game laws. Because of the way they eat and the conditions of their habitat, mussels may ingest bacteria harmful to humans. Fish and game authorities close areas of tainted water to mussel-hunters. Most states now require that shoreline shellfish-seekers have a state license. And all shorelines have areas where underwater tidal currents make deep wading dangerous. Be sure you learn what you're getting into before you wade out.

As you can see, you need only a bit of know-how and the most primitive bits and pieces of tackle in order to harvest the shorelines. Now, let's see how to pre-

After the purging, clean up the shells of mussels and clams to finish removing any foreign matter. This is again a job of wire-brushing, swishing the brush often through a bucket of water and dipping the shellfish into water now and again to rinse them.

Crabs must be cleaned. This is a simple matter of folding back the heavy membrane at the rear apex of their triangular shells and scooping out the sponge-like intestines with the tip of a knife. You should be ready to cook crabs as soon as this has been done.

Now, at last you're ready to cook.

COOKING SHORE FOODS

These foods are the simplest of all to prepare, for it's not the cooking that makes the dish, it's the saucing.

Freshwater crayfish are cooked by dropping them into a pot of lukewarm water and then bringing the water slowly to a boil. Two or three minutes of actual boiling is all that's needed. The lukewarm-to-boiling cooking in theory produces a tastier flesh; professionals who cultivate and cook crayfish claim that the shock of being dropped into a pot of bubbling water causes the crustacean to tighten its muscles and the result is tough flesh.

Mussels, clams, and crabs are all cooked by steaming or boiling, though steaming is by far the best way to go. Put the shellfish on a rack in a deep pan that has a tight-fitting cover; pour enough water into the pan to cover its bottom to a depth of half an inch, and put the pot over high surface heat. When steam stops leaking out of invisible crevices around the lid, the shellfish are ready to eat.

Broth from the pots in which mussels and clams have been steamed is often served as an appetizer before a seafood meal, so when you steam these shellfish be sure to preserve the liquid left in the bottom of the pot. It can be used in some of the sauces which are given later in this chapter or used as the base for a soup to which bits of the shellfish's flesh have been added or as a fish stock in cooking other dishes. Strain the liquid, of course.

What you eat when you devour a sea urchin is its roe, which is scooped out with a spoon after cutting off the urchin's top membrane with a sharp knife. Sprinkle the roe with lemon juice.

Like caviar, sea urchins are an acquired taste.

SAUCES FOR SHELLFISH AND CRUSTACEANS

To emphasize an earlier remark, among cooks it's axiomatic that the sauce makes the dish. When you serve crayfish, mussels, clams, or crabs, the sauce almost always *is* the dish.

Sauces need not be elaborate. Crayfish, clams, crabs can all be eaten just as they come from their shells, dunking the morsels of sweet flesh in Lemon Butter, which is simply good creamery butter heated and blended with a dash of fresh lemon juice. Or, eat them in a cocktail, the sauce prepared by stirring a short dash of furnace-hot Tabasco or a smidge of horseradish into canned tomato paste or puree, not catsup (which today is overloaded with sugar). Or, add a dash of dry sherry to bottled Pickapeppa sauce for a crab cocktail base.

Brew up your own sauce with tomatoes fresh from the garden. If you use a blender or food processor to make the puree, the tomatoes must be plunged into boiling water, skinned, and seeded. You can save this coolie labor by using an old-fashioned puree cone, which will pass only the juice and pulp. Then mix the fresh puree with a bit of tarragon vinegar and a sprinkle of salt before stirring in the crabmeat.

Creamed crabmeat can be prepared using the Basic White Sauce recipe given later in this chapter. For baked crab, modify the sauce by adding a bit of dry sherry and saffron, some paprika and onions cooked until they are very soft. Then stir in enough fine dry breadcrumbs and a generous amount of crabmeat into the sauce to stiffen it, mound it high in the crab shells, and bake 5 to 10 minutes. If you're using canned or frozen crabmeat and have no shells, fill small individual soufflé dishes with the mixture. Always top the filling with a thin slice of lemon and sprinkle with paprika.

SAUCES FOR FISH

Use sauces with either freshwater or saltwater fish. They add immeasurably to plain broiled, boiled, steamed, grilled, baked, or fried fish.

There are two basic sauce bases, the Cream Sauce and the Basic Brown Sauce, which appear first. In later recipes you'll find examples of how combining is handled. But with the two basic sauces you can produce dozens of others.

Don't be afraid to give your imagination a free hand in creating sauces. If you come up with a bad one, it can be tossed out with little loss; if you do succeed in creating a new one, you'll make history, for in spite of the claims of "brand-new" sauces made in the cooking sections of women's magazines, there have been no absolutely new sauces created since around 1892.

BASIC CREAM SAUCE

1 **Tbsp butter**
1 **Tbsp all-purpose flour**
1 **cup milk**
½ **tsp salt**
⅛ **tsp freshly ground white pepper**
1 **egg yolk, beaten**

Melt the butter and over low heat stir in the flour to form a white paste called the roux. Do not let it brown. Add the milk and seasonings while stirring; remove from heat when the mixture begins to bubble. Quickly whip in the egg yolk. Do not reheat without constantly stirring, or the sauce will curdle.

This cream sauce can be made thicker by doubling the amount of butter and flour, still thicker by tripling the quantities of these two ingredients.

BASIC BROWN SAUCE

6 Tbsp butter
3 Tbsp all-purpose flour
1½ cups stock or broth (meat for meat dishes or vegetable dishes, consommé for vegetable dishes, fish for fish dishes)
1 tsp fresh lemon juice

Divide the butter into two equal portions. Melt 3 tablespoons in a saucepan over low heat, and when melted add the flour bit by bit while stirring constantly to form a paste or roux. This will range in color from tan to brown, depending on the length of time it is allowed to cook, but be careful not to allow the flour to burn. When the roux has formed, add the stock while continuing to stir until the desired consistency is reached. Finally, add the lemon juice.

HORSERADISH SAUCE

1½ cups plain yoghurt or dairy sour cream
2 to 3 Tbsp well-drained prepared horseradish

¼ tsp mustard seed

Combine the yoghurt or sour cream with the horseradish. The best way to drain horseradish thoroughly is to put a dollop into the center of a small square of clean white cloth, bring the corners of the cloth together, and twist until the liquid has been expelled. Then use a whisk to blend in the mustard seed.

GREEN SAUCE

1¼ cups dairy sour cream
¼ tsp powdered ginger
½ cup minced watercress
¼ tsp green chartreuse
   Small pinch of salt

Mix ingredients together in a bowl with a wooden spoon or in a blender. Chill before serving.

CELERY SAUCE

¾ cup minced celery
1 cup broth or meat stock

Boil briskly until the celery is soft. Strain the stock through a square of white cloth, leaving the celery in the cloth. Fold the corners of the cloth together and twist to extract all the liquid from the celery. Discard the remaining shreds of celery.

Make up a batch of Basic Cream Sauce, substituting the broth in which the celery was cooked for the milk, and adding as a final ingredient ¾ cup sour cream.

MUSTARD SAUCE

1 cup Basic Brown Sauce from recipe #2
1 Tbsp Dijon mustard

Heat the Brown Sauce and when warm stir in the mustard. Do not allow to boil.

This section on sauces could be extended indefinitely, but you now have all the tools you need to work with, and there's still a bit more cooking to be done before we get through here.

It's fitting, I think, to cap off this chapter with a formidable dish that gathers the fullest bounty of the ocean. Here's an Italian stew, which almost certainly is a Neapolitan version of Marseilles's famed bouillabaisse.

CIOPPINO

To serve 10 or 12:
1 pint unshelled shrimp
1 quart unshelled clams or mussels
2 pounds firm ocean fish, halibut, sea bass, etc.
1 medium-sized lobster
3 cups crabmeat in large pieces
1 large red onion
1 green pepper
4 ripe tomatoes or 4 cups drained solid-pack canned tomatoes
2 cloves garlic
2 Tbsp light olive oil
3 cups dry red wine
2 tsp tomato paste
1 tsp salt

Prepare the shellfish by scrubbing their shells well, trim beards from mussels, etc. Leave the shellfish in their shells. Cut the fish into thumb-sized chunks. Clean the lobster by splitting it down the back and removing the gritty sac in the head and the dark intestinal vein running down the center of the tail. Cut lobster into chunks, leaving the shell on the pieces.

Peel the onion, clean the pepper, chop coarsely. Mince the garlic. Sauté the vegetables lightly in the oil; stir in the wine, tomato paste, and salt.

Put the shrimp, clams, the lobster and fish pieces into a large pot that can be covered, such as a Dutch oven. Pour the vegetable mixture over them, close the pot, and cook over low heat 20 minutes.

Traditionally, this dish is served in soup bowls with tablespoons used in eating it; a portion of each kind of the fish and shellfish should be in each serving.

This is the only seafood dish I know of with which red wine *must* be served.

16 PREPARING GAME FOR THE TABLE

As every hunter who's been around the block knows, game of all kinds returns the greatest rewards at the dining table to those who give it proper care in the field. There are a number of things that must be done immediately after game is brought down if you want to enjoy it to the utmost when you get around to cooking and eating it. The game must first be cleaned and skinned. Then the carcass must be transported home in a manner that will assure it arrives in good condition. Finally, big game animals must be butchered and made ready to cook.

Small game animals and birds require equivalent treatment if they are to do credit to the cook when they are placed on the table. Based on my own observations over the years, about half the hunter-chefs who enjoy reputations as outstanding performers over the campfire's coals or in the kitchen owe that reputation to the field care they give their trophies rather than to cooking skill.

If you've brought down a large antlered game animal—deer, elk, moose, caribou, antelope—with a shot that's gone cleanly through the heart or lungs, count yourself lucky even if the animal has run a short distance after it was hit. Most of the time, the type of rifle bullet used in the high-velocity weapons so popular today will begin expanding even if it strikes the soft and inedible tissue that fills the chest cavity of antlered game. As it expands the slug also makes a wide path which serves as a blood-drain. This reduces the time required to bleed a dead animal and makes cleaning easier by helping to drain the blood from the animal's circulatory system.

On the other hand, when you gut-shoot antlered game, and the slug plows through the belly and intestinal organs, the animal may still be able to run a good distance. While it's running, its body temperature increases with dramatic swiftness, and the bacterial organisms which

Equipment is basically the same for field-dressing all game. When dealing with larger animals such as elk and moose, a combination knife/saw comes in handy.

the expanding rifle slug has spread into its innards may have entered the bloodstream and be multiplying rapidly. You must therefore work fast when you reach the fallen animal, because delay in cleaning multiplies the amount of flesh that may spoil.

If you've never tasted soured venison, be grateful. If you have tasted it, you don't need any description of the sensation of repulsion that grips you with the first bite. If you're wise, the first bite will also be your last. No matter where you're

dining, the best thing to do is to suffer a sudden loss of appetite and excuse yourself from the table, or simply sit and wait and watch your fellow-diners struggle.

When and if you kill any antlered game, or any game at all, remove its insides without delay, and get it started cooling just as fast as you can. The methods of cleaning antlered game animals are the same regardless of their species, so let's take the most common, deer, as our example.

FIELD DRESSING DEER

1. Roll animal onto its back with its head positioned slightly uphill. This way, when you open the abdomen, blood and entrails spilling out will flow downhill and away from your work area. Remove genitals by cutting around them and pulling them away. Be careful your knife does not go too deeply or you may damage the precious hindquarter meat located directly below.

2. With the edge of knife blade facing upward, to avoid cutting into the intestines, open abdominal cavity by running knife from genitals to base of rib cage or sternum. This cut gives easy access to intestines and paunch. It is not necessary to open chest cavity of animal as this only allows dirt and other debris to enter. Nor is it necessary to cut the animal's throat to bleed it. Animal will have bled itself automatically and the majority of blood will have collected in the chest and abdominal cavity and spilled out when you made the initial abdominal incision. Pull out intestines and paunch, cutting restraining ligaments to free them, and bring out liver and kidneys.

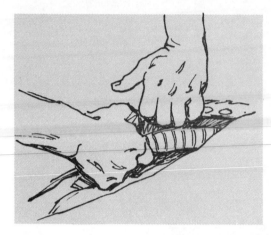

3. With your sleeves rolled up, reach high up into chest cavity and with your knife sever the windpipe and esophagus tubes. Grab this twin-tube assembly and pull backward; the heart and lungs will come right out.

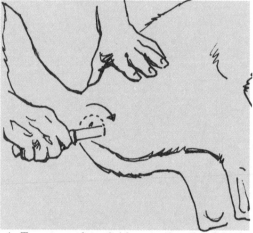

4. Turn around to finish removing the digestive tract. Cut around anus (above), then very carefully cut around bladder (left) and eventually internal organs will come free.

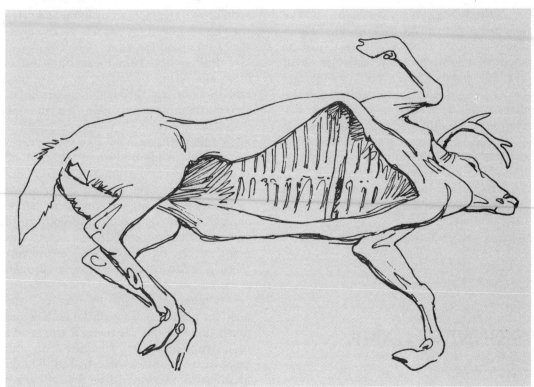

5. After swabbing out body cavity with dry grass or moss, place sticks crosswise inside to spread body walls and speed cooling.

This is the point at which field-dressing stops. Now, there are two schools of thought about field-dressing. Some hunters prefer to do only the most necessary cleaning jobs where an animal fell, and defer the finishing until they get the carcass to camp, or even until it's been taken home. Others want to get the entire job out of the way at one time.

It's your option, of course, but a suggestion or two might be worth your consideration. You're already well along on the cleaning job when you've reached the stage where field cleaning ends. It will take very little more time and effort to finish the job. Of course, you'll be able to do a more thorough piece of work where you have better facilities, and unless you're going to have a long trip home, or you're taking the carcass to where the weather's unusually warm, field cleaning is logical. The logic stops at the point where deferring what's left to be done might damage the meat that will provide so many enjoyable dishes. Weigh all the factors before you decide.

Whatever your decision, you've reached a plateau in the cleaning where you can afford to stop and rest, just as soon as you've found a short stick of deadfall wood which you'll wedge between the haunches. This will spread the carcass and let it start to cool. After this, stop for a breather. If you plan to finish the job at home, get the animal started to camp as soon as one of your hunting buddies shows up to give you a hand.

Basically, the same routine you'll follow in cleaning a deer will work for all other antlered game.

SKINNING GAME

While you can wait a few days to skin other animals, skin antelope or any of the other horned game—horned as opposed to antlered—as quickly as possible. The skin of a horned animal will transmit a strong taste to its flesh if not removed at once.

With the animal hanging head-down, slit up the insides of the hind legs and work your fingers into the slit. Pull the skin away from the bones, which are very close to the skin at their extremities, and begin pulling downward. Some hunters who don't choose to exert themselves in this aspect of the job save time by choosing an exceptionally sturdy tree limb from which to hang the animal; then they nitch their cars or trucks to the first strip of skin they loosen by hand and drive the vehicle ahead for the few yards necessary to strip off the skin.

Pulling the skin loose by hand is often slowed up by having to pause now and then to cut through a tough bit of stringy membranous tissue, but the job goes fast enough. All you need to do is keep pulling the skin off, like you're turning a glove inside out when taking it off your hand. Work around each leg and around the carcass, pulling down a few inches at a time and moving your hands along the parting around the body until you reach the base of the skull. At this point, cut the flesh of the neck to the vertebra, and saw through it or chop through it with a hatchet.

Unless you want to preserve the head for mounting, saw off the antlers and finish skinning out the head. If the head's to be cape-mounted, take the skin and head with the antlers attached to the taxidermist who's going to be doing the job and let him push the wheelbarrow from that point on.

As far as procedure's concerned, skinning a bear's not a great deal different from skinning horned or antlered game. All vertebrate creatures, including man, have remarkably similar anatomical structures. You'd make basically the same cuts in the same sequence when cleaning a bear that are made when cleaning a deer or any other game animal. However, when cleaning a bear, there is one major difference between it and other large game in handling the interior organs. Do not eat bear liver or feed it to your pets. Bears sometimes secrete Vitamin A in their livers in amounts that can be toxic to humans and dogs or cats. Discard the liver with the intestines.

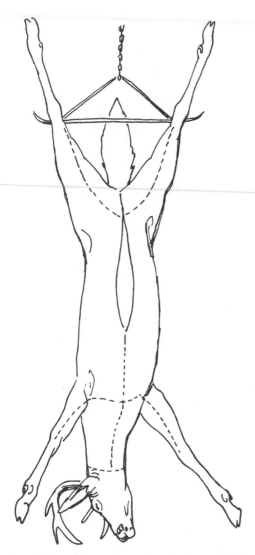

Hang deer in this manner: First make small slits through the thin skin at the Achilles tendon and then insert a game gambrel. The reason for hanging animal by the rear legs is to allow rising body heat to escape quickly; if you hang deer by the head, rising body heat will be trapped in the chest cavity. Removing hide is easy. Just make shallow cuts as indicated, then begin pulling the hide away mostly with your hands, using your knife only in those few places where it is securely attached around the legs and across the brisket.

If the bear is to be cleaned and skinned for eating, cut off its paws and bake them in coals; bear paws are a great delicacy. The meat's a bit gelatinous, but the flavor's superb. You'd take the claws out before cooking, of course, and remove the skin beginning just above the pads. However, if the bear's going to be mounted, leave the skin on the paws as well as the head and let the taxidermist do the skilled work required to get the skull and paws freed.

Whatever kind of wild game carcass you're dealing with, do get off as much fat as possible during the cleaning. Few of the antlered or horned species have a great deal of fat on them, but even a little bit of fat will turn rancid very, very quickly and taint the meat to which it's attached. Bears are fatter than most wild animals, and their fat is about the rankest you're likely to encounter, so de-fat thoroughly to protect your meat.

Procedures that you'd follow for cleaning and skinning a wild boar are so much the same as those applicable to bears that to repeat them would be needlessly repetitive. You don't have to worry about the liver of a wild boar being toxic, but it's too rank to be enjoyable. If the boar is of a peccary subspecies, which in the Southwest is called javelina, there are musk glands on its sides, near the backbone, between the rib cage and hip joints, which should be removed at once. Make a cut along the spine from the hips to the ribs and pull the skin back to get to these glands, and avoid cutting into the glands. The easiest way to remove them is to take out a piece of the flank meat along with the glands.

SAW
CUT

Field-dressing a bear is essentially the same, but the procedure for hide removal differs somewhat. You'll want to save the hide so a taxidermist can transform it into a handsome rug, so make your knife cuts as indicated here. Note how neither the head nor the paws has been removed. Don't try to skin-out the head or paws. Just leave them attached to the hide, salt thoroughly, and deliver to your taxidermist.

HANDLING BIG-GAME CARCASSES

Handling even a small deer carcass is a two-man job. A lone hunter can do it, even over rough ground, but it'll take a lot of time and at least two trips. I recall one night in a hunting camp by a small lake in the Sierra Nevada when our party had been sleeping for a couple of hours before we were roused by a man calling. Flashlights began to flicker, and they quickly focused on a young fellow just out of his teens, standing outside our tarp shelter with the forequarters of a deer on his back, the forelegs over his shoulders, tied together in front of his chest.

He explained that he'd gone "up the hill" as he put it just before dark, looking for a good spot to hunt at daybreak. He'd jumped a three-point buck on the trail up, and knocked it over with a single shot. It was, he confessed, the first deer he'd ever shot, and he knew that if he didn't clean it the meat would be tainted by morning.

He'd tried to field-dress it, working in the dark, by touch alone, but the job had been too much for him. He was unable to lift the deer by himself, so he'd just cut it in half and brought the forequarters down, hoping he could make it to his car, get a flashlight, and go back for the hindquarters, but he was tired out after lugging the forequarters as far as he had.

All of us knew what "up the hill" meant; it was country we'd hunted in before. The vestigial lumber trail that led up the side of the small mountain didn't call for any real climbing, but it was a pretty steep walk. Our sympathies were with the young hunter, of course. After we'd given

him a hand in getting the forequarters dressed out, we went with him up the hill, helped him clean the hindquarters, and carry both halves of the carcass to his car, which was about a half-mile from our camp.

By the time the job was finished, so was most of the night. Now, we didn't really grudge losing a morning of hunting, because to have let the hindquarters of a good buck lie on the ground and go bad would have been unthinkable. We were just glad that it had been a 140-pound deer instead of an 800-pound elk. We did wish, though, that the young hunter hadn't been so quick on the trigger so late in the evening while he was hunting alone. A more experienced hunter would have let the opportunity pass, knowing that if his shot did knock down the deer at that time and place, he'd be in trouble.

Being a brave lone-wolf hunter is fine in theory, but if you're going to hunt in good game country, especially where the going's rough, do it with a companion, or you'll risk losing a lot of venison simply because you can't get a deer carcass to the place where you've left your car. There've been a lot of times when I've had sure shots at game in inaccessible places, and have decided not to shoot because getting a carcass out would be next to impossible. Still, if I'd been the young hunter, I'd probably have done what he did, in his eagerness to get that first deer.

There are differences of opinion about the best way to handle the cleaned carcass of a big game animal while getting it home or to a refrigeration plant. One is to leave the skin on the carcass to protect it while it's being transported, the other is to skin and halve or quarter the carcass to make it easier to carry. My own method is to let conditions shape the decision. If it's brisk weather, chilly, and with a fine fresh wind blowing, the skin stays on. If it's at all warm, or if I'm going to be on a warm road most of the way home, the carcass gets quartered and wrapped, because I think it'll stay cooler that way.

A deer bag, or even enough coarse-mesh gauze to wrap a carcass or its quarters is a must if you're in warm country where there are a lot of insects buzzing around. It's not that I have any fear of the hornets that freshly butchered venison seems to attract, or the pathological fear of blowflies that a dentist friend of mine showed. Stan and I were on a mountain hunting trip once when a fly lighted on the stick of salami we'd brought along for iron rations. Stan yelled "Blowfly!" as he jumped up and started flicking a dish-towel wildly to drive the fly away. He also refused to touch that salami, even after I'd jokingly offered to scrub its still-un-broken casing to remove any eggs the fly might have deposited. Now, it's true that some species of flies do deposit eggs on raw meat, and the eggs will, if given time, develop into maggots. The deer bag or gauze is a good precaution in fly country in warm weather.

When you do reach the car or trunk or van, don't drape the animal's carcass over the fender or top. If you've quartered the carcass, don't stuff the pieces in the trunk. Even the tiniest of today's midget sedans will accommodate the entire car-cass of an average-sized deer, if you do a bit of judicious folding of legs and twisting of the neck.

But, whole or quartered, get that carcass inside the car. And before you begin loading, work out a way to use rocks or a length or two of tree branch to hold the carcass or quarters off the floor or

seat. Prop your load in a way that will let the air circulate all around it. In even mildly warm weather, travel with every-thing open or the air-conditioning turned on. If you're in a short-cab pickup, stretch a tarp over the bed, leaving big gaps at front and back to get the best ventilation.

BUTCHERING

Before getting into the cutting, you'll want to hang that carcass to let it age. Be-fore it's consigned to the walk-in icebox of your friendly neighborhood butcher or the chilled holding room of a meat plant or locker plant, check the carcass care-fully for any areas around bullet holes that might be getting a bit high. Cut them out, taking in an inch of flesh around the spots themselves for safety. Also, go over the carcass inside and out and remove all the fatty tissue and stringy membranes left after your cleaning.

How long a big-game animal's car-cass should hang is a matter of individual opinion. Some will settle for a few days, others like to let the carcass wait a week to give the meat a chance to grow tender with age.

Up in Del Norte County, California, which had the only year-around open sea-son on bear in the United States while I was there (and may still have, for all I know), my bear-hunting friends generally let a bear carcass hang for 6 to 8 days in a cold room. And I remember one year when Vern Johnson brought down a rouge she-bear in the high Sierra lake where he made his summer headquarters, and glazed the carcass every night for a month. The season was late, getting close to snow time, and every morning there was a film of ice on the water bucket. Vern sprinkled the hanging carcass every evening, the glaze melted for an hour or so in midafternoon, and the new glaze encased the meat every night. The meat was the sweetest bear meat ever.

You've got a carcass waiting to be reduced to steaks, chops, roasts, stew meat, and trimmings that will make a batch of the finest chili you've ever tasted, or that can be used in making a very superior mincemeat, or be ground up to form the base for an excellent meatloaf, or, as a last resort, used in venisonburgers. (I don't much care for the latter, by the way. Venison or any other game meat except that from a bear is too lean and dry to make good fried meat patties. Anyhow, good venison is a scarce commodity. It deserves a better fate and you deserve a more taste-rewarding dish.)

First, let's check off the equipment you'll need. Not precisely equipment— but necessary—is enough room in which to work. If the kitchen's too small, and you don't want to set up a temporary butcher shop on the parlor rug, move the base of operations to the garage or, better yet, to the basement (if you have one). Plan in advance where you're going to stack the different cuts, because you won't want to slow down to mark each package while you're cutting.

As for the gear itself, and the supplies, your basic tool is the best knife you can get your hands on. I'd suggest two knives, one a traditional butcher knife, the other a boning knife with a short,

sturdy blade. I still prefer old-fashioned knives with good carbon-steel blades, but the stainless steels have been improved a great deal since I developed my prejudice against them. If you can locate a pair of knives with stainless steel blades that rate in the neighborhood of Rockwell 56–58, and don't object to the price you'll pay for them, buy them.

Other tools needed are a sharpening steel, a meat saw or a hacksaw with a coarse blade, and more freezer paper than you think you'll ever use, with the special tape required to seal the packages. Some old rags to keep things cleaned up as you go are the final essential. Perhaps you can get a friend to help in return for a small share of the meat; if so, that second pair of hands will come in very handy (no pun intended).

Your first job will show you the need for some help. One method is to split the carcass from the rump to the neck, first marking the saw's path with a knife-cut along the backbone. This cut should be made while the carcass is hanging, the second-best position for it is spread flat on the floor. Draw the blade of the knife down the backbone until the vertebrae are exposed; then follow the line with the saw-blade. Now, the carcass is reduced to a size that's easier to handle. The accompanying butchering charts are not supposed to show in what order the cuts are made, but to identify the types of cuts each part of a carcass yields.

Or, use the second butchering method to produce slightly different cuts of boneless meat. With either method, of course, you'll save all the trimmings that are made as you cut to be chopped for stews or ground up to be used in a meatloaf. Meatloaves don't dry out as do fried ground meat patties. All game meat tends

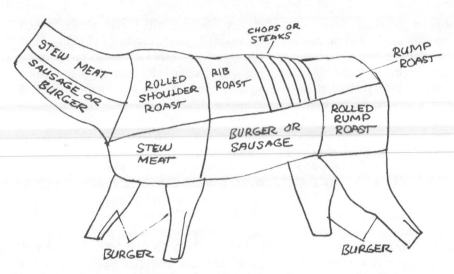

There are two traditional methods of butchering deer and other big game. This first method is the desired approach if you want steaks and chops. Use a meat saw or hacksaw to cut the carcass in half, lengthwise, down the center of the spinal column. Then make the other cuts as indicated.

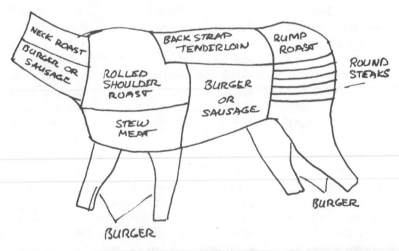

If you prefer entirely boneless cuts of venison instead, do not cut the carcass in half lengthwise. What you want to do now is use a fish fillet knife, or preferably a boning knife, to remove large chunks of meat from the carcass as indicated.

to be dry and needs the added moisture that can be given it in cooking.

Except for size, elk and moose carcasses are butchered using the same zones that I've used here to guide the cutting. The anatomy of a bear isn't too greatly different from that of other animals. The same organs are in much the same place, and the sequence in which you work is also quite similar. Rather than put in a lot of repetitious detail, I'll leave you to apply your common sense to the cleaning and butchering of Bruin. Just adapt the scenario already outlined and you should have no trouble.

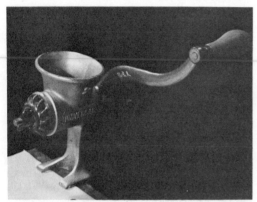

A meat grinder is an essential piece of equipment for making burger. Follow the instructions that come with the particular grinder you purchase.

The same grinder used for making burger can also be used to make sausage, by means of a special spout-type attachment that fits on the front.

I've never had the opportunity to hunt either the native wild boar, or even the exotic species that have begun to be imported and freed in more or less controlled country for hunting. However, as one of yesterday's humorists pointed out, "Pigs is pigs." I ask a butcher friend about the way to handle a boar's carcass, and his opinion is the same as the humorist's. Again, you have a commonality of anatomy on your side. A boar has the same organs in much the same place that other four-footed animals do, so I don't think you'd have any trouble in handling one if a chance to do a bit of boar-hunting comes your way.

SMALL GAME

Over the years, as the wilderness has diminished and the frontiers faded, we've come to shun most of the small animals that were subsistence for our ancestors. When great-grandfather or great-great-grandfather announced that he was taking his grandsons out for supper, he meant they were going into the woods to shoot meat for the meal; when father or grandfather makes a similar announcement today, it means he's taking the youngsters down to the franchised fast-food hamburger joint on the corner.

Powder and lead are no longer precious and scarce commodities to be used only when required to put meat in the family pot. We shoot at woodchucks today for target practice, not to take them home to eat. The day has passed when the raccoon that provided Daniel Boone's coonskin cap wasn't shot for headgear, but to provide a meal for Mrs. Boone and the youngsters.

These facts aren't mentioned as a basis for any moral judgment, or to score points against the Bambi cultists. They are the unconscious victims of several decades of watching animated cartoons in which animals are equated with humans. However, I look at the rising tide of metropolitan violence, and wonder if these propagandizing fantasies on the motion picture and television screens have had a reverse effect. Instead of teaching youth to lift animals to the level of humanity, they very well may have contributed to what can only be described as animalizing humans.

However, this isn't a philosophical treatise. It's a cookbook designed to help those who value the outdoors, and we'd better get on with it. The real reason behind the foregoing paragraphs is to point out that today our small game horizons are pretty much limited to rabbits and squirrels. Opossum, raccoons, and woodchucks, eaten and enjoyed by the pioneers, today are foods as exotic as pizza

was in the 1930s when Gino's in New York and Lupo's in San Francisco were the only two restaurants in the U.S. where pizza could be found.

There are many wooded and swampy areas where the animals our forefathers ate routinely still live and can be hunted, and they can contribute new flavors to your daily fare. Most of the recipes that will follow in a later chapter can be readily adapted to cooking them. In the event that you decide to try such small game as beaver, muskrat, opossum, and woodchuck in addition to the more usual rabbit and squirrel, the special precautions which must be taken during cleaning all small wild animals follow:

Beaver

Musk glands under forelegs must be removed. Also, remove a wide strip of flesh surrounding the genitals in the early stages of cleaning. Beaver tail is a delicacy; braise it with liquid over low heat.

Muskrat

Musk glands are in the abdominal cavity and these will come out when the animal is gutted. Wash cavity with two or three changes of salted water immediately after cleaning. Remove a wide strip of flesh when cutting out the genitals. Cut off tail and first joints of legs before cooking.

Opossum

Do not skin; gut, dip in boiling water, and scrape clean like a pig. Before dipping in water, remove small red musk glands under forelegs and at end of rib cage against backbone. Remove head, feet, and tail before cooking. Opossum are easily captured alive, and any that are to be eaten should be taken this way and fed a vegetable diet for three to four days before cooking. An opossum that has not been fed a controlled diet should be soaked 8 to 12 hours in salt water before being cooked.

Rabbit

No special care needed; has no musk glands.

Squirrel

Musk glands under forelegs and on backbone at top of hips; remove before cooking.

Woodchuck

Musk sacs under forelegs and four sacs spaced along backbone must be removed before cooking; also remove feet.

A lot of hunters don't clean small game for several hours. They prefer to keep hunting and defer cleaning until they stop at noon or in the evening. This is fine, under certain conditions. In cool weather, when you're carrying rabbits or squirrels with belt-thongs instead of a bag or the pocket built onto the back of your coat, you'll come out quite well, for the carcasses will be cooled by the air circulating between them. If the weather's warm or if you're tucking the game into a confined carrier, it's not such a good idea, for even the small creatures don't lose their body heat for quite a while when packed together in an airless game bag or coat compartment.

There are no special problems in gutting a squirrel or a rabbit, as the procedures are the same for both animals. Merely slit their abdomens and remove the intestines and genitals. In fact, you can follow the same routine in field-dressing just about any of the small game animals that come to mind.

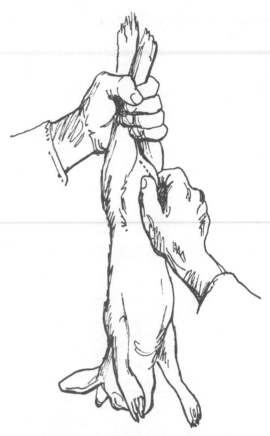

Field-dressing rabbits, squirrels, and other small-game animals takes less than a minute and is the same regardless of species. Make a small, lengthwise abdominal incision with your knife. Then use your fingers to pull out the internal organs. Finally, use a handful of dry grass to swab out the inside of the body cavity.

To skin rabbits, follow the step-by-step drawings in this chapter. Skinning squirrels and other small game is entirely different because their hides are quite tough and far more securely attached than the soft fur of rabbits. See the accompanying drawings for the proper way to skin squirrels and similar tough-skinned small game.

SKINNING A RABBIT

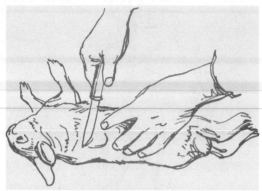

1. Use your knife to make a shallow cut through the skin in the middle of the back.

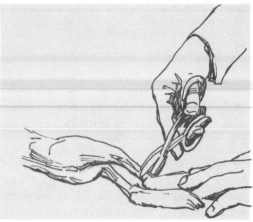

3. Now use shears to cut the lower leg bones.

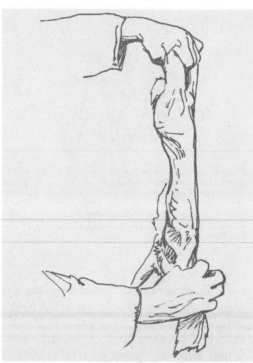

2. Rabbit skin is very soft, and it's now easy to place two fingers of the left hand and two fingers of the right hand in the cut you've just made. Pull your hands in opposite directions, and the hide will peel back and away the length of the carcass, over the head and front legs at one end and over the rear legs at the other.

4. With a heavy knife, cut the head free at the neck.

Whether skinning a rabbit or squirrel, the point will be reached in which the hide has been pulled as far as practical down the neck to the base of the head, and down each leg to the paws. Now, use a heavy-bladed knife or pair of game shears to sever the head and feet so they may be discarded with the hide still intact.

Butchering rabbits and squirrels is relatively easy. Using a sharp knife, first remove the front legs by running the blade beneath the scapulae (shoulder bones). Then remove the rear legs by running the blade around the hip or rump meat and down through the ball and socket ligament.

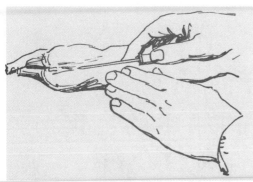

5. Run your knife blade beneath the scapulae of the front shoulders to remove the front legs, then down through the ball-and-socket joints to remove the rear legs.

This procedure should leave five pieces of meat: two front legs, two rear legs, and the long shoulder and backbone which contains the tenderloin meat. On especially large animals such as snowshoe rabbits, hares, raccoons and such, you'll probably want to cut the large backbone section into two or three smaller, more easily handled pieces.

Shotgunners will need to check the carcass and pick out any pellets that remain in the flesh. Do this job thoroughly, for nothing is more disconcerting or annoying than to bite down on a #6 shot pellet at the dinner table, unless it's to chomp the molars down on a #5 or #4.

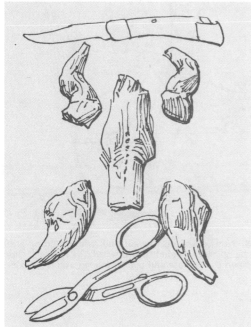

Whether rabbit, squirrel, or any other species, you should end up with five pieces of meat. With larger small-game species such as hares and jackrabbits, you may wish to cut the backbone-rib section into two or three pieces.

Even small game animals need to be aged a short while before they go to the pot. There's a popular belief, totally erroneous, that freezing meat somehow replaces aging. What happens when meat is aged is the result of enzyme action, which is speeded up by heat and retarded by cold. All that freezing does is to stop the enzymes from doing their work. If you're going to age small game by hanging it a few days, do it before it goes to the freezer and when you cook it, begin cooking be-

SKINNING A SQUIRREL

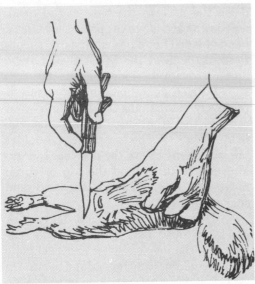

1. Skinning squirrels differs from skinning rabbits and other small game because their hides are so securely attached. Begin by making a cut just beneath the tail to sever the tailbone, but do not cut the tail entirely free.

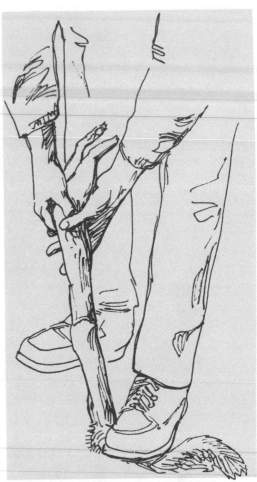

2. Extend the first cut around the flanks until it meets the verticle cut made in the abdomen during field-dressing. Be careful to make this a shallow cut so the meat is not damaged.

3. Now, stand on the tail and, while holding onto the rear legs, begin lifting upward; the hide will slide down the carcass and over the head and front legs.

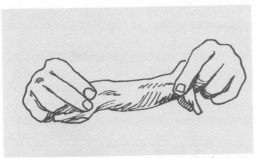

4. With fingers and knife blade, remove the small amount of remaining skin on the rear legs. Last, use tin snips or game shears to cut the leg bones just above the paws, and then cut the neckbone.

5. Completely skinned squirrel should look like this, clean and undamaged.

fore the carcass is completely thawed. Deterioration of meat is rapid once it's been frozen; deterioration and thawing begin almost simultaneously, so get your small game into the pot as soon as the flesh begins to soften after the carcasses come out of the freezer.

Recipes for small game dishes will be found in Chapter 18.

GAME BIRDS

For openers, let's be sure we're playing in the same ball park. "Game birds" means different things to different hunters, and the shades of meaning go deeper than just the major dividing-line between waterfowl and upland birds. If we wanted to shoot with a shotgun, we'd simply stay with that basic distinction, because whether a bird is lean like upland species or fat like waterfowl dictates the manner in which they'll reach the table.

Taking aim with a reasonably accurate rifle instead, we'll go along with the waterfowl/upland distinction, but carry it a step further as far as the upland birds are concerned and divide them into large, medium-sized, and small birds. Deciding precisely where to draw that line is the tricky part, because there often are birds of slightly different body sizes within a given species.

For example, a few days before sitting down to write this, I was talking with my friend Gene Schneider about a turkey hunt he'd just made. Gene's a county judge in the Texas Panhandle, and in that flat and generally treeless country a lot of turkey hunting is done with a rifle. Gene said that a turkey he'd shot looked as big as an ostrich in his scope, but when he'd cleaned it and plucked it, the turkey looked more like a pheasant.

In waterfowl, we'll put the large/small division line between ducks and geese; leave jacksnipe with the ducks and put such really big birds as sandhill cranes with the geese. Sandhills don't fall into a classification easily. Like jacksnipe, they should really be classified as shore or reed birds. Sandhills are as tricky to shoot as jacksnipe, too, but in a different way. They're big birds, and they fly faster than you think, so at first you never lead them far enough. They're even deceptive in the pot, because they taste more like beef than any bird has a right to.

With our dividing lines drawn, then, we can forge ahead.

UPLAND BIRDS

Doves, pigeons, quail, ruffed grouse, woodcock, and partridges, including chukars, all have dry flesh, and it's not at all necessary to age them beyond the few hours between the end of the hunt and the time you sit down and eat them. I don't argue with those who prefer to hang these birds a short while, but it's not really necessary.

Pheasant, prairie chickens, and sage grouse can be hung in a cool, dry place for 2 days, turkeys and sandhill cranes, a longer time.

Quail are quite a bit fatter than the other birds in this group, and if you age very fat quail too long it may go rancid. If you hold quail a few days, keep them cool. The short aging will make plucking them a bit easier. Pull their intestines out with a gut-hook before putting them aside, though. Matter of fact, use the gut-hook as soon as you pick the bird up after your shot has dropped it.

Using a gut-hook usually starts the bird to bleeding, which doesn't matter much if you're carrying them as you should be, with leather thongs or J- or S-hooks on your belt. If you object to this, some grass inserted in the incision you

made for the gut-hook can be used to swab away blood residue, which otherwise is a breeding ground for bacteria.

When you're dressing small upland birds, pluck their bellies first, then open the cavities and clean them before continuing to pluck. The reason for this is that you've probably got several pellets in each bird, and the chances are good that at least one of those bits of lead has punctured a crop or intestine. The less you handle the bird before it's plucked, the less the likelihood that you'll squeeze out fecal matter to taint their cavities.

When you've removed the intestines, wash the cavity with warm water in which a bit of baking soda has been dissolved, about a half-teaspoon of soda per quart. Then rinse the cavity with ice water, and the bird's ready for hanging or plucking. But let's have the plucking wait until we've looked at the pros and cons of hanging.

Almost all the upland game hunters I know hang their birds for at least a day or so. None of them follow the pattern of greatly extended hanging periods which is common abroad. To borrow an anglicism, the English fashion of hanging pheasant and grouse by the beak and letting them hang until the bird drops off the beak is not my cuppa.

Hanging large upland birds not more than 3 days in humid or warm weather and not more than a week in cold weather or 10 days in a chilled conditioning room will result in a better bird on the table. When you can tweak out a breast feather easily is as good a rule of thumb as any to determine when one of these birds is ready to go to the pot.

Now back to plucking. Usually, the tail feathers are tackled first, and before going any further, the first thing to attend

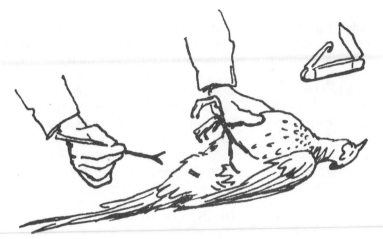

To field-dress medium-size game birds and ducks, slightly enlarge the vent with your penknife. Then insert a forked stick and twist to ensnare the entrails for quick removal. Or use a knife specially made for the purpose that has a bird-cleaning hook in place of one of the blades.

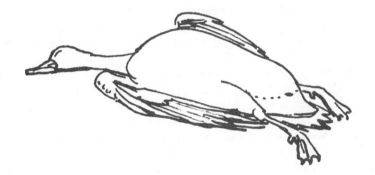

To handle the smallest game birds such as quail and doves, slightly enlarge the vent with your knife. Then insert one finger, curl your fingertip, and pull out the innards.

to before you forget it is to trim off the bird's preen gland. This is a little oil-filled sac that looks like a bump with a nozzle, and it's on the upper side of the tail. Just slice it off, cutting right down to the bone. Leaving it in while the bird cooks is an invitation to disaster. After the gland's disposed of, finish your plucking. Unless you plan to use wax, you'll strip the bird as thoroughly as possible, then singe off the bits of down that simply can't be grasped tightly enough to be pulled out.

Next comes singeing. If you're going to use plucking wax, you naturally skip singeing. To singe, roll up several pages of

a newspaper (outdoors), light one end, and while turning the bird pass it through the flames several times. That's all there is to it. Or, you can pass the bird over the flame of a gas stove burner.

Wax-plucking takes a bit more time, but does a cleaner job. It doesn't save as much time as its advocates claim, but does do away with all but a few of the occasional pinfeathers that have to be tweezered out of a carcass. You can buy a product labeled "plucking wax" at sports supply stores, but all you really need is the paraffin wax sold at supermarkets for sealing jars of home-canned foods. Allow three cakes of wax for each 1½ gallons of water when planning your mix, and if you measure the rate of wax consumption with a duck as a standard, the ratio of mix required is roughly ¾ gallon per bird.

A regular laundry pail holds 2 gallons, give or take a gill or so, but you can't mix a pailful because the birds you'll dip in the wax will displace a certain amount of liquid. If you mix a full pail and dip a duck in it you'll have a mess to clean up. If you've got a lot of birds to pluck, you can speed things up by using three pails; alternate two of them on the heater so you'll always have a hot solution, and use the third for a cold-water rinse to harden the wax after each bird's been coated.

Put three bars of wax in ¾ pail of water and heat it until the wax melts and floats on the surface. Dip the rough-plucked bird twice in the pail; dunk it in the cool water long enough to let the wax harden but not set solidly. Open a crack in the wax by wriggling a leg or wing back and forth, then peel off the wax by pushing it away from the skin with your fingers.

Whether you singe or wax, when the birds are plucked wipe the carcasses with a cloth moistened in lightly salted water and put them aside in a cool place. Cover them with a moist cloth to retard further dehydration. If they're going to be frozen, do so at once, being sure each bird is well-wrapped and the parcel tightly sealed.

WATERFOWL

Inevitably, there's going to be a bit of repetition in this section of the material contained in the preceding section, for to paraphrase what was said earlier about wild boar, birds is birds. But I'll try to hold repetition to a minimum and offer cogent reasons for any data duplicated.

To refresh your memory, we've put jacksnipe in this group, though jacksnipe and teal really belong to a subgroup of their own, because both are smaller than such ducks as mallard, canvasback, pintail, and what-have-you. It's in the cooking, though, that the size difference really counts, and we'll take care of that in Chapter 16.

In a large waterfowl group are the geese and the offbeat sandhill crane. The sandhill, incidentally, is not on the endangered species list, as many seem to think. There are only a handful of whooping cranes, but there are millions of sandhills, which migrate annually to the granaries of the nation, in north Texas, Kansas, and Oklahoma, where hunters may take them during short open seasons.

Getting rid of repetitious details first, you'll have better-flavored waterfowl on the table if you pull their intestines out with a gut-hook at once. Using a gut-hook usually results in bleeding, which isn't too important unless you object to its messing up a boat or a permanent blind. A wad of facial tissue or a little grass swabbed in the incision you made for the gut-hook will sop up the blood.

It's really a good idea to clean waterfowl as soon as possible, mainly to get the lead out of their flesh. Without any comment on the Great White Father's ruling on the use of steel shot, steel tears through a duck's innards and causes about the same amount of flesh-taint as lead pellets did. Steel shot also crack teeth and dentures even more effectively than lead did.

To field-dress the largest gamebirds such as geese and wild turkeys, make an incision as indicated so that you may insert your hand or a gut hook to withdraw the entrails.

Waterfowl seem to attract more pellets than do upland birds, even though most waterfowl are shot at longer range. This is probably because duck hunters favor 12-gauge full-choked guns, while most upland shooters tend to choose a 20-gauge with a wider shot pattern. Regardless of the gun used, pellets through the intestines of a duck or goose will quickly taint its flesh, so gut and clean the birds as soon as possible, and hang or store them in a cool spot for 3 or 4 days to let nature's friendly enzymes tenderize their flesh a bit.

An old-fashioned wooden ice chest is ideal for keeping ducks or other birds at a safe aging temperature. At one time you could buy one for about $3 or $4, but now that they're classified as collectibles and sell for as much as $500, they're luxuries few of us can afford. You might pick up a used soda-pop cooler of the kind used before the days of mechanical refrigeration, if you have space for one and shoot enough ducks to make having it worthwhile.

When you clean ducks, be sure to use a soda bath (see page 314) followed by

Since upland game birds and wildfowl are often taken in warm weather, it may not be wise to delay plucking and rough-dressing until you arrive home. Keep an ice-filled cooler in your car and attend to the chore before leaving the hunting location. Here, spruce grouse are being removed from plastic bags that were submerged in ice during a long drive.

an ice-water rinse of their cavities, especially if the birds are to be held over a few days. Save the giblets or not, as you choose. Some like them, some don't. Whether you pluck at once or later is another matter of personal choice; though, as is the case with upland birds, delay makes for easier plucking.

I've been tempted not to mention plucking, but it'd be a cop-out just to dismiss it and say that plucking's your problem. If you don't enjoy pulling feathers out of ducks, there are usually small boys in any neighborhood who'll do the job for a modest fee. Or, you can use plucking wax or take the ducks to a chicken farm where mechanical pluckers are used.

birds. Remember, when you're singeing a bird, you're not cooking it, so don't overdo. Remove the oil sac just before you singe; getting rid of this preening organ is more important when you're preparing waterfowl than when you're working with upland birds. A rinse in saltwater or vinegar water, followed by a cold-water wipedown will remove any taste the singeing might have left.

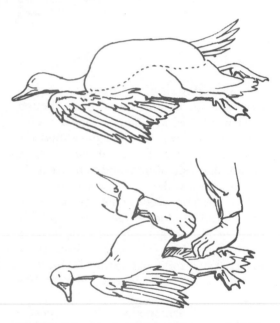

The final step before preparing game birds or waterfowl for the table, after wax-dunking or dry-plucking them, is to singe off any remaining down. The easiest way is to pass the bird quickly over a flame.

Whether it is an upland-bird species or waterfowl, many hunters like to "breast out" their game because the legs, wings, and other body parts generally contain so little meat. To breast out fowl species, cut through the skin and ribs as indicated (top). Then, while pressing down on the lower part of the body, lift sharply upward with the other hand and the breast will come away, leaving only shoulder attachments to be severed with a knife or shears.

Because neither human fingers or wax or machines ever get all the down off a duck, singeing should follow plucking. Use the method described for upland

Jacksnipe don't need to be hung to age; just keep them in the refrigerator if you're going to wait more than a day or two before cooking them. Teal are clean feeders, and usually sweet and tender, and they don't need aging, either. We've already gone into the middle-sized waterfowl group; now all that's left are the geese and sandhills.

There's very little variation required for the procedures already detailed except in the matter of aging. Geese do need a bit of time to mellow in a cool spot for 4 or 5 days before they're plucked. Sandhills require a week or more, depending on their size, but we're talking about big birds now, in the 8- to 12-pound class. Again, you should keep them in a cool place. After about 4 days begin testing by plucking out a breast feather. When the feather comes out easily it's time to pluck and cook.

THE DRUGSTORE FOLD

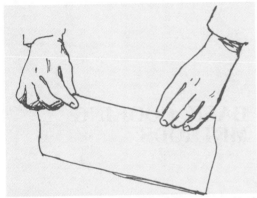

1. The drugstore fold utilizes a minimum amount of paper and yet ensures a tight seal so dry freezer air does not contact meat. Lay the meat in the center of the paper and bring up the two opposite sides.

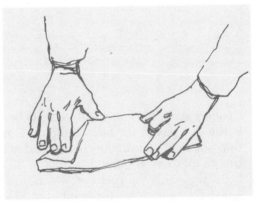

3. Make triangular folds at each end of the package, pressing the edges tightly.

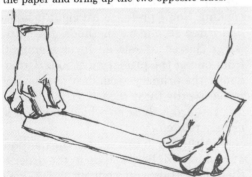

2. Fold over the two edges until they come down flat upon the surface of the package.

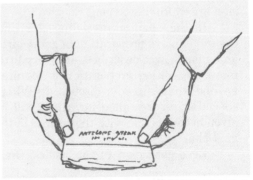

4. Finally, tuck the triangular tails underneath and secure with masking tape. Be sure to mark the contents of package and date frozen in indelible ink.

17 BASIC GAME COOKERY

Cooking game so that it will taste its best is the real payoff for most hunters. Now that you're in your home kitchen and getting to that payoff point, it's time to do a little reviewing of matters which until now have been taken for granted or have been mentioned only in passing. This time, they'll be treated in depth, as the actors who dramatize the news on television are so fond of saying.

In the chapter preceding this one, the preliminary preparation of game birds and animals was described, and very little more precooking preparation is required beyond that already discussed. Where special steps are called for, these will be given in connection with the recipes in the next chapter.

Let's get down to the basics, then.

BASIC COOKING METHODS

There's no general agreement among chefs or cookbook-writers on the precise classification of the major methods of cooking. Some prefer to list eight primary and three secondary methods, the latter being classed as related to or stemming from one of the primary methods. Others ignore the primary-secondary system and recognize the three secondary methods as separate from those to which they are so closely related.

Although in this section the methods of cooking will be taken up in the order of their importance in cooking game, we'll list them in alphabetical order, using the primary/secondary way of classifying them. They are:

Baking

Braising

Broiling, with Grilling a secondary method

Frying, with Deep-fat Frying considered to be the traditional or primary and Pan-frying the secondary method

Roasting, with Pot-roasting secondary

Sautéing

Steaming

Stewing

For all practical purposes, you can omit both styles of frying from the methods useful in cooking game and game birds. This has been mentioned before, and is being repeated purposely for emphasis. Please don't think that I'm stressing this out of personal prejudice; if you'll recall, frying is recommended in many of the fish recipes in Chapter 13.

Frying is eminently suitable for fish, because their flesh is structured quite differently from that of animals and birds. Frying is also suitable for the battery-raised chickens whose feet never touch the ground, and which make up around 90 percent of all commercially sold poultry. Chickens raised in this fashion have no muscles, just soft fleshy tissues. Wild birds, active from the time they can fly, develop quite tough bodies. Don't equate them with domestic fowl, or try to cook them in the same style.

This is equally true of meats. Hogs destined for slaughter are penned up in sheltered enclosures where they can barely move, and fed almost continuously. Except for a few places in Wyoming and Montana, where cattle are still grass-fed on open range, the feedlot has taken over insofar as beef production is concerned. Feedlots are made up of a lot of little pens where cattle are packed so tightly that they can move only a few steps. In these pens they are watered copiously and fed frequently.

In spite of the federal ban in 1972 against use of the chemical growth hormone diethylstilbesterol—DES—which is suspected of being a carcinogen, court cases against feedlots using it were still being filed in 1981. DES promotes cattle growth in terms of fat and soft tissue rather than solid meat. The point I'm making is that you will rarely encounter naturally fed, solid meat in any butcher-shop meats. The meat you do get is suited best for frying, and in connection with incessant promotion of the fried foods featured at most of the franchised fast-food joints this has accustomed U.S. cooks to rely far too heavily on frying.

By now, cooks have grown accustomed to timing recipes in terms of soft-fleshed domestic poultry, pork, and beef. You cannot time your cooking in this frame of reference when you are cooking game.

What we're really doing in game cooking is going back 50 or 100 years, when most meat was relatively tough, when time spent in the kitchen was not stolen from some kind of entertainment or sport, and when there were none of what today we call convenience foods, although both "convenience" and "food" are in some cases arguable designations. Please note that I'm not suggesting you follow these older methods in your everyday cooking routines. Game is no longer an everyday food, and a meal based on a game dish is something special, an event that requires extra attention.

Although we've already touched on most of the cooking styles to which game responds best, let's take a moment now to look at them more closely.

Braising and stewing are first cousins to one another and distant relatives of sautéing. All three require gentle heat and liquid in the pan or pot. The chief difference between the three is the quantity and type of liquid used, though sautéing, which is also considered as a cousin to frying, is generally done in an open pan.

When you braise meat, you cook it on low surface heat or in a low oven, in a closed pan, with a liquid which is generally thickened to form a sauce. The liquid should not cover the meat being cooked. This liquid may be a meat- or vegetable-based stock or broth, and accessory ingredients are often added to braised dishes. The virtue of braising game dishes is that steam from the liquid in the pan collects on the lid and condenses into drops that fall on the food below, further moistening it.

Stewing is done over very low surface heat in a deep closed pot; the liquid—most often water, but sometimes a thin stock or broth—covers the meat being cooked. Accessory ingredients are always included in a stew. Only the toughest, most recalcitrant meats are normally stewed, the better cuts being reserved for other cooking styles.

Sautéing is done over moderate to high surface heat in an open pan, usually a skillet, with a very small quantity of fat. The fat is most often one of the cooking fats which has a character of its own, butter or olive oil. When these or other fats are used they may be lightly seasoned. Additional seasonings may be rubbed into the meat before cooking begins, or added to the pan juices after the meat has been removed. The juices are then brought to a quick boil, perhaps being thickened slightly, to form a sauce that is served over or with the meat.

Roasting is done in an open utensil in the oven. The meat is normally seared at high heat and the temperature then reduced while cooking is completed. Roast meats are usually rubbed with a good coating of seasonings before cooking. When the meat is basted as it cooks, these seasonings combine with the pan juices and form a thin gravy that is served with the meat. Basting also adds a glaze to the surface of the meat and intensifies its flavor. Roasted meats are always large cuts and are usually brought whole to the table and carved for serving.

Broiling and grilling are essentially the same process, though broiling is done in an oven with the heat-source above the meat, which rests on a rack in a shallow pan. Grilling is done on a grid over the heat source. Broiled or grilled meats, game meats especially, must be basted. Pan juices may be used for basting when meat is broiled, or a seasoned fat or sauce may be used. Grilling creates no pan juices, so a separate basting liquid is required.

Spit-cooked meats may be either broiled or grilled; when the pieces of meat are small and several pieces cooked on an individual spit or skewer, they are called kebabs. A variation of this cooking style is called rotisserie cooking, in which the heat source is vertical, with the meats rotated in front of the heat by a mechanical device.

Baking is generally thought of as being confined to cakes or pastries, but it has some use in cooking game. Meat *en croûte* is a large cut of meat encased in a pastry shell and baked. So is a meat pot pie—tiny pieces of meat or disjointed squirrels or rabbits or game birds, cooked with a sauce or gravy in a deep baking dish with either a top crust or a full crust of pastry dough. A thin cut of flank, pounded even thinner, may be rolled with a layer of pastry and chopped vegetables and baked.

Given the wide choice provided by these methods of cooking and the many recipes that can be used to vary dishes cooked in each style, you should never be stumped for a new way to prepare and serve game.

RECIPE SELECTION

Selecting a recipe that's compatible with the game you're going to be cooking is one of the main keys to a successful dish. You would not, for example, want to broil venison chops cut from an old buck whose muscles had been toughened by years of use. Nor would you want to toss pieces from a veteran pheasant into a skillet for frying. In fact, there are virtually no game meats that do respond well to frying, but we'll get around to that in a later paragraph.

Looking at the matter of recipe selection from another angle, you have a pair of rabbits on hand, but you want to cook them by a recipe that specifies squir-

rels. Can you successfully interchange the type of game called for in a given recipe? The answer is generally yes, as was mentioned earlier.

Choosing a recipe for a specific type of game is more often than not a question of the age of the animal or bird you're going to be cooking. Go by the axiom, "the older, the tougher," and for older game select a recipe that involves marinating and long, gentle cooking. Since game birds and animals don't get wrinkled faces as we humans do, and don't carry ID cards or driver's licenses giving their age, you must be able to determine the approximate age bracket of an animal or bird.

This isn't as hard as it might appear to be at first. Most game animals and birds carry on their bodies clues to their age. Antlered game animals have the most obvious clues, in their antler points, but except for caribou, antlers grow only on the males. When you set out to guess the age of a doe, you'll have to depend on such clues as teeth, coat, and hide condition.

Teeth are the most reliable indicators of a game animal's age, just as they are to the age of domestic stock. Worn or broken teeth mean you're dealing with a veteran. So does a coat that's dull instead of glossy, and if a close inspection shows a lot of scars and scratches on the hide, that's another sign that the animal's been around a long time, as animal life spans are measured. Stiff ears are another indication of age on a doe, though using this as a clue depends on testing soon after the deer has been killed. But the ear tissue on a young animal is thinner and much more pliable than that of an older animal.

All the age signs that help you to date a deer appear on other antlered and horned game. The things you'd look for on the carcass of an elk or moose are very much the same, if you don't have the antlers to go by. Horned animals, which don't shed as do the antlered species, carry age indications in their teeth and on their hides in the case of antelope and on their horns in the case of sheep.

Bighorn sheep add a ring to their curved horns each year, but even from a distance you can get a rough idea of their age by observing how badly their horns show the marks of combat, places where the horns have been splintered or battered in year after year of head-on butting combats. A bear's teeth are the best indications of its age; if they're dark yellow, almost brown, and snaggled or broken, you've got an old bear to cook.

Again using deer as an example, you obviously don't want to cook an older deer by the same recipe you'd follow for a tender young spike buck or forked-horn. For old animals of any species, choose recipes that tenderize with marinades, moisture in a closed pot, and gentle-heat cooking. Save for younger animals recipes that call for broiling, grilling, or sautéing.

Interchangeability of recipes between species of big game animals is no problem. Chops or steaks or roasts from an elk, deer, or any other big game animal can be cooked by the same methods and seasoned in the same manner, as long as the cuts being cooked are approximately the same size. Remember, the meat of all antlered game animals is properly referred to as venison.

Size and weight as well as weight in proportion to size are the basic indicators of the age of small game animals. All these reach a maximum size, usually toward the end of their first year of life. As they grow older, though, their muscles tend to get a bit bigger and thus their weight increases, though the increase in small game is a matter of only a few ounces.

You can tell a lot about the age of rabbits and squirrels by examining their teeth and claws. The younger the animal, the sharper its teeth will be, and its claws will also be sharper and more flexible. Young rabbits have a very narrow split in their upper lips, which grows wider as the animal ages. Its ears also grow thicker and less flexible with age. Squirrels are not only accident-prone, snagging their skins quite frequently on the splintered stumps of limbs, but they're fierce fighters as well. You can pretty well judge whether you're about to cook an old squirrel or a young one by looking for scar marks on the inside of its pelt after you've skinned it; the more scars, the older the squirrel.

At the risk of being repetitious, cook older small game in a stew or let it rest in a marinade if it's going to be broiled. And, when cooking small game, squirrels and rabbits can be interchanged in recipes without doing anything except adjusting the cooking time to the size and age of the animals in the pot.

Game birds are a bit more cooperative in giving away their age. In all species of ducks and geese, the skin covering their legs and the webbing of their feet get rougher as the birds age. Young waterfowl have flexible, almost soft breastbones which grow less pliable and harder as the bird grows older. Young birds have a plentiful growth of pinfeathers which have not yet grown to quill or body feathers, while on old ducks and geese you'll find a number of thin, almost hairlike feathers mixed with their broader body feathers.

When establishing the age of upland birds, check the skin of their legs, which gets rougher with age, and the condition of their claws, which become blunt and splintered with use. The size of their leg muscles or drumsticks also increase as the birds grow older.

Some species have very specific age indicators. Grouse show age in the circle around their eye-pupils; it deepens in color with age until in old birds the circle is a deep red. To judge the age of a pheasant, look at the legs and claws, but look also at the first wingtip primary feather. In young birds it has a round tip, which grows sharper as the bird matures. Test quail for age by prodding with a fingertip at breast and rump, where it accumulates small pockets of fat. In young birds the fat is soft and almost liquid, but as the bird ages the fat hardens. The wattles of wild turkeys grow thicker and their reticulations more pronounced as the bird ages, there are the usual leg and claw signs to give you an idea of age, and the "beards" of toms are longer.

To return to the twice-repeated refrain, the older the bird, the tougher it's likely to be. Cook old birds slowly, with ingredients that add moisture to the dish, and use marinades. Save the younger specimens for spit-cooking or broiling.

In cooking game birds, you can interchange these just as readily as you can cuts of big game or squirrels for rabbits. You can swap ducks for pheasant, doves for pigeons, quail for woodcock, and vice versa. Again by adjusting the cooking time you can interchange ducks for geese. Turkey and sandhill cranes can be cooked using the same recipes.

GAME COOKING AIDS

Perhaps the most important thing you must remember about wild meats, one that can't be stressed too often, is that the flesh of *all* wild game, animals or birds, is inherently dry. When cooking game, the wise chef forgets that the cooking method loosely called frying ever existed. This ban should be observed rigidly, whether it's pan-frying or frying in deep fat. Choose to sauté instead.

When roasting or grilling or broiling wild meats of any kind you should baste the meat often with fat or with a moisturizing sauce. And wild meats roasted or grilled should not be undercooked any more than they should be overcooked. The line you must follow here is a thin one, but important. Forget about the blood-rare roast or steak. Aim for meat that is fully cooked but still moist. A tinge of pink, yes. That's when game is at its best, not when it's cooked dry and hard, or when it's rawly red and drips blood while being carved.

Acquire the habit of larding or barding when you cook game. Larding is done with a special needle that draws thin strips of blanched salt pork or firm pork fat into the meat. During cooking, the fat from the pork penetrates the fibers of the meat. Be sure the salt pork is blanched; this simply means dunking it in boiling water for a few seconds to draw out excess salt. Bacon isn't suitable for larding. It's not rich enough in fat and it has a characteristic flavor of its own which it will transmit to any meat with which it's cooked.

Barding, mentioned in an earlier chapter, is a technique which is especially useful when you want to spit-cook small game birds. It simply means covering the birds with thin slices of blanched salt pork. Use it also with venison if you wish to add a bit of fat to that always dry meat. Cook the meat until it's almost done, then remove the barding to let the surface brown.

Although not all game meats require marinating, it's a good idea to be generous in using marinades. In many respects they are as important as larding and barding in game cookery. However, you as the cook must be the final judge as to whether the meat being cooked should or should not be marinated. Your decision will be based on the age and condition of the animal or bird you're cooking. Not all the recipes that you'll encounter later will specify marinating—but it's understood that if you think a marinade is necessary, you'll certainly use one.

Birds as well as cuts from large animals can be marinated quite successfully. When cooking a stew or a casserole dish or sautéing chops or steaks, or even when broiling or roasting, a marinade is often used to smooth the flavor of the meat before cooking, and not infrequently the same marinade can be converted into a sauce which will enhance the flavor of the accessory ingredients to produce a superior dish.

Most marinades have a base of an acidic liquid such as wine or vinegar or lemon juice, to which are added herbs and occasionally spices and more frequently pungent seasoning ingredients such as garlic or onions. Just beware of getting your marinade too strong. You don't want a marinade so overwhelmingly potent that it masks the wild flavor of the game.

When you mix a marinade, a good rule of thumb to follow is to taste it—not swallowing it, just holding a teaspoonful in your mouth for a few seconds. If the marinade begins to assault your taste buds within 3 or 4 seconds after you've put it in your mouth, it's far too strong. You should be able to hold a spoonful of marinade in your mouth for at least a minute without feeling overpowered.

There are certain synthetics which you should avoid, not only in marinades and saucing, not only in game cooking, but in all cooking. These include all the powders which claim to produce lemon juice or any other natural juice, and most of the liquids which purport to be juices of a citrus plant or other commonly used seasoning. Most of the liquid products are manufactured by mixing water and an emulsifier with the powders.

These powders are related to lemon juice as closely as polyester is related to cotton. Many of them are totally synthetic, the products of chemicals mixed according to a laboratory formula to imitate the real thing; some are made from dehydrated citric acid that has been extracted from lemon rinds, from which the essential oils of lemon have been removed.

Even in their liquid form, the imitations do not contain the oil of lemon present in the fruit's rind. Diluted in a sugared lemonade, the synthetics taste remarkably like lemon juice, but the chemicals in their formulation may react unfavorably (and unflavorably) with some foods.

Any pure citric juice that is bottled will turn dark and become unappetizing-looking in a very short time. To prevent this, an antioxidant is mixed with the few frozen juices that are genuinely squeezed from citrus fruits. The antioxidant can have an adverse effect on the flavor of a sauce in which it is used or a marinade of which it becomes an ingredient. Don't risk spoiling a dish for lack of a real lemon. Squeeze the juice yourself when lemon juice is called for in a recipe.

Use discretion in selecting your cooking fats. Time after time, I see olive oil praised for its "lovely greenish hue, which shows that it is pure virgin oil." Pure virgin oil it may be, but it will not be first quality oil if it has a greenish tinge. I've been closely acquainted with a couple of small-scale olive oil producers who produced oil of such high quality that their entire output was spoken for two years in advance of pressing by a few superior restaurants and fortunate individuals.

Because these men were good friends, I visited them in their plants quite frequently, heard them arguing about quality, got intimately acquainted with their products. They always managed to hold back enough oil for their own household use and were very generous in sharing it with me. From this experience, I learned that the best first-press olive oil is not green or amber. It is absolutely clear and colorless and is so delicate that it can be used in baking cakes. During World War II, when kitchen shortenings were in such limited supply, this olive oil was all we used in our own cakes.

Unfortunately, oil of this quality seldom reaches the commercial market because it is in such limited supply. There are two or three top-grade olive oils imported from Italy, most of them in gallon and half-gallon tins. Recently, a few superior Italian and Spanish olive oils have begun to appear in quart and smaller bottles, which does away with the relatively large outlay that was required to buying any top-grade olive oil. These small containers of fine olive oil can usually be found in specialty food stores; look for them too in ethnic neighborhoods.

Otherwise, use safflower oil, peanut oil, or corn oil. But for some dishes, you must use butter, which has attributes lacking in most liquid shortenings, not the least of which is the ability to impart a distinctive flavor and texture to dishes in which it is used.

Always remind yourself that oleomargarine is not butter, but a substitute for, or imitation of, butter. Butter is made from milk, not beef suet or pork fat mixed with synthetic softeners and chemical coloring. It might fool your taste buds; it might even fool Mother Nature's taste buds; but it won't fool the mysterious natural reactions that occur in a cooking pot. You simply don't get the same results with margarine that you do when you use butter.

These things aren't matters of opinion, they're matters of cooking chemistry, which is far more subtle than the overseers of the food conglomerates realize. To draw an analogy which isn't really too farfetched: For centuries men have been trying to find the philosopher's stone which would transmute base metal to gold; for several decades, men have been trying to duplicate diamonds in laboratories. Neither effort has been completely successful. There are some things which only nature is capable of doing.

MARINADES AND SAUCES

Both marinades and sauces hold a high place in game cookery. Neither needs to be an elaborate concoction involving exotic or hard-to-find ingredients. Usually, you want the simplest combinations you can create, using the marinade or sauce to complement the meat, not overwhelm it. So far, we've only skimmed the froth from the broth, so let's dive into the subject a bit deeper instead of deferring it to the next chapter, which will be devoted to recipes.

First, don't confuse marinating with *pickling*. Pickling is a process of preserving meats, marinating tenderizes and adds flavor to them. When you pickle a piece of meat, it must be submerged completely and kept submerged, which usually means adding a bit more of the pickling liquid from time to time.

You can marinate a good-sized piece of meat in a relatively small quantity of liquid, simply by turning the meat from time to time. If you're marinating a large piece of meat and the recipe you're using doesn't produce what you think is enough liquid, increase all the ingredients in proportion rather than simply adding more liquid.

When making a marinade, don't feel compelled to stay rigidly with the recipe. If the ingredients list calls for garlic, and you don't like garlic, leave the garlic out. No need to substitute anything in its place, just omit. If you have a special liking for one of the herbs listed, go on and add a pinch more than the recipe calls for.

After meat has been marinated it should be drained well and wiped dry before cooking.

Just keep one thing in mind, though. The purpose of a marinade, like that of a sauce, is to flavor the meat, and at the same time to tenderize its fibers. Marinating meats adds to their savor and makes them easier to cook. Just don't get carried away and keep heaping flavor on top of flavor, and don't overload the marinade with too much of any single flavor, or you will be defeating your purpose.

ALL-PURPOSE MARINADE

Use this as a base from which to work, and modify it as you feel called on to do so. It's a basic or generic marinade useful for all types of wild meats, animal as well as fowl. The quantities given will cover a piece of meat weighing about 5 pounds, and they can be decreased or increased as required for smaller or larger marinating jobs.

2 **large sweet onions, sliced**
1 **large carrot, sliced**
2 **or 3 whole cloves**
3 **or 4 whole peppercorns, cracked**
1 **bay leaf**
2 **sprigs parsley**
2 **juniper berries**

1 pint red wine
3 Tbsp olive oil
1 Tbsp cider vinegar

Combine all ingredients in a large crock or other nonmetal container. Meat or small game being marinated should be held off the bottom with a cup or inverted sauce-dish, and moved occasionally and the marinade stirred. Normal marinating time is 2 to 3 days, but it may be extended as required. Discard the marinade after it has been used a couple of times.

COOKED MARINADE

To make 1 gallon:

½ pint olive oil or light cooking oil
½ pound minced carrots
½ pound minced onions
6 minced shallots
1 clove garlic, mashed
   Herb bunch: 2 sprigs each rosemary and thyme, 4 sprigs parsley, 2 bay leaves, tied with thread
1 pint cider vinegar
1 bottle dry white wine
3 quarts water
2 tsp salt
4 crushed peppercorns
3 Tbsp brown sugar

Heat the oil; sauté the carrots, onions, shallots, and garlic until they begin to brown. Add the herb bunch, vinegar, wine, and water. Bring to high heat, but do not let the mixture boil. Cook 15 to 20 minutes; add the salt, peppercorns, and sugar. Cook 10 minutes and strain through a clean white cloth into a crock or bottle for storing in the refrigerator. It is used at room temperature. Marinate thin cuts such as chops or steaks 2 to 3 hours; marinate roasts from 6 to 8 hours.

If you do not have fresh herbs, substitute the equivalent in dried herbs; the usual rule in herb substitutions is that a pinch equals a sprig.

This marinade can be reused if it is heated almost to a boil and strained after each use. It is designed for venison but works equally well with other game. For small game or birds, marinate for half to two-thirds the time given to thin cuts.

MARINADE FOR SMALL GAME

To make 1 quart:

1 pint dry red wine
1 pint water
2 Tbsp brandy
2 bay leaves
½ tsp crushed dry basil
3 or 4 cracked peppercorns
1 tsp salt

Combine ingredients; let stand an hour or so before using. If more than a quart is needed the recipe can be doubled.

Marinate 1 to 2 hours; the larger the animal, the longer the marinating time that will be required. Turn the animals often, every 15 to 20 minutes. The marinade cannot be reused.

MARINADE FOR LARGE GAME

To make 1 quart:

2 cups peanut or safflower seed oil
¾ cup brandy
6 Tbsp fresh lemon juice (juice of 2 lemons)
2 crushed or crumbled bay leaves
2 cups hot water

Combine ingredients in the order listed, adding the water after stirring those already mixed. Stir well, and stir each time meat being marinated is turned.

Marinate thin cuts 1½ to 3 hours, depending on age of game. Turn 3 or 4 times during the marinating period.

DRY MARINADE MIX

Technically, this is not a marinade, but a tenderizing and flavor-enhancing mixture. It becomes a marinade when wine is added after the meat with which it is being used has been in contact with the ingredients for several hours, and then left to absorb the flavor and be additionally tenderized by the wine.

6 to 8 minced carrots
6 large yellow onions
1 cup minced shallots
1 cup chopped parsley
1 tsp powdered allspice
¼ tsp powdered or ½ tsp crushed coriander
½ cup peanut oil
¼ cup red wine vinegar

Combine all ingredients except the oil and vinegar. Spread half the mixture on the bottom of a large platter or other non-metal bowl. Combine oil and vinegar and rub on the meat to be treated. Place the meat on the mixture in the platter and spread the remainder of the mixed seasonings over it. Cover with a cloth and place in a cool place.

For thin cuts such as steaks and chops, marinate 3 to 4 hours, turning approximately every 2 hours. Be sure to spread the mixture over the top of the meat when it is turned. If you are preparing a roast, marinate 12 to 16 hours, turning as before. If the surface of the roast appears too dry, mix a bit more oil and vinegar and rub over it.

A FEW MORE HINTS

If you want to give commercial meat a touch of game-meat flavor, add one or two crushed juniper berries to a marinade in which these are not included as ingredients. Remember, not all wild meats need their wild taste amplified. Marinades can be used to impart a wild flavor to commercial meat; for example, a leg of lamb in a marinade containing juniper berries takes on a flavor akin to that of venison.

To add to the crust of a roast, which some people value as a special tidbit, rub the surface well with a generous quantity of warmed 100-proof vodka and light it. Begin cooking after the vodka burns away. The liquor *must be warmed* if you want it to light readily.

To give extra crackle to the skins of game birds, use the method described above, substituting brandy for vodka. Remember, the liquor must be warmed in advance. The best way to do this is to pour it into a metal container, preferably stainless steel, and hold it in a pan of hot water for a few moments.

To cook a roast of game meat without marinating, hang the meat in a cool place—though not a refrigerator—at least 4 days to a week, depending on the animal's age. Before cooking, rub the meat with a very thin coating of flour and cover the surface with thin slices of blanched salt pork. Hold the barding in place with small skewers. Roast as usual, and remove the pork before the roast is done to let the surface brown nicely.

If a roast of game being cooked has been marinated too long, it will weep during cooking and be difficult to brown nicely. To prevent this, slice a potato thickly and put the slices in the roasting pan beside the meat. The potato will drink up the excess liquid and keep the roast from becoming unpleasantly soggy. Discard the potato pieces; they're not good eating.

WINES

This time around, our target is red wines, specifically, the pairing of red wines with the different kinds of game dishes that you will be cooking. Again, the wines of France will not be listed, as page after page would be required to cover the scores of vintages, which can only be identified by the chateaus whose names they bear. If you are knowledgeable about wines you will know them and be able to select without advice. If you want to know more about wines, there are hundreds of establishments which sell both imported and domestic vintages, and the only way you will really learn about wine is by tasting it.

Domestic wines are easier to identify in little space. The jug wines which are so inexpensive that they can be used in cooking are labeled generically; that is, by type: Burgundy, claret, or simply as mountain red, or "Smith Vineyards" red. A few varietals, wines made from a specific variety of grape, are bottled in jugs; the most common of these is zinfandel, but you will find Barbera and Charbono among the jug varietals. Many of the jug wines are very palatable, though a bit light-bodied, and are quite suitable for both drinking and cooking. By using them for cooking you can reduce the cost of preparing marinades quite substantially.

Within recent years, flavored wines and fruit wines have appeared in the United States. These may or may not be labeled as wine; most of them bear proprietary names after the fashion of soft drinks and seek market recognition by the use of odd-shaped containers which do not resemble traditional wine bottles. These are useless in cooking as well as unsuitable for drinking.

When you buy wines to be served with game, you will be looking for red wines bearing varietal labels; that is, the name of the grape comprising more than 50 percent of the pressing will be given.

Let's dispose of the rosés first, and I'll start with a confession that I don't admire them or consider them a wine suitable for service with any meal other than a light summer snack of pickup dishes. Call this another personal prejudice if you wish, but rosés have always struck me as being a cop-out wine, without enough character to stand up to the assertive flavors of wild game. To accompany game dishes, a positive wine is required.

During 25 years in the California wine country, I've tried perhaps 15 rosés, and my opinion's unchanged. I must admit that the rosés began improving during the 1970s, and they're certainly better suited to mealtime service than colas or iced tea or mixed liquor drinks.

Names of the most trustworthy California winemakers have already been listed in an earlier chapter, but here are those who have earned a reputation for producing consistently dependable and frequently superior red wines: Beaulieu, Buena Vista, Concannon, Heitz, Inglenook, Krug, Martini, Mirassou, Mondavi.

Look for varietals such as Cabernet and Cabernet sauvignon, Pinot and Pinot noir, Gamay and Gamay beaujolais, zinfandel, Barbera, and Charbono. Some of the wineries listed also produce very good wines which do not have enough grapes of a single type in their blend to be classed as varietal. These are labeled simply as Burgundy, but don't mistake them for the lighter jug wines bearing that generic name. These better-grade generics are usually sold in corked bottles.

If you want a white wine to serve chilled with a game dinner, try a Pinot blanc, a Pinot chardonnay, or a Chenin blanc. A number of California vintners now bottle a white chablis, and a few produce dry sauvignon and dry semillon wines that have the sturdiness of character required to hold their own when served with game dishes.

Now, with the basics firmly established, let's get on to the pleasant task of doing some actual cooking.

18 GAME AND WILDFOWL RECIPES

For centuries before history began to be recorded mankind has depended for his food, in whole or in part, on wild birds and animals and on fish, shellfish, and crustaceans. Some of the wild creatures that provided food for the nomads and cavemen of prehistory have vanished from the earth, and even in modern times we have witnessed the extinction of several edible species, while others are in danger today.

Today, though, the danger of extinction does not threaten any of the animals or birds which in civilized lands are hunted for sport and eaten as food by the hunters. Sportsmen and outdoorsmen are uniting in efforts to see that yesterday's mistakes do not recur today or tomorrow. We can cook and eat the wild foods which we garner by exercising the ancient inherited skills which we exercise when we hunt or fish today, and enjoy exercising the equally ancient and inherited art of cooking wild foods. This latter art has been practiced for so many centuries and

has resulted in such a proliferation of game dishes that a lifetime spent dining on nothing but game and fish would not allow enough time for us to sample all of them.

What I've tried to do in this final chapter is to strip game cookery down to its essentials, to give you a foundation on which you can build your own creations. Inevitably, you're going to find that someone has anticipated virtually every ingenious twist you think of, for there's really very little that is new in cookery. Don't feel brought-down, then, when you discover belatedly that your new creation was anticipated a hundred years ago. This happens to everybody who's ever cooked anything.

In the first section of this chapter you'll find a few traditional sauces, beginning with the basic brown and white mother sauces. These can be altered by the introduction of additional ingredients to produce dozens of others; those which are detailed are just a sampling of what can be done.

From the sauces we'll go to recipes for large game, then to those designed for small game, and wind up with recipes for the preparation of both upland birds and waterfowl. Finally, there'll be a few go-withs to start you to thinking of others.

Remember that cooking wild meats is something of a family matter; it's not as important which family the game comes from as it is that the recipe by which it's prepared will bring out its most pleasing flavor. By adjusting the quantities of seasonings and other ingredients, you can use almost all the recipes in this chapter for any kind of game. Some of the recipes by tradition are associated with a specific animal or bird, but that should not inhibit you from using them as a guide to cooking others.

SAUCES

Never begrudge any amount of time or effort required to make a sauce, especially one of the basic sauces. Never scant on the ingredients used in a sauce. A game dish without a sauce is like a pretty woman without her makeup. In her natural state she may be attractive, but with just a touch of help from the makeup box she becomes a vision of beauty.

BASIC BROWN SAUCE FOR GAME BIRDS

To make 1 quart:

½ cup olive oil or safflower oil
¾ cup minced carrots
½ cup minced sweet onion
3 Tbsp minced shallots
¼ cup minced fresh mushrooms
1 tsp salt
2 or 3 crushed peppercorns
2 whole cloves
1½ pint beef stock (not canned soup or bouillon cubes; boil a beef soup bone or a few rounds of marrowbone, skimming away the froth as they cook, and strain the stock before using)
½ pint dry red wine
1 tsp (plus or minus) arrowroot or cornstarch

Heat the oil; add carrots, onions, shallots, and mushrooms, then salt, peppercorns, and cloves. Cook over low heat, stirring often, until the carrots can be pulped easily with a spoon.

Add the wine and beef stock and simmer for 1 hour without allowing to boil. Pour the liquid into a clean pot. If evaporation during cooking has reduced the quantity to less than a quart, add equal parts broth and wine to bring the level up and reheat at a simmer. Cool or chill and skim off any fat.

Strain the skimmed liquid into a clean saucepan through a cloth and reheat to simmer. Stir in the arrowroot or cornstarch that has been moistened with an equal amount of cold water. The liquid should be the consistency of very heavy cream. You may need more or less of the thickener than the 1 teaspoon. Stored in the refrigerator in a tightly closed jar, it will keep for about a month.

This base sauce can be used as is, slightly thinned with broth or pan juices, or it can be modified by adding seasonings such as herbs to it to make different sauces.

Heat the butter in a saucepan and stir in the flour a little at a time. Stir almost constantly; the roux should not be allowed to brown. When the butter and flour are well mixed—the process should take 5 to 10 minutes, to allow the flour to cook thoroughly—combine the stock and wine and add to the roux slowly while stirring constantly. Add the thyme, rosemary, and nutmeg soon after all the stock has been added.

Cook over low heat, not allowing to boil, until the mixture is the consistency of light cream. Pour in a scalded jar, seal, and store in the refrigerator, where it will keep for about 2 weeks. Use as needed as a stock base or thicken with butter and flour kneaded together and added a bit at a time to produce a white sauce.

BASIC WHITE SAUCE

To make 1 quart:

- 2 Tbsp butter
- 3 Tbsp all-purpose flour
- 7 cups (about 1¾ pint) chicken stock (not a canned soup or bouillon cube); boil two or three chicken backs in 1 quart water, with ½ tsp salt, ½ bay leaf, and a single white peppercorn; skim, strain
- ½ cup dry white wine
- 2 sprigs fresh thyme or 2 pinches dry thyme
- 2 sprigs fresh rosemary or 2 pinches dry rosemary
  Large pinch freshly grated nutmeg

HUNTER'S SAUCE

- 1 cup chopped fresh mushrooms
- 1 Tbsp butter
- 1½ tsp all-purpose flour
- 2 Tbsp dry white wine
- 1 tsp chopped parsley
  Pinch each of chervil and tarragon
- 1 Tbsp tomato sauce
- 1½ cups Basic Brown Sauce

Sauté the mushrooms in the butter for a few minutes, drain them from pan, and reserve. Combine flour with the butter remaining in the pan, stir until lightly browned. Combine remaining ingredients, add to the roux in the pan, and stir until smooth; return the mushrooms to the pan; simmer until they are reheated.

This sauce is suitable for any game dish, but is at its best when served with roasts, chops, or steaks that have been sautéd, or small game and birds that have been roasted.

BRITISH BREAD SAUCE

3 cups breadcrumbs made by drying good-quality fresh bread and grating until the crumbs are rice-grain size
2 tsp butter
3 cups beef or chicken stock
1½ cups very lean uncooked ham minced very fine
1 tsp minced shallots
2 cups Basic Brown Sauce
1 Tbsp brandy (to vary, substitute lemon juice)

In the saucepan, fry the breadcrumbs in the butter until they are quite crisp. Strain from pan, leaving in the pan any butter that has not been absorbed by the bread. Put the crumbs on a paper towel and spread them to let the towel absorb excess butter.

Add the stock, ham, and shallots to the butter remaining in the saucepan;

simmer briskly for 10 minutes. Stir in the Brown Sauce and brandy and simmer 3 to 5 minutes.

Just before serving, add the breadcrumbs to the sauce, stir, and spoon over the meat on its platter or serving plates.

This sauce was once traditionally served in England over roast grouse, but strikingly similar recipes for venison sauce are found in cookbooks dating back 300 years. I strongly suspect the British lifted it and anglicized it. Whatever its origin, serve it over game birds or small game or plain broiled fish.

MADEIRA SAUCE

¼ cup butter
1 Tbsp minced onion
3 Tbsp flour
2 cups canned condensed consommé, undiluted
⅓ cup white raisins, soaked 10 minutes in hot water and drained thoroughly
⅓ cup Madeira
  Small pinch of cayenne

Melt the butter over low heat in a small saucepan, add onion and cook until golden brown, stirring often. Sprinkle the flour over the onions and continue to stir until the flour is assimilated. Cooking time after adding the flour is about 3 minutes; be careful not to overcook and scorch the flour.

Stir in the consommé and continue to stir until the mixture thickens to a creamy consistency.

Add raisins, Madeira, and cayenne. Cook 1 to 2 minutes, *do not boil.* Serve in a thick gravy boat or bowl, the sauce should be hot when used.

This is one of the great classic sauces for all kinds of wild game, large and small, as well as for game birds. It is also very good with ham. Makes about 2½ cups sauce.

MEXICAN-STYLE SALSA

- 2 **cups tomatoes, chopped coarsely**
- ½ **cup sweet white onion, chopped coarsely**
- 1 **fresh ancho chile or ½ red bell pepper, pith and seeds removed, chopped coarsely**
- ½ **tsp white vinegar**

Combine all ingredients in a bowl, stir well, and chill. Makes about 2 cups.

ONION SAUCE

- ¾ **cup chopped sweet onions**
- 1½ **cups water**
- ½ **tsp salt**
  Pinch of ground white pepper
  Large pinch freshly grated nutmeg
- 1 **Tbsp flour**
- 2 **cups Basic White Sauce**
- ½ **cup (more or less) dry white wine**

Put onions, salt, and pepper in the water and boil until the onions are very soft; drain through a sieve and discard the cooking water. Mash the onions into a smooth paste (or put in a blender) adding the nutmeg and flour.

Combine Basic White Sauce and wine in a saucepan; stir in the onion paste a bit at a time while simmering. Do not boil. Pour the sauce thinly over sautéd game chops or steaks, or over roasted small game or upland wildfowl.

BIGARADE SAUCE FOR DUCKS

- 1 **orange**
- ½ **cup water**

2 **cups Basic Brown Sauce**
1 **tsp butter**

Peel the zest from the orange in thin strips (the zest is the semitransparent outer skin); when peeling avoid cutting deeply and taking off any bits of the bitter pith. Chop the zest coarsely. Bring the water to boil in a saucepan, add the chopped zest, cook 3 to 4 minutes. Drain the zest, combine it with the warmed Basic Brown Sauce and the juice squeezed from the peeled orange. Bring to a quick boil, remove from heat, quickly stir in the butter and serve hot with the roasted ducks.

SOUR CREAM SAUCE

2 **Tbsp dry white wine**
1 **Tbsp fresh lemon juice**
2 **Tbsp coarsely chopped green onion, including tops**
1 **tsp chopped parsley**
¼ **tsp dry tarragon, powdered**
½ **cup dairy sour cream**
1 **egg yolk**

Combine the wine and lemon juice in a small saucepan and add the onion, parsley, and tarragon. Bring to a boil and let boil for about 2 to 3 minutes, until the liquids are reduced by one-half.

Blend the sour cream and egg yolk in a bowl and slowly add the wine mixture, stirring as it is added. Stir until smooth, return to the saucepan and cook over low heat for 3 to 4 minutes. *Do not allow to boil.* Makes about ¾ cup of sauce; recipe can be doubled.

RED CURRANT SAUCE

8 **ounces tart red currant jelly**
1 **Tbsp water**
2 **lemons**

Dissolve the jelly in the water over the lowest possible heat. Grate the lemon rinds and add to the jelly. Be careful not to let the grater bite into the lemon pith. Peel the pith from the lemons and squeeze their juice. Strain the juice; add it to the jelly. Simmer 3 to 4 minutes, stirring, until the flavors marry.

This is a traditional sauce for quail, but it's equally good on other wildfowl and small game.

BASTING SAUCE FOR ALL GAME

2 **Tbsp butter**

2 **Tbsp brandy**
   Large pinch nutmeg

Melt butter, combine with brandy, and add nutmeg. Brush over game while it is being broiled or grilled.

penned up in a feedlot does for the meat of cattle.

And, to repeat what has already been mentioned, recipes for venison can be used to prepare almost all small game animals as well as game birds, so feel free to interchange.

COOKING VENISON AND OTHER LARGE GAME

If the point hasn't been made often enough, let me repeat it now. Cooking large game differs from cooking market meats in one important aspect: The ingredients and processes must tenderize as well as enhance flavor. The object is not to emphasize the wild taste of game, but to control the strong flavor common to all game meats and to civilize it. The only part of a large game animal that requires no special handling is the liver of a deer. To do anything to deer liver besides sautéing it gently with butter is a waste of effort.

When you're cooking the muscle meats of wild animals, it's an entirely different ball game. Even the tenderest cuts, such as the chops, are far more tooth-resistant than the toughest cuts of beef. This is why the acidic liquids, wines and vinegars, play such a prominent part in game recipes. Their chemistry does for the meat of active animals what being

BRAISED VENISON

Dry marinade
4 **to 6 cups dry red wine, as re-**
   quired
2½ **to 3 pounds venison: deer, elk,**
   etc., cut in chunks
1 **to 2 tsp flour and an equal**
   quantity butter (optional)

Prepare marinade, marinate meat dry for 3 to 4 hours, add red wine to cover, let stand an additional 3 to 4 hours.

Transfer meat to a large covered saucepan. Strain marinade, discard the solids, and pour the liquid over the meat; the liquid should not cover the meat; if there is too much, reserve excess and add if the pan becomes too dry. There should always be enough liquid in the pan to cover the meat about ⅓ to ½. If no excess marinade remains, add wine to maintain this level.

Cook 2 to 2½ hours, with the pan covered, on low surface heat. Stir occasionally. When meat is done, the pan juices should be reduced to a thick sauce-like consistency. If it is too thin, or too strongly flavored for your taste, knead flour and butter into a paste and dissolve it by quarter-teaspoonfuls in the liquid. Always stir until each addition of the paste dissolves completely before adding more. Serves 4-6.

BROILED OR GRILLED VENISON

All the large game animals yield cuts that lend themselves to broiling or grilling, the broiling being done with the meat on a rack in an oven drip-pan, the grilling over coals. Choose thin cuts to cook in this style—chops, steak, flank. If flank is used, score it at right angles to the grain in several places.

Game meats being grilled or broiled should be basted often and turned several times. Broiling yields a bonus of drippings that can be used as a sauce base or added to a sauce:

2 chops per serving, or a cut of steak or flank large enough to serve four
3 Tbsp butter or light cooking oil
1 cup Basic White Sauce

To broil: Wipe meat dry with cloth and rub with butter or oil. Place on a rack over a drip-pan, cook until top side begins to brown, brush with butter, turn meat and brush with butter, then combine remaining butter with sauce and brush at fairly frequent intervals. When meat is done, combine pan drippings with remaining sauce and serve as a gravy.

To grill: Wipe meat dry; brush with butter or oil. Place over coals; combine remaining butter with sauce and use as a basting liquid.

You can use Basic Brown Sauce instead of White if desired.

VENISON STEWED IN BEER

2 to 3 pounds venison cut in stew-sized chunks
¼ to ½ cup all-purpose flour
   Large pinch of salt
   Small dash of freshly ground pepper
2 to 3 Tbsp butter or light cooking oil
3 or 4 shallots, minced
1 bottle beer, at room temperature
   Bay leaf
2 sprigs thyme or ½ tsp dried thyme
½ pint sour cream

Wipe the pieces of meat with a cloth; combine flour, salt, and pepper and dredge the meat with the seasoned flour, shaking or brushing off any excess. Heat butter or oil and brown meat well. Add the shallots while browning.

Reduce heat and pour the beer into the pan. Add bay leaf and thyme. Cook covered over moderate heat until meat is tender. Cooking time will vary according to age and condition of the animal from which the meat came and the section of carcass from which it was cut. If liquid level gets too low, add as much additional beer as needed to keep the meat covered.

When meat is tender, raise the heat until the liquid is just short of boiling; stir in the sour cream. Stir until the liquid is smooth and serve in stew bowls. Serves 4-6.

time will vary according to the thickness of the meat and the age and condition of the animal from which it was taken. About 15 to 20 minutes is a fair estimate. When the meat begins to become tender, add the chopped mushrooms. Stir them occasionally.

In a small saucepan, heat the sauce and to it add the tomato puree and mustard. Rinse the gherkins under running water, slice them into thin rounds, drain on paper towel until ready to use.

When the meat is ready to serve, add the warm sauce to it before taking it from the pan and keep on very low heat 3 or 4 minutes. If the sauce is too thick, add wine sparingly, stirring until it reaches the right consistency. Add the gherkin slices, stir well, and serve. Serves 4.

SAUTÉD VENISON CHOPS OR STEAKS, BUTCHER'S SAUCE

- 8 venison chops (2 per person) or large steak
- 3 Tbsp butter or light cooking oil
- 3 large fresh mushrooms, chopped coarsely
- 1 cup Basic Brown Sauce
- 1 Tbsp tomato puree
- ½ tsp dry mustard
- ¾ cup sweet or dill gherkins
- ¼ cup (more or less) dry white wine

Wipe the meat well and sauté it in the butter over moderate heat until it is almost done, turning as necessary. Cooking

Parslied brown rice makes a good accompaniment for venison cooked in this style. Steam the rice until tender, stir in a bit of butter and some minced parsley, make a foundation of the rice on each plate with the chops or a portion of steak, and pour some sauce over the meat.

VENISON CHOPS OR STEAKS VINAIGRETTE

8 chops (2 per serving) or a suit-
  ably sized steak
2 Tbsp all-purpose flour
  Pinch of salt and freshly
  ground pepper
4 Tbsp butter or light cooking oil
3 Tbsp white wine vinegar
½ cup chicken stock
1 Tbsp capers

Wipe the meat; mix flour, salt, and pepper. At high heat, brown the meat quickly in the oil, then reduce heat to moderate and cook until done, turning the meat as needed. Transfer meat to warmed platter or warmed dinner plates.

There should be about 2 to 2½ tablespoons of fat remaining in the skillet; if too much fat has been absorbed by the meat, add a bit more and heat. Dash the vinegar into the fat in the skillet, swirl it around, scrape the pan well as the vinegar bubbles. Add the broth, stir well over high heat until it is reduced slightly, have the capers drained and ready. Add the capers and stir; put a bit of the sauce on the meat or serve in a gravy bowl.

SAUCED VENISON STRIPS

1 pound of strips of venison
  about ¼ to ½ inch thick and
  1 to 2 inches wide, cut from the
  forearm or flank of deer, elk,
  antelope.
2 Tbsp flour
¼ tsp freshly ground pepper
2 Tbsp peanut or safflower oil
½ clove garlic, peeled and minced
  very fine
3 cups tomatoes, peeled, pureed
  in a blender or minced very
  fine
⅛ tsp salt

Rub the meat well with flour and sprinkle with pepper, then sauté very lightly in the oil; cook about 1 minute per side over high heat. Drain to a paper-covered platter or mixing board, and pour off any oil remaining in the skillet.

Reduce heat to medium and put the bits of garlic in the skillet, cook until they are a golden brown, shaking the pan now and then. Add the tomatoes and salt, stir to blend them, and cook until the tomatoes begin to bubble.

Return the venison strips to the skillet, immerse in the sauce, and simmer 5 to 7 minutes, depending on the thickness of the meat.

Arrange the venison strips on plates and divide the sauce over them. Serve with crusty French or Italian bread. Serves 4 to 6.

VENISON STEW, BASQUE STYLE

2 slices bacon, diced
1 Tbsp butter
¾ lb small pearl onions, peeled
1½ lbs venison neck or flank, cut in 1-inch cubes.
1 clove garlic, peeled and minced
2 Tbsp flour
1½ cups dry red wine
1 tsp salt
¼ tsp freshly ground pepper
¼ cup brandy

In a Dutch oven or heavy stew-pot, sauté the bacon bits in the butter until they are translucent. Add the onions and cook until they are lightly browned, stirring often. Remove the bacon bits and onion (use a slotted spoon and leave as much fat in the pan as possible) and set them aside.

Put the venison pieces in the pan and cook with frequent stirring until they are brown. Sprinkle the meat with flour while stirring. Add the wine, salt, pepper, and return the bacon bits and onions to the pan. Bring to a boil, reduce heat, and simmer for about an hour, until the meat is fork-tender.

Stir in the brandy, let simmer while stirring for three or four minutes and serve in bowls with crusty bread. Serves 6.

VENISON GOULASH

2 Tbsp oil
1½ lbs venison, from neck, flank, shanks, cut into cubes 1 to 1½ inches
3 medium-sized onions, peeled and sliced very thin
2 Tbsp paprika (paprika comes in three heats: mild, medium and hot; the quantity given here is for the medium, so increase or decrease the quantity to your taste if you get a milder or hotter version)
1 tsp salt
1 medium-sized bell pepper, sliced thinly, seeds and pith removed
½ cup water

In a Dutch oven, heat the oil and brown the venison, stirring often. Add the onions, sprinkle with paprika and salt while stirring, sauté over medium-low heat until the onions are soft. Put in the green pepper and water, cover the Dutch oven but do not put coals on top. Cook 1 to 1½ hours, until the venison is fork-tender. Traditionally, goulash is served over wide noodles. Serves 6.

VENISON WITH KRAUT

1¼ pounds venison, from neck, flank, or forelegs, cubed ¾ to 1 inch
1 Tbsp flour
2 Tbsp butter (cooking oil can be substituted)
½ tsp caraway seeds, crushed very lightly
1 cup hot water
1 pound sauerkraut, well-drained
½ cup dairy sour cream

Rub the meat well with the flour. Heat the oil in a Dutch oven over medium heat and brown the venison lightly. Cover the pot and cook over low heat for 10 to 15 minutes, stirring now and then to turn the meat.

Add caraway seeds and water, close the Dutch oven and cook over low heat for 35 to 45 minutes, until the venison is fork-tender. Do not add more water.

Add the kraut, stir in the sour cream, mixing well. Close the pot and simmer 5 to 10 minutes. Serves 6.

VENISON BORSCH

1½ lbs venison, from neck, flank, or forearm, cubed about 1 inch

Water to cover meat in pot
2 medium-sized potatoes, peeled and diced
3 or 4 beets peeled and diced (about 1½ cups)
1 large onion, peeled and grated
1 small head (about 1 pound) red cabbage, sliced thinly across its diameter
1 cup broth from boiled venison bones, strained
2 tsp salt
¼ tsp freshly ground pepper
1 large bay leaf
1 8-ounce can tomato juice

Place meat in Dutch oven with water barely covering it, bring to a boil, reduce to simmer and after skimming froth cover the pot. Cook 45 minutes to 1 hour, until meat is tender.

Add remaining ingredients, stir well. Cover Dutch oven and let simmer gently for 15 to 20 minutes, until potatoes and cabbage are tender. Remove bay leaf before serving in bowls. A dollop of sour cream can be floated on the surface just before serving. The borsch can be served hot or lightly chilled. Serves 6.

BRAISED ANTELOPE SHANKS

6 to 8 pieces of antelope forearm, cut about 3 inches long
1½ lbs (about 5 cups) antelope

neck meat cubed ¾ to 1 inch
2 tsp salt
¼ tsp freshly ground pepper
½ cup cooking oil
3 leeks, white bottom portion only, sliced ½ inch thick
2 cups coarsely chopped mushrooms
1 cup dry white wine
1 cup undiluted canned consommé
¼ pint coffee cream
2 egg yolks
½ tsp Dijon mustard

Rub the meat well with salt and pepper, put the oil in a Dutch oven, add the meat and cook uncovered over medium heat, turning and stirring the meat occasionally, for about 20 minutes. Add the leeks, mushrooms, wine, and consommé, cover the pot and cook 15 to 20 minutes, until the leeks are tender.

Drain the solid ingredients from the pot. Beat the cream, egg yolks and mustard together, and add to the liquid in the pot, stirring until it is blended smoothly. Return the solids to the pot and cook long enough to reheat them. Serves 4.

ANTELOPE STEW

3 lbs antelope neck and flank meat cubed 1 to 2 inches
1 Tbsp flour
1 tsp salt

¼ tsp freshly ground pepper
6 medium-sized potatoes, peeled and cut into chunks
4 large (3-inch diameter) onions, peeled and sliced thickly
1 Tbsp coarsely-chopped parsley
1 Tbsp crushed thyme
1½ to 2 cups water

Dredge the pieces of meat in the mixed flour, salt and pepper. Arrange half the potatoes and onions in a layer on the bottom of a Dutch oven or heavy stew-pot, sprinkle them with half the parsley and thyme. Arrange the meat in a single layer on top of the potatoes and onions and cover the meat with a second layer using the remaining potatoes and onions, sprinkle on the remaining seasonings. Add water to cover. Bring slowly to a boil, then reduce heat to low, cover the pot, and simmer gently for 1 to 1½ hours, until the ingredients are tender. Serve in bowls.
Serves 4 to 6.

SWEET ANTELOPE ROAST

3 pound piece of antelope from the shoulder or haunch, boned and trimmed
1 tsp ground ginger
3 Tbsp soy sauce

2 tsp Worchestershire Sauce
1 small bell pepper, halved, seeded and pith removed
1 clove garlic
½ cup currant jam
½ cup sweet Vermouth
1 tsp salt
2 Tbsp butter

Rub the meat with the ginger and place it in the roasting pan in which it will be cooked. Mix the soy and Worcestershire sauces, add the pepper and garlic, pour over the meat and marinate in the refrigerator 6 to 8 hours; a longer time, such as overnight, will do no harm. Turn the meat five or six times during the marinating period.

Let the meat come to room temperature before cooking, and remove the pepper and garlic from the marinade. Spread the currant jam over the top surface of the meat, and cook in a preheated 350-degree oven for 1¼ hour.

Drain the meat from the pan liquids, place on a heated serving platter, garnish with fruit or green lettuce.

With the roasting pan over a surface burner at medium-high heat, add the Vermouth, salt, and butter to the pan liquids, stir well, scraping the pan. Strain into a sauceboat and serve with the roast. Serves 4 very generously, 6 with a little stretching.

SKEWER-COOKED ANTELOPE

1½ pounds of meat from neck, flank or forearm, cut into fairly uniform cubes of about 1 inch
¼ cup cooking oil
2 Tbsp lemon juice (approximately the juice of one lemon)
1 Tbsp grated sweet white onion
½ clove garlic, minced very fine
¼ tsp ground coriander or cumin
½ tsp salt
Large pinch of cayenne

Combine the oil and lemon juice and roll the cubes of meat in the mixture, divide them among 4 or 6 skewers. Combine the onion and garlic, roll the moistened meat in this mixture, using enough pressure to cause some of the onion to cling to the meat. Mix the cumin (or coriander) with the salt and cayenne and dust over the cubes.

Broil over a grill or under a broiler for 10 to 12 minutes, and serve with boiled rice or on toasted bread. Serves 4 to 6.

COOKING SMALL GAME

Small game animals have two chief enemies in addition to the predators created by nature. One is the hunter, the other is the cook bearing a skillet.

Small game animals and skillets are natural opponents. Even in a hunting camp, there is no need to insult small game by frying it. Braise, bake, roast, or broil, using sauces generously with the last three methods, but don't inflict on anyone a dish of fried wild rabbit or squirrel, or what-have-you.

In recent years, of course, the "what-have-you" seems to have vanished. It was not always so. Our ancestors ate raccoon, woodchuck, muskrats, beaver, opossum, even porcupine (in spite of its resiny flavor). In fact, just about anything on four legs was pot meat to the pioneers. The only exceptions were skunks and the canines, wolves and coyotes, and in the Southwest, the prairie dog. I've talked to a few old cowhands who admitted to having tried prairie dogs, and all of them have had the same story, that the meat of these little rodents is so rank that they "couldn't gag it down."

Granted that the pioneers had tougher stomachs than we have today, I've tried all the small animals named except prairie dogs and porcupine, and feel that in some cases their names—such as muskrat, which identifies the animal as a rodent—have tended to discourage their consumption. Possum is fat, but tender and flavorful; beaver is a bit on the fat side, and coon is tough and stringy; but in a pinch, I could make a meal off any of them. If you feel like trying some of what we've come to consider nonedible small animals, almost any of the recipes that follow will yield dishes about as tasty as the more commonplace rabbit and squirrel.

You'll notice that these small-game recipes lean pretty heavily on "made" dishes such as stews and casseroles. There are two reasons for this. First, small game isn't really plentiful enough any more to cook a whole rabbit or squirrel per serving, unless you're exceptionally skilled or downright lucky, and made dishes are the best way I know of to extend the available meat over a lot of plates. But the real reason is that small game is much easier to cook satisfactorily in a stew or casserole than it is to roast or sauté. Look on this as aiming and shooting once and scoring twice. And always, always keep in mind that frying is the enemy of all small game animals.

SQUIRREL FRICASSEE

- 2 or 3 squirrels, cut up
- 2 thick slices salt pork, trimmed and blanched in boiling water to remove excess salt
- 1 clove garlic, mashed
- ½ cup onions, chopped coarsely
- 2 carrots, cut into small chunks
- 1 Tbsp minced parsley
- 1 bay leaf
- 1 tsp powdered thyme
- 1½ cup dry red wine
- 2 Tbsp cooking oil (butter's better, but we'll settle for oil, this time)
- 20 small pearl onions (marble-sized), peeled
- ½ tsp sugar

20 small mushroom caps
1 Tbsp lemon juice

Cut the salt pork into cubes and in a deep skillet sauté over medium heat until dark tan. Remove the cubes and drain. In the fat, simmer the garlic pulp and onions over low heat until the garlic dissolves and the onions become soft enough to mash into a paste. Drain onions from pan and brown the pieces of squirrel; be careful not to overcook. Return the pork bits and mashed garlic to the pan, add the parsley, bay leaf, and thyme, and the wine. Cover the pan and transfer it to a preheated 325-degree oven. Cook 45 minutes or more, until the squirrel is very tender.

In a skillet, sauté the onions in the oil, rolling them around and sprinkling them with the sugar, until they are brown and beginning to soften. Add them with the mushroom caps and lemon juice to the squirrel and stir well; cover the pan and cook about 10 minutes to give the flavors time to marry.

Brown squirrel pieces in a skillet. Then add other ingredients, cover pan and transfer it to a 325-degree oven to bake for 45 minutes or until tender.

SQUIRREL STEW

2 squirrels, cut up
2 Tbsp cooking oil
1 cup chicken stock
1 Tbsp flour
1 cup dry white wine
¼ tsp powdered bay leaf
1 tsp salt
¼ tsp freshly ground white pepper
2 slices bacon, cooked very crisp, drained

Grate the following ingredients in a Mouli grater or put them through the grating cycle of a food processor:
1 clove garlic
¼ cup onion
¾ cup almonds

Over low heat, brown the pieces of squirrel lightly in the oil; remove before it begins to harden. Remove to a baking dish.

Simmer the chicken stock; stir in the flour until it is dissolved; add wine, bay leaf, salt, and pepper. Combine with the grated ingredients to form the sauce.

Pour the sauce over the pieces of squirrel; cook in a 325-degree oven 25 to 30 minutes, until the squirrel is tender. Crumble the bacon over the top of the dish as a garnish.

GRILLED SQUIRREL

4 squirrels, cleaned, skinned, the
  carcasses split lengthwise
⅔ cup tomato juice
¼ cup cooking oil
1 Tbsp hot pepper sauce
⅓ cup dry sherry
1 tsp garlic salt

You will also need a heavy plastic bag
large enough to hold the halved squirrel
carcasses and the marinade.

Combine in the bag the tomato juice,
oil, pepper sauce, sherry and garlic salt,
put in the squirrel pieces and tie the
mouth of the bag tightly. Shake the bag
well, then marinate for at least 3 to 4
hours in the refrigerator. Marinating time
can be extended to overnight, if you wish.
During the marinating period, shake the
bag and turn it several times. Reserve the
marinade liquid in a bowl or pan when the
squirrel halves are removed from the bag.

Cook over coals on a charcoal grill,
or under the broiler of a kitchen range.
The approximate cooking time over coals
is 25 to 30 minutes, start cooking with the
halves bone side down and baste often
with the marinade. Turn and cook flesh
side down during the final 10 minutes of
cooking. Under a broiler, cooking time
will be 35 to 40 minutes; have the bone
side to the heat source for one-third the
cooking time and baste often. Serves 4,
one squirrel per serving.

MOCK HASSENPFEFFER

You can always cook a rabbit by the standard hassenpfeffer recipe you'll find in
any cookbook, but this one's quicker and
easier.

2 rabbits, cut up
½ cup flour
1 tsp basil
1 tsp salt
½ tsp freshly ground pepper
½ cup cooking oil
½ cup water
2 Tbsp red wine vinegar
1 Tbsp sugar
1 tsp honey
1 Tbsp chopped parsley
1 cup sour cream or yoghurt

Combine flour, basil, salt, and pepper and
rub well into the pieces of rabbit. Heat the
oil and sauté the rabbit pieces until they
brown lightly; don't overcook, or they'll
toughen up. Over low heat, in a separate
pan, combine water, vinegar, sugar, and
honey and simmer—not boil—for 2 or 3
minutes. Pour this over the rabbit and
cover the skillet; cook in a 325-degree
oven 45 minutes or until the rabbit is
tender. Stir in the sour cream and cook
covered an additional 5 to 6 minutes to
blend the flavors. Sprinkle with chopped
parsley. Serve good cold beer with hassenpfeffer in preference to even the finest
wine. Serves 6.

Continued . . .

MOCK HASSENPFEFFER

1. Begin by dredging rabbit pieces in seasoned flour.

2. Brown the rabbit pieces in a skillet.

3. Transfer the skillet to oven and pour over the top the mixture of water, vinegar, sugar, and honey. Bake, covered, for 45 minutes at 325 degrees.

4. When rabbit pieces are tender, spoon in sour cream and cook 5 minutes longer.

5. Cold beer, in an appropriate mug, goes better with Hassenpfeffer than even the finest wine.

GRILLED RABBIT

2 rabbits, skinned and cleaned
⅓ cup grated sweet onion
1 clove garlic, crushed
⅓ cup orange juice
2 tsp lemon juice
2 Tbsp cooking oil
2 Tbsp dry white wine
3 green bell peppers, cleaned and chopped coarsely

Split the rabbits lengthwise along the spine, wipe well. Combine remaining ingredients in a shallow dish and marinate the rabbit halves a minimum of 2 hours; they can marinate longer if you wish. Turn the pieces several times while marinating.

Drain the rabbit halves from the marinade and cook 25 to 30 minutes over medium-bright coals on a grill. Start cooking bone-side down, turn at midpoint. Baste frequently with the marinade mixture. In a kitchen range, broil 15 to 20 minutes, starting with the bone side toward the heat source, and turning at midpoint of the cooking. Baste often with the marinade. Serves 4.

RABBIT STEW

3 or 4 rabbits, skinned, cleaned, quartered
¼ cup peanut or safflower oil
12 pearl onions, peeled
4 small (6-inch) summer squash, halved
2 bell peppers, seeds and pith removed, cut in strips
½ clove garlic, mashed
½ tsp salt
¼ tsp dried oregano, powdered
¼ tsp dried thyme, powdered
Dash freshly ground pepper
½ cup white wine vinegar
1 cup water

In a Dutch oven or stew-pot, brown the rabbit pieces lightly, turning them often. Remove the rabbit pieces and brown the onions. Return rabbit pieces to the pot, add remaining ingredients and simmer slowly for 45 minutes to 1 hour, with the pot covered. Do not add additional liquid. Serves 4 to 6.

RABBIT-SAUSAGE STEW

2 rabbits, cleaned and quartered
3 Tbsp butter (cooking oil can be

used, but butter will give the
stew additional flavor)
24 pearl onions, peeled
 1 lb chorizo or cervelat or other
    dry sausage
 1 large sweet red pepper, seeded
    and pith removed, cut into
    strips lengthwise
 4 white potatoes, peeled and cut
    into eighths
 2 Tbsp tomato paste
 1 tsp salt
 2 cups water

 2 tsp salt
 5 or 6 peppercorns
 4 Tbsp butter (no substitutes)
 2 onions, chopped
 2 carrots, scraped and sliced
    thinly
 2 ribs celery, chopped coarsely,
    with leaves left on
 2 small young turnips, peeled and
    chopped coarsely
 2 Tbsp flour
 ¼ cup chopped parsley

Heat butter in a heavy stew-pot over medium heat and brown the pieces of rabbit
very lightly. Drain the pieces from the pot
and brown the onions. Return rabbit
pieces to the pot, add the remaining ingredients; stir the tomato paste and water
together before adding. Cover the pot and
cook at medium heat for 45 minutes to 1
hour.

To serve, divide the solid ingredients
equally in bowls, each serving should include a bit of everything. Serves 4 very
generously, can be stretched to serve 6.

RABBIT SOUP, VIENNA STYLE

 1 lonely rabbit, cleaned and quar-
    tered
 8 cups water

Simmer the rabbit in water with the salt
and peppercorns until it is quite tender.
While the rabbit cooks, sauté the onions,
carrots, celery, and turnips in the butter
until they begin to soften.

Remove the rabbit from the soup
pot and take the meat off its bones. Strain
the broth through cloth, reserve 2 cups,
return the rest to the soup pot. Sprinkle
the flour a little at a time over the soft-
ened vegetables, stirring it in, then add
the 2 cups reserved broth while continuing to stir.

When the flour is dissolved, cut up
the pieces of rabbit if necessary and return it to the pot. Add the parsley. Cook
for a few minutes—just enough to bring
things to a simmer—and serve it up. A
nice way to serve it is over lightly toasted
French bread, with a lightly chilled Rhine
or Moselle wine. Serves 4.

SALMIS

This is one of the great classic game dishes. It is a method of cooking rather than a recipe for preparing one kind of game, for you can make a *salmis* using the complete carcass of any small game animal or game bird, or you can make one from a partial cut of any large game animal. To serve four you would require four small birds, two large birds or small animals, or an equivalent quantity of the trimmings that are left after butchering out a deer or other large game animal.

Only one step in the preparation of a *salmis* is tricky, and that is the first step in cooking. The dish requires that the meat be preroasted at high temperature, so that it is only partly done. For small game birds this generally means 5 to 10 minutes in a 425- to 450-degree oven; for large birds and small animals such as squirrel and rabbit, 15 to 20 minutes; for pieces cut from large animals, 20 to 25 minutes. Birds and small animals are precooked whole with the liver inside the cavity.

Ingredients used in addition to the meat are given here in quantities sufficient to prepare a *salmis* that will serve four, and are listed in the order they will be used:

½ cup dry white wine
½ cup meat stock
1 lemon
½ tsp salt
⅛ tsp freshly ground pepper
Large pinch freshly grated nutmeg

1 Tbsp dry mustard
2 Tbsp butter
1 cup minced sweet white onion
1 cup fresh mushrooms, chopped or sliced
2 Tbsp chopped parsley

Roast the meat as indicated above, adjusting timing as required. The meat should be quite rare when it is taken from the oven. While the meat roasts, combine wine and meat stock and put to boil. Grate the peel from half the lemon, squeeze all juice from both halves, reserve.

Remove meat, and cut up on a prewarmed deep platter to catch the juices it will release. If small birds have been used, disjoint and quarter them. Large birds, remove legs and wings and slice the breasts thinly. Small game, disjoint and quarter. Roasts from large game, slice thinly. Reserve the juices, which should be quite a dark pink, almost red.

Rub livers through a sieve or put them through a blender. Combine liver paste with the juices from the platter and reserve. In a small saucepan, boil the wine/stock mixture to reduce it by half. Add to it the liver paste and pan juices, the grated lemon rind, juice, and seasonings.

Melt butter in the pan—preferably a chafing dish—in which the cooking will be completed. Add onions and mushrooms and the pieces or slices of meat; cook until redness is gone.

(Directions for preparing the *salmis* seem more complicated than they actually are when being carried out. Not only is the finished dish excellent, but think of the show you're staging for your guests.)

COOKING UPLAND GAME BIRDS

When choosing a recipe for cooking upland game birds, thoughtful cooks will always keep in mind the differences between these species and waterfowl. Upland birds lack the busy oil glands and the warming layer of fatty tissues with which nature provides waterfowl. The diets of upland birds are invariably low in liquid; they drink sparingly and less often than do their cousins of the wetlands.

It follows, then, that the ingredients and cooking processes by which upland birds are prepared must have a much higher proportion of moisture than is required for water birds.

PIGEONS PORTUGUESE STYLE

8 pigeons, pot-ready
1 Tbsp fine olive oil (or peanut or safflower oil)
8 large slices of very thin salt pork
½ cup chopped green onions, including tops
½ clove garlic, minced
½ bell pepper cut in toothpick-thin strips
1 cup cabbage, cut like the pepper
1½ cups chicken stock
½ cup port wine

Rub the birds with part of the oil; rub a shallow baking dish with the remainder. Wrap each pigeon separately in a slice of the salt pork. Spread the onion, garlic, pepper, and cabbage over the bottom of the baking dish and arrange the birds on the vegetables. Mix stock and wine and pour over the birds.

Cook in a moderate oven—350 degrees—20 minutes. Remove the pork and continue cooking 4 to 5 minutes, long enough to brown the birds' breasts.

Serves 6-8.

QUAIL WITH GRAPES

8 quail, pot-ready
3 Tbsp cognac or brandy
3 to 4 Tbsp light cooking oil (peanut or safflower)
2 tsp powdered rosemary
2 cups dry white wine
1 tsp butter
1 tsp flour
20 or 30 seedless grapes

Lay the quail breast-up in a shallow roasting pan and warm the cognac; pour it over the birds and flame them. Cover the birds with an oiled cloth and cook for 8 to 10 minutes in a 400-degree oven.

Combine the rosemary and wine and pour it over the cloth; continue cooking for 10 minutes. Knead together the butter and flour, form it into a ball, and chill if necessary until it is firm enough to handle. Remove the cloth and rub the breasts of the birds with the butter-flour ball. Strew the grapes over the birds; return to the oven long enough to brown their breasts.

DOVES WITH ORANGE SAUCE

8 doves, drawn and plucked (pigeons and quail are equally good cooked this way)
2 Tbsp butter
3 oranges
2 stalks celery cut in small pieces
1 medium-sized sweet onion, quartered
¼ tsp dry mustard

Take thin center slices from the oranges. You will need two slices for each bird. Peel the ends of the oranges very thinly, taking off only the aromatic skin and avoiding cutting into the bitter pith. Squeeze the orange pieces and reserve the juice.

Rub the birds with about half the butter, and sprinkle the mustard over their breasts very scantily. Put pieces of celery, onion, and orange peel in the cavity of each bird. Place the birds breast-up in a shallow roasting pan. Spread a piece of clean white cloth with the remaining butter; the cloth should be large enough to cover the pan, but do not cover at once.

Preheat oven to 450 degrees, put the pan containing the birds in the oven, and leave for about 10 minutes, until the skin on their breasts turns golden. Remove the pan; reduce oven heat to 325 degrees. Brush the breasts of the birds generously with orange juice and cover with the buttered cloth. Tuck the cloth in at the edges of the pan so it will touch the bottom.

This turns the cloth into a basting wick; it will draw up juices from the bottom of the pan to keep the birds moist, but will allow steam to escape and keep their flesh from getting mushy.

Return birds to oven for 15 to 20 minutes. They should not be overdone. Remove cloth, place orange slices on birds' breasts, return to oven just long enough to heat the orange slices, transfer to warmed plates, and serve at once.

Place the doves and mushroom caps on the onions in the pan, sprinkle the herbs and salt over the birds and vegetables.

Cover the pan and cook in a 325-degree oven for 20 to 25 minutes.

Serve on toast slices; spoon a layer of the onions on each slice, then top the onions with a brace of doves flanked by mushroom caps. Serves 4.

DOVES, HUNTER STYLE

8 doves, plucked and cleaned
2 slices bacon
2 Tbsp butter
½ cup grated sweet onion
24 large mushrooms or 1 pound button mushrooms, parboiled
¼ tsp powdered thyme
¼ tsp powdered rosemary
½ tsp salt

Cut one slice of bacon into eight equal pieces and roll each piece, insert a piece in the cavity of each bird.

Chop the remaining bacon coarsely and sauté until translucent in a shallow pan. Add the grated onion and cook 5 to 10 minutes, until the onion is beginning to soften. Remove the mushroom stems, chop coarsely, add them to the onions.

JACKSNIPE WITH SOUR CREAM

Though technically jacksnipe are shore or marsh birds, they are more akin to small upland birds when they get to the kitchen.

6 jacksnipe, drawn and plucked
½ onion
1 egg, beaten with a fork
1 Tbsp melted butter
½ tsp salt
    Large pinch freshly ground white pepper
1 cup chicken stock
1 Tbsp all-purpose flour
½ cup sour cream

Divide the onion into six parts and put a piece in the cavity of each bird. Arrange the birds in a shallow baking dish; beat the butter, salt, and pepper into the egg; brush the breasts of the birds with the mixture. Cook in a moderate—350 degree—oven for 12 to 15 minutes.

Heat the stock until it simmers, remove from heat and with a mixer beat the flour into it; when the flour has been absorbed, slowly beat in the sour cream. Pour this over the birds and cook an additional 5 to 7 minutes; serve at once, with a portion of the sauce poured over each bird.

BORDEAUX-STYLE PHEASANT

2 dressed pheasants
1 cup diced blanched salt pork
4 shallots, chopped
2 carrots, chopped
2 Tbsp cognac or brandy
3 or 4 sprigs each of fresh parsley, thyme, and rosemary
¾ tsp salt
⅛ tsp freshly ground white pepper
1 cup dry white wine
1 cup chicken stock
1½ cups fresh button mushrooms
1 cup tiny sweet onions
2 tsp minced parsley

Remove the wings from the pheasants and halve the birds by cutting along their spines.

Sauté the diced pork in a skillet, stirring frequently to brown the cubes evenly. Drain the bacon pieces from the pan and reserve. In the fat, brown the pheasant halves lightly, just enough to color the skin sides a golden tan. Over low heat, sauté the shallots and carrots until the carrots begin to soften; drain and reserve.

Arrange the pheasant halves in the bottom of a large covered baking dish skin-sides-up. Warm the cognac, pour over the pheasants, and flame. Strew the pork dice and vegetables over the pheasants; add wine and stock. Tie the parsley, thyme, and rosemary sprigs together and add to the pot. (If you use dry herbs, powder them finely or tie up in a square of clean white cloth.)

Cover the dish and cook in a moderate 300-degree oven for 30 to 40 minutes, until the pheasant breasts can be readily pierced with a fork. Add the mushrooms and onions, sprinkle on the parsley, cook 10 minutes. Remove the *bouquet garni* and serve.

PHEASANT POT PIE

This dish got its name because nobody who writes can resist the lure of an alliterative title. The pie is based on the very ancient game dish called "Hotchpotch" or "Hot Pot," in which pieces of several small game animals and birds were mixed up. You can mix other small game with the pheasant, of course, just as you can cook other game birds or small animals according to the recipe. You'll find it a good dish for opening day, when you're hungry for a taste of pheasant and don't want to wait for the birds to age. It's also nearly as good as Venison Chili when you want to use up bits and pieces of deer left from butchering.

2 pheasants, cut up, or the equivalent in other kinds of game
½ cup olive oil or peanut oil
1 cup dry vermouth
1 lemon
2 cups cold water
¾ cup blanched salt pork cubes
1 tsp salt
Small dash freshly ground pepper
¾ cup all-purpose flour
1 large sweet onion
2 tomatoes, peeled, seeded, and drained, chopped coarsely
Pie crust or biscuit dough to cover the baking dish

Disjoint the pheasant and cut each carcass into four pieces. Combine oil, vermouth, and the juice squeezed from the lemon; add the cold water. Marinate the pieces of pheasant in this for 3 to 4 hours.

Fry the salt pork. Combine the flour, salt, and pepper. When the time comes to take the pheasant from the marinade, drain the pieces well, wipe them, and roll in the seasoned flour. Brush off excess flour; brown the pieces of pheasant with the pork. As soon as the pheasant pieces are nicely colored, add boiling water to cover them and simmer 30 minutes with the pan covered tightly.

Drain the pieces of pork and pheasant (who was that in the wings who called out "Poet and Peasant?") from the skillet, pour off the fat, but do not wipe the pan. Pour the marinade liquid into the skillet and let it boil furiously until reduced by half.

Oil a deep baking dish, put the meat in it, grate the onion into the dish, add the tomatoes, stir to distribute the ingredients. Add enough marinade to cover the meat. Place the crust over the top of the dish, slash several times to allow steam to escape, and bake until the crust is lightly browned. To glaze the crust (optional, but a nice touch), brush with egg white.

SKILLET-COOKED PHEASANT

2 pheasants, preferably young birds, quartered
¼ cup peanut or safflower oil
2 large sweet onions, sliced about ½ inch thick
1 clove garlic, mashed
1 bay leaf
1 tsp dried thyme, crushed coarsely
¼ tsp nutmeg
1 tsp salt
1 tsp chopped parsley
1½ cups condensed chicken broth (canned)
1 cup water
1 tsp flour

Heat the oil in a deep, heavy skillet and brown the pieces of pheasant lightly. Remove the pieces and put them to drain on paper towels. In the remaining fat, sauté the onions, adding the garlic and bay leaf to the fat and sprinkling the garlic, thyme, and nutmeg over the onions as they cook.

When the onions begin to become transparent, return the pieces of pheasant to the skillet, add the salt and parsley. Combine the broth and water and pour into the skillet. Reduce the heat until the broth is just simmering, cover the skillet and cook 35 to 45 minutes, until the pheasant is so tender that the pointed end of a wooden toothpick pierces the drumstick.

Drain solid ingredients from the skillet to a warmed platter or serving plates, bring the liquid in the pan to a slow boil and stir in the flour to thicken. Pour the resulting sauce over the pheasant and onions and serve. Serves 4.

ROAST WILD TURKEY

Wild turkeys tend to be lean and dry of flesh, unlike the gorged commercial birds whose feet never touch the earth and whose flesh is further insulated by being shot full of tenderizing chemicals and soybean oil during the process of making them "self-basting." The wild turkey is very like the market birds which were all that were available when I was a boy.

Kids helped around the house in that period, and my chores included kitchen duty on special days such as

Roast wild turkey is a superb dish. Because the flesh is lean and dry, the bird must be cooked in a special way to keep it moist.

Thanksgiving, when they also extended to beheading the live turkey bought for the feast. Precleaned birds weren't sold in rural areas, then. You bought poultry on the claw from the nearest farmer who had a surplus and did your own killing and cleaning.

Turkeys of recent yesterdays were very like the wild birds, lean and dry, and it was common kitchen practice to parboil the bird before roasting. I've since discovered that even a wild turkey doesn't need parboiling to reach the table with its flesh tender enough to be carved. Here's how it's done.

1 turkey, 8 to 12 pounds
2 Tbsp butter
2 large yellow onions
1 green apple
2 tsp salt

Before trussing the turkey, slather its carcass generously with the butter; use more than the amount indicated if necessary.

Don't overlook the creases at the wings and thighs. Then peel and halve the onions, halve the apple, and press the cut surfaces in salt until they carry a generous coating. Put these in the cavity, and truss.

Place the bird in a roasting pan that has a well or a concave bottom where juices will collect. Tear or cut a rectangular piece of clean well-washed white cloth big enough to drape loosely over the bird and be tucked around it at the bottom of the pan.

Cook the turkey 30 to 40 minutes per pound in a 300-degree oven. You will not need to baste. The cloth acts as a wick to pull melted butter up and over the bird's breast and the onions and apple in the cavity give off just enough steam to moisten the flesh during the long cooking process.

Remove and discard the stuffing ingredients before serving. Serves 8.

TEXAS TURKEY

6 **to 8 pound turkey, cut into serving pieces**
4 **tsp cooking oil**
2 **cups chicken broth (can be diluted canned broth)**
1 **to 2 cups water**
1 **tsp salt**
8 **ancho peppers, seeded and cleaned of pith**
2 **or 3 small hot red peppers, chile tepines, seeded and cleaned of pith**
1 **large onion, peeled and chopped coarsely**
1 **pound fresh tomatoes, scalded and peeled, chopped coarsely**
2 **cloves garlic, peeled and minced**
1½ **ounces bitter chocolate, broken into thumb-sized bits (do not use milk chocolate)**

This is a north of the border version of the ancient Aztec dish called molé, which is several centuries old. Both kinds of the peppers needed can be found at ethnic markets in most places, and can also be ordered from many of the specialty food shops listed in the appendix. If you buy dried peppers, they can be plumped by soaking 15 to 20 minutes in warm water before they are cleaned.

Heat the oil in a large, deep skillet or Dutch oven and sauté the turkey pieces over medium-low heat to brown them lightly. Drain the pieces on paper towels, discard the remaining oil, but do not wipe or wash the pan.

Return the turkey pieces to the skillet, pour in the broth and add water to cover the turkey, simmer at very low heat with the pan covered.

Remove seeds and pith from the peppers. Using a mortar and pestle or a food processor or blender, reduce the peppers, onions, tomatoes, and garlic to a pulp and pour into the pot over the turkey. Stir in the chocolate bits.

Cover the pot and simmer at very low heat until the turkey is tender and the sauce thickened, 1 to 1½ hours. Serve over plain rice, or with hot tortillas. Serves 6.

COOKING WATERFOWL

Ducks are about the only wild game which should always be marinated. To marinate or not to marinate is always cook's choice, of course, but if you'll refer to Chapter 15, you'll find some guidelines that may be helpful. Ducks are oily birds, and the only way I know to remove the excess oil from their flesh is to use a marinade. You'll find suitable marinades and suggestions on their use in Chapter 17.

ROAST DUCK

If you're wondering why this plain-Jane recipe is used to start the section on waterfowl, it's because I remember having given a nonhunting friend a pair of wild ducks. He wasn't at home when I delivered them, so I handed them to his wife. Not until some months later did my spouse hear via the wives' grapevine that my friend's wife had sat staring at those two ducks all afternoon, weeping from time to time, because she had no idea how to go about preparing them. Not everybody, it seems, can roast a duck, even in the plainest possible fashion. This, then, is dedicated to neophyte wildfowl cooks.

2 ducks, drawn and plucked
4 stalks celery, cut in chunks
2 apples, quartered
1 Tbsp salt (more or less)
½ tsp freshly ground pepper
1 cup olive oil (or other cooking oil)
½ cup fresh lemon juice

Divide the celery and apple between the ducks, putting them in the cavity. Truss by pulling the legs together and tying and by tying the wings close to the body with string pulled across the backs of the birds.

Rub the birds well with mixed salt and pepper. Roast with the breasts up in a roasting pan, brushing frequently with the mixed oil and lemon juice. Cooking time in a 375-degree oven is about 45 to 55 minutes for a 4- to 5-pound bird. If fat bubbles form under the skin, pierce them with a knife-tip.

DUCK IN RED WINE

2 ducks, quartered, wings and giblets removed and saved
1 cup chopped celery
1½ cups scraped chopped carrots
½ cup chopped sweet onion
½ cup cognac or brandy
1¼ cups dry red wine
1 tsp lemon juice
1 clove garlic, peeled
Butter or olive oil
2 sprigs each parsley and thyme
½ bay leaf

Cover the wings and giblets with water to which has been added ½ teaspoon salt; cook until giblets are very tender. Drain and discard cooking liquid. Put giblets in covered dish and refrigerate.

Put the pieces of duck in an earthenware or other nonmetal dish and strew the celery, carrots, and onion over them. Combine the liquid ingredients; pour over the duck pieces and marinate overnight in a cool place.

Approximately 2 hours before dish is to be served, drain duck pieces, reserving the marinade. Wipe the pieces of duck with a cloth to dry them, and brown them at low heat in oil or butter. Reserve any fat left in pan.

Mash the liver and garlic together; mince the heart fine, or put through the blender. Combine the paste with fat left when the duck was browned.

Tie parsley, thyme, and bay leaf with string, or prepare a small bag with the dry equivalents.

Put duck pieces in casserole, strain the marinade liquid and pour over them, add herbs, and cook covered in 350-degree oven 40 to 45 minutes, until duck is tender. Drain duck pieces to warm platter. Remove and discard herbs. On surface heat, bring the marinade to a boil, stir in the liver-garlic paste, simmer to reduce by ¼ to ⅓. Skim any fat that rises to surface after pot is removed from heat.

Garnish platter with parsley or other ingredients as desired and serve with the sauce in a separate bowl.

DUCK BREASTS PAPRIKASH

4 duck breasts
2 Tbsp butter
2 large onions, chopped coarsely
2 tsp paprika
1 cup chicken stock (or stock made from the legs and wings of the ducks)
½ pound mushrooms
4 slices good, firm bread, toasted

Sauté the duck breasts in the butter over low heat, about 4 to 5 minutes per side. Sprinkle the onions with the paprika and smother the breasts with them. Add the mushrooms and broth. Cover the pan and

ROAST DUCK

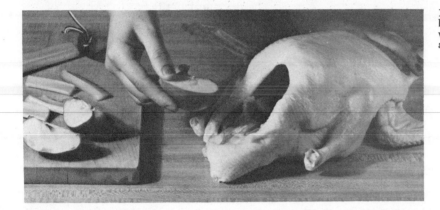

1. After plucking the bird, fill body cavity with slices of apple and celery.

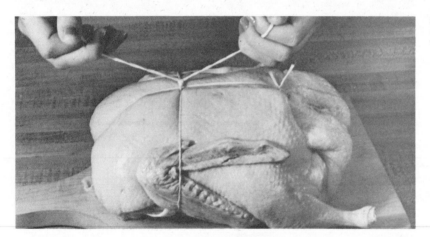

2. Truss bird with cotton string to fold wings close to body.

3. Rub salt and pepper liberally into skin.

4. Roast in an oven preheated to 375 degrees, basting frequently with a mixture of olive oil and lemon juice. Cooking time will average between 60 and 70 minutes.

5. Duck should never be roasted until it is well-done. It should be brown and crisp on the outside, but slightly pink, tender inside.

cook in a 300-degree oven 25 to 30 minutes, until the onions are soft and transparent. Cut the toast slices into triangles, place the breasts on the toast, and cover with the onions. Serves 4.

can be served from the baking dish or can be turned out to a small plate and garnished by surrounding it with sprigs of parsley. Yields approximately 2½ cups.

DUCK PATÉ

1 **duck, cleaned, plucked and skinned, the liver reserved**
1 **cup fresh orange juice**
¼ **cup Grand Marnier or Tequila Almendrada**
1 **tsp ground dry marjoram**
½ **tsp ground dry sage**
½ **tsp ground dry tarragon**
1 **tsp salt**
¾ **cup shelled pistachio nuts**

Cut the duck meat into thumb-sized chunks and marinate 8 to 12 hours in the orange juice and liqueur. Turn and stir several times during the marinating period.

Sprinkle the herbs and salt over the meat and put through a food grinder or processor. Reserve juices and add them to the ground meat mixture, together with the pistachio nuts.

Press the meat mixture firmly into a terrine or small baking dish (a small soufflé dish does nicely) and cover. Use foil pressed tightly to the sides if the baking dish has no cover.

Bake in a medium-low oven, 275 degrees, for 1½ hours, until no moisture remains in the mixture. The resulting paté

GAME BIRD GIBLETS

1 **pound giblets: hearts, livers, gizzards**
2 **tsp peanut or safflower oil**
½ **cup coarsely chopped sweet onion**
1 **Tbsp flour**
½ **cup dry red wine**
1½ **cups condensed canned consommé (water in which 2 chicken bouillon cubes have been dissolved can be substituted)**
1 **cup carrots, peeled and cut into ½-inch chunks**
1 **cup celery, chopped very coarsely**
1 **small bay leaf**
⅛ **tsp freshly ground pepper**

Clean the giblets, removing the fell (the white membrane) from the gizzards. Cut giblets into bite-size pieces.

Heat the oil in a deep, heavy skillet or saucepan, stir in the onion and cook until it is golden brown. Sprinkle on the flour and stir until it is assimilated, then add the wine. Raise the heat to bring the wine to a quick boil, lower heat and cook about 10 minutes, until almost all the liquid in the pan has evaporated, then put in the giblets, consommé, carrots, celery, bay leaf, and pepper.

Cover the pot and simmer very gently for 45 minutes to 1 hour, until the giblets are tender. Remove the bay leaf before serving. Serve over rice or with boiled or mashed potatoes. Serves 4 to 6.

ALSATIAN STYLE GOOSE

1 goose, 6 to 8 pounds, pan-ready
4 to 6 slices blanched salt pork

4 cups sauerkraut, drained and rinsed
2 apples, chopped coarsely
1 tsp caraway seeds
1 cup dry white wine
1 Tbsp flour

Try out the pork until it is brown and firm; remove and reserve. In a deep ovenware pot, brown the goose in some of the pork fat until it is a light tan. Cut the pork into dice. Put a layer of sauerkraut on the bottom of the pan, and add a few of the pieces of apple and a few caraway seeds. Lay the goose on this foundation and cover with the remaining kraut, apples, and caraway seeds. Pour the wine in; cook covered in a 325-degree oven for 1 to 1½ hours. Before serving, drain off the pan juices and thicken them with the flour before pouring them back over the goose.

Serves 6-8.

A FEW GO-WITHS

Dishes served to accompany game should not be too highly seasoned nor too heavy, and their seasonings should not conflict with the flavors of the main course. Here are some suggestions:

WATERCRESS SOUP

6 cups chicken stock
1 tsp salt
1 or 2 bunches watercress (or use wild cress which you gathered on a hunting or fishing trip)
1 cup mushrooms, chopped coarsely or sliced thinly from the stem ends
2 small green onions, sliced diagonally
2 cups Basic White Sauce
2 Tbsp very dry sherry

Add salt to stock. Wash the cress, blot dry, remove the lower ends of the stems, chop coarsely, add to stock. Add mushrooms and onions; simmer 10 minutes. Add Basic White Sauce and sherry (suggestion: Tío Pepe) and simmer another 5 minutes, stirring occasionally.

GREEN TOMATOES PARMIGIANA

For this dish, please do not use the dreadful dead-white pregrated soap-flavored granules labeled Parmesan which are sold in little plastic packets in the chain supermarkets. Find an Italian food store and buy a chunk of genuine rock-hard Parmesan and grate it yourself.

6 to 8 firm green tomatoes (depending on size)
½ cup olive oil
¼ cup minced onion
1 clove garlic, mashed
1 can tomato paste (4 oz.)
½ pound mozzarella cheese
¾ cup freshly grated Parmesan cheese
2 eggs
2 Tbsp white Chianti or dry semillon
   Dash of salt

Wash and slice the tomatoes, discarding stem-scars. Rub a shallow baking dish with part of the oil. Combine the onion, garlic, and tomato paste in a mixing bowl. Grate the mozzarella and combine with it half the Parmesan. Beat the eggs with the wine and salt; work in the cheese mixture a little at a time.

Arrange a layer of tomato slices in the pan, sprinkle it with part of the tomato paste mixture, pour over this part of the cheese mixture. Build a second and, if necessary, a third layer, covering each layer as described. Be sure to reserve enough of the egg-cheese mixture to cover the top.

Sprinkle the remaining Parmesan over the top; bake uncovered for 15 to 20 minutes in a 350-degree oven, until the top is golden brown and bubbly. Slice like a pie to serve.

TOMATOES PROVENÇALE

4 large, firm ripe tomatoes
1 tsp salt
¼ tsp freshly ground pepper
6 to 8 Tbsp medium-fine bread-crumbs
1 clove garlic, minced
1 Tbsp fresh lemon juice

Scald and peel the tomatoes; cut in halves. Sprinkle with salt and pepper; arrange cut-side-up in a shallow baking pan.

Combine breadcrumbs, parsley, oregano, and garlic; sprinkle over the tops of the tomatoes. Cook under the broiler 5 to 7 minutes, until the breadcrumbs are nicely browned. Sprinkle with lemon juice just before serving. Serve hot.

CRANBERRY CONSERVE

Serve this as a side dish or as an appetite fillip at any meal where game is a main course.

½ pound cranberries
2 oranges, peeled and seeded, chopped coarsely
¾ cup fresh pineapple, chopped very coarsely

½ apple, unpeeled but cored, chopped coarsely
4 tsp fresh lime juice
½ cup walnuts, chopped very coarsely
2 Tbsp Cointreau, Triple Sec, or Tequila Almendrada

Combine all ingredients; let rest in the refrigerator overnight. Remove in time for the dish to have warmed a bit; it should be cool but not icy when served.

ORANGES DIABLO

Game dinners tend to be on the heavy side, and a light dessert is indicated. Unless oranges have been used as a garnish in one of the dinner dishes, they can refresh taste buds as a dessert.

2 dessert-sized (4 ounce) cans mandarin oranges
2 Tbsp fresh lime juice
1 cup Tequila Almendrada or Triple Sec

Drain the oranges; boil the juice to reduce it by half. When the juice cools, add to it the lime juice and liqueur, pour over the oranges, and chill overnight. Stir occasionally. Allow to come to a bit below room temperature before serving.

POACHED FRESH PEARS

6 firm-ripe pears
2 to 3 cups unsweetened pineapple juice (orange juice can be
   used)
½ cup water
¼ cup grenadine
1 piece stick cinnamon, 2 to 3
   inches long
1 Tbsp unsweetened chocolate,
   grated

Peel the pears without removing the stems. Place a heatproof plate on the bottom of a deep saucepan or stewing-pot large enough and deep enough to accommodate the pears in an upright position. Combine the liquid ingredients and pour into the pan; they should cover the pears completely. Add the cinnamon.

Bring the liquid to a boil over high heat, reduce heat to simmer and cook uncovered 30 minutes, or until pears are tender but not soft. Remove the pears with a slotted spoon or lifter and place upright in dessert plates.

Divide the liquid over the pears, discarding the cinnamon stick. Chill for 1 to 2 hours before serving. Just before serving, dust the pears with the grated chocolate. Serves 6.

PINEAPPLE FRUIT CUP

1 large pineapple
1 to 2 pints fresh strawberries,
   stems removed, washed and
   well-drained, or use ripe cherries, pitted and cut in half, or
   blackberries or boysenberries
⅓ cup liqueur (Kirsch, Cointreau,
   Grand Marnier, Triple Sec,
   Curacao)

Cut the top off the pineapple about 1 inch below the leaves and with a long sharp boning knife remove its center, leaving a shell about ½ inch thick. Reserve the top. Cut the center portion into cubes.

In the refrigerator, marinate the fruit or fruits selected together with the pineapple cubes in the liqueur. Stir often. The use of a small quantity of sugar—½ to 1 tsp—is optional. If sugar is used, a light hand is suggested; too much sugar will detract from the natural flavors of the fruits.

A half hour before serving, fill the pineapple with the fruits or berries, pouring the juices into the shell as well. Replace the top. To serve, spoon the fruits and some of the liquid from the center into dessert plates. Serves 6 to 8.

ORANGE SNOW

1 cup fresh orange juice
1 packet unflavored gelatine
2 Tbsp fresh lemon juice
½ cup eggwhites (3 large or 4 small eggs)
  Small pinch of salt
¼ cup granulated sugar

Pour the orange juice into a small saucepan and empty the gelatine into it. Stir, and let stand 5 to 10 minutes to allow the gelatin to dissolve. Bring to a boil over high heat, take pan off heat at once when boiling begins.

Add lemon juice, stir well, and place pan in a large bowl of ice cubes or crushed ice and stir occasionally until the mixture thickens to the consistency of unbeaten egg whites; this should take about 10 to 12 minutes.

In a mixing bowl, add salt to eggwhites and beat—or use an electric mixer—until the eggwhites begin to foam. Begin adding the sugar by teaspoonful, continuing to beat until the whites form a soft rounded peak when the beater is lifted from them.

Beat the gelatine mixture until foamy. Using a rubber scraper or a wire whisk and a light touch, combine the gelatine with the eggwhites until they amalgamate smoothly.

Refrigerate the snow for at least 2 hours before serving. It can be refrigerated in the mixing bowl and spooned into dessert plates, or can be turned into a melon mold and turned out on a chilled platter to serve in slices. Makes 8 servings.

LEMON SNOW

1 cup fresh lemon juice
2 Tbsp pineapple juice
1 packet unflavored gelatine
½ cup eggwhites (3 large or 4 small eggs)
  Small pinch of salt
⅓ cup granulated sugar

Combine lemon juice and pineapple juice in a small saucepan and empty the gelatine into it. Stir, and allow to stand 5 to 10 minutes until the gelatine dissolves. Bring the mixture to a boil over high heat and remove from heat at once when boiling begins.

Place the pan in a bowl of ice cubes or crushed ice and beat until the mixture is the consistency of eggwhites; this should be 5 to 10 minutes.

In a mixing bowl, add salt to eggwhites and beat with a whisk or eggbeater or power mixer until the eggwhites begin to foam. Continue beating while adding the sugar by teaspoonful until the eggwhites form a softly rounded dome when the beater is lifted from them.

Beat the juice-gelatine mixture until it is foamy, and combine this with the eggwhites, using a spatula or whisk.

Refrigerate the mixture for at least 2 hours before serving. It can be spooned into dessert dishes or poured into a melon mold before refrigerating, and the mold turned out on a chilled platter and the snow served at the table by slicing it. Serves 8.

POSTSCRIPT

To close, I'd like to share with you a little wish that might be repeated by an outdoorsman:

Let me cherish the land where I go for
    my hunt,
Let me work with quiet strength to
    keep it unspoiled,
So that those who come later will
    have it to use.
May my gun be fired only to provide
    me with food,

Let my game be brought down with a
    clean quick shot,
And at dusk when I'm tending the fire
    where I cook,
May its coals be a beacon to guide
    through the dark
Good friends who will share the game
    I bring home.

APPENDIX

A SOURCES OF SUPPLY FOR GAME, WILDFOWL AND FISH

This list is for hunters who don't fish, fishermen who don't hunt, and for cooks who want to try species of game, fish or shellfish not available in the areas where they live.

While most seafoods are now shipped without restrictions and can be found nationwide in the specialty foods sections of large foodstores, there is a maze of state laws which govern the sale and/or shipment of game meats. Federal laws prohibit shipment of any wild waterfowl across state lines, but this does not apply to waterfowl bred on game farms. Some states prohibit the shipment of any game meats, whether wild or raised on game farms. You should investigate your own state's laws before ordering.

Some items from the following suppliers are available only seasonally; minimum purchases of some items may be required, so check with any supplier from whom you plan to order.

Archbold Associates, East Aurora, NY 14502 – pheasant, quail, chukar partridges, wild turkey.

Battistella's Seafood, Inc., 910 Touro St., New Orleans, LA 70116 – fresh, canned and frozen crab, crawfish, shrimp, oysters, Gulf of Mexico fish including shark; freshwater fish as well as turtle and alligator.

B-Bar Ranch, Gillette, WY 84716 – buffalo.

Bird Island Resort, Rt 2 Box 142, Afton, OK 74331 – ducks and geese.

Booth Fisheries, 600 Lombard St., San Francisco, CA 95537 – Dungeness crabs in shell.

Brittain Ranch, Conway, TX 79020 – buffalo.

Capn's Corners, Camden, ME 04543 – clams and lobsters in shell.

Cavin Game Bird Farm, North Little Rock, AR 72114 – pheasant, quail, chukar partridges.

Cotuit Oyster Co., P.O. Box 563, Little River Rd., Cotuit, ME 02635 – fresh oysters.

Czimer Foods Co., 953 West 63 St., Chicago, IL 60621 – most kinds of venison, wild boar, ducks, geese, pheasant, quail.

Dark Harbor Lobster Co., Box 406K, Belfast, ME 04915 – fresh lobsters, frozen lobster tails and crab.

Embassy Seafoods, Inc., P.O. Box 268, Winthrop, MA 02152 – fresh lobster, crabs, scallops.

Eureka Fisheries, Box 217, Fields Landing, CA 95537 – abalone.

Feby's Fishery, 1111 New Rd., Elsmere, DE 19805 – fresh Atlantic and Gulf of Mexico fish and shellfish, including blue crab; a specialty is Pacific Ocean abalone.

H & L Game Farms, Baldwin, MS 38824 or Box 123, Ridge Farm IL 61870 – pheasant, quail, chukar partridges, wild turkey.

Mrs. Loren Holcomb, North Branch, MI 55056 – most upland game birds and waterfowl.

Iron Gate Products Co., 424 West 54th St., New York, NY 10019 – pheasant, quail, chukar partridges, wild turkey.

J. & J. W. Ellworth Co., Greenpoint, Long Island, NY 11944 – oysters in shell.

JA Ranch, Clarendon, TX 79226 – buffalo.

E. Joseph, 183 Van Brunt St., Brooklyn, NY 11231 – pheasant, quail, chukar partridges, wild turkey.

Jurgensen's, 601 South Lake St., Pasadena, CA 91109 – most kinds of venison, wild boar, upland game birds and waterfowl.

Kraft's Game Farm, Princess Anne, MD 21853 – pheasant, quail, chukar partridges, wild turkey.

L & M Quail Farm, 1730 Picher, Joplin, MO 64801 – pheasant, quail, chukar partridges, wild turkey.

LeJune's Quail Farm, Box 112, Sulphur, LA 70663 – pheasant, quail, chukar partridges.

Les Eschalottes, Ramsey, NJ 07466 –
most kinds of venison, wild boar.

Maryland Gourmet Mart, 414 Amsterdam
Ave., New York, NY 10024 – pheasant,
quail, chukar partridges, ducks, geese.

Meadowbrook Game Farm, Richfield,
PA 17086 – pheasant, quail, chukar
partridges, wild turkey.

Saltwater Farms, Damariscotta,
ME 04543 – fresh clams and lobsters
in shell.

Saunders Poultry Shop, 3rd & Fairfax, Los
Angeles, CA 90036 – pheasant, quail,
chukar partridges, ducks, geese.

Geo. H. Schafer Market, 1097 Third Ave.,
New York, NY 10028 – pheasant, quail,
chukar partridges, ducks, geese.

Sun Sportsman's Supply, Box 856, Salina,
KS 67401 – pheasants, quail, chukar
partridges.

Wakefield Food Sales, 32 S. Fifth Ave.,
Mt. Vernon, NY 10550 – crabs in shell.

Wichita Mountain Wildlife Reserve,
Cache, OK 73527 – buffalo, elk. This is
a U.S. government game reserve which
has a yearly sale of surplus animals;
you must order 90 days before the sale,
which takes place at a different time
each year, and take delivery at the
Reserve; you buy a whole or half animal
on the hoof at far below market prices.
Reserve employees slaughter and field-
dress, but you do your own butchering.
The hide is extra if you buy a half-
carcass.

Wickford Shellfish Co., 67 Esmond Ave.,
Wickford, RI 02852 – will supply a
complete clambake with all seafood,
vegetables, and accessories; also
lobster, fresh Atlantic seaboard fish.

B SOURCES OF EQUIPMENT AND SUPPLIES

Arlene's, 3736 Millswood Drive (P.O. Box 396), Irving, TX 75062 – specializes in cutlery.

Better Living Laboratories, Inc., 2893 Southaire Dr., Memphis, TN 38118. Manufacturers of H20K Water Filter; write for name of nearest dealers.

Brookstone, 5 Vose Farm Rd., Peterborough NH 03458. Utensils, cutlery.

Coleman Company, Wichita, KS 67201. Manufacturers of camp stoves, coolers, utensils, packs, etc. Sold through sports and hardware stores, etc., nationwide.

C. W. Foods, Inc., Woburn, MA 01801. Makers of Bolton Biscuit and Pilot Bread.

Dacor, 102 North Brand Blvd., Suite 322, Glendale, CA 91203. Manufacturers of kitchen grill and spit cooktops; write for name of nearest dealer.

Ducane Heating Corp., 600 Dutch Square Blvd., Columbia, SC 29210. Manufacturers propane-fueled outdoor grills; write for name of nearest dealers.

Hammacher Schlemmer, 145 East 57th St., New York, NY 10022. Retail and mail order dealers in grills, utensils, cutlery, etc., write for catalog.

JennAir Corporation, 3035 Shadeland, Indianapolis, IN 46226. Manufacturers of JennAir Range, kitchen grill and spit-cooking provision; write for name of nearest dealers.

Koolatron Industries, Ltd., 56 Harvester Avenue, Batavia, NY 14020. Manufacturer of portable electronic refrigerators; write for name of nearest dealer.

Leyse Aluminum Co., Kewaunee, WI 54216. Manufacturers camping-grade aluminum Dutch ovens and other cookware; write for name of nearest dealer.

L. L. Bean, Inc., Freeport, ME 04033. Mail order dealer in grills, utensils, cutlery, backpacks, etc.; write for catalog.

Oregon Freeze Dried Foods Co., P.O. Box 1048, Albany, OR 97321. Makers of compressed foods, write for names of dealers.

Orvis, 10 River Road, Manchester, VT 05254. Mail order dealer in grills, utensils, cutlery, backpacks; write for catalog.

Richmoor, Inc., 14801 Oxnard St., Van Nuys, CA 91411. Distributors of pouch foods; write for names of dealers.

Ronco, Inc., 1200 Arthur Ave., Elk Grove Village, IL 60007. Makers of food dehydrator; write for names of dealers.

Skylab Foods, Inc., 4 Warehouse Lane, Elmsford, NY 10523. Makers of retort foods; write for names of nearest dealers.

INDEX